Sherry Smith

Moscow
and Its Environs

PROGRESS PUBLISHERS MOSCOW

Emmanuil Dvinsky

Moscow
and Its Environs

A Guide

ЭММАНУИЛ ДВИНСКИЙ

МОСКВА И ЕЕ ПРИГОРОДЫ

На английском языке

Редакция литературы по спорту
и туризму

Translated from the Russian by
Barry Jones
Editor of the Russian text *I. Rakhmanina*
Assistant editor of the Russian text
L. Andrianova
Editors of the English text *N. Efendieva
and Yu. Semyonov*
Designed by *Yu. Kopylov, D. Kulchinsky,
N. Sokolov*
Art Editor *A. Tomchinskaya*
Photos by *N. Rakhmanov, A. Markelov*
Maps by *L. Cheltsova*
Layout by *V. Shits*

© Издательство «Прогресс», 1981

English translation © Progress Publishers
1981

$\frac{20904-579}{014(01)-81}$ 103-81   1905040100

CONTENTS

Moscow Yesterday, Today, Tomorrow	8
A Little History	11
Moscow Since the Revolution	20
Trips Around Moscow	43
The Kremlin	45
Red Square and Kitaigorod	71
Karl Marx Avenue and the Central Square	88
The Zamoskvorechye	107
The Boulevards Ring	121
Sadovoye Ring (I. From Crimean Square to Lermontov Square II. From Sadovaya-Chernogryazskaya Street to Crimean Bridge)	134
Luzhniki (Volkhonka–Metro-Builders Street–Komsomol Avenue)	155
Kalinin Avenue–Arbat	175
Kutuzov Avenue–Mozhaisk Highway	187
Herzen Street and Vorovsky Street	198
Krasnaya Presnya–Serebryany Bor	211
Gorky Street	221
The Leningrad Highway (Leningrad Avenue–Leningrad Highway)	237
Towards Dmitrov (Pushkin Street–Novoslobodskaya Street–Dmitrov Highway)	250
Petrovka Street–Kuznetsky Most Street	262
Northern Radial Road (Neglinnaya Street–Commune Square–Altufyevo Highway)	271
Peace Avenue (Dzerzhinsky Street–Peace Avenue–Yaroslavl Highway)	284
The Road to the North-East (Kirov Street–Komsomol Square–Sokolniki Park–Shchelkovo Highway)	298
The Road to Izmailovo (Bogdan Khmelnitsky Street–Chernyshevsky Street–Karl Marx Street–Lefortovo–Izmailovo)	311
Solyanka–Zayauzye–Enthusiasts Highway	327
The South-East (I. Taganka Street–Ryazan Avenue. II. Marxists Street–Volgograd Avenue)	338
Proletarian Avenue–Kashira Highway	351
The Route South (Lyusinova Street–Greater Tula Street–Warsaw Highway)	366
The South-West (I. Lenin Avenue–60th Anniversary of October Revolution Street–Trade Unions Street. II. Vernadsky Avenue–Troparyovo)	373
Practical Information	393
Name Index	427

Millions of people from all over the world come to Moscow to see the capital of the first ever socialist state.

We hope that during your stay in Moscow this book will serve as a guide and good companion. The itineraries and excursions set out here are arranged in conformity with the radial and circular lay-out of the city itself. We have divided them into two groups the first being devoted to the ancient parts of Moscow: the Kremlin, Red Square, Kitaigorod, Zamoskvorechye, the central squares, Marx Avenue and the two inner circular roads, the Boulevards and the Sadovoye. Then follow the radial main roads that run from the centre of the city to the outer ring road, which marks the city boundary.

Thus a panoramic picture of Moscow will unfold before you: old town, new districts, construction sites, and zones of the past preserved, with their numerous historical and cultural relics. The book will tell you about the memorials of revolutionary and military events and peace-time endeavours, about industrial enterprises and research centres, educational establishments, museums, theatres and sports grounds, and sculpture and architecture.

What attracts one so much about Moscow today is its rapid development, the pounding rhythm of its life and the irresistible charm of its youth—most important in a city which is more than 800 years old! There is something new going up in Moscow every year, every month, every day. Moscow is growing and expanding at a faster rate than any other capital city in the world.

This guide book has been so arranged that you can follow any of the suggested itineraries either right through from the beginning to the end or select that particular part which appeals to you most. Each itinerary is accompanied by an illustrated plan. On the longer excursions we would advise you in the interests of economizing on time to follow our recommendations as to the most interesting things to see (these have been marked on the plans). The book also contains a plan of the whole of the city, with the aid of which and the illustrated plans you may make up itineraries to suit your own needs.

Thus Moscow extends her invitation to you. So take a stroll down the streets of the old town, visit the famous theatres and arts galleries, admire the Kremlin, go on the Moscow underground railway—the Metro, order a table at the restaurants famous for their national cuisine, and be sure not to miss the new Olympic stadiums. You will soon feel the driving energy that the city radiates and experience something of the fullness and variety of life in Moscow.

But there is also a wealth of sights to see in the region beyond the city limits (the Moscow Region) and in the ancient Russian towns that lie near the capital.

The road runs through the beautiful Russian countryside with its forests and copses, rivers and small streams, meadows and fields. There you will see monuments immortalizing the heroism of the Soviet people as well as the classical architecture of the pre-revolutionary country estates turned into museums. There are the churches and monasteries of the past and the urban panoramas of the modern housing estates.

So it only remains for us to wish you a good journey and a pleasant stay in Moscow and the Soviet Union.

Moscow yesterda

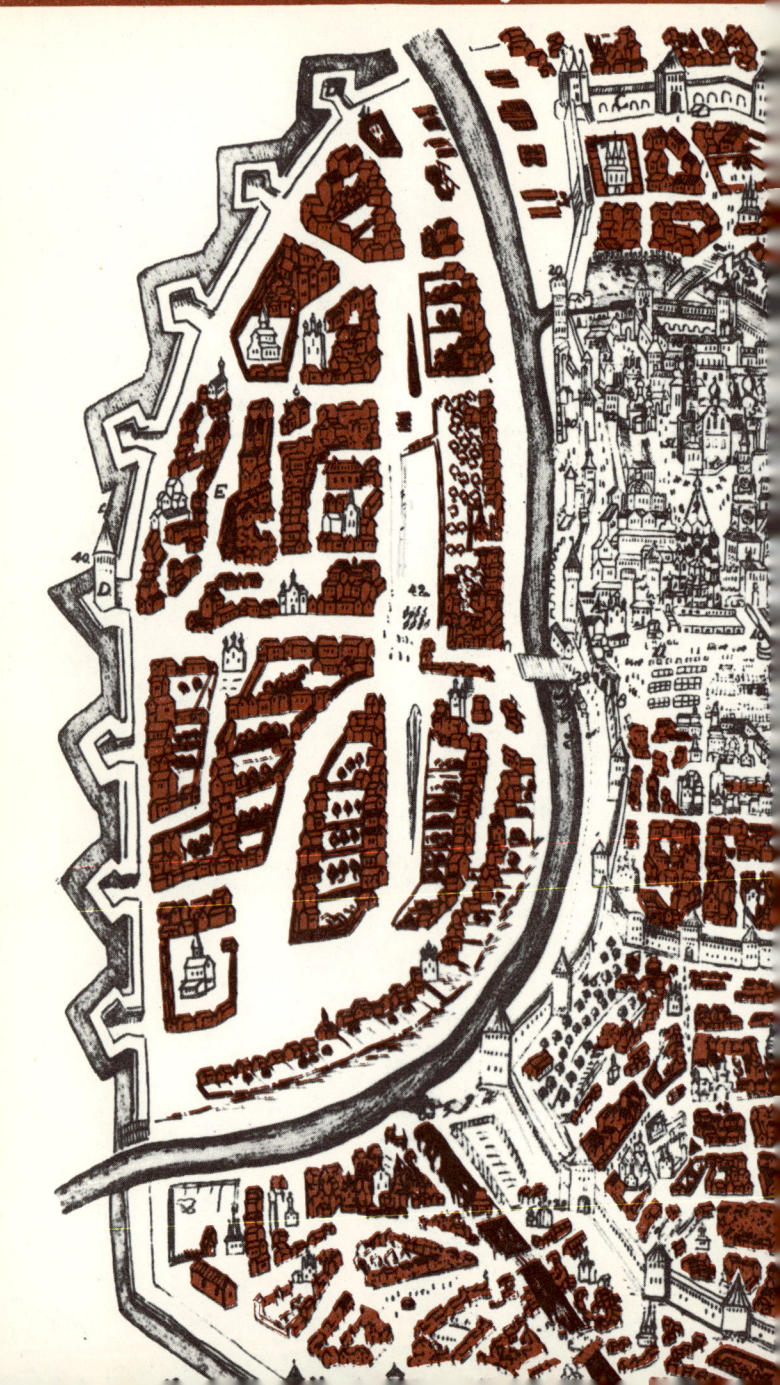

oday, tomorrow

A LITTLE HISTORY

The history of Moscow is the history of Russia herself. In ancient times the country was even called Muscovia and the people Muscovites. Over the centuries Moscow led the way to the unification of all the Russian principalities, a complex process which ended with the formation of the Russian state. The first written reference to Moscow is found in one of the ancient chronicles, the Hypatian Chronicles of April 1147 A.D., which together with other manuscripts inform us that the city was founded in that same year by Prince Yuri Dolgoruky, who strengthened it with wooden walls and a ditch.

From tiny little streams a mighty river flows,
From sources no less humble our Mother Moscow rose...

so ran the words of the old song. Today Moscow is a huge city spread over a vast area of 878,7 square kilometres, but originally it was a settlement occupying no more than one tenth of the area of the Modern Kremlin. The fortress built by Yuri Dolgoruky stood on a rampart 8 metres in height and 40 metres across at the base. The walls were built of huge wooden beams 3 metres high. There were two or three wooden towers and a set of double gates.

But Yuri Dolgoruky did not build his *grad* or town on an empty spot. Recent archaeological discoveries show that well before Moscow was mentioned in the surviving written records a feudal settlement also surrounded by wooden walls and a defensive ditch had already existed on its site. The area around the fortress became inhabited with merchants, tradesmen and artisans. East of the Kremlin, near the site of the present Rossia Hotel, part of another ancient settlement has been discovered along the banks of the River Moskva. Judging from the archaeological finds made here (which can be seen on permanent display in the Cathedral of the Annunciation in the Kremlin) the settlement had wide trading connections and an extensive handicrafts industry, which included iron-working, smelting, forging, tanning and pottery. It also had a developed shoe-making industry and produced women's jewelry, combs, buttons and household utensils. The growth of a town depends to a large extent on its geographical position. In this respect ancient Moscow was very advantageously situated. It was built on top of a hill, with the approaches on either side protected by two rivers, the Moskva and the Neglinnaya, which made it easily defendable. The River Moskva connected Moscow through a system of other rivers and portages with many other Russian principalities and eventually led to the Volga and the Dnieper. Many ancient roads also ran through Moscow (they will be mentioned later when describing different Moscow districts), linking Moscow with the main towns of Russia. The basin of the River Moskva was rich in natural resources including iron ore, limestone, sandstone and clay, which contributed to the development of the artisan industries and trade. One further condition for the rise of Moscow was its central position relative to the other lands of ancient Rus. It became a place of retreat for the inhabitants of the other Russian lands, when their own territory was under foreign invasion.

In 1237 Russia was struck by a terrible calamity. The Tartar hordes of Batu Khan took Ryazan by storm and poured into the depths of the country. The Russian principalities, weakened by internal discord, could not withstand the Mongol-Tartar invasion and Batu's hordes swept on destroying all before them. Cities were laid waste and men and women put to the sword. By early 1238 they reached Moscow and burned the city to the ground. They then went on to take Vladimir, the capital of the Vladimir-Suzdal principality, where they won a decisive victory. Russia, stricken and shattered, was now in the hands of the Mongol-Tartar invaders. But Moscow hadn't completely perished. Gradually the people rebuilt their gutted houses and churches, the artisans began to ply their trade once more and life was slowly brought back to normal. Henceforth it was Moscow that headed the long and stubborn struggle against the Tartar invaders. In 1263 Moscow became the capital city of the Moscow principality which steadily began to occupy the whole basin of the River Moskva. At the same time the building of the city of Moscow continued. Along the roads that led away from the Kremlin to lands far and near proper streets began to be laid and buildings to be built. More and more people came to live in Moscow and around it, which naturally led to the development of the city's economy and the accumulation of considerable material wealth. As modern historians see it, it was the labour of the artisans and peasants in the Moscow region that provided the material conditions for Moscow to become the centre of the Great Russian nation then being formed and later unify the peoples of the country into a single, powerful state.

In the 14th century the principality of Moscow was considerably extended by Prince Ivan Kalità, who annexed a number of neighbouring lands. After two fires in 1331 and 1337, Kalita undertook a number of major building projects in the Kremlin. The head of the Russian Church now changed his seat from Vladimir to Moscow and the Kremlin became the centre of all-Russian ecclesiastical power. During that century Moscow suffered considerably. Besides the fires, which destroyed considerable parts of the city, many of the inhabitants were carried off by the Black Death, which raged through Europe at the time. But again and again the city rose from the ashes bigger and stronger than before as new palaces, churches and defence works were built. Moscow began to amass the strength of the whole Russian nation for the struggle against Tartar oppression. In 1365 the grandson of Ivan Kalita, Dmitri Donskoy, Prince of Moscow, made preparations for a decisive struggle with the Tartars by strengthening the defences of the capital. The wooden walls of the Kremlin were replaced with a powerful whitestone wall interspersed with turrets and the whole area of the Kremlin was increased almost to its present dimensions. A ring of monasteries was built round the approaches to the city for added protection.

In 1368 and again in 1370 Olgerd, Prince of Lithuania tested the strength of the new defences when he tried to storm the new whitestone walls and was resoundingly defeated. In 1378 Dmitri Donskoy fought and defeated the Khan's army at the River Vozha. In the words of Karl Marx, "it was the first real battle with the Mongols that the Russians won". Soon afterwards, on September 8, 1380 Dmitri Donskoy inflicted a crushing defeat on the army of Mamai Khan at Kulikovo Field. This victory, won by a prince of Moscow, increased still further the prestige of the city in the eyes of the Russian people.

The 15th century saw the unification of more and more of the Russian lands under the principality of Moscow. By the beginning of the 16th century this process was almost complete and a single Russian state was established. During the 15th century Russia finally threw off the Tartar yoke, which had oppressed the country for more than 250 years and saved the peoples of Europe from enslavement. Ivan III, Prince of Moscow, acquired a title of the Great Prince of all Rus.

The growth of the political and economic might of Moscow was accompanied by a period of intensive construction. Ivan III undertook the massive reconstruction of the Kremlin, for which purpose he invited to the capital a number of famous Italian masters. From 1485 to 1495 powerful new brick walls were erected with massive towers, new cathedrals were put up, stone churches constructed and a palace for the Great Prince built. Much construction work went on outside the Kremlin as well. By the late 15th century Moscow occupied an area of 5.4 square kilometres and had become one of the largest cities in the world.

In the 16th century new defences were built around Moscow against possible enemy incursions on the ever expanding city. During the first half of the century the main market, which was situated near the walls of the Kremlin, was surrounded with a towered wall. This area received the name "Kitaigorod" (the derivation from the Old Slavonic *kita,* which meant a bundle of stakes, for these bundles formed the basis of the earthworks which surrounded the original area). At the end of the century Fyodor Kon, a stone mason, built the third fortification ring around the city, also consisting of brick walls and towers and enclosed a whole new part of Moscow. This new area, known as the Bely Gorod (White City), had grown up around the Kremlin and Kitaigorod. The points at which the radial roads met this circular defence wall were marked with towers and double gates *(vorota).* The names of some of them like the Nikitskiye Gates and the Pokrovskiye Gates have been retained to this day. Almost simultaneously a further defence boundary was erected in the form of a 15 kilometre earthen rampart with an oak wall and numerous towers. This fourth ring in the defence works encompassed the Zemlyanoi Gorod (Earthworks City) and included the outskirts of Moscow and the Zamoskvorechye (the district lying beyond the River Moskva). Later when the town expanded even further, these defences were taken down. The walls of the Bely Gorod were replaced with the Boulevards, which are still part of Moscow today and the former earthen rampart is now the Sadovoye Ring (Sadovoye Koltso).

Thus Moscow grew in a series of rings with radial roads and has retained that pattern to this day.

In the 16th century industry and trade developed considerably and new major enterprises and workshops were set up. The weapons industry became particularly developed with the Moscow Cannon Factory gaining considerable fame and the royal arsenals turning out gunpowder, sword-blades and armour. But the workshops of Moscow won equal acclaim for their manufacture of peace-time goods, particularly expensive pottery. The development of production naturally led to an increase in trade and Moscow established trade links not only with her near neighbours, but with far off lands as well. The 16th century was also a time of great cultural upsurge. It saw such great architectural achievements as the building of the Cathedral of the Archangel Michael, the Bell Tower of Ivan the Great in the Kremlin, and St. Basil's Cathedral (Cathedral of the Intercession) in Red Square, as well as the opening of Russia's first printing-house in Moscow and the appearance of the first printed books.

The early 17th century has gone down in history as the "Time of Troubles". In 1610 Moscow was occupied by Polish and Lithuanian troops, but within two years the people's volunteer corps, which had been called together by the merchant Kuzma Minin and Prince Dmitri Pozharsky liberated the city. When the interventionists had been finally driven out, Moscow lay in ruins. Where once there had been streets, there remained only wasteland, and the palaces and cathedrals of the Kremlin stood roofless. Over the next twelve years intense rebuilding once more went on in the city. New stone palaces and government buildings were erected in the Kremlin and the main towers in the wall were given ornamental hipped roofs. Stone was now used widely as the medium for building outside as well as inside the Kremlin. The 17th century historian and traveller Paul of Aleppo has left this description of Moscow: "The town can be seen 15 versts away, enchanting the eye with its beauty and magnificence, its loftiness and its many towers and shapely domes that flash with gold." During the 17th century Moscow continued to develop as an economic and trading centre, becoming the "market of all Russia" and by the early 18th century it had become the largest industrial town in Russia, producing a variety of manufactured articles, particularly textiles.

In 1712 Peter the Great transferred the capital from Moscow to the new city of St. Petersburg, which he had built on the shores of the Gulf of Finland. But Moscow continued to play an important role in political, economic and cultural life of the country. The city remained the centre of Russian national culture, and continued to grow and develop architecturally as well as industrially. Moscow as the "second capital" of Russia retained a considerable amount of the state apparatus of the Russian empire including the offices of the two central institutions—the Senate and the Collegiate.

In 1755 the first Russian university was opened and the production of books began to be increased considerably. The work of many famous Russian 18th century writers is connected with Moscow, which still remained the heart of Russia and the bearer of the national and patriotic feelings of the people.

This was made particularly clear during the Patriotic War of 1812. In the struggle against the Napoleonic invasion Moscow was the centre of popular resistance. When the French armies reached the outskirts of the city, the inhabitants left it, destroying all reserves of food. Soon afterwards a major fire broke out in Moscow which lasted six days and nights and burned down three-quarters of the town. When the French left Moscow they destroyed many of the buildings in the Kremlin and damaged its walls and towers. Fortunately, the majority of the great architectural buildings were left intact and others were later restored. From that memorable time no foreign invader has ever set foot on Moscow soil. Once again after the Napoleonic invasion Moscow was reborn. New brick buildings were built to replace the gutted wooden ones and some of these still adorn the capital today.

Nineteenth-century Moscow strengthened her reputation as a major centre of national culture. Here many of the famous writers and poets, scholars and painters, musicians and artists, who made a significant contribution not only to the culture of Russia but to that of the world, lived and worked.

Throughout the whole of its history Moscow has held an outstanding place in the liberation movement of the country. The working people of Moscow, worn out by unbearable suffering and bent beneath the yoke of serfdom frequently rose against their oppressors. In autumn 1606 the forces of Ivan Bolotnikov, leader of one of the largest peasant risings in Russia, laid siege to the capital, winning over many of the inhabitants of the city. There was popular unrest throughout the 17th and 18th centuries and many times Red Square saw crowds of insurgent tradespeople, *streltsy* (royal guards), and other participants in the various uprisings such as the Salt Revolt, the Copper Revolt and the Black Death Revolt.

Moscow was also closely linked with the Decembrists' (the revolutionary nobility who took part in an uprising in Senate Square in St. Petersburg on December 14, 1825) movement, for it was here that the leading ideologists and organizers of the movement were born. For many of the revolutionaries the road to Senate Square led via Moscow, where in 1817-18 one of the first Decembrist organizations was founded.

It was in Moscow that the activity of two of the famous revolutionaries of the next generation, Alexander Herzen and Nikolai Ogarev, began. One of the main centres for the Russian liberation movement was Moscow University, where many student groups met to discuss and develop the ideas of the famous revolutionary democrats of the 1860s, Nikolai Chernyshevsky and Nikolai Dobrolyubov, who called upon the whole of progressive Russia to support a peasant revolution.

After the emancipation of the serfs in 1861 industry began to expand rapidly in Moscow. By 1890 there were one and a half times more enterprises than there were in the pre-emancipation period and the cost of industrial production increased 4.5 times. By the last third of the nineteenth century Moscow had become the largest transport junction in the whole of Russia.

The expansion of industry meant a concomitant increase in the strength of the proletariat and the development of the workers' movement. More and more strikes took place at the factories and the first Marxist organizations appeared. A decisive role in the strengthening and development of these latter in Moscow was played by the arrival here of Lenin, then still a young man. In 1895 the first all-Moscow Marxist organization, the "Workers' Union" was set up which later developed after the pattern of "The League of Struggle for the Emancipation of the Working Class" formed by Lenin in St. Petersburg. In 1898 the Moscow committee of the Russian Social-Democratic Labour Party was formed. The development of a mass workers' movement and its adoption of socialist principles ushered in the new, proletarian stage of revolutionary struggle.

Moscow was one of the centres of the revolutionary struggle of the proletariat in all three revolutions in Russia: in the first Russian revolution of 1905-1907, the February Revolution of 1917 and the Great October Socialist Revolution of 1917.

"The movement started in St. Petersburg, spread through all the marginal regions of Russia, and mobilized Riga, Poland, Odessa, and the Caucasus; the conflagration has now spread to the very heart of Russia," Lenin wrote at the beginning of the first Russian revolution. In October 1905 the Moscow committee of the party decided to stage a general strike in Moscow. In a very short time this wave engulfed the whole of Russia and involved more than 2 million workers who came out in support of the overthrow of autocracy. In Moscow and a number of other cities Soviets of Workers' Deputies sprang up. These mass organizations of the working class were to become the prototype of the new Soviet political system established in 1917. The highest stage in the development of the 1905-1907 revolution in Russia was the armed uprising of the Moscow proletariat in December 1905. The Presnya, Zamoskvorechye and workers' districts in the South-East of Moscow became the centres of the uprising. Exceptional heroism was shown by the workers in the battles in the Presnya district. The December uprising had a tremendous influence on the growth of revolutionary consciousness among the workers. The experience gained by the Moscow workers helped the revolutionary proletariat in winning their victory in October 1917. The struggle for the victory of the socialist revolution was one of the finest pages in the history of Moscow. On October 25 (November 7, new style) 1917 the Moscow Bolsheviks, on receiving information from Petrograd that the revolution had begun, immediately formed a revolutionary centre for controlling the transfer of power to the Soviets.

A complicated situation developed in Moscow. Having suffered defeat in Petrograd, the counter-revolutionaries were relying on a victory in Moscow. They had powerful forces on their side, including the well-armed and well-trained officers and cadets, and were grouped around the Alexandrovskoye Cadet College on Arbat Street, the Alexeyevskoye Military College, the Cadet Training Centres at Lefortovo and the headquarters of the Moscow Military District, which was situated on Prechistenka (now Kropotkin Street). Their objective was to take the Kremlin and the Moscow Soviet, destroy the revolutionary centre and ensure the arrival in Moscow of military units with whose help they hoped to crush the revolution.

In this difficult situation the Bolsheviks suggested the formation of a Military Revolutionary Committee. The basic forces of the revolution were located in the workers' districts and in the military barracks. On October 27 the headquarters of the counter-revolutionary forces declared a state of martial law in the city and sent the Military Revolutionary Committee an ultimatum demanding its liquidation and the disarmament of all revolutionary units. The ultimatum was rejected. On October 29 revolutionary troops from Moscow supported by detachments of the Red Guard from the surrounding towns went over to the offensive. In the heavy fighting that followed the Red Guard units suffered considerable losses, but the revolutionary storm could not be abated and one by one the positions of the counter-revolution fell. Between October 30 and November 2 the basic objectives in the centre of Moscow, where counter-revolutionary forces had lain entrenched, were liberated. The building of the Duma (pre-revolutionary parliament), where the counter-revolutionary headquarters were located, was taken. On November 2 Red Guards entered Red Square amid heavy fire and on the following morning workers' and soldiers' detachments took the Kremlin. Soviet power was established in Moscow.

The places connected with the revolutionary fighting both in 1905 and 1917 are sacred to the hearts of Muscovites. They are marked throughout the city with memorial plaques and monuments. In Moscow and the Moscow Region there are more than 170 buildings including factories, institutes, houses and flats where Lenin either visited, lived in, worked or spoke at. Many of them you will come across in your walk through the city, so the city itself will amplify our brief historical account.

In March 1918 a very memorable event took place—the Soviet government headed by Lenin moved from Petrograd to Moscow. This made Moscow the capital of the Soviet state. In December 1922 at the First All-Union Congress of Soviets the formation of the Union of Soviet Socialist Republics was proclaimed. Since then Moscow has been the capital of the USSR.

MOSCOW SINCE THE REVOLUTION

Moscow is the largest town in the Soviet Union. It is the capital of the Union of Soviet Socialist Republics and the Russian Soviet Federative Socialist Republic (RSFSR). It is the largest political, economic, industrial, scientific, educational and cultural centre in the entire USSR.

Moscow is the seat of the Central Committee of the Communist Party of the Soviet Union, the Presidium of the Supreme Soviet of the USSR and the Soviet Government, the Union and republican ministries, the All-Union Central Trade Union Council and the Central Committee of the Young Communist League.

In Moscow representatives of the Union republics and all the Soviet peoples meet at party congresses and sessions of the Supreme Soviet of the USSR to decide the fundamental issues relating to the national economy and determine the domestic and foreign policy of the Soviet state.

For millions of people throughout the world Moscow is the herald of peace. On the eve of the 60th Anniversary of the Great October Socialist Revolution the Supreme Soviet of the USSR, expressing the will of the whole Soviet people, adopted in Moscow a new Constitution of the USSR, Article 28 of which reads: "In the USSR war propaganda is banned." Thus the Fundamental Law of the USSR reflects the peace policy of the Soviet state, which has been consistently implemented since its first days when Lenin's "Decree on Peace" was published. This policy is based on the fundamental principles of friendship and international cooperation.

Moscow is a major international centre. Here meetings take place at which representatives from different countries throughout the world discuss matters relating to the struggle for peace, freedom and social progress. Each year there are international scientific symposia, exhibitions and art festivals, many of which have become traditional attractions. In 1980 the 22nd Olympic Games were held in Moscow.

The foundations for Moscow's magnificent present were laid by the Great October Socialist Revolution.

THE IMMEDIATE POST-REVOLUTIONARY PERIOD

The Soviet state, the Communist Party and the Soviet Government have always regarded the development of Moscow, the improvement of housing conditions and the better provision of amenities as a matter of considerable importance.

In that difficult year of 1918, when foreign intervention and internal counter-revolution unleashed civil war upon the country, when the weakened land of the Soviets was compelled to wage war in defence of the gains of the socialist revolution, work began on the first project for the reconstruction of Moscow, both central and suburban. The aims of this project were to get rid of the slums, the overcrowding and the unsanitary housing conditions, radically reconstruct the workers' districts making them healthier places to live in and improve street planning so as to achieve an organic combination of the new and the old.

In the twenties Moscow took the first steps towards transforming her suburbs. Workers' estates began to be built in the industrial districts which were to become the foundations of a socialist town, where there are no social distinction between its various districts. Also during the twenties a number of major civic buildings were erected such as the factory palaces of culture, which are still to be seen in the city today as reminders of the lively and energetic quest for new forms in architecture, which characterized the period.

Thanks to the hard work and determination of the working people the twenties also saw a revival of Moscow's industry. The Moscow workers began the Communist Subbotniks (a Saturday worked without pay for the benefit of society), which has since become a glorious national tradition. In this desire to work without reward for the good of the state and society as a whole, Lenin saw the beginnings of a new, conscious, communist attitude to work.

During these early years Moscow gave all the help she could to the working people of the Soviet republics. In 1921 when the electrification of Baku, the capital of Azerbaijan, began, the workers at the Moscow Dynamo factory sent the city electric locomotives. The Ukraine, which suffered terribly during the years of intervention and civil war, received from Moscow machinery, metals and textiles. Then again, in 1922 the working people of Moscow collected and sent to Kirghizia 10,000 million roubles for the development of a transport system. These were examples of genuine proletarian internationalism and fraternal aid, which only became possible in conditions of Soviet power. By the mid 1920s the restoration of the economy was almost complete, but this was no time for the new Soviet state to stop since it had only achieved the economic level of poor agrarian Russia ...

In 1927 the 15th Party Congress opened in Moscow. It adopted the directives for drawing up a five-year plan of national economic development, the first in the history of the Soviet Union. Its objective was the creation of the country's own advanced technological base for the socialist reconstruction of the entire economy.

During the prewar five-year plans Moscow factories produced the first Soviet cars and ballbearings as well as the palatial underground railway stations.

New and gigantic plants were built on the sites of the old enterprises. These included the Moscow Automobile Factory, the Dynamo, Hammer and Sickle, and Red Proletarian factories, and the Vladimir Ilyich Factory. A tremendous role in the achievement of national economic targets was played by the scientists and technologists of Moscow, many of whose physicists, mathematicians, chemists, biologists, doctors, and geologists gained world renown in the years before the Second World War. From the thirties onwards Moscow became an international scientific centre. New schools, colleges and higher educational establishments were built taking students from the Union and autonomous republics, who would become the country's specialists in all branches of the economy.

Moscow also became the centre of a new socialist culture and as such was visited by Henri Barbusse, Upton Sinclair, Rabindranath Tagore, Bernard Shaw and Romain Rolland.

Moscow architects developed new principles of architecture which were based on an all-round regard for social objectives.

In 1931 Soviet town planners began to draw up a General Plan for the Development and Reconstruction of Moscow.

THE RECONSTRUCTION OF MOSCOW

When the idea of the reconstruction of Moscow was mooted some specialists wishing to preserve the old town as a city-museum suggested the building of a new Moscow beyond the limits of the city. Others wished to pull down the old city in its entirety and build in its place a new capital with a completely different lay-out. Neither of these two suggestions met with approval. The General Plan for the Development and Reconstruction of Moscow, which was finally adopted in 1935, preserved as its basis the historically formed radial and circular lay-out of the city. The plan incorporated a massive campaign to increase the city's housing, develop its economy, widen and improve the street network, pull down old buildings that had no historic or artistic value and put up new ones in their place. Transformation on such a scale had never been known by any other city in the world. It was the world's first overall reconstruction plan for a capital city, that put the interests of the people ahead of any other.

Work was begun in the thirties on the main highways and squares of the city, and the first lines of the underground railway system were laid. In 1937 work was completed on the world's largest river canal which linked the River Moskva with the Volga. As a result the River Moskva received an annual increase of a billion cubic metres of water from the Volga, which made it navigable again.

In 1936-1938 ten wide bridges were built across the River Moskva together with a drainage canal running parallel to it and seven bridges across the River Yauza. In 1939 the All-Union Agricultural Exhibition (now known as the Exhibition of National Economic Achievement) was opened, which became a popular attraction. The city was literally transforming before the eyes.

But the peaceful toil of the Soviet people was violently disrupted in 1941. On June 22 of that year fascist Germany invaded the Soviet Union.

THE WAR YEARS. THE BATTLE FOR MOSCOW

The outbreak of the Great Patriotic War meant the beginning of a period of great suffering for the city of Moscow and her people. The nazis planned to take Moscow in the shortest possible time. Seventy-seven German divisions, including 23 motorized and tank units, were thrown against the city. By October 1941 the Front reached its very suburbs. On October 19 the State Defence Committee announced that Moscow was in a state of siege. More than 500 thousand inhabitants of the city began to build defence fortifications, while a further 120 thousand formed 12 divisions of the home-guard. Meanwhile the partisans, Muscovites and inhabitants of the region round Moscow, fought valiantly in the rear of Hitler's troops. The whole country came to Moscow's aid and the enemy's October offensive was held back.

On November 7, 1941 a parade was held as usual in Red Square before Lenin's Mausoleum in honour of the 24th anniversary of the October Revolution. The main slogan declared the will of the Soviet people for all the world to see—"Moscow will never surrender!"

In mid-November the nazi troops began a second offensive. But the desire of the enemy to take Moscow at any price floundered upon the firm determination of the Soviet people to defend it. In the battle that ensued the Soviet soldiers performed feats of untold heroism and self-sacrifice. The whole country was aroused by the words of political officer V. Klochkov, hero of the defence of Moscow: "Russia is vast, but there is nowhere to retreat. Behind us lies Moscow."

In early December, 1941 the Soviet Army launched a counter-offensive and by the end of February 1942 had advanced over 400 kilometres westwards. Thus at the gates of the Soviet capital the nazi troops suffered their first major defeat in the Second World War, and this brought about a radical turning point in its course. It was in the Battle of Moscow that the Soviet troops finally frustrated the nazi plan for a *Blitzkrieg* and dispelled the myth of the invincibility of Hitler's army.

But the war was to continue for another four years, and Moscow, where the State Defence Committee, the Central Committee of the CPSU and the government of the USSR were located, controlled the people's struggle with the fascist invaders, organizing and directing the country's forces for the final defeat of the enemy. Moscow also performed hitherto untold feats of labour heroism and throughout these dark days remained the heart of the country.

In commemoration of the 20th anniversary of the victory of the Soviet people in the Great Patriotic War (1941-1945) Moscow was awarded the honorary title of Hero-City for outstanding services to the Motherland, and the mass heroism, courage and fortitude shown by the working people of the capital in the struggle with the nazi invaders.

All over the city in the streets and squares, factories and institutions, schools and colleges there are sculptural compositions set up in honour of the defenders of Moscow. The names of many of the streets recall their heroic deeds. Their memory will live on in the hearts of the people. Young Muscovite couples, on their wedding day, go from the palace of marriages to the Tomb of the Unknown Soldier in the Alexander Gardens outside the Kremlin to pay tribute to the courage of the Soviet soldiers and place flowers by the monument.

MOSCOW EXTENDS ITS BOUNDARIES

After the victorious conclusion of the Great Patriotic War the housing programme in Moscow, outlined in the reconstruction plan, was given the go-ahead. By 1960 more than 30 million square metres of housing space had been built and new blocks of high-rise flats erected round the outskirts of the city.

Further building demanded an extension of the city limits. In August 1960 a decision was taken to form a new outer limit to the city, which was to be marked with a 109 kilometre outer ring road. The city boundaries now included a number of small towns and villages that had previously been part of the Moscow Region. From 1961 to 1975 the Moscow housing fund was almost doubled. 76.7 million square metres of housing space were built, and 5.4 million Muscovites moved into new modern flats. In June 1971 a new General Plan for the Development of Moscow was approved, designed to cover the next 25-30 years and containing a forecast of likely developments over an even longer period.

The main objective of the plan is to make Moscow a well-planned city with a modern architecture, a well organized transport system and all the latest amenities to ensure favourable conditions of work and rest for its inhabitants. The city area has been broken down into major planning zones, each of which includes housing estates, industrial zones and places of recreation and leisure. The General Plan also takes care of industrial development around Moscow with all enterprises producing or using harmful products being moved out of the living areas. Dozens of new housing estates have already been completed and any of our itineraries along the radial highways will pass through new districts which have only recently appeared on the map, so the reader can see for himself how the General Plan is being implemented.

The General Plan also covers the second important problem for any city—transport. The radial-circular system of roads is supplemented by a network of fast automobile highways. These roads link the peripheral districts of the city without passing through the centre (they will be mentioned in more detail later on). A third and a fourth ring roads are also planned together with radial highways, 45 new bridges across the Rivers Moskva, Yauza and Setun, more than 150 road junctions and 100 overpasses across the railways. The underground system is to be increased approximately three times and the bus, trolleybus and tram routes extended.

The city gardens and parks and the green belt around the capital, which are designed as places of rest and leisure, will accommodate up to three times the number of citizens they do at present. New boarding houses, rest homes, sanatoria, tourist camps and fishing and hunting lodges are being built here as well as special summer holiday camps for children.

THE CENTRE

Ideas on the limits of the centre have changed many times throughout the long history of the capital. Until not so very long ago the centre referred to the area which incorporated the Kremlin and what is now Sverdlov, Revolution and the 50th Anniversary of the October Revolution Squares, i.e. the very ancient nucleus of the city. Later on Muscovites began to call the centre the whole area bounded by the Boulevards Ring, and now everything within the Sadovoye Ring is called the centre and even many of the streets and avenues beyond it. This is the oldest part of the city and is consequently undergoing considerable reconstruction, since there are many cramped yards and delapidated houses, and altogether insufficient greenery. According to the General Plan for the Development of Moscow the city centre is designed as an integral, artistically organized system. As well as residential apartment blocks it contains the main buildings of the party and government institutions, the ministries and departments, museums, theatres, concert halls, hotels, shops and restaurants. The city centre is to retain its impressive appearance and here, as in the past, Muscovites will gather on days of national celebrations.

The focal point of the centre of Moscow is the unique architectural composition of the Kremlin. This is emphasized by ensuring proportional symmetry between the Kremlin itself and the surrounding buildings of more recent design, whose height increases gradually the further they stand away from the Kremlin and the nearer they are to the Sadovoye Ring.

Some 1,800 buildings and monuments of historical and architectural value, the majority of which are concentrated in the centre, have been taken under state protection as being of great value to the city. They have not only been preserved and restored, but in most cases given the kind of surroundings that will contribute best to their emotional impact, and their harmonious connection with the new buildings of the city.

The Moscow City Soviet has declared nine zones in the city centre as subject to special protection. These are: Kitaigorod, Kropotkin Street, Kirov Street, the Arbat, Petrovka and Kuznetsky Most Streets, Herzen and Vorovsky Streets, Bogdan Khmelnitsky and Chernyshevsky Streets, the Zamoskvorechye and the Zayauzye. These protected zones have been designated not with the intention of mummifying the old districts of Moscow and making them purely museum exhibits or places of tourist interest only, that are cut off from the everyday life of the city. The reconstruction is rather intended to care for individual monuments and their historical and architectural environment and at the same time to clear these areas of dilapidated buildings that are mere encumbrances. These latter buildings are of no artistic or historical value and therefore not worth preserving. They must consequently make way for new buildings, gardens and squares which are essential in a large city. Housing conditions and the provision of amenities in these protected zones are being improved enormously, for the restoration plans nave taken account of the internal design of these old buildings and carried out improvements to bring them into line with modern standards of comfort.

The long-term development programme envisages a polycentric capital with a constellation of architectural ensembles grouped around its central nucleus.

A PANORAMIC VIEW OF MOSCOW

With its unique skyline and the beauty of its picturesque views, seen from the heights within the city, Moscow never fails to astonish and delight the eye.

As the great Russian poet Mikhail Lermontov wrote in the early 19th century: "One who has never cast his eye over the vast expanses of our ancient capital, one who has never seen this magnificent, limitless view, does not know what Moscow is—for Moscow is not just another city, not a faceless, cold, symmetrical pattern of buildings... No, it has a spirit and a life of its own... Every stone in Moscow bears a message inscribed by time ... a message that vibrates with thought, feeling and inspiration to the scholar, patriot and poet! ... The craftsmen of ancient times knew how to create a wonderful interplay of architecture and nature."

The old masters knew how to create wonderful ensembles, where architecture and nature meet in a process of mutual enrichment.

Now the canvas has been extended and the picture of contemporary Moscow enlarged. But the artistry of Soviet town planners has given expressive force to the natural features of the city—the picturesque terraces with their gently sloping inclines which gradually open out into wide plains, the variety of relief, the sharp bends in the River Moskva—and enriched them afresh. By developing and extending the traditions of Russian architecture the builders of the new Moscow give their work the scale and content that conforms to the needs of the times. The new General Plan for the Development of Moscow continues to implement the ideas set down by Lenin for the expansion of the city. In a speech on March 6, 1920 to a meeting of the Moscow Soviet on the question of improving the amenities, transport and the organization of the city's economic life Lenin said, "We must do this so as to set an example to the whole country... We must set this example, here in Moscow, an example such as Moscow has set many times before." The tremendous work involved in the reconstruction of Moscow was based on one of the fundamental principles of socialism and was written into the Programme of the Communist Party of the Soviet Union: "Everything for the sake of man, for the benefit of man."

Today all these ideas, projects and plans are being realized to make Moscow a city in which the great architectural ensembles of the past and the modern spatial composition of the present are united in one integral and harmonious whole.

GEOGRAPHY AND STATISTICS

Moscow is situated in the European part of the country, between 55 and 56 degrees latitude and 37 and 38 degrees longitude. The city is 42 kilometres from north to south and 35 kilometres from east to west. In the past geographers liked to say that Moscow stood on seven hills. The well-known nineteenth century expert on Moscow, I. Snegirev, for example, believed that the seven hills were the Borovitsky, the Sretensky, the Tverskoi, the Tryokhgorie at Presnya, the Vorobyovy Hills and the heights around Taganka and Lefortovo. But in the strict geographic sense of the word it is impossible to call these hills. The territory of Moscow should rather be seen as a plain whose essential surface area lies at a height of thirty to thirty-five metres above the River Moskva (which is approximately 150 metres above sea level). The relief rises in three terraces above the river. To the south and south-west lie the highest parts of Moscow—the Tyoply Stan, a preglacial eminence which rises 250 metres above sea level. The northern part of this eminence—the former Vorobyovy Hills, now the Lenin Hills—rises to a height of 80 metres above the river.

The River Moskva enters the capital from the north-west, near the Volokolamsk Highway and flows in a number of huge loops in a general south-easterly direction. Outside the city limits, near the town of Kolomna, the river flows into the Oka, which is a tributary of the Volga. Within the city it is some 80 kilometres long, stretching across the city 35 kilometres as the crow flies.

Within the city limits there are something like one hundred small rivers and streams, but practically all of them today have been piped to run underground. The largest tributary of the River Moskva is the Yauza which runs almost 34 kilometres from its source near the town of Mytishchi outside Moscow. After the building of the Moscow Canal, the Yauza like the Moskva became navigable thanks to the influx of water from the Volga.

The climate of Moscow is moderate continental. As a rule the frosts in winter are not harsh nor the heat in summer excessive. The average temperature for winter is 9 below and for summer 17°C. Moscow has on average 228 days a year in which the temperature is above zero. But the climate is, nevertheless, very changeable and deviations from the average are fairly frequent. December, for example, may have frosts or long periods of thaw. In summer heat-waves of 30°C may suddenly give way to cold spells and rain. An experienced tourist can therefore draw the conclusion that an umbrella and a mackintosh may well be necessary in summer and warm clothes in winter.

Administrative zones. In Moscow there are 32 administrative districts. One of these—Zelenograd— has been built 40 kilometres from Moscow and is considered the 32nd district of the capital.

The population of Moscow is over 8 million.

More than 4 million Muscovites work in industry, in building, at scientific institutions, on the transport services, in the trade and catering service, in educational and cultural institutions, in health and social security, in the housing and social services and in management. 56 per cent of all workers in Moscow are women. There are representatives from more than one hundred of the various Soviet nations and ethnic groups living in Moscow, 90 per cent of the population are Russians.

Moscow is administered by the City Soviet and the District Soviets of People's Deputies. Under the jurisdiction of the Soviets of People's Deputies come all matters relating to the economy, culture, education, health, transport, building, the social services, trade and so on.

There are 1,000 deputies in the Moscow City Soviet, 471 of whom are workers. Also included among the deputies are management executives, scientific workers, technologists and other specialists, party, Soviet, trade-union and Komsomol workers, teachers, students and workers in culture and education, medical practitioners, journalists, prominent figures in literature and the arts, and members of the armed forces. 513 of the deputies are members or candidate members of the CPSU, and 447 are women.

By way of comparison it is interesting to note that before the Great October Socialist Revolution there were 146 members in the Moscow City Duma (Parliament) from 1912 to 1916, 63 of whom were industrialists, 32 traders, 24 house-holders and 27 "persons of free profession." The Duma contained not one representative of the working class, nor a single woman (women were not entitled to be elected).

The Budget of the Moscow City Soviet. The annual expenditure of the Moscow City Soviet on economic and cultural development comes largely from the enterprises and institutions that are subordinate to it. Local taxes and contributions from the population comprise no more than 5 per cent of the total.

More than half of the annual budget goes on housing and urban development, the rest goes on education, health and social security. The increase of total volume of capital investments over each five-year period is approximately 35 per cent.

The Housing Fund. 85 per cent of all apartment space in the capital was built since the war. Each year 120 thousand new flats are built. From 1971 to 1975, 2.4 million Muscovites received new accommodation and 25.8 million square metres of housing space were made available for exploitation. Before the Revolution there were 190 thousand flats in Moscow with a combined area of 16.9 million square metres. At present the housing fund amounts to 130 million square metres. Rent in the USSR amounts to no more than 3-5 per cent of the average family budget. It was established in 1926 and since then has remained unchanged. Almost the whole housing fund of Moscow today consists of apartment blocks with central heating, double glazing and insulation, hot and cold water, gas, electricity and all the modern conveniences.

Public Services. Moscow has more than 3,500 streets, avenues, embankments, squares and boulevards, their combined length amounting to more than 3,600 kilometres. There are 360 bridges, tunnels and overpasses as well as 150 underground crossings.

There are more than 9,000 machines of different kinds for sweeping and cleaning the streets and pavements, breaking up ice and clearing away the snow. Moscow, therefore, tends to astonish visitors by its cleanness. The water and sewage system has been almost entirely relaid since the Revolution. The city spends more than 6 million cubic metres of water (i.e. 700 litres for every member of the population) on its needs.

One-third of the total area of the city is made up of parkland, and other forms of greenery. Per head of the population there is twice as much verdure in Moscow as in Vienna and four times as much as in Paris. The city has 11 park and forest areas, 26 city and 58 district parks, 21 of which are for children, 14 large gardens and more than 800 flower gardens and boulevards. The streets are adorned with trees, lawns and flower-beds.

Environmental Protection. A considerable amount of work is carried out in Moscow on environmental protection. In recent years dust and pollution in the city have been reduced 3-4 times. There are no smogs in Moscow. A model drainage and sewage system ensure the freshness and transparency of the Rivers Moskva and Yauza. There is nothing unusual about bathers on the city beaches or fishermen on the river embankments. Noise abatement, green belts, and underground transport and other facilities—it is difficult to list all the ways in which ecological problems are being tackled in Moscow. Between 1976 and 1980 more than 800 million roubles were spent on environmental protection.

City Transport. There are in excess of 5,500 kilometres of city transport in Moscow including Metro, bus, trolleybus and tram routes. The cost of transport—3-5 kopecks—was fixed just after the war and has never been increased since. Every day more than 15 million people use public transport in Moscow.

The Metro is the Moscow underground transport system. It is the fastest and one of the most convenient forms of transport in the city. By 1980 there was 185 kilometres of rail in the Metro system and 115 stations. During rush hour trains run every 90 seconds.

The **trolleybus** has certain advantages, especially for tourists, for their broad windows allow an excellent view of the streets and everything in them that is of interest and that there is no time to see more closely. There are a total of 1,000 kilometres of trolleybus routes throughout the city and the total number of passengers carried throughout the year amounts to something like 1,000 million.

Bus routes comprise the longest transport system in Moscow—3,700 kilometres—and each year they carry 1,765 million people.

Trams are the oldest form of city transport, having been in existence in Moscow for more than 80 years. The oldest inhabitants of the city still remember the precursor of the tram—the horse-drawn tram. The quiet comfortable trams of today carry 600,000 passengers a year.

There are more than 16 thousand **taxis** at the services of Muscovites and visitors to the capital.

Fixed-price (15 kopecks) taxi-buses have become very popular in Moscow. They are mini-buses seating up to ten passengers and following a set route.

Intercity Communication. There are nine **railway** stations in the capital taking up to 2 million passengers a day. Moscow is the largest railroad junction in the USSR and in Europe.

Air Transport. Moscow is linked by air with 210 cities in the USSR and 83 capitals and major towns in 70 different countries. Moscow's four airports—Vnukovo, Domodedovo, Sheremetyevo and Bykovo handle up to 1,000 flights daily on internal lines. Aeroflot cooperates with all airlines of the socialist countries as well as with such companies as Sabena, Air Canada, Pan American, Lufthansa, SAS, Air India, British Airways, Alitalia, KLM, JAL and others. Most international air routes are serviced by IL 62, TU 154 and TU 134.

Moscow is a port for five **seas**. It has direct water communications with the Caspian Sea, the Sea of Azov, the Black Sea, the Baltic and the White Sea.

In Moscow there are 13 **highways** connected by the outer ring road.

The Health Services. As everyone knows, the health services in the USSR are free. In Moscow there are more than 3 thousand hospitals, polyclinics, specialist consultation bureaux and health centres. There are more than 80 medical research institutions housed in new buildings and equipped with laboratories and clinics. Recently two major complexes were opened belonging to the USSR Academy of Medical Sciences—the Cancer Research Centre on the Kashira Highway and the All-Union Cardiological Research Centre at Kuntsevo. There are also preventative medicine clinics attached to the enterprises and institutions as well as health resorts.

Children's health is one of the most important concerns of the Soviet health services. There are children's polyclinics all over Moscow, as well as nurseries and kindergartens for the very young, which are situated near to their homes. The General Plan for the Development of Moscow envisages the building of branch schools situated outside the city limits.

Education. Education in the USSR is free. There are 3,720 thousand people engaged in some form of educational activity in Moscow, which is to say almost half of the population. In pre-revolutionary times one-third of the population between the ages of 9 and 49 were illiterate.

Now almost everyone in the country has **secondary education**. Young workers are able to complete their education while still at work by attending evening schools and sandwich courses.

New schools are being built every year in the capital, chiefly in the new housing estates. They are spacious, convenient and well equipped with studies, workshops, laboratories, gymnasiums and sports grounds, and some have swimming pools. There are special classes for extended day groups in which children do their homework under the supervision of teachers and take part in various school societies after school proper has finished.

There are also boarding schools in Moscow, where the children live and study. For specially gifted children there are music schools and art schools, as well as 130 children's sports schools with more than sixty thousand pupils.

There is a wide network of **colleges and vocational-training schools**. Between 1971 and 1975, 275 thousand students completed secondary technical education courses at the colleges and 243 thousand graduated as qualified specialists in 200 different fields from the vocational-training schools. Approximately half of those graduating also completed secondary general education courses and received official leaving certificates, thereby gaining the right to seek entry into the universities and the higher educational establishments.

In Moscow's **higher educational establishments** there are more than 635 thousand young men and women from all the nations and ethnic groups of the USSR receiving full-time or part-time extra-mural education. The city has become an international centre of higher education. Young people come here to study from the socialist countries, the developing countries of Asia,

Africa and Latin America and the capitalist countries. There are 12 thousand foreign students from 130 countries studying in Moscow. The largest and best known higher educational establishments will be mentioned in more detail under the specific itineraries later on in this book.

Extra-mural studies and evening classes have become very popular in the USSR. Those who have elected to improve their qualifications in this way receive a supplementary 30-40 days paid holiday from work for examination preparation, four months paid holiday for the presentation of a diploma or thesis, 50 per cent discount on travel during examinations (if the student lives in a different town), one additional day off per week for senior students and a number of other privileges and concessions. Enterprises have the right to send their employees to higher educational establishments and technical colleges and pay them a grant which is 15 per cent higher than that paid by the state.

At the Likhachov Automobile Plant a new type of educational establishment has been set up in a new building whereby hundreds of workers from the plant and neighbouring enterprises can receive specialised engineering qualifications without interrupting their work at the factory itself. This idea has since been copied by other major enterprises throughout the country.

Industry. Moscow was once thought of as being largely a cotton town. In 1913 more than 38 per cent of the work force of the city were engaged in the textile industry, while only 18 per cent were employed in the engineering and metallurgical industries. But this pattern was decisively altered during the first five-year plans. Moscow became a major producer of the means of production. Now more than half the industrial work force of the city is employed at the engineering, toolmaking and metallurgical plants. Furthermore Moscow now has automobile, instrument-building, ballbearing, electronics, aviation and radio-electronics industries together with a massive building industry, geared to the production of pre-fabricated housing units. There are now more than 100 specialized plants manufacturing standardized sections and finishing materials ready for on-site assembly.

Moscow also makes a large contribution to the country's consumer goods industry, producing 19 per cent of the RSFSR's manufactured silk, 10 per cent of television sets, 24 per cent of watches and clocks and 39 per cent of vacuum cleaners.

Almost half of Moscow's labour force works at major enterprises which employ thousands of workers. By way of comparison it should be borne in mind that in 1920 75 per cent of all enterprises in Moscow employed less than 100 workers.

Goods produced in Moscow are in demand in other countries as well as the USSR. The city currently exports lathes and instruments, automobiles, electric motors, ballbearings, refrigerators, television sets, medical equipment and medicines, fabrics, watches and clocks, perfume and other commodities.

Moscow's "second" industry, in terms of its labour force, is **scientific research.** Over the last few decades scientists from Moscow have carried out fundamental research and made advances that have furthered the development of science and technology throughout the world, especially in space exploration. Moscow scientists have made outstanding advances in laser technology, the production of artificial diamonds and controlled thermonuclear fusion, which is one of the most important problems in science today. Moscow scientists are also renowned for their work in social sciences, chemistry, biochemistry, molecular biology, medicine, geology, energetics, radio-electronics and computer technology and in the development of new materials and technological processes.

Moscow is the seat of the state's highest scientific institution—the USSR Academy of Sciences as well as the Academies of medical sciences, agricultural sciences, pedagogical sciences and the Academy of Arts.

Research and development in various fields is carried out by specialized institutes, laboratories, higher educational establishments and museums, which are all installed with the latest equipment and housed in their own individual premises. The Amalgamated Institute of Nuclear Research, for example at Dubna near Moscow, is internationally famous. Here scientists from the socialist countries work on joint projects.

After the victory of the Great October Socialist Revolution Lenin set Soviet scientists the task of studying the country's productive forces and the principles governing their rational distribution and utilization, and analysing the ways to achieve rapid economic growth. Today this work is being successfully fulfilled. The creation of a highly developed economy in the USSR, the raising of the living standards of the Soviet people and the development of education and culture are closely linked with scientific progress.

Culture. Museums and Exhibitions. There are literally dozens of **museums** in Moscow catering for every taste and interest, whether it be history, medicine, industry, painting, archaeology or space exploration. Every year the museums of Moscow are visited by almost 30 million people. The internationally famous museums include: the Central Lenin Museum, the Tretyakov Gallery, the Pushkin Museum of Fine Arts, the History Museum, the Central Museum of the Revolution of the USSR, the Kremlin Museums, and the Exhibition of National Economic Achievement.

The *Information* section at the end of this book contains a full list of all the museums and exhibitions in Moscow together with their addresses and telephone numbers.

Entertainment. In Moscow the theatre season is all the year round. Posters all over the city advertise a choice of plays, concerts, choral recitals and dance performances. Altogether there are 25 permanent **theatres** in Moscow and many concert halls as well as the summer theatres and open concert stages located in the parks, at the Exhibition of National Economic Achievement, and various halls where visiting drama companies and the amateur theatre groups perform. The permanent theatres are attended by an audience of about 15 million a year.

Eight Moscow theatres bear the honorary title "Academic", which is awarded by the government for outstanding services to the theatrical arts. The first theatres to receive this title were the Bolshoi, the Maly and the Art theatres.

In summer when the theatre companies of the capital usually go on tour, the Moscow theatres are far from being empty, for this is when visiting drama companies from other parts of the USSR and abroad begin their season.

Moscow's **concert** life is rich and varied and her symphonic orchestras, dance and choral ensembles, instrumentalists and vocalists have won world renown. In the concert halls of the capital prize winners of national and international music competitions can be seen performing as can famous actors and actresses, recitalists and visiting performers from the Union republics and abroad.

The concert halls of the capital are comfortable and have excellent acoustics. On the new housing estates cinemas have been built equipped with multi-purpose halls, which can be used for concerts. Also the hundreds of clubs, houses and palaces of culture have excellent facilities for concerts.

Every year two festivals for music lovers are held in Moscow: the spring festival "Moscow Stars" (5-15 May) and the winter festival "Russian Winter" (December 25-January 5). These festivals include opera, ballet and drama performances by the best artists and companies in the capital. Thousands of visitors from abroad and tens of thousands from all parts of the Soviet Union come to Moscow for these arts festivals.

The Moscow State **Circus** has the best performers in the USSR, and many of them are equally famous abroad. Moscow has two permanent circuses and in summer circuses also perform in the Gorky Central Park and Izmailovo Park as well as at the Exhibition of National Economic Achievement.

The Cinema. Moscow is the centre of the Soviet film industry. There are six film studios located in the capital, the largest of which is Mosfilm. In 1979 Mosfilm celebrated its 55th anniversary. The Mosfilm village occupies an area of more than 40 hectares. Throughout its long history the studio has produced many films of international acclaim. The Gorky Studios have the distinction of being probably the only studios in the world producing chiefly for a child audience. Among the film studios not mentioned in the separate itineraries it is worth mentioning the Central Studios of Popular Scientific and Educational Films, whose work is devoted to the advances made in contemporary science and technology. These film studios produce, as their name suggests, educational films for schools, higher educational establishments and technical colleges.

Every two years international Moscow film festival is held in July, which is attended by major figures in the film world from many different countries. There are three competitions at the festival: for a full length feature films, documentaries and children's films. The motto of the festival is "For Humanism in Cinema Art, for Peace and Friendship Among Nations."

Moscow has more than 520 cinemas seating in all 105 thousand. In 1977 more than 102 million people visited the cinema. Dozens of new cinemas have been opened in recent years especially in the new housing estates.

In Moscow there are 315 **social clubs, Houses and Palaces of Culture**, all equipped with auditoria which are in no respect inferior to those in professional theatres and concert halls. Every club has its own amateur arts group engaged in various art forms such as drama, opera, choreography, choral music, symphonic and wind music, painting, sculpture, film-making, vaudeville and the circus. Many of these amateur groups have been in existence for many decades and have achieved a high level of artistic performance. 75 of the best of these groups have been awarded the honorary title *Narodny* (People's).

The majority of social clubs are attached to the various enterprises, institutes and higher educational establishments in the city. There are also clubs which bring people together according to their occupation. These include clubs for railway workers, teachers, medical workers, etc. Considerably active are the Clubs of Unions of the arts intelligentsia which include Artistes' Club, Actors' Club, Writers' Club, Journalists' Club, Architects' Club, Film-makers' Club, Composers' Club, and Painters' Club. These societies organize discussions of new works, plays, and meetings with audiences and readers, etc.

There is also an international club, the House of Friendship with Foreign Countries (see Chapter *Kalinin Avenue—Arbat*).

The Parks of Culture and Rest. The parks of Moscow are noted above all for their beautiful avenues of trees, their fountains, ponds, flower beds, their pleasant summer houses and their secluded walks. But there are also dozens of fairgrounds, amusement arcades, bowling alleys, courts for tennis or volleyball and places where chess can be played. There are summer theatres in all the parks as well as open concert stages, cinemas and dance halls. In winter skating-rinks are formed and forest clearings and hillsides are set aside for skiing. During the festivals the parks are crowded with people, singing and dancing and holding carnivals. Various exhibitions are also held in the parks. (More details on the largest parks will be given under the itineraries in which they occur.)

Moscow is the largest **publishing centre** in the country. 37 daily newspapers with a combined daily circulation of 79 million are published here, including *Pravda, Izvestia, Komsomolskaya Pravda, Selskaya Zhizn, Trud, Pionerskaya Pravda* and many others.

At the same time Moscow publishes more than 3,600 periodicals covering the arts, the social sciences, and science and technology as well as other magazines, almanacs and collections.

There are over 60 publishing houses in Moscow, including the largest in the world: Politicheskaya Literatura, Khudozhestvennaya Literatura, Sovetsky Pisatel, Molodaya Gvardia, Detskaya Literatura, Progress, Iskusstvo, Prosveshcheniye, Russky Yazyk, and many others. In 1977 alone Moscow produced 40 thousand titles of books and pamphlets with a total circulation of 1,800 million copies.

Muscovites' love of reading is well known. No one is surprised at the fact that underground trains often look rather like reading libraries with almost everyone holding a book or a newspaper. A similar picture is to be seen on the other means of public transport as well as in the boulevards and parks. There are 4.3 thousand state and public libraries in Moscow, all of which are free, while Moscow book shops have an annual turnover of 900 million. Details of the Moscow **radio and television studios** will be met in chapters *Zamoskvorechye* and *Northern Radial Road.*

Sports. Moscow and the Olympics. Some 1.5 million Muscovites practise one or other of the various sports in the stadiums, clubs and circles, which are either attached to their place of work or study or situated near to where they live. The state does everything it can to promote the development of physical culture and there are stadiums, sports halls, water stations, swimming pools, ski-jumps, skating-rinks, tourist centres and tennis courts readily available for all. Use of these facilities, which include equipment and attire is free.

Physical education is taught at school from the first form and schools specializing in the teaching of sports are very popular. The students' sports clubs are among the largest in the capital.

Moscow has also led the field in starting sports clubs for the middle-aged and the elderly, and these now have a total membership of 630 thousand with stadiums and sports halls at their disposal.

Naturally enough Moscow is also a town of great sporting attainment. 800 Muscovites have attained the highest sports class and more than 9,000, the second highest. More than 200 Muscovites in different years became Olympic champions, which makes Moscow the leading city in the world in the numbers of

Olympic winners living therein. Every year there are something like 1,500 international, national and local sports competitions including world and European championships. Every four years the USSR holds a national Spartakiad and the finals in 25 sports in which 10 thousand sportsmen participate are held in Moscow.

Moscow was chosen as the Olympic city for 1980 and all Muscovites took part in preparing the city for this great festival of sport, peace and friendship.

In 1974 when the International Olympic Committee decided to hold the 22nd Olympic Games in Moscow, the Soviet capital had 60 stadiums, 1,300 sports halls, 29 swimming pools, a rowing canal and some 3,000 sports courts. 78 sports stadiums were newly built or reconstructed for the 1979 USSR Spartakiad and the 1980 Olympic Games forming altogether six sports centres: the Central Lenin Stadium; a covered stadium seating 45 thousand and Olympic swimming pool in Peace Avenue; sports complexes in Leningrad Avenue and Khimki-Khovrino; sports complex of the State Institute of Physical Culture in Izmailovo; equestrian centre in Bitsa Park; Canal for rowing and canoeing at Krylatskoye and Krylatskoye Olympic Ring and shooting range. Details on these centres, Olympic Village and new hotels are included in corresponding itineraries.

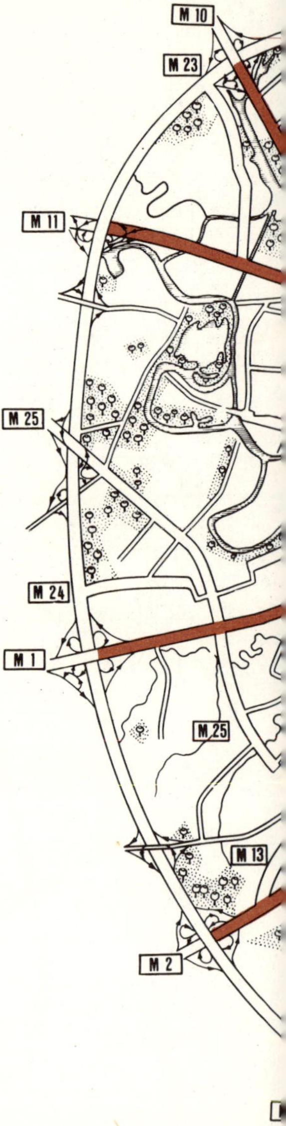
M 10
M 23
M 11
M 25
M 24
M 1
M 25
M 13
M 2

Trips around Moscow

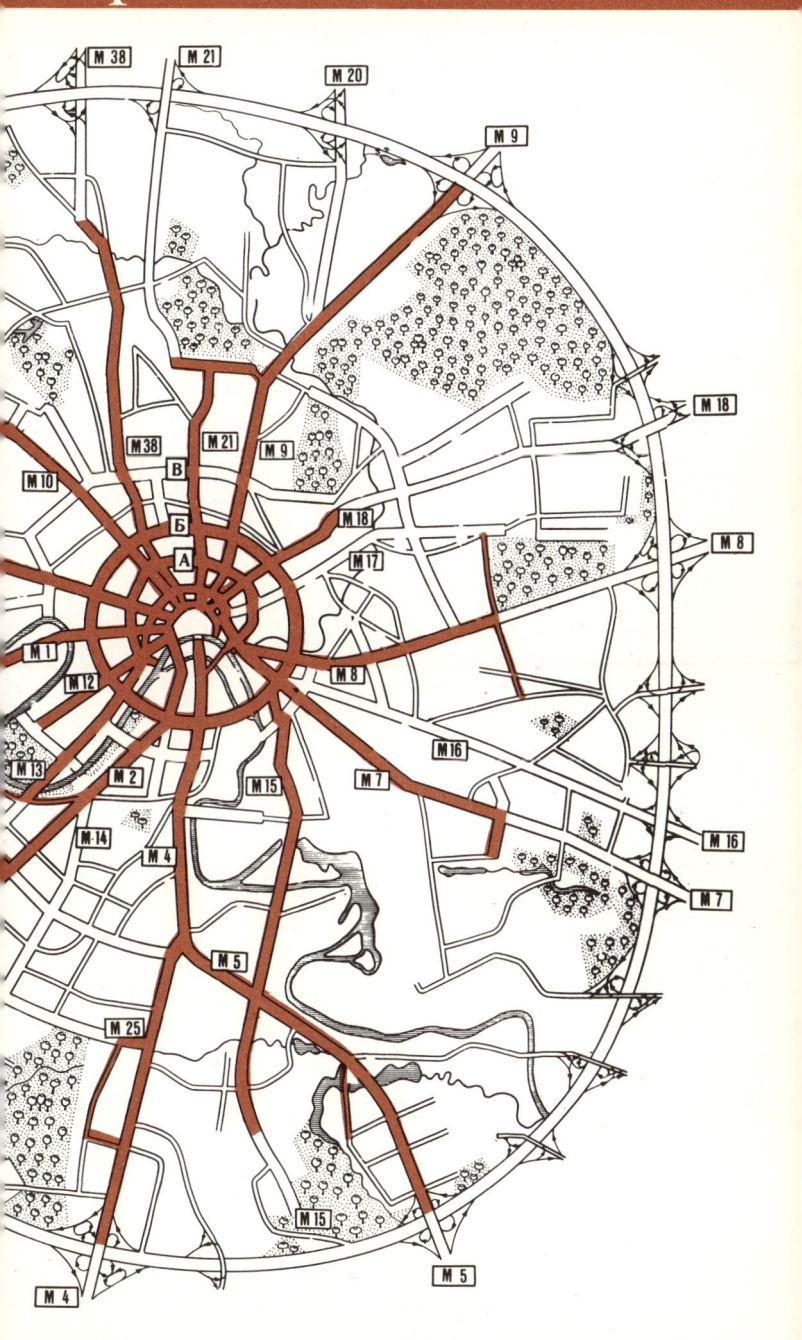

THE KREMLIN

*The Kremlin Walls and Towers—Cathedral Square—
Cathedral of the Dormition—Cathedral of the Annunciation—
Church of the Deposition of the Virgin's Robe—Cathedral
of St. Michael the Archangel—Bell Tower of Ivan the
Great—Tsar Bell—Tsar Cannon—Great Kremlin Palace—
Palace of Facets and Sacred Vestibule—Poteshny Palace—
Patriarch's Palace and Cathedral of the Twelve Apostles—
The Arsenal—The Presidium of the Supreme Soviet of
the USSR—Places Associated with Lenin—the Government
Building—Lenin's Apartment and Study Museum—
Monument to Lenin—State Armoury—Diamond Collection
of the USSR—Palace of Congresses*

The Kremlin is the heart of Moscow, the heart of the whole Soviet Union. It is the seat of the main Soviet governmental institutions—The Presidium of the Supreme Soviet of the USSR and the Council of Ministers of the USSR. It is here that the Communist Party of the Soviet Union holds its congresses and

50th Anniversary
of the October Revolution
Square

MARX AVENUE

Alexander Gardens

Borovitskaya
Square

Tainitsky Gardens

KREMLIN EMBANK

MOSKVA

MAURICE THOREZ EMBANK

KREMLIN

1. Water Tower
2. Annunciation Tower
3. Tower of Secrets
4. First Nameless Tower
5. Second Nameless Tower
6. Petrovskaya Tower
7. Beklemishev Tower
8. Constantine and Hellen Tower
9. Tocsin Tower
10. Tsar's Tower
11. Saviour's Tower
12. Senate Tower
13. St. Nicholas Tower
14. Corner Arsenal Tower
15. Intermediate Arsenal Tower
16. Kutafia Tower. Entrance to Kremlin through Trinity Gates
17. Trinity Bridge
18. Trinity Tower
19. Commandant's Tower
20. Armoury Tower
21. Borovitskaya Tower
22. Cathedral Square
23. Cathedral of the Dormition
24. Cathedral of the Annunciation
25. Church of the Deposition of the Virgin's Robe
26. Cathedral of St. Michael the Archangel
27. Bell Tower of Ivan the Great
28. Tsar-Bell
29. Tsar-Cannon
30. Great Kremlin Palace
31. Palace of Facets (Granovitaya Palata)
32. Terem Palace
33. Poteshny Palace
34. Cathedral of the Twelve Apostles and Patriarch's Palace
35. Monument to Lenin
36. Armoury
37. Kremlin Palace of Congresses
38. Biblioteka Imeni Lenina Metro Station
39. Ploshchad Revolyutsii Metro Station
40. Moskvoretsky Bridge
41. Bolshoi Kamenny Bridge

sessions of the Supreme Soviets of the USSR and the RSFSR take place.

But the Kremlin is also the cradle of Moscow. It is here that the ancient Russian capital grew and developed and its walls have looked down on the most important events in the history of the Russian state and the world's first socialist country. The art treasures of the Kremlin are preserved with great care by the Soviet people and many of its churches and palaces have become museums. But the enormous work involved in restoration continues as historians, architects and builders apply their skills and knowledge to revealing more and more of the beauty that lies hidden in the ancient Kremlin.

Before beginning your tour of the Kremlin, it is well worth looking at it from the far side of the River Moskva and from the Moskvoretsky or Bolshoi Kamenny Bridge. Here you get a unique panorama of the whole ensemble as it stretches down the incline and can view to best advantage one of the finest works of Russian national art and architecture.

At its centre the snow-white Bell Tower of Ivan the Great rises up amid clusters of golden cupolas, while spread out on either side are the various palaces and chambers of the Kremlin. On the crest of the hill is the Great Kremlin Palace and on its right above the dome of the USSR Government Building flies the Red Flag of the Union of Soviet Socialist Republics.

Down below surrounding the steep hill on which the Kremlin stands are the huge walls and towers which are usually made the starting point for excursions round the Kremlin.

The Kremlin Walls and Towers

The Kremlin walls are 2,235 m long, from 3.5 to 6.5 m thick and from 5 to 19 metres high, depending on the terrain. Atop the walls stand 1,045 bifurcated merlons, from 2 to 2.5 metres in height and fitted with narrow embrasures. Behind the merlons and running round inside the wall is a rampart from 2 to 4.5 metres wide. The present walls of the Kremlin were built in the 15th century.

Above the walls there are 20 towers, four of which have entrances. These latter are somewhat larger than the others.

The gate-towers were built where in ancient times roads led to the Kremlin. The high, distinctive hipped roofs on the towers were added later in the 17th century.

The wall that runs along the bank of the River Moskva is the oldest of the Kremlin walls, being built in 1485, for it was from this side that Tartar attacks could be expected.

The round corner turret on the far left (looking from across the Moskva), near to the Bolshoi Kamenny Bridge, is almost 59 metres high and is called the **Vodovzvodnaya** (Water) **Tower**. The name dates back to 1633, when machines for drawing up water were installed here and the first pressure water supply in Russia was used to carry water through lead pipes from the River Moskva to the tsar's palaces and gardens. In 1812 the tower was destroyed by the Napoleonic army, but it was restored soon afterwards.

Going from the Water Tower along the wall parallel to the embankment you come to the rectangular **Blagoveshchenskaya** (Annunciation) **Tower**, which is comparatively small, 30 metres in height. At the foot of the tower is a white limestone slab, preserved from the ancient whitestone Kremlin of the 14th century.

Further to the left stands the **Tainitskaya Tower** (Tower of Secrets). This tower is 38.4 metres high and is the oldest tower in the Kremlin, for it was from here that the Kremlin fortifications were begun. The name of the tower comes from the secret well that was hidden inside it. At one time the Tower of Secrets had considerable strategic significance and a supplementary fortification was attached to it with entrance gates and an underground passage to the river.

Next along the embankment we come to the **First** and **Second Bezymyanniye** (Nameless) **Towers**, the **Petrovskaya Tower** and, finally, at the corner the round **Beklemishev Tower** (46.2 metres). This tower was built in 1487 by the Italian architect Marco Ruffo, and is frequently referred to nowadays as the **Moskvoretskaya Tower**, because of its proximity to the Moskvoretsky Bridge.

From this tower wall turns sharply and rises up the incline towards Red Square. The first tower we come to is the **Konstantino-Yeleninskaya** (Constantine and Hellen) **Tower** (36.8 metres). In the reign of Dmitri Donskoy a whitestone gate-tower stood here, through which in 1380 the prince led his troops to the historic battle of Kulikovo, where the Tartar-Mongol hordes were decisively beaten. The present tower was built in 1490 by Pietro-Antonio Solario.

Higher up is the **Nabatnaya** (Tocsin) **Tower**. Although this tower is not very high (38 m), being situated on a hill it commanded a broad view of the southern planes. The tower takes its name from the tocsin that once hung from it, which day and night used to be guarded by the watch. At the sign of the approaching enemy the watch would sound the tocsin and the inhabitants would rush to take shelter within the fortress or the monastery. In 1771 at a time of popular unrest the insurgent citizens sounded the tocsin calling the people to the Kremlin. After the revolt had been put down Catherine the Great ordered the "tongue to be pulled from the seditious bell." Now the tocsin is kept in the Armoury.

The next tower in line is the youngest in the Kremlin. It is called the **Tsarskaya** (Tsar's) **Tower** and was built in 1680 to replace the older wooden tower. To be precise it is not really a tower, but a stone turret placed on the wall and reaching to a height of 11.4 metres above the merlons. From here, according to legend, the tsar's family would watch the ceremonies and important events taking place in Red Square.

The gates of the **Spasskaya** (Saviour's) **Tower** have for centuries been the main official entrance to the Kremlin. The tower was built under the guidance of Pietro-Antonio Solario in 1491, was rectangular in form and approximately half its present height. In the 16th century it was fitted with a clock and in 1625 the Russian architect Bazhen Ogurtsov built the octagonal multi-tiered turret which now surmounts the rectangular tower. A new clock was built on the turret equipped with a revolving face and a carillon by the Englishman, Christopher Halloway. The bells of the carillon were cast by Kirill Samoilov. In the reign of Peter the Great the clock was replaced.

The clock we see now was installed in 1851-52. During the October Revolution the tower and the clock were damaged by a shell, and on Lenin's instructions the carillon was repaired by the clock-maker, N. Behrens. Today the chimes of the Kremlin clock can be heard on the radio at 6 a.m. and midnight, Moscow time, while in Red Square the clock chimes every quarter of an hour with its "quarter bells" as they are called, and rings on the hour with its big bell. The big bell weighs two tons and the whole carillon 25 tons. It occupies three floors of the tower. The length of the minute hand on the clock is 3.28 metres.

The Spasskaya Tower is the most beautiful tower in the Kremlin. Its architecture combines elegance and monumental grandeur. The tower is 67.3 metres high.

The next tower along Red Square is the **Senatskaya** (Senate) **Tower,** 34.3 m, behind which stands the Government Building and in front of which lies Lenin's Mausoleum.

Further along Red Square we come to the **Nikolskaya** (St. Nicholas) **Tower,** 67.1 metres, which can easily be distinguished for its Gothic style. The most powerful of all the Kremlin towers is the **Uglovaya Arsenalnaya** (Corner Arsenal) **Tower** 60.2 metres. This tower goes deep into the ground and its walls reach a thickness of 4 metres. The tower was not only used for defence purposes, but concealed a hidden spring, which was indispensable to the defenders of the fortress in the event of a siege. This hidden spring is still in existence today.

Moving now along the north-western side of the Kremlin wall we pass through the Alexander Gardens and come to the **Srednaya Arsenalnaya** (Intermediate Arsenal) **Tower**. Further along is the tallest tower in the Kremlin, the **Troitskaya** (Trinity) **Tower** which is 76.35 metres in height. This tower is almost 10 metres higher than the Spasskaya Tower. The **Troitskiye Vorota** (Trinity Gates) here have long been one of the official entrances to the Kremlin. Opposite the Troitskaya Tower, on the other side of the River Neglinnaya, which once served as a moat round the Kremlin, is another smaller tower, the **Kutafia**, connected to the Troitskaya Tower by a bridge. This, the first stone bridge in Moscow, is now the main entrance for tourists and visitors.

Further along the wall we come to the **Komendantskaya** (Commandant's) **Tower** and the **Oruzheinaya** (Armoury) **Tower** and finally, the **Borovitskaya Tower** (50.7 m). This tower stands at the foot of the Borovitsky Hill, whence the Kremlin arose. The name of the tower comes from a pinewood *(bor),* which once covered the whole hill and where Yuri Dolgoruky first founded his settlement. This tower differs from the others by its gradational form.

Above the five highest towers in the Kremlin walls— the Spasskaya, Troitskaya, Nikolskaya, Borovitskaya and Vodovzvodnaya—there are red five-pointed stars glowing day and night.

They were put up in 1937 for the twentieth anniversary of the October Revolution. Their framework is made of stainless steel covered with rolled gold and they are faced in ruby glass. Each star is lit by a 5 thousand watt bulb and is so constructed that it can revolve smoothly in the wind, even though its weight is between 1 and 1.5 tons. The points of the star are 3-3.75 m apart.

Cathedral Square

In the centre of the Kremlin is Cathedral Square, a rectangular courtyard bounded by the cathedrals of the Dormition, the Annunciation and the Archangel Michael, the Church of the Deposition of the Virgin's Robe and the Bell Tower of Ivan the Great. (See schematic plan.) Cathedral Square is one of the most ancient squares in Moscow, dating back to the early 14th century. The present architectural ensemble was largely built in the early 16th century.

The Cathedral of the Dormition

The Cathedral of the Dormition stands on the site of the first stone cathedral which was built by Ivan Kalita in 1326-27 and which in its turn replaced the churches that were even older— 12th-century wooden and 13th-century stone ones. It was the largest building of its period in Russia and is one of the most perfect examples of 15th-century architecture. Building was begun on the Cathedral of the Dormition in 1475 under the supervision of the Italian architect, Aristotle Fioravanti, after the model of the 12th-century Cathedral of the Dormition in the ancient Russian town of Vladimir (thus emphasizing the continuity of tradition from one of the oldest towns in Russia). The Cathedral was finally completed in 1479.

For four centuries the Cathedral of the Dormition in the Moscow Kremlin was the main cathedral in Russia. It was here that tsars were crowned, acts of state proclaimed and other important ceremonies held. The Cathedral also served as the burial vault for the Moscow metropolitans and patriarchs (their tombs lie along the walls).

The central part of the Cathedral is separated from the chancel by a five-tier iconostasis (17th century) which is approximately 16 metres high and which was covered in the late 19th century with embossed gilt silver. Here there is a collection of icons from the 11th to the 17th century which are of enormous historical and artistic value. They include such unique works as *Our Lady of Vladimir* (14th century), *St. George* (12th cent.), the *Archangel Michael* (12-13th century), the *Trinity* (14th century) and many others. Soviet restorers have recently succeeded in uncovering part of the original 15th-16th century murals, which had once been thought to be irrevocably lost.

The Cathedral also contains many remarkable works of applied art including the throne of Vladimir Monomakh, or the imperial seat of Ivan the Terrible, as it is also known, which is an outstanding example of Russian woodcarving and dates back to 1551; the whitestone seat of the Patriarch (16th century); the bronze open-work canopy by Dmitri Sverchkov (1625); twelve censers of gilded bronze; multi-tiered candelabra (17th century) and many others. During the Patriotic War of 1812 the Cathedral was plundered by Napoleon's troops. From the silver that was later taken by the Cossacks from the retreating Napoleonic armies a huge chandelier was made which now hangs in the centre of the Cathedral. The oldest monument of applied art in the Cathedral are its southern doors, which were brought to Moscow from Suzdal in 1410. They contain twenty paintings in gold and black varnish on biblical themes.

The Cathedral of the Annunciation

The Cathedral of the Annunciation unites in one artistic whole the works of 14th-16th century Russian masters.

Being at one time the private chapel of the royal family, the Cathedral of the Annunciation is not very big. It has beautiful portals leading from the inner court to the central part of the church. The oldest of these is the southern which was restored in 1950 from fragments and which preserves the ancient traditions of wooden architecture which required that it be framed with columns in the form of sheafs of corn. The northern and western portals are 16th-century and decorated with whitestone carving.

The floor of the Cathedral dates back to the reign of Ivan the Terrible and is faced in ornamental jasper.

The ancient frescoes of the Cathedral were thought to have perished under centuries of redecoration, but in 1946 Soviet specialists began the work of cleaning and restoring the frescoes to reveal the remarkable works of Feodosy executed in 1508.

The iconostasis of the Cathedral is of enormous historical and artistic value. It was designed and most of the icons were painted by Theophanes the Greek, but on the third tier of the iconostasis the works of Andrei Rublyov can be seen. It is in connection with the Cathedral of the Annunciation that the name of Andrei Rublyov first occurs for in all probability it was here that he began his work.

In the ancient crypt of the Cathedral a permanent archaeological exhibition has been opened, which displays the most important finds made in excavations within the Kremlin walls.

The Church of the Deposition of the Virgin's Robe

The little Church of the Deposition of the Virgin's Robe was built between 1484 and 1486 by architects from Pskov as a private chapel for Russian metropolitans and patriarchs.

The iconostasis is of great artistic value, being designed in 1627 by a group of Russian painters headed by Nazary Istomin.

After work of restoration in the church was completed, a small exhibition of ancient Russian pictorial art was opened. The western and northern galleries house a unique collection of ancient wooden sculpture and stone masonry. Here there are rare carved icons, 15th-18th century crosses and other works by Russian folk artists.

The Cathedral of St. Michael the Archangel

The Cathedral of St. Michael the Archangel was built between 1505 and 1509 by the Italian architect, Alevisio Novi in the style of traditional Russian architecture. The rich decoration in the Cathedral, however, is more characteristic of the Italian Renaissance.

The original murals have not been preserved, having been removed together with the plaster in the mid-17th century. The present frescoes were painted in the 17th century by artists gathered from all over Russia under the supervision of master painters from the Armoury. They depict battle scenes from the history of the struggle for Russian independence as well as other scenes from daily life. The murals also include full-length portraits of the Muscovite princes. On one of the columns there is a painting of the outstanding 13th-century statesman and soldier Alexander Nevsky.

The iconostasis (1680-1681) is beautifully decorated in ornamental gold fretwork. Most of the icons were painted by such famous icon-painters as Dorofei Ermolayev, Ermolai Zolotarev and Mikhail Milyutin who are noted for their realistic style. The icon of St. Michael the Archangel is late 14th century and there are also 15th and 16th century icons.

From the 14th century the Cathedral of St. Michael the Archangel contained the sepulchre of the Muscovite princes and tsars, who continued to be buried there until 1700. There are 46 tombs with whitestone epitaphs, etched in intricate Slavonic characters and giving the names and dates of the deceased. The earliest tomb is that of Ivan Kalita who died in 1340 and the Cathedral also contains the tombs of such famous historical personages as Dmitri Donskoy, the great prince and soldier, Ivan III (the Great), Ivan IV (the Terrible) and his sons.

The 17th century frescoes which had been almost completely obliterated over the years were fully restored in 1953-54.

The Bell Tower of Ivan the Great

Rising high above Cathedral Square and uniting its churches into a single artistic ensemble, the 81 metre Bell Tower of Ivan the Great presents a magnificent example of early 16th century architecture. It was designed between 1505 and 1508 by the Italian architect Marco Bono. In 1600 a further two tiers were added, making it the main watch-tower in the Kremlin with a view over 25 to 30 kilometres.

The admiration of contemporaries was aroused not only by the height of the tower, but also by its beauty, its balanced proportions and its perfection of form. The grandeur and harmony of the structure seemed to embody the strength of the centralized Russian state, and the Bell Tower of Ivan the Great became the prototype for many Russian towered churches.

Between 1532 and 1543 on the north side of the Bell Tower the architect Petrok Maly built a campanile—a huge building for housing the large bells. In 1624 Bazhen Ogurtsov built another campanile, known as the Filaret.

When Napoleon left Moscow in 1812 he ordered the Bell Tower to be blown up, but the magnificent column withstood the blast and only the campaniles were destroyed. In 1819 these were restored by Domenico Gilardi.

Altogether there are 21 bells in the belfry and campaniles, all decorated with bas-reliefs and ranging from the 16th to the 19th centuries, when the finest of Russia's bells were cast. The largest is the "Dormition" bell, weighing 70 tons.

Beside the Bell Tower of Ivan the Great, outside Cathedral Square, stands the heaviest bell in the world, the **Tsar Bell** (Tsar-Kolokol). Cast in 1733-35, by Ivan Motorin and his son, Mikhail, it is 5.80 m high, 6.60 m in diameter and weighs more than 200 tons. Artistically it has no equal in the world. During the great fire of 1737 the bell still lay in its casting pit and attempts to extinguish the fire led to water falling on the red-hot bronze. The result was that a huge chunk weighing 11.5 tons fell off the bell. After that the Tsar Bell remained in the earth for almost 100 years. In 1836 it was raised and put on a granite pedestal by the architect Montferrand, where it stands today.

Another fine example of the advanced standard of Russian metallurgy is the **Tsar Cannon** (Tsar-Pushka), which also stands near the Bell Tower of Ivan the Great. It is older than the Tsar Bell, being cast in 1586 by Andrei Chokhov. The cannon weighs 40 tons, is 5.32 metres long and has a bore of 0.917 m. The gun-carriage and cannon-balls lying near the cannon are purely decorative and were made in the 19th century. The cannon itself was designed to fire not cannon-balls but grape-shot.

The Great Kremlin Palace

On the crest of the Borovitsky Hill in the southern part of the Kremlin, where Yuri Dolgoruky once founded his settlement stands the Great Kremlin Palace.

It was here that Ivan III built the first of many stone palaces. But fire and enemy invasion again and again necessitated their rebuilding. By the late 17th century the palaces here, like the churches of the Kremlin, had acquired a certain grandeur. But when the capital moved to St. Petersburg, all building in the Kremlin was discontinued. In the 1740s the famous architect Bartolomeo Rastrelli renovated the tsar's palace which had fallen into delapidation making it splendidly ornamental.

But the Great Kremlin Palace took on its present form in 1849 when it replaced the Rastrelli building. The new palace was 125 metres long and contained more than 700 rooms including several private suites that were occupied by the royal family: the Palace of Facets (Granovitaya Palata), the Sacred Vestibule (Svyatiye Seni), the Golden Chamber of the Tsarina (Zolotaya Tsarytsina Palata) and the Terem Palace (Teremnoi Dvorets). The Great Kremlin Palace was designed by K. Thon and built by P. Gerasimov, D. Chichagov and other famous architects. Its main façade faces the River Moskva and appears to be three storeys high, but in fact there are only two, the upper having its windows in two tiers.

The Great Kremlin Palace today has retained much of its traditional ceremonial significance. It has witnessed many important historical events in the social and political life of the Soviet Union. Party congresses have taken place here as have many CPSU Central Committee Plenums. Here in the Great Kremlin Palace state treaties are signed as well as communiques and protocols on mutual cooperation between the USSR and other countries. Here government awards are presented and government and diplomatic receptions held.

It is in the Great Kremlin Palace that sessions of the highest legislative bodies of the USSR and the RSFSR–the Supreme Soviet of the USSR and the Supreme Soviet of the RSFSR– are held. In the vast Meeting Hall of the Supreme Soviet the two chambers of the Soviet parliament—the Soviet of the Union and the Soviet of Nationalities—gather to hold their sessions. Entirely built in 1934 by I. A. Ivanov-Schitz this huge hall (it has 3,000 seats) combines the former St. Alexander and St. Andrew Halls. From 1920 to 1922 the St. Andrew Hall was the scene of the first congresses of the Communist International and sessions of the All-Russia Central Executive Committee at which many of the speeches were delivered by Lenin. In memory of this a white marble statue of Lenin by S. Merkurov was placed in 1939 at the back of the hall, behind the presidium seats.

Next in size after the Meeting Hall of the Supreme Soviet is the Georgiyevsky Hall (1,250 square metres in area and 17.5 metres high). The hall is devoted to the commemoration of Russian military glory. The columns along the walls contain sculptures by Giovanni Vitali which personify Russia's victories. The hemispherical vaults of the hall, which rest on huge pillars are decorated with moulded ornamentation. In the recesses between the pillars there are marble plaques on which the names of the soldiers and regiments who distinguished themselves in battle are carved in gold. It is in the Georgiyevsky Hall that receptions are held in honour of veterans of the Revolution, the Civil War, the Great Patriotic War and heroes of labour.

Next to the Georgiyevsky Hall is the Vladimirsky Hall, an octagonal room which was also designed for ceremonial occasions. This hall links the 19th-century palace with the ancient civic buildings that are part of the latter's ensemble.

The former royal suites in the Great Kremlin Palace are now kept up as museums.

From 1966 to 1973 the façades and interiors of most the rooms that make up the Great Kremlin Palace were restored.

The Palace of Facets and the Sacred Vestibule

The Palace of Facets is one of the few remaining parts of the Tsar's palace that was built in the late 15th century by Ivan III. It functioned as his reception room and is the oldest stone civic building in Moscow. Building was begun on the Palace of Facets by Russian masters under the supervision of the Italian architects Marco Ruffo and Pietro-Antonio Solari in 1487 and completed in 1491. The main façade of the building looks out on to Cathedral Square and is faced in cut stone slabs, from which its name is taken.

This ceremonial palace is 9 metres high and has an area of 495 square metres, which made it the largest hall in Moscow. The cruciform vaults of the Palace of Facets are supported by a rectangular column in the centre of the hall which gives an impression of great space and lightness. On the walls and on the vaults the Belousov brothers, masters from Palekh (a village renowned for centuries for its distinctive paintings), reproduced in the 19th century according to an exact description left by the famous Russian icon-painter Simon Ushakov subjects taken from the ancient 16th-century murals.

In ancient times the entrance from Cathedral Square to the Palace of Facets led through the Sacred Vestibule (Svyatiye Seni), a small room which was changed considerably in the 19th century. The Sacred Vestibule is decorated with whitestone portals which have the appearance of being entwined with gold and silver lattice-work—such was the craft of the Russian stonemasons. On the second floor above the vestibule, the window of a *tainik* (secret chamber) can be seen. It was from here that the tsarinas and princesses would watch the ceremonies taking place in the Palace of Facets, since custom forbad their personal participation.

In 1968 major restoration work was completed on the Palace of Facets and the Sacred Vestibule. Modern master craftsmen have restored the stone lattice-work and the frescoes as well as the three-tiered crystal chandelier and the parquet.

The Terem Palace

The Terem Palace is a fascinating monument of 17th century Russian architecture and social life. It was built by Bazhen Ogurtsov, Antip Konstantinov, Trefil Sharutin and Larion Ushakov, who put three additional storeys on to the parts of the older 16th-century palace. The tiered structure of the Terem Palace and especially its old-style window frames of white stone, the tiles on its portals and its cornices and parapets offer a fine example of Russian traditional architecture. The Terem Palace contains 17th century royal suites.

The Terem Palace also includes a group of churches: the Cathedral of the Redemption (Verkhospassky Sobor), the tsars' private chapel, St. Catherine's Church, the private chapel of the tsarinas and the princesses, the Church of the Resurrection of Lazarus (Voskreshenye Lazarya), the oldest church in the Kremlin (1393) and others. In 1680-81 they were all united by a single cornice and roof, decorated with eleven elegant cupolas on slender drums, and faced in coloured tiles. This was the work of Osip Startsev.

The Tsarina's Golden Chamber was built in the late 16th century as the official reception room of the tsarina. Its walls and vaults are covered with frescoes and three of its windows look out on to Cathedral Square.

The Poteshny Palace

Almost the same age as the Terem Palace, the Poteshny (Amusements) Palace was rebult in 1679 as a theatre. It was here that the royal court put on various theatrical performances and other "amusements".

The Poteshny Palace has been rebuilt several times, but its basic southern and northern façades and the official entrance with its small pitcher-shaped columns and its intricately designed windows have retained their original form.

The Patriarch's Palace and the Cathedral of the Twelve Apostles

The Patriarch's Palace and the small five-domed Cathedral of the Twelve Apostles (both 17th century) were built by the David Okhlebinin, Antip Konstantinov and Averky Mokeyev on the instructions of Patriarch Nikon, who tried to assert the domination of the church over the state. The Patriarch's Palace is no less luxurious than the tsar's and consists of many chambers and churches linked by passageways and staircases. Several of the living and other rooms have been preserved together with the Cathedral and the main part of the palace, the huge Room of the Cross, or the Myrrh Chamber, as it is called.

The well-known 17th century traveller, Paul of Aleppo, left the following description of the chamber: "Particularly remarkable is its wide vault without central support... It is laid with beautiful coloured tiles. The huge windows look out on to the cathedral (Cathedral of the Dormition—*Ed.*) and contained small windows fashioned from a wonderful mica and ornamented with seemingly real flowers... Near the door is a huge stove of fine tiles."

Specialists worked for more than 40 years to restore the ancient monument to its original form.

In the Room of the Cross a museum of 17th century art and culture has been opened. Here you can see exhibitions of bronze, tin and silverware, crystal and glass, and embossed plate. There is also an exhibition of 17th century dress and ornaments. One of the rooms in the museum shows what the Patriarch's office looked like.

The Arsenal

The Arsenal is a remarkable example of 18th century architecture. Its rectangular form is distinguished by its monumental simplicity. It was built by Peter the Great in 1702 for the manufacture and storage of weapons, and as a museum for the display of military accoutrements captured in battle with foreign invaders. The Arsenal was built by two outstanding Russian architects, Mikhail Cheglokov and Dmitri Ivanov with the participation of the German architect, Christoph Konrad. As a result of the war with Sweden (1700-21) building was discontinued and not begun again until 1722. In 1737 the partially finished building was severely damaged by fire and not restored until 1754. In 1812 it was again badly damaged by Napoleon's troops and restored once again, this time by Osip Bove. Since then it has remained intact.

Along the walls of the Arsenal are cannons cast by Russian masters as well as hundreds of others captured from the French.

The Arsenal has also strong historic connections with the Revolution. In October 1917 the Arsenal was manned by a unit which had come over to the side of the revolutionaries. These were given short shrift by the Cadets who managed to take the Kremlin by a trick. They were lined up in Senate Square unsuspectingly and machine gunned. A memorial plaque on the south façade of the Arsenal bears the names of the fallen and the following inscription: "On this spot our comrades, soldiers of the Kremlin Arsenal, were shot by Cadets for their part in the defence of the Kremlin during the October Revolution (October 28, 1917). Eternal be their memory!"

There are two other memorial plaques on the left of the Arsenal's south entrance arch. These are dedicated to the officers and men of the Kremlin Garrison who died in the defence of Moscow and the Moscow Kremlin in the German bombardment during the Great Patriotic War.

The Presidium of the Supreme Soviet of the USSR

In 1932 building was started near the Spassky Gates of the All-Russia Central Executive Committee Military School. Designed by I. Rerberg this was the first building to be put up inside the Kremlin during the Soviet period and was intended for students who would both study in the Kremlin and defend it. Work was completed in 1934. Afterwards the purpose of the building was changed to house the Sverdlov Club and, in 1958, the Kremlin Theatre, where it staged the performance of all-Union reviews as well as plays put on by the people's and professional theatres and visiting drama companies from abroad.

After the building of the Kremlin Palace of Congresses, this building was redesigned as the office of the Presidium of the Supreme Soviet of the USSR and now houses the offices of the Soviet Parliament and its standing commissions.

During sessions of the Supreme Soviet its chambers—the Soviet of the Union and the Soviet of Nationalities—occupy the building in turn. This is also the meeting place for the Council of Elders, which consists of representatives from the groups of deputies.

It is to this office that ambassadors and other representatives of foreign states come to present their credentials, and here meetings and talks are held between Soviet state officials and foreign delegations.

It is here that the Chairman of the Presidium of the Supreme Soviet, who is President of the Soviet Union, carries out his work.

The central room in the building is the Conference Hall, seating 1,000 and equipped with a relay system which provides a simultaneous translation of the speaker into any one of the languages of the Union Republics. The balcony running round the hall is designed for visitors, foreign journalists and diplomats.

In the tradition of the palatial halls of the Kremlin the decor of the Conference Hall is finished in rare woods, polished stone and crystal.

Places Associated with Lenin

Brief in time, but immeasurable in significance—such was the period of Lenin's life connected with the Kremlin. Here he lived and worked from 1918 to 1922 and from here he guided the revolutionary transformation of Russia; here he grappled with the most difficult problems of defending the country against the counter-revolution and foreign intervention and restoring the economy and here he planned the building of the world's first socialist state.

... On March 12, 1918 Vladimir Ilyich Lenin passed through the Troitskiye Gates to enter the Kremlin for the first time. As head of state he had come to examine the new premises designed for the revolutionary Government of the Soviet Republic.

The Government Building

One of the finest works of the great Russian architect, M. Kazakov, this building was originally built in 1776-88 to house the Senate.

The building is triangular in form and has three internal courtyards. The main room is a domed hall about 27 metres high and some 25 metres in diameter making it one of the largest halls in old Moscow. Along the walls there are 24 columns and in the gaps between them, 18 multi-figured bas-relief panels. The high dome of the vault is richly covered in moulded ornamentation.

In terms of its architecture and decor this hall is one of the masterpieces of Russian classicism and has been called the Russian Pantheon. The hall aroused the astonishment of contemporaries not only for its artistic perfection but also for the technique of the architect who raised such a cupola and made it no more than one brick in thickness.

After the Soviet government moved to Moscow the Council of People's Commissars and the All-Russia Central Executive Committee were housed here. In spring 1918 the red flag was raised above the huge dome.

The State Flag itself was the subject of discussion at a meeting of the All-Russia Central Executive Committee under the chairmanship of Lenin on April 8, 1918, and the revolutionary red banner was approved as the national flag of the new Soviet Republic. Later the hammer and sickle appeared in the top left hand corner as symbols of the union of the working class and the peasantry.

If you stand in Red Square and look towards the Kremlin, you will see the upper storey of the Government Building rising above the Kremlin wall and surmounted by the state flag of the USSR. This is part of the architectural composition that opens with the Lenin Mausoleum.

In 1919 the round hall was named the Sverdlov Hall in memory of Yakov Sverdlov, the first chairman of the All-Russia Central Executive Committee. Here between 1919 and 1922 Party Congresses and conferences took place under the chairmanship of Lenin. Nowadays Plenums of the Central Committee of the CPSU are held here, government honours are bestowed and the International Lenin Prizes ("For the Promotion of Peace Among Nations") are awarded. The building contains the offices of the Council of Ministers of the USSR, the highest executive and administrative organ of state power in the USSR.

The third floor of the building contains Lenin's apartment and study.

Lenin's Apartment and Study Museum

Lenin's study is a small room with two windows. On the desk there is nothing at all superfluous—just an ink-stand, a number of pens and pencils, a couple of telephones and a lamp. At the desk is a high-backed wicker chair. Standing a little to one side is another desk surrounded by soft leather chairs, intended for visitors. In one corner stands a revolving bookcase full of reference books and some two thousand books line the walls.

This library was collected by Lenin himself. In 1918 Lenin first catalogued his books, but in subsequent years their numbers grew considerably so that they had to be placed in one of the rooms of the Sovnarkom (Council of People's Commissars) and in Lenin's flat itself. In all there are more than ten thousand books, periodicals and pamphlets in twenty different languages on such varied subjects as the social sciences, literature, mathematics and physics, technology, agriculture, medicine, geography, chemistry and military matters.

Though involved in work on the urgent problems that faced the Soviet state at its inception, Lenin nevertheless continued to develop Marxist revolutionary theory. It was here that he wrote *The Immediate Tasks of the Soviet Government* and finished his book, *The Proletarian Revolution and the Renegade Kautsky.*

During the Civil War it was from this room that Lenin organized the defence of the new Soviet Republic. By the door of the study is a table covered with atlases and maps. Two large maps hang on the wall with small flags indicating the various front lines. The pencil marks here were made by Lenin himself. To this room all important information connected with the progress of the war came pouring in...

But Lenin never thought of his work as something that cut him off from the people. Large numbers of people were received in the Kremlin including petition-bearers from the villages, delegations of workers, cultural figures, scientists, students, representatives of the communist and workers' parties and public figures from abroad.

December 12, 1922 was the last day on which Lenin worked in his study. Opposite his desk there is a large antique clock, which shows when Lenin left his study for the last time—8.15 p.m.

The room next to Lenin's study is a hall which was used as

the meeting place for the Council of People's Commissars, the Council of Labour and Defence and the Political Bureau of the Central Committee of the Party. In those days the situation facing the country was critical and work in this room was intense. In the first few months after the government had moved here it sat daily and the Council for Labour and Defence weekly. All these sittings were chaired by Lenin and those present at them were astounded at his remarkable clarity of thought, rapid understanding of the matter at hand, his bold, broad and principled solutions and his ability to instantly weigh up pros and cons and arrive at the correct decision. In memory of the fact that Lenin once worked here, his chair is still kept in the room.

Further along the corridor from Lenin's study is the apartment that was occupied by the Ulyanov family. It consists of four small rooms furnished in the simplest style. The largest room was occupied by Lenin's sister, Maria Ilyinichna and a smaller room by his wife, Nadezhda Konstantinovna Krupskaya. Next came their dining room and, finally, the smallest room in the apartment which belonged to Lenin. It served the dual function of bedroom and study and was furnished with the bare minimum—a bed, a few chairs, a bookcase and a writing desk. In the words of the Soviet writer Alexander Serafimovich: "Everything here was designed for work and very little for rest." It was here that between December 1922 and February 1923 when Lenin was suffering from a serious illness that he dictated his last articles and letters to the Central Committee: "Pages from a Diary," "On Co-operation," "How We Should Reorganize the Workers' and Peasants' Inspection," "Our Revolution," "Better Fewer, but Better" and a few others. In these articles and letters Lenin assessed the work of the Bolshevik party during the years of Soviet power and continued to examine problems confronting the building of socialism in the country.

* * *

On May 1, 1920 the first All-Russia Subbotnik (a Saturday worked voluntary without pay for the benefit of society) took place. Lenin himself took part in it helping to carry wooden beams and clear rubble inside the Kremlin. Now on this spot a flower garden has been laid and here on November 2, 1967 in honour of the 50th anniversary of the Great October Socialist Revolution a Monument to Lenin was unveiled.

Monument to Lenin

Looking at the monument you get the impression that Lenin has left his study for a few minutes and come to sit down for a rest under the shade of the trees. The small granite pedestal does not make the bronze figure of Lenin look any different from any of the other visitors who have come to the Kremlin. Lenin is there among them. The sculptor—V. Pinchuk and the architect S. Speransky—have contrived to bring out the simplicity and humanity in Lenin's features. At the foot of the monument there are always flowers. The strict, noble beauty of the sculpture harmonizes with the architecture of the Kremlin.

The State Armoury

The Armoury was built by K. Thon in 1851. It is the oldest Russian museum and contains rare examples of applied art and culture.

But the museum is far older than the present building which houses it, beginning as the treasure house of the great Muscovite princes in the 14th century. By the 16th century it had already taken on the features of a state repository, but at the same time it was also a workshop for the manufacture of weapons and armour. The finest craftsmen in all Russia including armourers, workers in metal and bone, embossers, jewelers, gold-embroiderers and painters were gathered here. Besides weapons, gold, silverware, jewelry, crockery and icons were made for the court.

When Peter the Great moved the majority of master craftsmen to St. Petersburg, this "arts academy," as it was known, ceased to exist in the Kremlin. The Armoury became simply a repository for armour, valuable military trophies and royal regalia. In the early 18th century it became a family museum for the Romanovs and was added to exclusively "at his majesty's request."

The Great October Socialist Revolution made the treasures in the Armoury the property of all the people, to whom they rightfully belonged. During the first years of the Soviet Republic the halls of the Armoury, as other museums throughout the country were made open to the public.

The basic collection of the Armoury consists of works created in the Kremlin workshops, of which the armoury was the biggest. The exhibition opens with weaponry, armour and sundry accoutrement from the 13th to the 18th century, and includes bows, quivers, arrows, chain-mail, hauberks, sabres, swords, maces, spears and ceremonial axes. The oldest exhibit is a late 12th century helmet supposedly belonging to Prince Yaroslav, the father of Alexander Nevsky. Pride of place in the museum goes to a collection of ceremonial fire-arms, the earliest examples of these weapons known. The collection also contains examples of the work of the famous armourers from Tula.

Two halls contain the remarkable works of Russian gold and silversmiths from the 12th to the 19th century.

The museum contains a unique collection of 14th-19th century cloths and dress showing the finest examples of weaving, gold, silver and pearl embroidery from Byzantium, Persia, Turkey, Italy, Spain, France and Russia.

Among the gifts presented to the Russian tsars from foreign states there are examples of the work of 15th to 19th century Polish, German, English, Dutch and French jewelers as well as articles of crystal, jasper and ivory from the East.

There is an exhibition of court vestments from various epochs, fashionable clothes from the 16th-17th centuries, ceremonial armour, Russian pre-revolutionary orders and orders bestowed by foreign states, Gobelin tapestries.

Also on display are ornamental saddles and harnesses, decorated by Russian and foreign craftsmen and a unique collection of stage coaches, each of which is a work of art in itself.

During the Soviet period a considerable amount of work has been done on studying the collections contained in the Armoury. They were carefully restored, classified and information about them published. The treasures of the Armoury are open to general viewing and every day the museum is visited by more than three thousand people.

The Diamond Collection of the Soviet Union

Continuing as it were the exhibition on display in the Armoury and housed in the same building is the Diamond Collection of the Soviet Union, containing some of the finest diamonds in the world.

Here you can see the legendary Orlov and Nadir Shah diamonds, whose history dates back to the 16th and 17th centuries, as well as other unique jewels from the historical treasures of Russia. There are 35 "named" uncut diamonds from Yakutia including the October, Komsomol, Golden Prague and Valentina Tereshkova diamonds. A special case contains rare gold and platinum nuggets.

The Diamond Collection of the Soviet Union presents a unique collection of the works of 18th-19th century Russian jewelers in gold, platinum and precious stones, as well as modern works.

The Kremlin Palace of Congresses

In 1961 the ancient ensemble of the Kremlin received a new addition—the Palace of Congresses. Though light and airy in appearance, it at the same time produces an impression of monumental magnificence arousing in the onlooker a surprisingly festive mood. The architecture is simple and functional. The façade, a plane surface of polished glass divided by narrow triangular white marble pylons, opens on to a spacious foyer and broad staircases. The Palace of Congresses looks especially impressive at night when all the lights are on and it is full of people.

The events that take place in this building attract attention throughout the world for it was here that the 22nd, 23rd, 24th and 25th Congresses of the Communist Party of the Soviet Union were held. Sessions of the Supreme Soviet of the USSR, ceremonial occasions in honour of important anniversaries in the life of the Soviet people and international forums and congresses take place in the Palace of Congresses.

But the Palace of Congresses is a building with many functions, one of the most important of which is the holding of various theatrical performances and other popular festivities. The huge auditorium is designed to seat six thousand. Special facilities are installed for simultaneous interpreting in 29 languages. A system of hoists allows various scenic and other transformations to take place. The proscenium and the seats of the Presidium are separated from the main stage by a decorative curtain in the centre of which is a bas-relief portrait of Lenin against a red background. This curtain was made by Latvian artists.

Here on the stage of the Palace of Congresses the Bolshoi Theatre gives special performances of ballet and opera.

The main foyer of the Palace is decorated with a frieze portraying the 15 arms of the Union republics and the arms of the Soviet Union, executed in mosaics after a drawing by the famous Soviet artist, Alexander Deineka.

The Palace has more than 800 separate rooms including halls, foyers, lobbies, cloakrooms, special rooms for the Presidium, the diplomatic corps and the press, rehearsal halls, changing rooms and rooms for the service and technical staff.

Above the auditorium there are buffets able to accommodate up to 2,500 people, and from the gallery which surrounds the auditorium there is a beautiful view over the Kremlin and the streets of Moscow.

The Palace of Congresses took no more than 16 months to build. And the architects and builders—M. Posokhin (chief designer), A. Mndoyants, Y. Stamo, P. Shteller, A. Kondratyev, G. Lvov and I. Kochetov—were awarded the Lenin Prize.

RED SQUARE AND KITAIGOROD

*Red Square—Lenin Mausoleum—Cathedral of St. Basil—
Monument to Minin and Pozharsky—Place of Execution—
GUM—State History Museum—Kitaigorod—October 25
Street—Kuibyshev Street—Razin Street*

The merchant settlements and their Great Trading Quarter (Veliky Posad), which lay next to the Kremlin have already been touched upon in the first Chapter *(A Little History)* of this book. The formation of settlements of this kind under the walls of a fortress was a fairly common phenomenon all over Europe, and all over the world for that matter. The Great Trading Quarter came almost right up to the walls of the Kremlin and only a little space was left for a market centre, the *Torg* as it was called. In the 14th century Ivan Kalita, who understood the advantage of a central market under the walls of his fortress, "turned" the Kremlin towards the Great Trading Quarter. He had all the merchants' shops placed along the eastern side of the wall and made the main entrance to the Kremlin on this side also. This is where

71

Red Square stands today. During the first half of the 16th century the Great Trading Quarter was surrounded with fortifications, which became part of the Kremlin walls. The importance of the square (after the fire of 1403 its area was considerably expanded) increased rapidly. Social life in the capital was transferred from Cathedral Square within the Kremlin to the broad square outside it. After the tall hipped roofs were added to the Spasskaya Tower and the other Kremlin towers in the 17th century and a number of stone buildings in the square were erected, the people began to call it Krasnaya, which in those days meant beautiful but now means red. By the mid 17th century this name became officially accepted.

RED SQUARE

Red Square (Krasnaya Ploshchad) has been the witness of many important events in the life of the Russian people. Here the popular revolts that shook the throne of the tsars usually had their beginning, and here autocracy held its courts to try the defeated insurgents. Red Square has been the scene of parades in celebration of Russian military glory and many other ceremonies and official functions. Though time has changed the face of Red Square it has remained the centre of the city and the main square in Moscow.

The Great October Revolution of 1917 gave new meaning to the name of Square, for the red flag of proletarian revolution now flew above it.

On November 10, 1917 proletarian Moscow accompanied the fallen heroes of the Revolution on their last journey. They were buried in a mass grave in the Kremlin wall.

Many times the voice of Lenin rang out over Red Square as he addressed crowds of revolutionary soldiers and workers, calling upon them to save and protect the gains of the Revolution and give all their strength in the struggle for a brighter future for mankind. Inspired by his words the revolutionary workers and soldiers would go out from Red Square to meet the enemy and grapple with hunger and destruction.

But on those sad days in January 1924 Red Square was hushed in silence, as the people, grieving at their loss, bid farewell to Lenin.

Across Red Square the first lorries, planes and tractors produced by Soviet industry passed, the heroes of the five-year plans, and pilots who had performed hitherto unheard of feats marched. On June 24, 1945 a Victory Parade was held in Red Square and the banners of the defeated fascist troops were cast at the foot of the Lenin Mausoleum.

On national holidays it has become the tradition for many thousands of Moscow's inhabitants to assemble in Red Square, and every year on the two revolutionary holidays (November 7 and May 1) demonstrations of the working people take place here. There are guest stands for distinguished citizens and foreign guests.

The Lenin Mausoleum

Stretching along one side of the Kremlin walls, Red Square has become a part of its overall architectural ensemble, with seven Kremlin towers standing along its western side.

The compositional centre of Red Square is the Lenin Mausoleum, wherein lies the body of the great revolutionary leader and founder of the Communist Party of the Soviet Union and the Soviet State.

The Lenin Mausoleum is a classic work of Soviet architecture. Its architect, A. Shchusev, employed a simple and expressive design in the form of a monumental edifice, faced in dark red granite and black labradorite, which embodies, as it were, the grief of the people and the power of Lenin's eternal teaching.

Every hour on the hour to the peal of the Kremlin chimes the guards are changed at the entrance to the Mausoleum. It is a solemn ceremony that remains long in the memories of those who have witnessed it. Summer and winter, rain or fine, an endless stream of people come to pay their respects to the memory of Lenin.

During national festivities the Mausoleum becomes a tribune before which pass the columns of demonstrators and participants in the military parades. On both sides of the Mausoleum there are stands of light-grey granite for the guests.

Behind the Mausoleum along the Kremlin wall the revolutionary necropolis is located. Here lie buried outstanding figures in the

Communist Party of the Soviet Union and the Soviet State, leaders of the international workers' and communist movement, scientists and men of culture, great soldiers and national heroes. The memories of many of these persons live on in the names of Moscow's streets and squares: Kirov Street, Gorky Street, Kuibyshev Street, Krupskaya Street, Maria Ulyanova Street, Sverdlov Square, Dzerzhinsky Square, Nogin Square, Gagarin Square, Korolev Street, Lyusinova Street, Vorovsky Street, Sapunov Street and many others.

In your excursions round Moscow you will frequently come across the names of those who are buried in Red Square.

The Cathedral of St. Basil the Blessed

The Cathedral of St. Basil (Khram Vasiliya Blazhennovo), also known as the Intercession Cathedral, stands in the southern part of Red Square near the Spasskiye Gates, and is easily distinguishable by its particoloured cupolas. Centuries of Russian architectural development are represented in Red Square and this remarkable building. It was built as a monument to an historical Russian victory, as a result of which the khanates of Kazan and Astrakhan were annexed to Russia in October 1552. It is a masterpiece of ancient Russian architectural art.

Building on St. Basil Cathedral began in 1555 on the orders of Ivan the Terrible and it was completed in 1561.

According to the ancient chronicles St. Basil Cathedral was built by architects Postnik and Barma.

Brought up on the works of Russian wooden architecture they reproduced in stone many of the traditional motifs of the ancient masters, and created a monument whose composition has no equal anywhere in the world. The Cathedral consists of nine dissimilar turriform churches united into a single artistic whole. The central, hip-roofed one has a height of 57 metres (until the additions had been made to the Bell Tower of Ivan the Great it was the tallest building in Moscow). It is encircled by four onion-shaped cupolas, below which are another four onion-shaped cupolas. The cathedral is supported by a single base and the second storey is encircled by a gallery with intersecting passages.

The external ornamentation on the Cathedral reflects a seemingly inexhaustible wealth of imagination on the part of the two architects.

The Cathedral of St. Basil is now a branch of the State History Museum.

The Monument to Minin and Pozharsky

Near the Cathedral of St. Basil stands a monument to the heroes of the national liberation struggle against the Polish and Lithuanian invaders in the early 17th century. This was the first monument in Moscow to be erected to civilians and it was executed by the famous sculptor Ivan Martos in 1818, being paid for out of public subscription. The inscription reads: "To Citizen Minin and Prince Pozharsky—Russia is thankful. 1818." True to the classical traditions of the time the sculptor clothed his heroes in Grecian garb, but they are typical Russians and equally clearly express the patriotic fervour of the liberation struggle against foreign invasion.

Place of Execution

Near the Cathedral of St. Basil is a low round stone mound. This was the Place of Execution (Lobnoye Mesto—in Old Russian this meant a place that could be seen from all round.) In the mid-16th century it was also used as a tribune for making royal proclamations and it was from here that Prince Dmitri Pozharsky proclaimed in 1612 the freedom of Moscow from foreign invasion. The Place of Execution was guarded by cannons including the famous Tsar Cannon.

As the name suggests, it was here that sentences of death were announced, but they were actually carried out nearby. In the 18th century the Place of Execution was faced in white stone by the famous Moscow architect M. Kazakov and in this form it has remained to the present day.

GUM—The State Department Store

For centuries the eastern side of Red Square had been associated with trading and the first stone shops were built here in the 1590s. Today on the site of the former commercial arcades of Red Square (Verkhniye Torgoviye Ryady) stands the State Department Store, better known as GUM, which was built in 1894 by architect A. Pomerantsev and engineer V. Shukhov and reconstructed in 1953. The design of the building incorporates many old Russian architectural elements. It is 250 metres in length and consists of three passages covered by a glass and metal roof. The overall length of the counters in GUM is 2.5 kilometres and the store serves some 400 thousand customers daily.

The State History Museum

At the far end of Red Square stands the red-brick building of the State History Museum. It was built in 1878-1883 by V. Sherwood in the style of the 17th century with ornamental façades, decorative porches and towers on its pyramid-shaped roof. Formerly this had been the site of the Zemstvo Offices and then in 1775 the first Russian university, which was founded by Mikhail Lomonosov and which was later transferred to a building on what is now Marx Avenue.

The State History Museum is more than 100 years old. To describe all the treasures which are housed in its 47 halls would be to write a whole history of the country from the earliest times to the present day. The museum holds something like four million exhibits and more than 10 million documents.

The museum contains an archaeological section showing the life and culture of the ancient peoples who inhabited the territory of what is now the Soviet Union.

Of exceptional value is the collection of coins and medals, of Russian, Eastern and West European weaponry, ancient utensils and furniture. Here is displayed the magnificent art of the Russian gold and silversmiths, cabinet makers, stone masons, gold embroiderers, lace workers and weavers.

Among the ancient books and manuscripts there are Russian, South Slavonic, and Byzantine monuments going back to the

13th century as well as 11th century Greek manuscripts, and 10th century script from Novgorod written on birch-bark. The autographed manuscripts include the originals of a number of important manifestos of the Russian liberation movement.

The visitor to the State History Museum will see recreated before him a panorama of the ancient past and the recent present. ... A hauberk from a Russian soldier who fought at the battle of Kulikovo in 1380, a school book on birch-bark once belonging to a boy who lived ten centuries ago in the city of Great Novgorod; the sabre of Dmitri Pozharsky and the seal of Kuzma Minin, leaders of the people's liberation movement in the early 17th century, a steam engine built in 1766 in the Urals by Ivan Polzunov, the clothes worn by Ivan the Terrible, the carriage of Peter the Great, the bed of Napoleon, left behind after his panic flight from Russia, the pikes of Stepan Razin's and Emelyan Pugachev's men used in the rebellions of the 17th and 18th centuries, weapons used on the revolutionary barricades in 1905 and 1917, the guns that smashed the last German pill-boxes in Berlin in 1945 and many more.

Side by side with these relics of the past are monuments to the contemporary achievements of the Soviet people: the tub which was used by the builders of the Krasnoyarsk Hydro-Electric Station in Siberia to pour the first concrete into the dam, the identity card of the world's first cosmonaut, Yuri Gagarin, a globe of the Moon, made after the lunar flight of the first Soviet automatic station and presented to its chief designer, Academician Sergei Korolev... The list is endless.

The exhibits of the Soviet period show clearly the path travelled by the Soviet people in more than 60 years of Soviet power.

* * *

The historical and architectural monuments in Red Square are sacred to the Soviet people. The 1970s saw the completion of a long period of restoration work that was carried out in Red Square on an enormous scale and included such important projects as the renovation of the Lenin Mausoleum, the cleaning of the Kremlin walls, during which almost a million bricks were replaced with new ones made according to the ancient methods, the redecoration of the Kremlin towers, in which the stone lattice

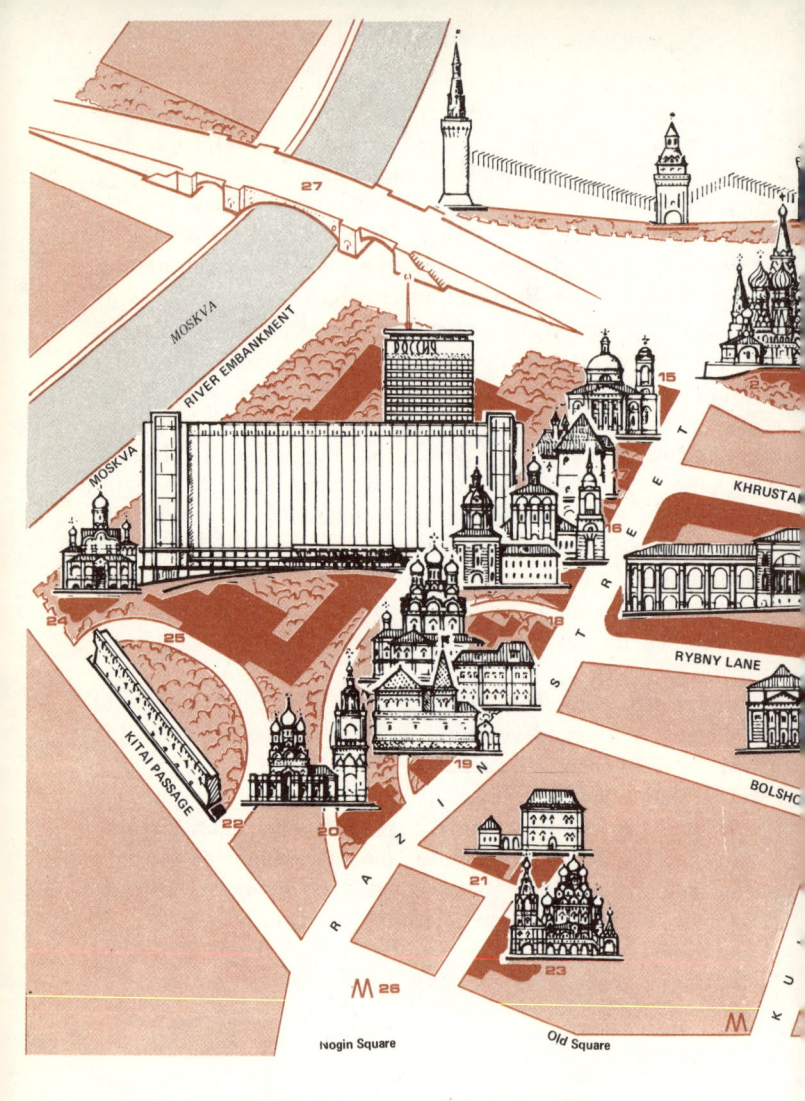

RED SQUARE AND KITAIGOROD

1. Lenin Mausoleum
2. Cathedral of St. Basil the Blessed, a branch of the History Museum
3. Monument to Minin and Pozharsky
4. Place of Execution (Lobnoye Mesto)
5. State Department Store (GUM)
6. Ploshchad Revolyutsii Metro Station
7. State History Museum
8. Provincial Government Building and Old Mint (18th cent.)
9. Saviour Behind the Icons Monastery (early 17th cent.)
10. Cathedral of the Epiphany (17th cent.)
11. Moscow Institute for Historian-Archivists (former Printing House, 16th cent.)
12. Slavyansky Bazar Restaurant

Red Square

HISTORY PASSAGE

Revolution Square

SAPUNOV PASSAGE

KUIBYSHEV PASSAGE

Sverdlov Square

OCTOBER STREET

MARX AVENUE

New Square   Dzerzhinsky Square

13. Old Merchants' Court
    (18th-early 19th cent.)
14. USSR Chamber of Commerce
    and Industry
    Zaryadye
    (15th-17th cent.)
15. Church of St. Barbara
16. Church of St. Maximus
17. Old English Tavern
18. Znamensky Monastery and
    the Old State Court
19. Boyar's House (16th-17th cent.),
    a branch of the History Museum
20. Church of St. George on
    Pskov Mount
21. House of Simon Ushakov
22. Parts of Kitaigorod Wall
23. Trinity Church in Nikitniki,
    a branch of the History Museum
24. Church of the Conception of
    St. Anne
25. Rossia Hotel
26. Ploshchad Nogina Metro Station
27. Moskvoretsky Bridge

ornamentation on the Nikolskaya Tower was made gleaming white and the steeple and chimes of the Spasskaya Tower were freshly gilded, and the renewal of the visitors' stands by the Lenin Mausoleum. All this work, carried out by architects, engineers, builders, granite masons, stone masons, gilders, engravers and other craftsmen, was done to make Red Square preserve its beauty for centuries, so that future generations can see the main square of the capital of the Soviet Union in exactly the way it was created by the genius of the people.

KITAIGOROD

After the Great Trading Quarter had been surrounded by fortifications, this part of Moscow began to be called the Kitaigorod (as we mentioned above, the name signified a type of fortification). Fragments of the old Kitaigorod wall can still be seen in Sverdlov Square (behind the Metropol Hotel) and in Kitai Passage (Kitaisky Proyezd) near Nogin Square (Ploshchad Nogina).

For centuries Kitaigorod was the centre of Muscovite trade, it being forbidden in the other parts of the city until the mid-18th century and Red Square was the centre of Kitaigorod. Three streets, now called October 25 Street (Ulitsa Dvadtsat Pyatovo Oktyabrya), Kuibyshev Street and Razin Street—led into the square and between them lay a warren of side streets, where the trading stalls were located. In the 17th century there were 72 of these side-streets or rows *(ryady)* as they were called crowded in between the three main streets and they contained as many as 700 stores. The names of many of the "rows" have still been preserved today in such side streets as Crystal (Khrustalny), Fish (Rybny) etc. The contemporary layout of Kitaigorod was largely formed in the late 19th and early 20th centuries, when the district gradually became the business centre of bourgeois Moscow. Here the major trading companies built their offices, banks, insurance companies, joint-stock companies and wholesale warehouses. Kitaigorod represents a unique collection of Russian architectural monuments from different ages and many of them today contain historical and art museums and exhibitions. Today Kitaigorod is one of the nine protected areas of Moscow and, as in Red Square, a considerable amount of restoration work is being carried out here. A number of major government institutions and ministries are now located in this area.

With the building of the Rossia Hotel Kitaigorod became one of the centres of Moscow's hospitality, but its life as a trading district is still maintained, for not only is GUM, the State Department Store located here, but so also is the USSR Chamber of Commerce and Industry.

Your excursion around Kitaigorod is best begun from October 25 Street (Ulitsa Dvadtsat Pyatovo Oktyabrya).

October 25 Street

The street begins opposite the Nikolskaya Tower from **History Passage** (Istorichesky Proyezd), where the former Iberian Gates used to stand and which served as the main entrance into Kitaigorod from the side of what is now Gorky Street. Formerly the Nikolskaya it was renamed in honour of the events of the Great October Socialist Revolution in Moscow. In October 1917 Red Guards fought with counter-revolutionary detachments along the Nikolskaya and finally broke out into Red Square where they joined up with other Red Guard units in order to take the Kremlin.

Many of the buildings on October 25 Street are connected with the history of the Russian liberation movement.

On the corner of History Passage (No 1) and October 25 Street stands what was formerly the **Provincial Government building** (built in 1740 by I. Heyden). Here was situated notorious "Yama" (the pit), a debtors' prison. A memorial plaque on the wall outside states that from September to October 1790 the famous revolutionary teacher, writer and philosopher, Alexander Radishchev was held here under guard on his way to exile in Siberia. Radishchev's ideas, and particularly his famous book *Journey from Petersburg to Moscow* which represented a bold challenge to autocracy and the serf-owners had tremendous influence over the development of progressive thought in Russia.

In the courtyard of the debtors' prison is an even older building, the **Old Mint** (Monetny Dvor), built in the late 17th century and one of the few industrial buildings of the time that have come down to us. It was here that in 1775 the leader of the greatest serf uprising in Russian history, Emelyan Pugachev, was held together with his followers before his execution.

Further along this side of the street in the courtyard of No 7 there are several old buildings, which formed the **Zaikonospassky** (Saviour Behind the Icons) **Monastery**, which was founded in 1600. In the reign of Peter the Great the monastery was extended and new buildings were added by the Russian architect Ivan Zarudny. The octagonal top and rotunda of the monastery cathedral rise above the top of the Kitaigorod wall and can be easily seen from Sverdlov Square. It was here that the first higher educational institute in Russia—the Slavonic, Greek and Latin Academy—was opened in 1687. Among the more famous pupils of this academy were Lomonosov, Bazhenov, the famous architect, Kantemir and Trediyakovsky, the poets, Magnitsky, the author of the first arithmetical textbook to be published in Russian and Krasheninnikov, the renowned geographer and explorer.

On the right, in **Kuibyshev Passage** (Kuibyshevsky Proyezd) there is a remarkable work of 17th century architecture, the **Cathedral of the Bogoyavlensky Monastery**. This tall turriform church is pure Moscow baroque, full of rich, decorative ornamentation.

But this street not only saw the beginning of higher education in Russia, but also of printing. On March 1, 1564 Ivan Fyodorov and his assistant, Pyotr Mstislavets published at the Printing House the first Russian book, the *Acts of the Apostles* in 267 pages. Later in 1703 during the reign of Peter the Great the **State Printing House** published the first Russian newspaper, *Vedomosti* (the Gazette). Only two rooms of the first Russian printing house have survived in the courtyard of No 15. They later became part of the Synodal Printing House, which was built on the same spot in 1814. Today the building houses Moscow Institute for Historian-Archivists. The green walls of the building are covered with white stone carving and the façade has been decorated by A. Bakarev and I. Mironovsky with spiral columns, lancet windows, ancient porches and a sun-dial above the entrance— a whimsical combination of Gothic elements with ancient Russian architectural motifs.

The next building, No 17, once the Slavyansky Bazar Hotel, has gone down in the annals of the history of the theatre, for it was here on June 21, 1898 that the famous meeting took place in the restaurant of the hotel between Vladimir Nemirovich-Danchenko and Konstantin Stanislavsky, which led to the formation of the Moscow Arts Theatre. Today this building houses **Slavyansky Bazar restaurant**, which is famed for its traditional Russian cuisine.

A little further up the street on the left is the short **Tretyakov Passage** (Tretyakovsky Proyezd). It was built by the Tretyakov brothers who owned the estate, which was situated here, and whose collection of art works became the foundation of the famous Tretyakov Gallery. The passage was built in 1870-73 by A. Kaminsky, with elegant archways at each end in the style of ancient Russian architecture. It links October 25 Street with Marx Avenue.

At the end of the street there once stood the fortified wall and towered gates which marked the eastern boundary of Kitaigorod.

Kuibyshev Street

Kuibyshev Street (Ulitsa Kuibysheva) was named in 1935 after Valerian Kuibyshev, an eminent figure in the Communist Party and the Soviet State. In the past it was the main street of Kitaigorod.

In the 19th and early 20th centuries the bourgeoisie bought up much of the property belonging to the old nobility with its spacious palaces and gardens and built in their place larger buildings with richly ornamented façades and smart interiors. The classical buildings of the great Russian architect, M. Kazakov, were rebuilt in the "art nouveau" style while the officially approved pseudo-Russian style was introduced.

One of the largest buildings in pre-revolutionary Moscow was the **Old Merchants' Court** (Stary Gostiny Dvor), No 4, which was built between 1790 and 1805 by I. Selekhov and S. Karin and designed by Giacomo Quarenghi. The monumental façades of the Old Merchants' Court are lined on all sides by huge Corinthian half-columns and arches.

Most of the buildings on Kuibyshev Street are occupied by various organizations and institutions. Behind the Old Merchants'

Court stands a collonnaded building (No 6) which was once the Stock Exchange. Built by A. Kaminsky in 1875, it now houses the central offices of the **USSR Chamber of Commerce and Industry**, an institution which promotes internal trade and strengthens commercial contacts between the USSR and foreign countries. Every year the USSR Chamber of Commerce with the participation of the various ministries and enterprises concerned organizes exhibitions of Soviet machinery, instruments and consumer goods, and provides facilities for foreign firms to exhibit their products in the USSR.

Razin Street

This street is named after Stepan Razin, the great leader of the peasant revolt against feudal oppression in the 17th century. It was along this street that on June 6, 1671 he was led to execution in Red Square.

Razin Street (Ulitsa Razina) was one of the boundaries of the area occupied by the trading rows. Further on, down the slope that leads to the River Moskva, lay the Zaryadye district (beyond the rows), which in ancient times was the nucleus of Kitaigorod serving as its port. According to a guide-book written in 1917 just before the October Revolution, the Zaryadye was "one of the dirtiest and most congested parts of Moscow, crammed full of traders and merchants, large and small."

Cleared of its humble dwellings, Razin Street is a veritable open-air architectural museum. Many years work have gone into restoring the original beauty, that was created by Muscovite architects of bygone age, and the street is now an officially protected area.

At the entrance to Razin Street near Red Square stands the small **Church of St. Barbara** (No 2)—a fine example of late 18th century Russian classicism—whose high ground floor is decorated with Corinthian porticoes. Next along the street at No 4 is the 17th century **Church of St. Maximus**, which today houses the permanent exhibition of the All-Russia Society for the Protection of the Environment.

Between these two churches and a little further down the incline that leads to the Rossia Hotel stands a white two-storeyed building, whose age can be judged from its high, four-sided sloping roof and its thick walls, broached here and there with tiny windows. This is the **Old English Tavern**, which was granted in 1556 by Ivan the Terrible to English merchants for use as their Moscow office. One floor of the English Tavern was used as living quarters and the other as stores. It was here that diplomats and envoys from England would stay while visiting the Russian court. In the early 17th century the building was destroyed and the ancient walls were later covered and built upon so that to all intents and purposes the English Tavern had disappeared forever. But recent restoration work recovered the original walls and even part of the ornamentation and today this unique monument has been fully restored with ancient whitestone blocks being used for its cupola vault. It now houses an exhibition of local archaeological finds, organized by the Institute of Archaeology of the USSR Academy of Sciences.

A little further down Razin Street on the right is the entrance to the north wing of the **Rossia Hotel**, which was built in 1969, Chief architect D. Chechulin. The hotel itself forms a rectangle 44 metres in height with the south wing running alongside the River Moskva where broad stairways lead up from the embankment, the west wing facing the Kremlin and the east wing opening on to Kitai Passage. The central section of the north wing is surmounted by a twenty-storey tower which commands a beautiful view over the Kremlin, Red Square and Kitaigorod. The Rossia Hotel can accommodate more than 5,000 guests. It has a two-studio **Zaryadye Cinema**, with seats for 1,550, a **Central Concert Hall** accommodating 2,500 and several restaurants and cafes. The hotel's decor is finished in aluminium, glass, marble and high quality woods. The concert hall has a large stage equipped with all the necessary facilities for the production of dramatic and musical works. Here congresses, receptions, exhibitions, balls, dances and New Year festivities are held. The chairs in the auditorium are equipped with headphones which provide simultaneous translations in seven languages.

Below the overpass that leads to the second floor of the Rossia Hotel from Razin Street is one of the most interesting monuments in the Zaryadye—a complex of buildings including the **Znamensky**

Monastery and the chambers of the **Old State Court** (Stary Gosudarev Dvor).

In 1613 Mikhail, grandson of the Romanov Boyars, was made tsar of Russia. On ascending the throne he took up his place of residence in the Kremlin, and in 1634 founded on the Old State Court, his former estate, the Znamensky Monastery, which subsequently enjoyed the patronage of the Romanov royal family.

The five-cupola, two-tier church which is the largest in the monastery complex was built between 1679 and 1684 by Fyodor Grigoriev and Grigory Anisimov, who are described as being "apprentice stonemasons". After restoration in 1976 the church was opened as a concert hall.

The monastery ensemble includes an 18th century belfry (which stands before the ramp leading to the hotel) and the boyar's house (16-17 cent.), which is a **branch of the State History Museum** (No 10). Here you can see the boyar's study, the dining hall and the women's rooms. In the vestibule there are chests and caskets and on the lower floor store-rooms with household utensils, weaponry, and trunks of clothes, valuables, money and tableware. The upper storey is used for various exhibitions put on by the State History Museum.

The row of churches on Razin Street ends with the small five-cupola **Church of St. George on Pskov Mount**, a characteristic example of 17th century ornamental architecture.

The side streets that run off to the left of Razin Street also contain a number of monuments of ancient Russian architecture that are worth seeing. At 12 Ipatyevsky Lane there stands the two-storey stone **House of Simon Ushakov**, the famous 17th-century painter, who renounced the traditional norms of icon painting and created beautiful realistic works, thereby exerting a tremendous influence on Russian 17th century iconography. Here were the living quarters and studio where he worked with his pupils. Of particular interest is the palatial façade of the House, with its ornamental lintels, cornices and inter-floor bands.

In neighbouring **Nikitnikov Lane**, No 3, stands one of the most beautiful churches in Moscow, the **Trinity Church in Nikitniki**. Built between 1631 and 1634 by the merchant, Grigory Nikitnikov, who was so wealthy he used to lend money to the tsar, the church is considered the finest example of mid-17th century Russian ornamental architecture. It is remarkable for its wealth of decorative ornamentation, particularly the beautiful *kokoshniki* (an architectural structure in the form of a Russian woman's hat) around the golden cupolas, and the complex creating intricate compositions in the tradition of old-time Russian housebuilding. This building incorporates the architectural techniques, which were later used in many of the buildings in Moscow of the time. The walls in the church are covered with frescoes by the "royal masters" of the Armoury which have remained in an excellent state of preservation. The upper tiers of the iconostasis are full of ancient icons, while the lower tier contains works by Simon Ushakov and other painters from the Armoury. In the 1930s the Trinity Church became a **branch of the State History Museum**.

Further along Razin Street we come to the end of Kitaigorod. On the right, along **Kitai Passage**, is a restored part of the Kitaigorod fortifications. The four metre thick wall, the embrasures designed for short, middle and long range firing and the rampart running round behind the merlons testify to the impregnability of this fortress.

Next to the Rossia Hotel is the late 15th century whitestone **Church of the Conception of St. Anne**. Restoration work has restored its original look, which was spoiled by later additions. This church is one of the oldest in Moscow outside the Kremlin.

KARL MARX AVENUE AND THE CENTRAL SQUARES

Marx Avenue—Borovitskaya Square—50th Anniversary of October Revolution Square—Alexander Gardens—Monument Tomb to the Unknown Soldier—Sverdlov Square—Revolution Square—Lenin Central Museum

Marx Avenue

The avenue which now bears the name of Karl Marx has always connected the various streets and squares that lie along the north-west wall of the Kremlin and the boundaries of Kitaigorod. It is one of the main thoroughfares of the city.

Borovitskaya Square

The Borovitskaya Square is situated by the Borovitskiye Gates of the Kremlin, which were formerly the only gates of the ancient fortress. According to the chronicles, in 1493 Ivan III, wishing to protect the Kremlin from destruction by fire, ordered a fairly large gap to be left between the walls of the Kremlin and the living quarters on the far side of the River Neglinnaya. This gap was very probably the origin of the street which is now Marx Avenue.

The south quarter of Borovitskaya Square opens on to the **Bolshoi Kamenny Most** over which a six-lane highway carries traffic across the River Moskva. The bridge is 187 metres long and was built in 1938 by N. Kalmykov and designed by V. Shchuko, V. Gelfreikh and M. Minkus. The parapet is surmounted by a monumental iron railing.

On the crest of the hill opposite the Borovitskiye Gates and commanding a view over Marx Avenue stands a beautiful palace— the finest work of the Russian architect, Vassily Bazhenov. Built in 1784-86 for the rich landowner, P. Pashkov and formerly known as the **Pashkov House**, it is now part of the **Lenin State Library**. The building is considered one of the most beautiful in old Moscow and a masterpiece of Russian classicism. The harmonious perfection of the Pashkov House and its ornamental façade have aroused the admiration of Muscovites and visitors to the city for more than 200 years.

In 1862 it housed the Rumyantsev Museum and Public Library, which was founded on the extensive collection of N. Rumyantsev, a famous collector of Russian books, chronicles, manuscripts and works of art. In 1925 this institution became the Lenin Library and a memorial plaque informs visitors that in August 1893 and February 1897 Lenin studied here in the reading room.

Between 1928 and 1958 a series of new buildings (3, Kalinin Avenue) were added to the Pashkov House by V. Shchuko and V. Gelfreikh as part of the plan to extend the Lenin Library. It is now the largest library in the world and its façades face two avenues—Marx Avenue and Kalinin Avenue. The façade along Marx Avenue is decorated with 14 allegorical figures—a worker, a collective-farmer, a soldier, etc.—and statues of the world's great writers and thinkers.

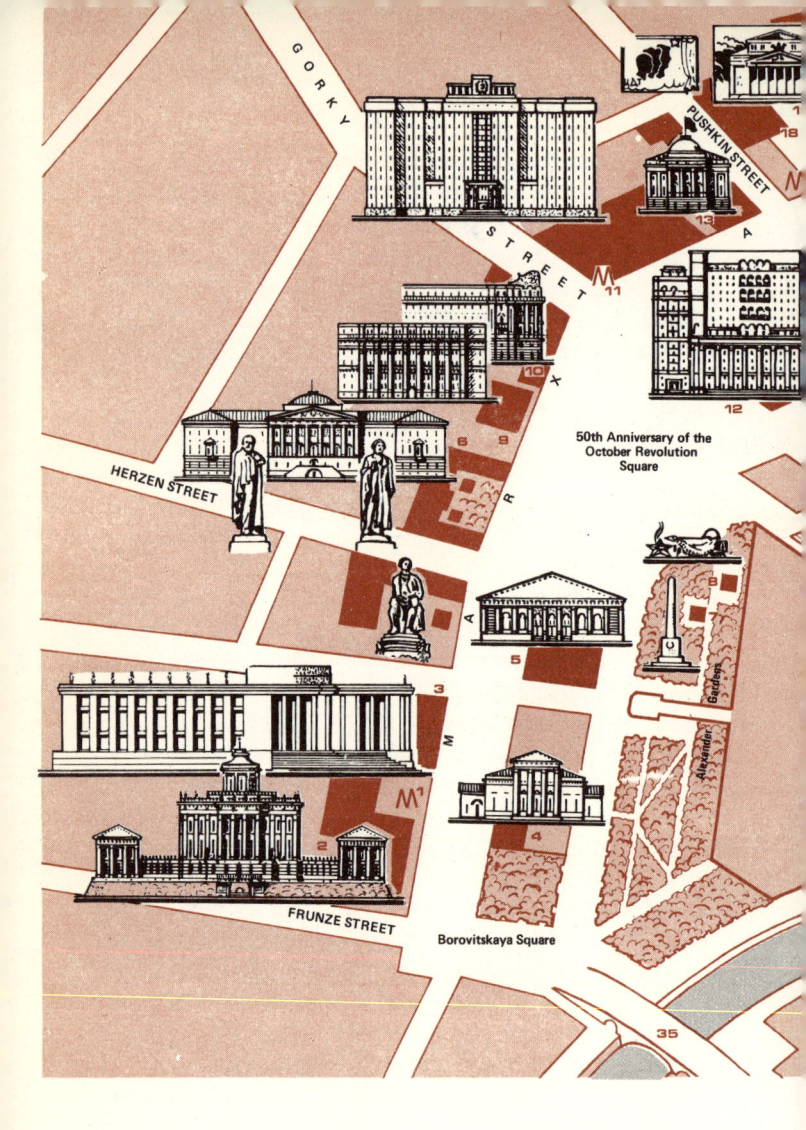

MARX AVENUE AND THE CENTRAL SQUARES

1. Biblioteka Imeni Lenina Metro Station
2. Pashkov House (18th cent.)
3. Lenin State Library
4. Kalinin Museum
5. Central Exhibition Hall (former Manège)
6. Moscow State University

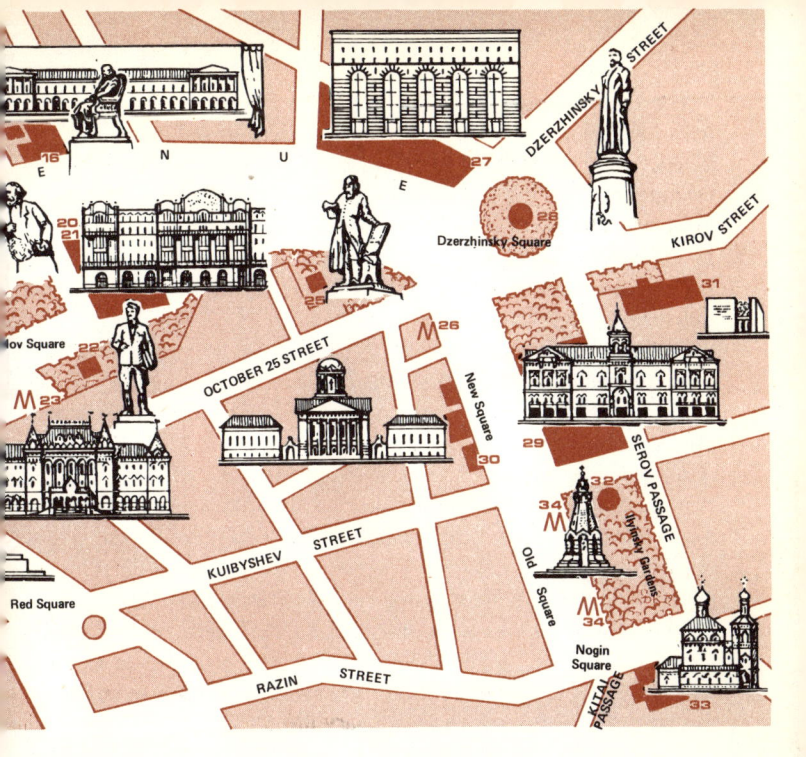

7. Obelisk set up in honour of the great Socialist philosophers and revolutionaries
8. Tomb of the Unknown Soldier
9. Intourist
10. Natsional Hotel
11. Prospekt Marksa Metro Station
12. Moskva Hotel
13. House of Trade Unions
14. Ploshchad Sverdlova Metro Station
15. Bolshoi Theatre
16. Maly Theatre
17. Monument to Alexander Ostrovsky
18. Central Children's Theatre
19. Monument to Karl Marx
20. Metropol Hotel
21. Intourist Central Travel Bureau
22. Monument to Sverdlov
23. Ploshchad Revolyutsii Metro Station
24. Central Lenin Museum
25. Monument to Ivan Fyodorov, the first Russian printer
26. Dzerzhinskaya Metro Station
27. Detsky Mir (Children's World) Department Store
28. Monument to Felix Dzerzhinsky
29. Polytechnical Museum
30. Museum of the History and Reconstruction of Moscow
31. Mayakovsky Museum
32. Monument to the Russian Grenadiers who fell in the glorious Battle of Plevna
33. Church of All Saints on Kulishki (14th cent.)
34. Ploshchad Nogina Metro Station
35. Bolshoi Kamenny Bridge

The Lenin Library contains more than 28 million books, periodicals and sets of newspapers in 89 languages of the peoples of the USSR and 109 foreign languages. Every years some 3 million readers visit the library, where there are 22 reading rooms at their disposal. The library also has one of the largest book museums in the world. The Lenin Library maintains a constant system of book exchanges with 3 thousand libraries and scientific institutions throughout the world.

The rare books and manuscripts section has a number of unique collections including Old Slavonic and Russian 11th century manuscripts, editions of the works of Kopernik and Giordano Bruno, published in their lifetime, the first off-prints made by Ivan Fyodorov as well as manuscripts and first editions of the works of famous Russian scientists and writers. The library also possesses a collection of the newspapers published by the French Communards during the Paris Commune, complete sets of the political newspaper *Kolokol* (the Bell), published by Herzen in London from 1857 to 1868 which exposed tsarist autocracy, a full set of Lenin's illegal newspaper, *Iskra* (The Spark), which was the first Russian newspaper of the revolutionary Marxists as well as many other editions of underground revolutionary literature.

Opposite the Lenin Library on Marx Avenue is the **Kalinin Museum** (No 21), devoted to a prominent member of the Communist Party and Lenin's comrade-in-arms. The son of a peasant, Mikhail Kalinin (1875-1946) started out on the shop floor as a turner and ended up Chairman of the Presidium of the Supreme Soviet of the USSR.

Across the road from the Lenin Library on the corner of Marx Avenue and Kalinin Avenue at No 22/4 is a reception hall, where Mikhail Kalinin used to receive visitors from all over the country. Now this building houses the **reception rooms of the Chairmen of the Presidium of the Supreme Soviet of the USSR** and **the Presidium of the Supreme Soviet of the RSFSR.**

A little further along on the other side of the road stands the huge edifice of the former Manège. The entrance to this vast building, which stretched the whole block, is on 50th Anniversary of the October Revolution Square. In its day it was considered a miracle of architectural construction. Despite its huge dimensions (170 m × 45 m) the building has no intermediate supports, its roof being held in place by a skilful interlacing of wooden beams and rafters. The Manège was built in 1817 by the military engineer A. Bétancourt and designed by Osip Bove. In 1957 the building was redesigned to function as the **Central Exhibition Hall**. It has an exposition area of 6,500 square metres and is used for holding exhibitions of Soviet and foreign paintings and photography etc., as well as for presenting architectural and sculptural projects for nation-wide viewing and discussion.

On the other side of Marx Avenue (No 18), behind iron railings stands one of the buildings of the **Moscow State University**. This used to be called the "new" University (as distinct from the "old" university building) until the Moscow State University (MGU) was built on the Lenin Hills. It was built in 1836 by Y. Tyurin in the style of Russian classicism. In 1941 both the building itself and a monument to the founder, Mikhail Lomonosov, were damaged during the fascist bombing, but the building was restored in 1943 and a new bronze **monument to Lomonosov** (by I. Kozlovsky) was put up in 1957. Today the building houses the faculty of journalism. (More information on the Moscow State University is contained in the Chapter *The South-West*.)

50th Anniversary of the October Revolution Square

This square (Ploshchad Pyatidesyatiletiya Oktyabrya) was built in the early 1930s as part of the reconstruction of the city centre.

In the centre of the square stands a two metre granite slab which was placed in position on the eve of the 50th anniversary of the October Revolution and which marks the spot where a future monument is to be built in honour of the Great October Socialist Revolution.

The Alexander Gardens

On the south side of 50th Anniversary of the October Revolution Square you can see the ancient Kremlin walls, the yellow building of the Arsenal rising above them, the round Arsenal Tower and, along the side of the wall, running parallel with the Square, the Alexander Gardens (Aleksandrovsky Sad). The gardens were laid in 1821-24 according to a design by O. Bove above the cover channel of the Neglinnaya, which had been piped underground. At the foot of the Intermediate Arsenal Tower Bove set an ornamental grotto, which he entitled "Ruins". The monument cast-iron gates of the gardens railings present a fine example of Russian foundary work.

In the central avenue of the garden stands an **obelisk, set up in honour of the great Socialist philosophers and revolutionaries**, which was the first Soviet monument. It was unveiled on November 7, 1918 following Lenin's decree "On the Removal of Monuments Erected in Honour of the Tsar and His Servants and the Designing of Monuments to the Russian Socialist Revolution." On Lenin's suggestion the names of the tsars and the double-headed eagle, the symbol of autocracy, were removed from a column that had been erected in 1913 to mark the tercentenary of Romanov dynasty, and replaced with the names of those great thinkers whose memory is dear to the people: Marx, Engels, Liebknecht, Lassalle, Bebel, Campanella, Meslier, Winstanley, Thomas More, Saint Simon, Vaillant, Fourier, Jaurès, Proudhon, Bakunin, Chernyshevsky, Lavrov, Mikhailovsky and Plekhanov.

In December 1966 during the 25th anniversary of the defeat of Hitler's forces outside Moscow, the ashes of the Unknown Soldier were taken from where they had lain—the 41st kilometre on the Leningrad Highway, a scene of bloody and vicious fighting— and ceremonially buried in the Alexander Gardens. On May 8, 1967 a memorial ensemble was opened above the **Tomb of the Unknown Soldier**, at the centre of which burns the Eternal Flame, which was lit in Leningrad from the undying flame that burns in the Field of Mars, where the bodies of the heroic fighters of the revolution lie buried. The Eternal Flame lights up a five-pointed military star and the inscription: "YOUR NAME IS UNKNOWN, YOUR FEAT IS IMMORTAL" is etched on the granite plaque of the gravestone. On a granite wall nearby are the words: "TO THOSE WHO DIED FOR THEIR COUNTRY. 1941-1945." Further to the right along the Kremlin wall is a row of ten blocks of dark-red porphyry under which are urns containing sacred earth from the Hero Cities: Leningrad, Kiev, Minsk, Volgograd, Sevastopol, Odessa, Kerch, Novorossiisk, Tula and Brest Fortress. Each block bears the name of the city and an embossed representation of the Golden Star medal. The gravestone at the Tomb of the Unknown Soldier is crowned with a large bronze emblem—a soldier's helmet, the flag and a laurel branch. On ceremonial guard at the grave stand two light-blue fir-trees (A distinct species of fir-trees which grow in the Caucasus.—*Tr.*). The ensemble was designed by architects D. Burdin, V. Klimov, Y. Rabayev and the sculptor, N. Tomsky.

Every year on May 9, the Victory Day, the whole country observes one minute silence in respect for the memory of the fallen and flowers are placed on the soldiers' graves. It has become the tradition for newlyweds, on the day of their wedding to come to the Tomb of the Unknown Soldier in order to pay their respects to those who died to give them the happiness they enjoy today.

From the Alexander Gardens you have a fine view over the whole 50th Anniversary of the October Revolution Square and all the buildings of various epochs that surround it.

On the right of Herzen Street is the "old" **University building** (1786-1793) whose harmonious lines and proportional structure are characteristic of the work of M. Kazakov. After the fire of 1812 it was restored by Gilardi, who rebuilt the façade and the semi-circular assembly hall. In 1922 monuments (by N. Andreyev) were set up in front of the building **to Herzen and Ogarev**, the great Russian revolutionary democrats who were graduates of the University.

The next building on this side of the square (No 16) was built in 1934 by I. Zholtovsky. The façade has half-columns with classical capitals, and magnificent cornices and balconies. The building houses The USSR Company for Foreign Travel better known as **Intourist**. Intourist makes all travel arrangements for foreigners within the USSR having cooperative arrangements with more than 700 firms and shipping agencies all over the world and organize foreign travel for Soviet citizens. There are departments of Intourist in more than 100 towns throughout the USSR. It has a staff of some 5,000 guides and interpreters to help visitors from abroad learn about the life and achievements of the USSR and see the famous sights and monuments of its history and culture. Intourist offers more than 20 types of excursion, including individual and package tours, coach and car camping holidays, treatment at health resorts, trips to arts festivals and sporting events, river and sea cruises, "friendship trains", and holidays for schoolchildren etc.

On the corner of 50th Anniversary of the October Revolution Square and Gorky Street stands the **Natsional Hotel**, built in 1903 by A. Ivanov. A memorial plaque commemorates the fact that in March 1918 Lenin stayed here after the Soviet government had moved to Moscow. He occupied room 107 on the second floor. In recent years the interior of the hotel has been completely renewed.

Further ahead lies that section of Marx Avenue which used to bear the name Okhotny Ryad (Game Market).

> In the 18th century the River Neglinnaya used to flow along the Kitaigorod wall where it formed ponds and small lakes. Here stood a water-mill, which ground flour and further along in Okhotny Ryad were the barns where the corn was stored. It was here that hunters and fishermen used to bring the meat, game and fish they had caught along the river and trade it for grain and flour.
>
> The commercial character of Okhotny Ryad was retained throughout the next century. By the late 19th century it was a dirty street, built up on both sides by two-storey houses, usually consisting of a shop on the ground floor and an inn on the first floor.

Looking at Marx Avenue as it is now, all this is very hard to imagine. Between 1933 and 1935 two new buildings were erected to give this part of Moscow the look it has today.

On the right hand side (looking from 50th Anniversary of the October Revolution Square) is the huge building of the **Moskva Hotel** faced in white marble. Designed by A. Shchusev, L. Savelyev and O. Stapran and accommodating 840 guests, the Moskva Hotel was the first hotel in Moscow to be built during the Soviet period. Recently the older buildings which were adjacent to the hotel were pulled down and two new wings were added, thus doubling the hotel accommodation.

On the left hand side of Marx Avenue is the twelve-storey building of the State Planning Committee (Gosplan) which controls all aspects of state planning in the USSR including drawing up the five-year national economic development plans, outlining more long-term projections and fixing annual targets. The austere grandeur of its lines, the plinth and entrance portals which are faced in polished granite and the huge relief of the national emblem of the USSR, the only ornamentation on its façade emphasize the social function of the building (architect—A. Langman).

Next to Gosplan stands the **House of Trade Unions** (Dom Soyuzov). This masterpiece of classical architecture was built in the 18th century by M. Kazakov as a club for the Moscow nobility. It was then the largest dance hall in the capital and such famous personages as Pushkin, Lermontov and Tolstoy attended balls here. The Hall of Columns with its rows of white Corinthian columns and the multi-tiered crystal chandeliers that hang between them, which today leaves such an unforgettable impression, was famed for its acoustics and here Tchaikovsky, Rimsky-Korsakov, Rakhmaninov and Liszt gave concerts.

The Hall of Columns has been the scene of many important congresses and conferences and Lenin spoke here many times. It was here, from 23rd to 27th January, 1924 that Lenin's body lay in state after his death.

Beyond the House of Trade Unions lies Sverdlov Square.

Sverdlov Square

The old square took on its present features in the early 19th century.

The fire of 1812 destroyed all the buildings that surrounded the square, and a new design by Osip Bove was adopted for reconstructing it as one of the main squares of the city and linking it with the old centre, the Kremlin and Red Square. The River Neglinnaya, which used to run through the square, caused frequent inundations and so between 1816 and 1820 it was piped underground and the whole area was drained and levelled. In 1824 the Bolshoi Theatre was built on the site of a former theatre that had been destroyed by the fire and the Maly Theatre was also erected nearby in the same square. The façades of all the other buildings round the square were designed in the same style as the Maly

Theatre. This strictly symmetrical architectural ensemble by the architect Bove was considered the finest in Moscow. In 1830 it was named Teatralnaya Ploshchad (Theatre Square) and it remains the theatrical centre of the city.

In 1919 the square was renamed after Yakov Sverdlov, a prominent member of the Communist Party, Lenin's comrade-in-arms and the first chairman of the All-Russia Central Executive Committee. In 1978 a **monument to Sverdlov** was opened in the square. The 5.6 m bronze figure by R. Ambartsumyan (sculptor) and B. Tkhor (architect) stands on a three metre high pedestal before the ancient merloned wall of Kitaigorod.

Marx Avenue crosses Sverdlov Square (Ploshchad Sverdlova) dividing it in two.

In the northern half stands the **Bolshoi Theatre** with a monumental colonnade and quadriga of bronze horses on its pediment. Built in 1821-24 by A. Mikhailov and O. Bove it is one of the finest theatrical buildings in the world, a monumental work of Russian 19th century classicism. After the fire of 1853 the building was restored and partially rebuilt by A. Kavos. The five-tier hall can accommodate an audience of 2,000 and its acoustics and decor rival any opera house in the world.

In 1976 the Bolshoi Theatre company celebrated its bicentenary. It is the oldest Russian opera and ballet company. Here the classics of world opera and ballet and the finest creations of Russian and Soviet composers like Glinka, Tchaikovsky, Musorgsky, Rakhmaninov, Shaporin, Kabalevsky, Prokofiev, Khachaturyan and others have been performed. The vault of the Bolshoi Theatre has echoed to the voice of Chaliapin, Sobinov and Nezhdanova. Today such Soviet artists famous throughout the world as Arkhipova, Vasilyev, Liepa, Maksimova and many others perform here. Today the Bolshoi Theatre Company has some 900 artistes making it the largest in the world and performs opera, ballet, orchestral and choral works. Wherever people gather to enjoy and appreciate the finest achievements in serious music the name of the Bolshoi Theatre is honoured and loved.

The building of the Bolshoi Theatre has been connected with many important events in the Soviet Union's history. It was here, at the 8th All-Russia Congress of Soviets in 1920 that Lenin's plan for the electrification of the country was adopted. A map of the European part of the Soviet Republic was shown there, to light which it took almost all the power generated by Moscow's power stations. Now the USSR holds first place in Europe and second place in the world for the production of electricity. During the first years of the new Soviet Republic party congresses, meetings and conferences used to take place in the great hall of the Bolshoi Theatre and a memorial plaque informs visitors that Lenin spoke here more than 30 times. Another memorial plaque contains the following inscription: "Here on December 30, 1922 the First All-Union Congress of Soviets proclaimed the formation of the USSR and adopted the declaration and treaty on the formation of the Union of Soviet Socialist Republics."

Next to the Bolshoi Theatre is the **Maly Theatre**. The Maly Theatre company was founded in the mid-18th century, but its permanent building was not erected until 1821. Three years later, in 1824, it was rebuilt by Bove. The Maly Theatre has played an important role in the history of Russian society and it has been called the second Moscow University. Some of the greatest Russian actors have played here including Shchepkin, Mochalov, the Sadovskys, Yuzhin, Ostuzhev, Yablochkina and others. Many of the plays put on by the Maly Theatre have become part of the essential repertoire of the Soviet dramatic theatre. The Maly Theatre has been called the "House of Ostrovsky" for almost all the plays of the great Russian playwright have been performed here, and in 1929 a **monument to A. Ostrovsky** by N. Andreyev was set up in front of the theatre.

On the other side of the square, opposite the Maly Theatre is the **Central Children's Theatre**. Founded in 1921, it was one of the first professional theatres in the USSR to cater for a young audience. The theatre produces pantomimes for the very young and for school children of various ages, and, thanks to the mastery of the directors and the actors every performance becomes a happy event to be remembered.

In the centre of the square in front of the theatres is a public garden, which is particularly pleasant in spring when the boughs of the apple trees are covered with white may-blossom. The fountain outside the Bolshoi Theatre is a favourite place for rendezvous.

On the other side of Marx Avenue, the south side of Servdlov Square, there is another public garden. Here on May 1, 1920

Lenin laid the first stone of the future **monument to** the founder of scientific communism, **Karl Marx**, and in 1961 that monument was unveiled. Designed by L. Kerbel the bust of the great thinker, upon whose teaching the lives of millions of people are founded, project from an enormous granite block.

The garden also has a fountain, built in 1826-35 by Vitali and decorated with a graceful sculptural composition.

The **Metropol Hotel** is also situated on the south side of Sverdlov Square. Built between 1899 and 1903 by V. Valkot, it is considered one of the most interesting works of the then fashionable Art Nouveau. On the pediment is a ceramic pannel representing the "La Princess Lointaine" by M. Vrubel. The hotel contains a three-studio cinema and a restaurant. The main entrance is on Sverdlov Square and to the right is the **Intourist Central Travel Bureau**.

A plaque on the wall of the Metropol Hotel recalls the fierce fighting that took place here in what was then Theatre Square between the Red Guards and the counter-revolutionaries in 1917. Other memorial plaques commemorate the fact that in 1918-19 the hotel was occupied by the All-Russia Central Executive Committee headed by Sverdlov, that Lenin spoke here on many occasions and that in November 1921 talks were held here on the establishment of friendly relations between the RSFSR and Mongolia, in which the founder of the Mongolian People's Revolutionary Party and the Mongolian People's Republic, D. Sukhe-Bator, took part.

Revolution Square

The south part of Sverdlov Square joins Revolution Square (Ploshchad Revolyutsii).

Soon after revolutionary units had liberated the Metropol Hotel, they succeeded on November 2, 1917 (Old style) in taking the City Duma (Municipal Council) building, which was the headquarters of the counter-revolutionary forces in Moscow. The city centre was now in the hands of the revolutionaries. In memory of these battles the former Resurrection Square (Voskresenskaya Ploshchad) was renamed Revolution Square on May 1, 1918.

The Central Lenin Museum

The former Municipal Council Building (No 2) was erected in 1891-92 by D. Chichagov in the style of ancient architecture with its high sloping roofs, towers and ceremonial porch. After the revolution the emblem of old Moscow which hung above the entrance was replaced with a sculpture, entitled "Worker and Peasant" by G. Alekseyev executed in relief.

In 1936 the building was made the Lenin Museum, and from that time more than 45 million people from all over the world have visited it. The museum contains some 400 thousand documents, manuscripts, first editions, and collected editions of the works of Lenin, published in every continent of the world and in many different languages. According to statistics published by UNESCO Lenin is the most widely-read author in the world.

Moving from one hall to the other is like reading the pages of Lenin's biography, tracing year by year the life of the leader of the Communist Party, the creator of the world's first socialist state and the man who was one of the greatest philosophers, revolutionaries and statesmen the world has ever known.

On display in the museum are many of Lenin's personal effects, like the things he used when in hiding from the bourgeois Provisional Government (in a hut on the Razliv near Leningrad) and the coat he wore, when an attempt was made on his life on August 30, 1918. One room contains an exact reproduction of Lenin's study in the Kremlin, and also on display is the motor car used by Lenin in 1920-22, which has been restored by workers of the Likhachov Automobile Plant.

Every visitor stands in silence before the mask of white gypsum which captures the features of the great man in death. It was made by S. Merkurov immediately after Lenin had died.

In 1970, to mark the centenary of the birth of Lenin the exposition area of the museum was increased to include ten new halls on the third floor: "The Ulyanov Family," "Places Associated with Lenin," "Gifts to Lenin from the Working People," "Lenin in the Cinema and Theatre," etc. Of particular interest is the section entitled "The Figure of Lenin in Pictoral Art." Here you can see dozens of life drawings made during meetings with Lenin, studies and the first castings of the famous "Leniniana" by sculptor N. Andreyev. There are also many other paintings, graphics, and sculptures of Lenin throughout the other sections of the museum.

The exhibits show Lenin as the founder of the Union of Soviet Socialist Republics, the triumph of Lenin's nationalities policy and the development of the ideological and theoretical heritage of Leninism today.

* * *

Beyond Sverdlov Square Marx Avenue rises up towards Dzerzhinsky Square (Ploshchad Dzerzhinskovo).

To the right as you ascend Marx Avenue you can see on the hillside **a monument to Ivan Fyodorov, the first Russian printer**. The monument, by S. Volnukhin, was unveiled in 1909 and placed next to the State Printing House in Kitaigorod and where the first Russian book was printed. Fyodorov stands holding a galley and looking anxiously at the first proof...

Behind the monument is one of the most popular second-hand bookshops in Moscow.

On the opposite side of Marx Avenue and occupying a whole block is a bright multi-storeyed building with high arches and windows. This is **Detsky Mir** (Children's World), the largest children's shop in the Soviet Union, built in 1957 by A. Dushkin. Together with its 24 branches in different parts of the city, the Detsky Mir sells clothing, footwear, toys, furniture, schoolbooks and sports equipment. But the shop also learns from its young customers: every year a competition is held for the best home-made toys and models, and the best entries are put on show in the shop.

Dzerzhinsky Square

Ascending Marx Avenue you come out into Dzerzhinsky Square (Ploshchad Dzerzhinskovo), where altogether nine roads meet. In the centre of the square stands a **monument to Felix Dzerzhinsky**, a prominent figure in the Communist Party and Soviet state and Lenin's comrade-in-arms. The statue of this fearless "knight of the Revolution" was made in 1958 by the sculptor, Yevgeny Vuchetich. Dzerzhinsky was head of the Cheka, the All-Russia

Special Commission for Combatting Counter-revolution, Sabotage and Speculation, but for many years he combined this work with many other important posts. He was put in charge of some of the most difficult and troublesome problems facing the party and sent wherever there was need of his organizational ability, energy and selfless dedication. Thus Dzerzhinsky headed the commission which was set up to try and improve the lot of children and which after the Civil War saved millions of children from hunger, illness and criminal influence. Later he was made People's Commissar for the railways and Chairman of the All-Union Economic Council.

Dzerzhinsky Square was formerly known as Lubyanskaya Square, being so named by the inhabitants of Novgorod who settled here in the 15th century in memory of the Lubyanitsa Street in their native city.

Over the last few decades Dzerzhinsky Square has changed its appearance twice. In the 1930s when work was begun on the first plan for the reconstruction of Moscow, the walls and towers of the old Kitaigorod were pulled down all the way from the square itself to the River Moskva and in their place a broad highway was laid. The second stage of the reconstruction took place in 1970s when the square was considerably enlarged, the old buildings around the Polytechnical Museum were pulled down and underground road-crossings built.

Beyond Detsky Mir on the far side of the square stands a nineteenth century building with a clock on its tower. This was the headquarters of the Cheka. In 1946 the former Cheka building was enlarged with a new multi-storeyed block, designed by A. Shchusev. Its side façade faces on to what is at present Kirov Street. Here it is planned to build the new Kirov Avenue which will connect the central squares of the city with Komsomol Square, or the Three Stations Square, as it is often called.

Opposite Detsky Mir on the other side of Dzerzhinsky Square between two of the city's main thoroughfares, **Serov Passage** (Proyezd Serova) and **New Square** (Novaya Ploshchad) stands the Polytechnical Museum (3/4 Novaya Ploshchad). In 1972 the Polytechnical Museum celebrated its centenary. The museum has 80 halls and takes up the whole street-block. It contains some 20 thousand exhibits showing the achievements of Soviet science and technology. Lectures are given here by prominent scientists, engineers, innovators and figures from the world of culture. The Polytechnical Museum maintains connections with 48 foreign countries and organize exhibitions at home and abroad.

The central part of the building (1877) and the right wing (1896) are stylized as traditional 17th century Russian architecture while the left wing, which was added later (1903-1907) is more in the Art Nouveau style.

Memorial plaques on the front of the Polytechnical Museum commemorate the revolutionary events that are linked with the building. In 1917 the Moscow Bolsheviks held meetings and conferences in the large auditorium (now the Central Lecture Theatre). It was here that on October 25th 1917 at a plenary meeting of the Soviets of Workers' and Soldiers' Deputies a communique on the revolution in Petrograd was read and a proposal adopted that the Bolsheviks should assume state power. On March 12, 1918 immediately after the government was moved from Petrograd a plenary meeting of the Moscow Soviet took place in the Polytechnical Museum at which Lenin made his first speech in Soviet Moscow.

There are two more museums in the region of Dzerzhinsky Square. The first is the **Museum of the History and Reconstruction of Moscow**, which is housed in the Church of John the Divine (12 New Square), an interesting example of the early 19th century Empire style. The museum contains a collection of plans, pictures, prints, lithographs, models and photographs showing the way the city looked in the various stages of its development from ancient times to the present day.

In 1974 the **Mayakovsky Museum** was opened at 3/6 Serov Passage. Here in a tiny room the great poet of the Revolution composed his works during the last eleven years of his life. The exhibition occupies five halls and Mayakovsky's room has been restored exactly as it was during the poet's life-time.

At 6/8 New Square is the **Central Council for the All-Union Organization of Pioneers** of which 25 million young children are members.

The building on the corner **Serov Passage** (No 13/3) houses the **Central Committee of Young Communist League**, better known as the Komsomol, which represents 34 million young communists. Here the Komsomol keeps its banner, which has been decorated with six Orders, awarded for the services performed by the organization in the building of socialism and communism and for its heroic exploits.

At the entrance to the Ilyinsky Gardens (its name has been retained in memory of the Ilyinskiye Gates in the Kitaigorod walls), which leads down from New Square to Nogin Square stands a monument in the form of a small octagonal shrine which bears the inscription: "To Our Comrades Who Fell in the Glorious Battle of Plevna, November 28, 1877. The Grenadiers." The monument was built by Sherwood from subscriptions collected by Russian soldiers, who took part in the heroic storming of the Turkish fortress of Plevna and liberated the Bulgarian people from Ottoman Empire. The bas-reliefs on the side of the monument depict scenes from the battle and the taking of Plevna.

On the right down one side of the green rectangular public garden which stretches as far as Nogin Square lies **Old Square** (Staraya Ploshchad), which dates back to 18th century Kitaigorod. The far side of Old Square is entirely taken up with the buildings of the Central Committee of the Communist Party of the Soviet Union and the Moscow City and Moscow Regional Party Committees.

Nogin Square

Since 1924 this square has born the name of Victor Nogin, an active participant in the three Russian revolutions and the first Bolshevik Chairman of the Executive Committee of the Moscow Soviet of Workers' and Soldiers' Deputies.

The main building in the square, opposite the Ilyinsky Gardens is known as the **Delovoi Dvor** (Business House), which was built in 1912 by I. Kuznetsov to house offices and banks. During the first years of Soviet power the 4th House of Soviets was located here as well as various institutions and a hostel for visitors. In Summer 1920 the guests included the well-known American journalist, John Reed, the author of the book on the Great October Socialist Revolution, entitled *Ten Days That Shook the World* and one of the founders of the US Communist Party. Later the building housed the Supreme Council on the National Economy of the USSR and it was here that two prominent party and state figures, V. Kuibyshev and G. Orjonikidze worked. Today the building

(No 2/5) is occupied by the Ministries of the Iron and Steel Industry and the Building Materials Industry.

Next to the Delovoi Dvor is one of the ancient churches of Moscow, the **Church of All Saints on Kulishki**, which was founded by Dmitri Donskoy and built on the road along which the Russian soldiers marched from the Kremlin to the battle of Kulikovo. Since then the church has been rebuilt many times. Recently archaelogists discovered fragments of a more ancient architecture and restoration work continues on this unique monument.

Leading down from Nogin Square to the River Moskva is **Kitai Passage** (which you already know from the first excursion) with its restored section of the old Kitaigorod wall. This completes the excursion which has taken you from the Bolshoi Kamenny Bridge by a series of squares and avenues round the centre to Kitai Passage, where a new bridge is planned to span the river in the near future.

THE ZAMOSKVORECHYE

*I. The Eastern Zamoskvorechye. Pyatnitskaya Street–
Bolshaya Ordynka–The Tretyakov Gallery. II. The Western
Zamoskvorechye. Serafimovich Street–Bolshaya
Polyanka–Dimitrov Street*

Opposite the Kremlin and enclosed by a broad bend in the River Moskva lies one of the oldest parts of the city–the Zamoskvorechye which means "beyond the River Moskva". This district is now a protected area.

> The first mention of the Zamoskvorechye occurs in the 14th century chronicles, where it is characterized as a densely populated district of traders and artisans. Here grain was brought from the south as well as herds of the fast, powerful steppe horses, which people would come to buy from all over Russia. Along the banks of the River Moskva was a wall of defences protecting the Kremlin from the south. The

outer limits of the Zamoskvorechye were protected by a powerful earth works, a ditch and a wooden wall with bastions. The defenders would use a special kind of mobile fortress, equipped with artillery which could be freely moved from one part of the wall to the other against the enemy's cavalry.

These ancient times are still recalled in the plan of the Zamoskvorechye streets as are the old 16 and 17th century trading settlements in the names of the streets.

In your excursion around this protected area you will come across many valuable 17th century monuments. The majority of the buildings here date back to the 18th and 19th centuries, when the Zamoskvorechye was largely a residential district for the bourgeoisie as can be seen by the detached private houses and the elegant churches and belfries. Nowhere in Moscow has such characteristic scenery remained.

The beautiful panorama of the Zamoskvorechye and its "river façade", the embankments, begins at the Moskvoretsky Bridge by which you enter the Zamoskvorechye from Red Square.

I. EASTERN ZAMOSKVORECHYE

Pyatnitskaya Street

Pyatnitskaya Street is the eastern boundary of the protected area and especially rich in 18th and 19th century houses in the Moscow classical and Empire style.

At the entrance to Pyatnitskaya Street on the left is the **Ovchinnikov Embankment** and the two **Ovchinnikov Lanes** (here in the 17th century was a settlement the inhabitants of which cured sheepskins and carded wool). During the restoration of the merchant's house (No 10) in **Intermediate Ovchinnikov Lane**, which was thought to be 19th century, it was found that the building was in fact a **17th century stone hall**—a rare phenomenon in Moscow of the times, where the buildings were largely wooden—and that 300 years ago it had been the office of the sheep-tanners settlement. Now the old terem has been restored to its original form.

There are two more buildings of interest in this street: the **Church of St. Michael the Archangel**, 1662 (No 7) and **the house** at No 1/13 (late 18th-early 19th century), part of which is 17th century.

The next road—**Chernigov Lane** (Chernigovsky Pereulok)—is also steeped in history. The **Church of St. Michael and St. Theodore** (No 3) which is 17th century and the **Church of St. John the Baptist at the Wood** (No 2), parts of which are 16th century, are both protected by the state as historical monuments. The former **Urban Mansion (late 18th-early 19th century)** at No 9/13 with its light-blue exterior, bas-reliefs and cupids is also of some interest. The mansion itself formerly comprised some of the neighbouring **17th century buildings** and is now used as a kindergarten.

At 12 Pyatnitskaya Street a memorial plaque with a portrait of Lev Tolstoy on it commemorates the fact that the great Russian writer lived here from 1857 to 1858 and worked on the short novel, *The Cossacks.*

No 18 with its decorative façade of Ionic columns is of interest. It was built by the great architect Osip Bove in the 1820s for the entrepreneur, Demidov. Opposite this house behind the little square outside the **Novokuznetskaya Metro Station** is one of the few modern buildings on Pyatnitskaya Street (No 25). This is the **State Television and Radio Committee**. Millions of people listen to Radio Moscow, which broadcasts 8 programmes for Soviet listeners in 68 languages and a number of programmes for listeners abroad in 69 languages. The thousands of letters from listeners abroad each year testify to the popularity of these programmes. Radio Moscow broadcasts the news 16 times a day and programmes every half hour on the **Mayak (Beacon) Station**.

On the corner of Pyatnitskaya Street and **Klimentovsky Lane**, the next turning on the right, stands the **Church of St. Clement** (No 26), one of the finest baroque monuments in Moscow, said to have been built by Trezini between 1762 and 1770. The high two-storey building with its many colonnaded porticoes, mouldings and other ornamentation is more reminiscent of a palace and its five cupolas stand out clearly above the Zamoskvorechye panorama as seen from the Kremlin.

On the right-hand side of Pyatnitskaya Street stands the house (No 33) where two former presidents of the USSR Academy

MOSKVA
MAURICE THORES EMBANKMENT
BOLOTNAYA EMBANKMENT
SERAFIMOVICH STREET
KADASHEVSKAYA
YAKIMANSKAYA EMBANKMENT
LAVRUSHIN LANE
DIMITROV STREET
BOLSHAYA POLYANKA STREET
BOLSHOI TOLMACHEVSKY
SHCHETININ LANE

ZAMOSKVORECHYE

Eastern Zamoskvorechye

1. Stone Hall (17th cent.)
2. Church of St. Michael the Archangel (17th cent.)
3. Church of St. Michael and St. Theodor (17th cent.)
4. Church of St. John the Baptist at the Wood (16th-17th cent.)
5. Urban Mansion (late 18th-early 19th cent.)
6. Novokuznetskaya Metro Station
7. Church of St. Clement (18th cent.)
8. Trinity Church in Vishnyaki (19th cent.)
9. Bolshoi Moskvoretsky Bridge
10. Maly Moskvoretsky Bridge
11. Church of the Resurrection in Kadashi (17th cent.)
12. Church of the Icon of the Mother of God "Consolation of All the Afflicted" (18th-19th cent.)
13. Urban Mansion (late 18th cent.)
14. Monument to Alexander Ostrovsky
15. Urban Mansion (18th-early 19th cent.) (Ushinsky Scientific and Pedagogical Library)
16. Tretyakov Gallery
17. Church of St. Nicholas in Pyzhi (17th cent.)
18. Tropinin Museum
19. I. Grabar Russian Art Restoration Centre
20. Dobryninskaya Metro Station

Western Zamoskvorechye

21. Variety Theatre
22. Palace of the Secretary of the Duma Averky Kirillov (17th cent.)
23. Udarnik Cinema
24. Monument to Repin
25. Wanda Shop
26. Church of St. Gregory Thaumaturgus (17th cent.)
27. Monument to Dimitrov
28. House of the Merchant Igumnov
29. Church of Ivan the Warrior
30. Exhibition Hall of the Union of Artists of the USSR
31. Arts Salon Khudozhnik RSFSR
32. Oktyabrskaya Metro Station
33. Bolshoi Kamenny Bridge
34. Maly Kamenny Bridge

of Sciences—A. Karpinsky, the geologist and V. Komarov, the botanist—used to live. Further along on the same side of the road at No 51 is the **Trinity Church in Vishnyaki** (1824-1826) built by the famous Moscow architect A. Grigoriev. At the end of Pyatnitskaya Street (No 71) is the 1st Model Printing House, the largest printers in Moscow, whose work is highly regarded by booklovers. The printing house was founded more than 100 years ago and belonged to I. Sytin, a famous Russian publisher and educationalist. In both 1905 and 1917 the printers were in the vanguard of the revolutionary struggle, and it was the walk-out strike of the workers at this printing house that sparked off the wave of political strikes in October, 1905.

Bolshaya Ordynka Street

Bolshaya Ordynka is the main thoroughfare in the Zamoskvorechye and derives its name from those ancient times when once this road led to the Zolotaya Orda (the Golden Horde). Today Bolshaya Ordynka is the beginning of a major southbound highway—the Warsaw Highway (see Chapter *The Route South*).

Bolshaya Ordynka begins from the Maly Moskvoretsky Bridge and runs parallel with Pyatnitskaya Street. The street is lined with interesting architectural monuments on which restoration work is being carried out. All the side-streets leading into Bolshaya Ordynka will be kept in the form in which they were built in the 17th, 18th and 19th centuries and places connected with the revolutions of 1905 and 1917 are to be marked with memorial plaques and sculptures, for many of these streets—Polyanka Street, Pyatnitskaya Street, Bolshaya Ordynka, and Yakimanka Street—are part of the history of the October Revolution. On Dobrynin Square (formerly Serpukhov Square), which lies at the far end of Bolshaya Ordynka, the Military Revolutionary Committee and the Zamoskvorechye Red Guard had their headquarters in 1917.

At the entrance to Bolshaya Ordynka, where it meets the **Kadashevskaya Embankment** there are a number of side-streets on the right-hand side which used to form the Kadashi, an old artisan quarter. Founded in the 15th century, it consisted largely of coopers who made barrels *(kadki)* for the court of the great prince. Later the quarter changed its trade and began to produce canvas and table cloths for the royal court. The **Church of the Resurrection in Kadashi** (7/2 Kadashevsky 2nd Lane) was built entirely at the expense of the artisans. With its red-brick walls, ornamental white-stone lintels, portals and colonnades it is a fine example of late 17th century Russian baroque. The unknown architects who built the church alongside traditional elements made many innovations. The pyramid of *kokoshniks* has been replaced by two tiers of decorative roof-trees which have no equal in Russian architecture. The bold ornamentation, the dynamic design and the architects' remarkable feeling for the material makes this church one of the finest works of Russian architecture of the period. At 32 Kadashevskaya Embankment another 17th century building has been recently discovered, which served as the inn and community centre of the quarter. After restoration it is planned to open here a museum of local social history, and the whole district lying between the Kadashevskaya Embankment and the Ordynka is to become a tourist centre with its own exhibition hall, lecture theatre, and trade centre (to be built at the entrance to Pyatniskaya Street).

The work of two outstanding architects went into the building of the **Church of the Icon of the Mother of God "Consolation of All the Afflicted"** which stands at 20 Bolshaya Ordynka. The refectory and the beautiful three-tiered belfry were built in 1792 by Bazhenov, and the classical style church with its rotunda and cupola were built in 1834-36 by Bove. The church's interior is decorated with late 18th-early 19th century frescoes, and the ornamental floor is made of cast-iron plates. Of considerable interest is the colonnaded iconostasis.

Services are still held in the church as they are in several other churches you will come across in your excursions round Moscow. In the USSR the Church is separated from the state, and orthodox churches, catholic churches, mosques, synagogues and other religious buildings continue to function.

On the opposite side of the street (No 21) is yet one more of the combined works of these two architects. The **Urban Mansion** (late 18th century) with its outbuildings and stone wall was originally built by Bazhenov and restored after the fire of 1812 by Bove.

Behind the new **Novokuznetskaya Metro Station** and running parallel with Bolshaya Ordynka is **Alexander Ostrovsky Street** (formerly Malaya Ordynka).

Alexander Ostrovsky, the great Russian dramatist, lived in the Zamoskvorechye for almost 20 years. He was well acquainted with the life of the Moscow mercantile class and most of his plays are devoted to exposing its acquisitiveness and the despotism of its petty-tyrants. At No 9, where Ostrovsky was born, a **memorial museum**, a branch of the Bakhrushin Central Theatrical Museum, will be opened. In the public gardens nearby stands a bronze bust of the great playwright by G. Motovilov.

On the right of the underground station is **Bolshoi Tolmachevsky Lane** which from the 15th to the 17th century lay in the heart of a quarter largely inhabited by interpreters. 3 Bolshoi Tolmachevsky Lane is a valuable architectural monument of the 18th and 19th centuries. Formerly an **urban mansion** belonging to the Demidov family, mining industrialists from the Urals, it now houses the **Ushinsky Scientific and Pedagogical Library**. The most interesting part of the former mansion is its beautiful wall and wrought iron gates, made by Urals blacksmiths.

On the right of the mansion is **Lavrushin Lane**—one of the most famous streets in Moscow, for here stands the Tretyakov Gallery.

Tretyakov Gallery

The façade of the building was built in 1906 according to a design by the famous Russian artist, Victor Vasnetsov but the right wing was added later by the Soviet architect, Alexei Shchusev.

The Tretyakov Gallery is the treasure-house of Russian pictorial art. It is a very popular museum receiving one million and a half visitors annually. Here are the finest examples of Russian and Soviet painting.

The founder of the Gallery, Pavel Tretyakov, began his collection of the finest Russian painters in 1856 and continued this work for a period of forty years. In 1892 Tretyakov added to his collection the paintings his brother had collected during his lifetime and presented the entire collection to the city of Moscow. It contained then 1,200 paintings as well as sculptural and graphic works.

After the October Revolution the Soviet state decided to retain the name Tretyakov in recognition of his services to the country. Over the years of Soviet power the collection has increased and now numbers some 50 thousand works including examples of ancient Russian art, canvas painting, sculpture, drawing, etchings, engravings and works of applied art.

Here you can see the works of such great painters as Andrei Rublyov (circa 1350-1430), Dionysius (15th century), Simon Ushakov (17th century) and others. Russian 18th century art is represented by the work of the portrait painters: A. Antropov, F. Rokotov, D. Levitsky, V. Borovikovsky and the brilliant sculptural works of F. Shubin and M. Kozlovsky.

The halls devoted to the early 19th century contain the remarkable canvas by Alexander Ivanov, *Christ's First Appearance to the People*, which took twenty years to paint and is considered as fine as anything painted by Raphael, Michelangelo and Leonardo da Vinci. Here too are portraits by Orest Kiprensky, paintings by Alexei Venetsianov, the founder of the first Russian school of genre painting, works by Carl Bryullov and genre paintings by Pavel Fedotov.

The next section is devoted to the second half of the 19th century—the period of the flowering of Russian realism. Here you can see the paintings of the Peredvizhniki, a circle of painters whose works are characterized by their revolutionary-democratic ideas and their selfless love for the people. Their paintings tell of the hard lot of the peasants and the cruel tyranny of the monarchy.

The two giants of Russian painting, Ilya Repin and Vasily Surikov have separate halls to themselves. The Tretyakov Gallery has the fullest collection of the works of Repin.

Also of world renown are the Russian landscape painters: Alexei Savrasov, Ivan Shishkin, Arkhip Kuindzhi, Vasily Polenov, Ivan Aivazovsky and Isaak Levitan.

Late nineteenth and early twentieth century painting is represented by the rich colours of Abram Arkhipov, Filipp Malyavin, Konstantin Korovin, and Boris Kustodiev, the historical canvases of Andrei Ryapushkin and Apollinary Vasnetsov, and the works of Alexander Benua, Konstantin Somov, Mikhail Vrubel. Also of note are the remarkable works of Valentin Serov.

The large section on Soviet art brings together the finest works of Soviet painting, sculpture and graphics. Continuing and developing the progressive traditions of the Russian realist painters, Soviet painters have created an impressive artistic chronicle of the great socialist epoch from the first days of the revolution. They give a profound and faithful portrait of the life of the Soviet people in the process of struggle, labour and creation. There are the works of the older generation of painters, like Mikhail Nesterov, Vasily Baksheyev, Igor Grabar, Vitold Byalynitsky-Birulya, Konstantin Yuon, Arkady Rylov, Isaak Brodsky and Mitrofan Grekov, and those who began painting during the Soviet period—Alexander Gerasimov, Boris Ioganson, Kukryniksy, Kuzma Petrov-Vodkin, Martiros Saryan, Pavel Kuznetsov, Pyotr Konchalovsky, Arkady Plastov and many others whose works are the pride of national pictorial art.

* * *

On your way to the Tretyakov Gallery you can see in the right-hand corner the multi-storeyed building (No 17) which in 1937 was built by I. Nikolayev for the Union of Writers of the USSR. It was here that Mikhail Prishvin, whose works were devoted to capturing the beauty of the Russian countryside, lived and worked as well as the great Soviet teacher and writer Anton Makarenko. Vsevolod Vishnevsky, Nikolai Pogodin and Alexei Faiko, who wrote some of the classics of Soviet drama, also lived and worked here, as did Iohannes Becher, the German anti-fascist poet. In the courtyard of the building work was recently finished on restoring the 17th century stone house.

Turning again into Bolshaya Ordynka you will see one of the most interesting monuments of mid-17th century architecture—the **Church of St. Nicholas in Pyzhy** (No 27a). It stands out from a distance with its complex design, its emphatically ornamental *kokoshniks* rising up to the drums of the five cupolas and its pyramid-shaped belfry with an ornamental portal.

Turning down **Cossacks 1st Lane** (Pervy Kazachy Pereulok) and crossing into **Shchetininsky Lane** you will find at No 10 a very interesting museum which has only recently been opened. It is devoted to the works **of Vassily Tropinin and the artists of his time**.

The museum was opened in 1971 thanks to a generous gift from the old Moscow art collector F. Vishnevsky, who made over to his native city his whole collection, amounting to more than 300 paintings and *objets d'art.*

The basis of the collection consists of 40 works by Vassily Tropinin, one of the major Russian early 19th century realist painters, who had been a former serf.

The museum also contains unknown and little-known canvases by the outstanding Moscow artists who were precursors or contemporaries of Tropinin— Alexei Antropov, Ivan Vishnyakov, Fyodor Rokotov, Dmitry Levitsky, Vladimir Borovikovsky, Orest Kiprensky and Pavel Sokolov.

On the right-hand side of Ordynka (No 34) is a group of buildings: that are well worth seeing. The house stands by the side of a pond with a squat church next to it, and both are encircled by a wall with double gates. The whole ensemble was specially designed in 1908-1912 by A. Shchusev, a connoisseur of Russian folk architecture, to give the impression of medieval Russia. The church was decorated by Mikhail Nesterov. Today it houses the **I. Grabar Russian Art Restoration Centre**.

II. THE WESTERN ZAMOSKVORECHYE

Your third excursion around the Zamoskvorechye begins at Bolshoi Kamenny Bridge (which you will have seen from Borovitskaya Square) and takes in the streets that have not been included into the protected area. Here you will see many new buildings and carefully preserved monuments, especially along the new fully reconstructed Dimitrov Street.

Serafimovich Street

Serafimovich Street lies to the right of the bridge between the River Moskva and the drainage canal which intersects the Zamoskvorechye. The canal was built in 1783-1786 along the old river bed to protect the city from flooding. The street is named in honour of Alexander Serafimovich, a prominent Soviet writer and author of *The Iron Flood*, a classic of Soviet literature about the Civil War and other books.

It was on this street that between 1928 and 1931 the first block of flats to be built in socialist Moscow was erected by the architect B. Iofan. The main façade of the building gives on to **Bersenevskaya Embankment**, where it incorporates the **Variety Theatre**, the entrance of which is marked with a portico of six rectangular columns. The building also houses the **Udarnik Cinema**, a department store, a library and a kindergarten. The Variety Theatre is the largest theatre of its kind in the capital and performances are put on here by companies from Leningrad, Kiev, Minsk and many other Soviet cities as well as by foreign variety companies.

Plaques on the building are dedicated to the memory of those figures from the party, the state, the army, the arts and the sciences who at one time lived in this building: G. Petrovsky, G. Dimitrov, P. Lepeshinsky, A. Serafimovich, M. Tukhachevsky, Y. Stasova, N. Podvoisky and others.

Next to the building along the embankment is a unique monument— the two-storeyed brick **palace of the Secretary of the Duma Averky Kirillov** (No 20). It is the only well-preserved mid-17th century boyar residence in Moscow. The palace is decorated with white-stone carving and parti-coloured tiles and a colonnaded porch has been added to the façade.

Nearby is the **Red October confectionery factory**. Before the revolution it used to be referred to as "sweet hell", because of the terrible conditions under which the workers toiled. Today it has been completely modernized and automated and is one of the best known factories in Moscow. The sweets made here are very popular in the USSR and abroad.

Just off Serafimovich Street lies **Repin Square** with its large public garden that contains a fountain from which music plays. In 1956 a **monument to Repin** by Matvei Manizer was unveiled.

Bolshaya Polyanka Street

Bolshaya Polyanka begins on the far side of the **Maly Kamenny Bridge,** which lies across the drainage canal as a continuation of the Bolshoi Kamenny Bridge. Here most of the buildings—6-7 storey blocks of flats—were put up around the 1930s. In 1971-72 a number of high-rise 14-storey blocks were erected with shops on the ground floor. One of these shops, **Wanda** (No 30) sells perfumery and other goods from Poland.

The rest of Bolshaya Polyanka has kept its old buildings, most of which are detached houses, former residences of the bourgeoisie, and old churches.

Early architecture is represented by the **Church of Gregory Thaumaturgus** (No 29a) built in 1667-69 by Ivan Kuznechik and Karp Guba. It has five cupolas, a refectory and a tent-shaped belfry and its brick walls are decorated with white-stone and ornamental ceramics.

Dimitrov Street

The name of the Bulgarian Communist Geogri Dimitrov, who was a prominent member of the international communist movement and whose boundless courage and indomitable will was a credit to his people, was given to this ancient Moscow street in 1957. In 1972 a **monument to Dimitrov** by K. and M. Merabishvili and R. Gvozdev was unveiled in the new public garden.

Until recently the street had maintained the characteristic features of the Zamoskvorechye. Now it has become one of the main thoroughfares of the city linking the centre with Lenin Avenue. The road has been widened from 18 to 50 metres and underground crossovers, high-rise flats and administrative and social buildings have been built on it.

But the historical and architectural monuments have been preserved and restored. These include a very original red-brick building, known as the **House of the Merchant Igumnov,** which was built by N. Pozdeyev at the end of the 19th century in the style of a 17th century wooden terem. Further along on the other side of the road the high-rise flats give way to another 18th century monument, the **Church of Ivan the Warrior** (No 46) built between 1709 and 1713 on the orders of Peter the Great in honour of the victory of Poltava (the decisive battle of the Russo-Swedish war).

In place of the old side-streets which used to lie on the right-hand side of the street a public garden has been built which runs in terraces down to the River Moskva and in the centre of which stands the Exhibition Hall of the USSR Union of Artists on Crimean Embankment (Krymskaya Naberezhnaya). Part of the square is to become a "Park of Fine Arts"—an open-air museum which will be part of the exhibition of the picture gallery. Here on open stands works of architecture and sculpture will be demonstrated.

It is in this part of the street that most of the new building has taken place. Multi-storey flats have gone up, and a café, an **arts salon Khudozhnik RSFSR** (Russian Artist) and an antique-shop have been opened here.

THE BOULEVARDS RING

*Gogol Boulevard–Suvorov Boulevard–Tver Boulevard–
Strastnoi Boulevard–Petrovsky Boulevard–Rozhdestvensky
Boulevard–Sretenka Boulevard–Chistoprudny Boulevard–
Pokrovsky Boulevard–Yauza Boulevard*

The ring of green boulevards which runs round the centre of the city is a favourite spot among Muscovites. All year round the gardens that run down the centre of the boulevards are never deserted—children play here, people meet their friends, sit over a game of chess or simply stroll under the trees.

The chain of boulevards is not really a ring at all, but a horseshoe, which encircles the centre and touches the River Moskva on either side. Here between 1586 and 1593 a fortified wall was built to protect the settlements that lay outside the limits of the Kitaigorod. The wall was 10 kilometres long and up to 6 metres thick in places and where it intersected the

BOULEVARDS RING

1. Monument to Engels
2. Moskva Open-Air Swimming Pool
3. Kropotkinskaya Metro Station
4. Soviet War Veterans' Committee
5. Exhibition Hall of the Union of Soviet Artists
6. Herzen Museum
7. Monument to Gogol (Sculptor N. Tomsky)
8. Arbatskaya Metro Station
9. Central Club of Journalists
10. Monument to Gogol (Sculptor N. Andreyev)
11. Lunins' House (19th cent.)
12. Monument to K. Timiryazev
13. Yermolova Museum
14. Malaya Bronnaya Drama Theatre
15. Pushkin Theatre
16. Moscow Arts Theatre, new building
17. Gorky Literary Institute

18. Monument to Pushkin
19. Rossia Cinema
20. Pushkinskaya Metro Station
21. Monument to Chekhov
22. Palacial building (18th cent.)
23. Vysoko-Petrovsky Monastery (17th cent.)

Rozhdestvensky Boulevard. Yauza Boulevard

24. Rozhdestvensky Convent (16th cent.)
25. Cathedral of the Sretensky Monastery (17th cent.)
26. Monument to N. Krupskaya
27. Kirovskaya Metro Station
28. Turgenevskaya Metro Station
29. Monument to A. Griboyedov
30. Menshikov Tower (Church of the Archangel Gabriel, early 18th cent.)
31. Sovremennik Theatre

radial roads, gates were built with towers. The wall itself was surrounded by a moat. The new fortress was built by Fyodor Kon and encircled an area of more than 500 hectares. It was called the Bely Gorod (White City).

By the end of the 18th century the fortifications had lost their military significance and were taken down. In their place ten boulevards were laid and where the former city gates had stood squares were now built, many of which have retained their former name: Nikitskiye Gates, Petrovskiye Gates, Pokrovskiye Gates, etc.

At the south-west end of the horseshoe lies **Kropotkin Square** (Kropotkinskaya Ploshchad) which has been recently enlarged with many of the old houses being pulled down. Between Kropotkin Street and Metro-Builders Street on the west side of Kropotkin Square a new public garden has been built, in the centre of which stands a **monument to Engels** by I. Kozlovsky, A. Zavarzin and A. Usachev which was opened in 1976.

Gogol Boulevard

We enter Gogol Boulevard (Gogolevsky Bulvar) from the Kropotkinskaya Metro Station. The boulevard was named in 1924 after the great Russian writer, Nikolai Gogol. The right-hand side of the boulevard is higher than the left, for here lay the ancient rampart on which once stood the wall of the Bely Gorod, and there was a steep drop from the top to a stream which flowed below.

The first turning on the left is **Ryleyev Street**, named after Kondraty Ryleyev, a prominent poet and one of the leaders of the Decembrist movement who took part in the Senate Square insurrection in St. Petersburg on December 14, 1825. Here at No 15 Ryleyev used to stay with his friends while in Moscow.

At 4 Gogol Boulevard is an old building which now houses the **Soviet War Veterans' Committee**. Here heroes of the Great Patriotic War, men who fought at the front or were partisans come to meet each other. The Committee also organizes international meetings with members of the Resistance movement in other countries.

The two-storeyed building at No 10 also warrants attention. Built in the style of Russian classicism with its six-columned portico, this house too has connections with Ryleyev, for it was here in 1824 that he used to read to his friends and fellow-thinkers his own seditious poetry. Later the literary and musical soirées that were held here were attended by such notable figures as Ostrovsky, Turgenev and Repin. Today exhibitions are put on here by the Board of the Union of Artists of the USSR and "Friday Concerts" are held jointly with Moskontsert.

The side streets off to the left of the boulevards—**Sivtsev Vrazhek** and **Starokonyushenny Lane**—are like an open-air museum of 18th-19th century Empire style wooden architecture and this little corner of Moscow has been carefully preserved. The façades of many of the buildings with their carved ornamentation and wrought-iron fences have been restored.

25 and 27 Sivtsev Vrazhek were the home of the great Russian revolutionary-democrat, thinker and writer, Alexander Herzen, of whom Lenin said: "In the feudal Russia of the forties of the nineteenth century, he rose to a height which placed him on a level with the greatest thinkers of his time." At No 25, which belonged to his father, Herzen was arrested in 1834 as a twenty year old student and sent into exile. In the neighbouring house, No 27, were Herzen moved after returning from exile in 1843, a **museum** in his memory was opened in 1976.

At the end of Gogol Boulevard, by Arbat Square stands a bronze **monument to Gogol** by N. Tomsky. The pedestal is inscribed with the words: "To the great Russian writer, Nikolai Vasilyevich Gogol from the Government of the Soviet Union. March 2, 1952."

Suvorov Boulevard

Beginning from Arbat Square, this boulevard takes its name from the famous Russian General Suvorov who at one time lived nearby (42 Herzen Street).

At the entrance to Suvorov Boulevard (Suvorovsky Bulvar) on the left a large two-winged building can be seen (No 7). The memorial plaque says that here in the right wing from December 1848 Gogol lived until his death on February 21, 1852. The building is now a library and the rooms occupied by the great writer have been kept just as they were during his lifetime. A **Gogol memorial exhibition** has also been opened here.

The windows of Gogol's study on the first floor look out on to the boulevard. Here Gogol received such famous writers as Aksakov, Turgenev, Ostrovsky, historian Pogodin and many other notable figures from the contemporary world of Russian culture. On November 5, 1851 Gogol read the text of his comedy *Inspector General* to an assembled group of artists from the Maly Theatre, headed by Shchepkin and a number of Moscow writers. Here in this house he worked on the second volume of his prose poem *Dead Souls* and, on the night of February 12, 1852— just ten days before his death—burnt the precious manuscript.

In the courtyard of the house stands a second monument to the great writer, which was made in 1909 by N. Andreyev and formerly stood in Gogol Boulevard on the site of the present monument, from where it was moved in 1954. Here Gogol is portrayed, according to the evidence of contemporaries, just as he was in the last years of his life—his head lowered, and sitting lost in gloomy reflection. The pedestal of the monument is encircled by a magnificent gallery of Gogolesque characters executed in bas-relief.

On the other side of the Boulevard at No 8a is the **Central Club of Journalists**, which used to be called Printers House. Here performances were frequently given by such famous Soviet poets as Alexander Blok, Sergei Yesenin, Demyan Bedny and Vladimir Mayakovsky, and here the journalists would meet Kalinin, Lunacharsky and other prominent party and public figures. The building itself is late 18th century, but it has not retained its original appearance. It is also claimed that here in 1829 Pushkin read to his friends his poem *Poltava* which he had just completed.

The most perfect example of early 19th century Empire style can be seen at No 12, known in Russian architectural history as **Lunins' House** from the Decembrist M. Lunin to whom it belonged. The building is one of the finest works by the architect

Domenico Gilardi. After restoration it is planned to open here a new exhibition of oriental art (see Chapter *Sadovoye Ring*).

Between Suvorov Boulevard and Tver Boulevard lies **Nikitskiye Gates Square** (see Chapter *Herzen Street and Vorovsky Street*).

Tver Boulevard

Tver Boulevard (Tverskoi Bulvar) opens in a broad square at the centre of which stands a granite monument to Kliment Timiryazev, the great Russian botanist and physiologist, built in 1923 by S. Merkurov. He is depicted wearing the gown of the University of Cambridge, of which he was elected honorary professor. The pedestal contains the inscription: "To K. A. Timiryazev, Striver and Thinker."

The oldest of the boulevards—it was built more than 180 years ago—has seen much history. Time was when Pushkin, Griboyedov and Lermontov would have strolled under its shady trees.

During the 1905 Revolution and again in the October Revolution of 1917 Tver Boulevard was the scene of much fighting. The granite cube near Pushkin Square (you can see it at the end of the Boulevard) marks the place, where on September 24, 1905 one of the first barricades in Moscow was erected.

Tver Boulevard is also the most theatrical of the city's boulevards.

On the left-hand side in the three-storey house at No 11 the great actress, Maria Yermolova, lived from 1889 to 1929. In 1970 the third floor of the house was opened as the **Yermolova Museum**, a branch of the Central Theatrical Museum.

> Stanislavsky said of Yermolova that she was "a whole epoch of the Russian theatre, a symbol of feminity, beauty, strength, enthusiasm, true simplicity and modesty." After the October Revolution Yermolova welcomed her new audience, now composed of the people. On Lenin's suggestion Yermolova was the first Russian actress to be awarded the title "People's Artist."

At 2/4 Malaya Bronnaya Street (one of the turnings off Tver Boulevard on the left-hand side) stands the building of the **drama theatre**. At 22 Tver Boulevard is the new building of the **Art Theatre** designed by V. Kubasov, V. Ulyashov, and A. Tsikunov and, on the opposite side of the road at No 23, the **Pushkin Theatre**. The new building of the Moscow Art Theatre can seat 1360 and contains facilities for simultaneous translation into four languages. The hall is compact and the greatest distance from the stage is 24 metres. The stage is equipped with all the latest developments in theatrical technology. (More information on the Art Theatre is given in Chapter *Towards Dmitrov*).

In the upper foyer during performances the branch of the Moscow Art Theatre Museum is open for visitors.

25 Tver Boulevard is an old detached house set in its own grounds and well known in Moscow as Herzen's House. Here in 1812 he was born, and here he spent his childhood. In 1959 a **monument to Herzen** by M. Milberger was set up in the courtyard of the house. A pillar at the entrance gates also contains a bas-relief portrait of Herzen by N. Andreyev. Today, this building houses the **Gorky Literary Institute**, which was founded fifty years ago by Gorky himself. Many famous Soviet writers attended the institute including Konstantin Simonov, Chenghis Aitmatov and Rasul Gamzatov. Now students of more than fifty nationalities of the Soviet Union study here on internal or external courses.

At the intersection of Tver Boulevard and Gorky Street lies Pushkin Square (see Chapter *Gorky Street*).

Strastnoi Boulevard

Strastnoi Boulevard, which continues on from Tver Boulevard is one of the widest (123 metres) and most picturesque of the boulevard ring.

At the entrance to the boulevard there will be a bronze **monument to** the great Russian writer **Anton Chekhov,** by M. Anikushin and V. Kamensky.

The detached house on the left-hand side of the Boulevard (No 11) once housed the editorial offices of the popular magazine *Ogonyok*. A memorial plaque on the façade of the house contains a bas-relief portrait and an inscription which runs: "In this building Mikhail Yefimovich Koltsov, the famous Soviet journalist and founder and editor-in-chief of *Ogonyok* worked from 1927 to 1938."

On the same side of the road at the far end of Strastnoi Boulevard (No 15) stands one of the most imposing classical buildings in Moscow with its twelve columned portico, built in 1790 by Kazakov.

> From 1802 to 1812 it housed the aristocratic English Club. The ceremonial dinner given in 1806 by the Moscow nobility in honour of the Russian general, Bagration, and described by Tolstoy in *War and Peace*, took place in the large hall. The French writer Stendhal, who served in the Napoleonic army in 1812 saw the building and later wrote to his sister: "Moscow is a town which is so far unknown to Europe. It has 600-800 palaces, whose beauty supercedes anything in Paris."

Since 1833 it has been a hospital.

Petrovsky Boulevard

Along the slopes of what was once the River Neglinnaya (the river has long since been piped underground) Petrovsky Boulevard descends to **Trubnaya Square**.

At the end of the Boulevard where it meets **Neglinnaya Street** at the entrance to the square (No 14) on the right stands a building which before the Revolution was famous as the Hermitage Restaurant. It was a favourite meeting place for Tchaikovsky, Turgenev and Chekhov and here in 1902 Gorky and the players of the Arts Theatre celebrated the première of the play *The Lower Depths*. It now houses the **Committee for Lenin and State Prizes in Science and Technology** which are presented every year for outstanding work and new discoveries. After a period of extensive discussion among the scientific community the Committee makes its choice for the various awards from among scientists, workers and engineers.

Rozhdestvensky Boulevard

From Trubnaya Square Rozhdestvensky Boulevard rises steeply to **Sretenka Street**. High on the right can be seen the buildings of the former **Rozhdestvensky Convent**—a unique 16th century architectural monument on which restoration work is at present being carried out. At the end of the boulevard are two 17th century architectural monuments: on the right the recently restored **Cathedral of the Sretensky Monastery**, and on the left, at the corner a small squat **17th century church**. The church now houses the **permanent exhibition of the Soviet Merchant Navy**, which shows the past, present and future of the USSR's merchant shipping. The exhibition includes models of the latest diesel and turbine ships, and tankers. It also contains much interesting material on Russian and Soviet expeditions to the Arctic and the Antarctic, the opening of the northern sea routes and the geographical discoveries made by Soviet scientists in the Far North and Far South of our planet.

Sretenka Boulevard

Sretenka Boulevard (Sretensky Bulvar) is the shortest in the chain of boulevards. In the small square at the entrance to the boulevard a **monument** was unveiled on June 1, 1976 **to Nadezhda Krupskaya**, the wife of Lenin and herself an important figure in the Communist Party and the Soviet state, who made a tremendous contribution to the development of education in the workers' state. The sculptors, Y. Belashova and A. Belashov, and the architect, V. Voskresensky, have created a romantic image of the young Krupskaya stressing her purposefulness and selflessness in the service of the people. The site for the monument was deliberately chosen, for No 6/1 on the right-hand side of the road housed the People's Commissariat for Education, where from 1920 to 1925 Krupskaya worked. At the beginning of the century this was the largest tenement house in Moscow, having been built by the Rossiya insurance agency and for many years it was one of the sights of the city.

Sretenka Boulevard ends at **Turgenev Square** (Turgenevskaya Ploshchad), which until recently was a narrow lane, but has now been considerably widened. At present a considerable amount of construction work is going on in the square in preparation for the New Kirov Avenue which will run through here.

Turgenev Square joins on to **Kirov Gates Square** (Ploshchad Kirovskiye Vorota), which is the entrance to the widest (135 metres) and most verdant boulevard in Moscow.

Chistroprudny Boulevard

At the entrance to Chistoprudny Boulevard in 1959 a **monument** was unveiled **to Alexander Griboyedov** (Sculptors: A. Manuilov and A. Zavarzin), the great Russian writer. A bronze theatrical curtain reveals a gallery of characters from his famous satyrical comedy, *Woe From Wit.*

On the right, on the corner of Telegraph Lane stands the building of the **RSFSR Ministry of Education** (No 6), which is one more place connected with the work of Nadezhda Krupskaya, for here she worked in the 1930s.

Further along this same little street is the famous Church of the Archangel Gabriel (No 4), which is also known as the **Menshikov Tower**. In 1704-07 on the orders of A. Menshikov, a member of the court of Peter the Great, who wished to have his own church, higher than that of Ivan the Great in the Kremlin, the architect Ivan Zarudny created one of the finest examples of early 18th century architecture. Light and graceful in form with rich ornamentation the tower combines the traditional architectural techniques employed in the Russian churches with those of classical architecture.

At the far end of the boulevard is the rectangular pond from which this boulevard gets its name.

Opposite the pond is a beautiful building with an antique colonnade (No 19), built in 1912-14 by the architect R. Klein and formerly the Coliseum Cinema. At the outbreak of the Great Patriotic War in autumn 1941 an assembly of those volunteering to go behind the enemy lines was held here. One of those attending that meeting was Zoya Kosmodemyanskaya.

> ...As an 18-year-old Moscow Komsomol, Zoya Kosmodemyanskaya joined a partisan detachment in autumn 1941. On November 26 she was captured

while on a mission to a village where the headquarters of an enemy unit was stationed. Though brutally tortured by the Germans, she did not give her comrades away nor even tell them her proper name. On November 29 Zoya was led to the scaffold and all the villagers driven out to watch the execution. But right to the last her courage never deserted her. Even as she stood on the scaffold tortured and maimed by the fascists and the rope was put round her neck, she cried to the villagers: "I'm not afraid to die, comrades! To die for the people is happiness!" Zoya was posthumously awarded the title of Hero of the Soviet Union and you will come across references to her many times in Moscow.

Recently the Coliseum Cinema was redesigned as the **Sovremennik** (Contemporary) drama **Theatre**. This theatre has become particularly popular with young audiences for youthful enthusiasm and up-to-dateness of its repertoire and the skill of its directors and performers. The new theatre has 800 seats.

At No 23 a memorial plaque commemorates the fact that this was the house of the famous film director, Sergei Eisenstein, who made among other films the inimitable *Battleship "Potemkin"*, one of the finest films in the history of world cinema.

Chistoprudny Boulevard ends at Pokrovskiye Gates Square (Ploshchad Pokrovskiye Vorota).

Pokrovsky Boulevard

Stretching for a distance of 200 metres on the left-hand side of Pokrovsky Boulevard is a three storey building built in the 1830s which was formerly the **Pokrovsky barracks** (No 3). In 1917 the soldiers stationed here joined the revolutionary proletariat and took part in the seizure of the city post-office, the inter-city telephone exchange and later the Kremlin.

No 11 is the main building of a late 18th century Moscow noble's mansion which was frequently been subject to alterations. Since 1932 the building has housed the **Kuibyshev Military Engineering Academy**. A plaque on the façade of the building is dedicated to the memory of General D. Karbyshev, Hero of the Soviet

Union, who graduated from this academy in 1911 and later taught there. During the second World War General Karbyshev was taken prisoner and held in the Mauthausen prisoner of war camp, where he was barbarically tortured to death by the fascists, being tied down naked in the freezing cold while water was slowly poured over him. The memorial plaque reproduces the scene of his death.

Yauza Boulevard

Yauza Boulevard (Yauzsky Bulvar) is the last in the chain of boulevards that encircle the centre of Moscow. To the right of the entrance to the Solyanka Street runs **Podkolokolny Lane**. This used to be the site of the infamous Khitrov Market, which was known for its dens and doss-houses. The living conditions of the inhabitants of this area were depicted by Gorky in his play *The Lower Depths* and here Vladimir Gilyarovsky the social writer brought the actors of the Art Theatre when they were rehearsing for a production of Gorky's play.

In 1903 Lenin wrote: "Both in town and country there are more and more people who can find no work at all. In the villages they starve, while in the towns they swell the ranks of the 'tramps' and 'down-and-outs', find refuge like beasts in dug-outs on the outskirts of towns, or in dreadful slums and cellars, such as those in the Khitrov Market in Moscow."

After the October Revolution Khitrov Market ceased to exist and in its place blocks of flats and a technical college were built.

The boulevards ring ends at **Yauza Gates Square** (Ploshchad Yauzskiye Vorota). From here there is a beautiful view over the embankments of the River Moskva with their new buildings which have become an organic part of the city's panorama.

According to the General Plan for the Development of Moscow the horseshoe of boulevards is to be made into a proper ring by including the Zamoskvorechye.

SADOVOYE RING

I. From Crimean Square to Lermontov Square. Crimean Square–Smolensk Square–Tchaikovsky Street–Insurrection Square–Sadovaya-Kudrinskaya Street–Sadovaya-Samotechnaya Street–Kolkhoz Square–Sadovaya-Spasskaya Street–Lermontov Square.

II. From Sadovaya-Chernogryazskaya Street to Crimean Bridge. Sadovaya-Chernogryazskaya Street–Chkalov Street–Kursk Station Square–Taganka Square–Lenin Square–Paveletsky Station–Dobrynin Square–October Square–Crimean Rampart Street

The chain of streets that go to form the 16-kilometre highway which encircles the centre of Moscow is called the Sadovoye Ring. It is the third ring you have met so far (the first was the fortification wall around the ancient Kitaigorod and the second was the Boulevards Ring which originally encircled the Bely Gorod) and shows how Moscow has grown and developed over the centuries. Altogether the Sadovoye Ring consists of 17 streets and 12 squares.

Almost simultaneously with the building of the walls around the Bely Gorod in the 16th century, a ring of fortifications was built to protect the artisan settlements which had sprung up outside its limits. The new fortifications consisted in an earth rampart surmounted by an oak fence and flanked by dozens of towers. It marked the new boundaries of the city. The names of many of the streets in Moscow today containing the word "Val" (Rampart) derive from these times: Krymsky Val (Crimean Rampart), Zatsepsky Val (Zatsepa Rampart), etc.

By the 18th century Moscow no longer had need for these fortifications and the earth rampart lost its significance. During the rebuilding after the fire of 1812 the rampart was removed and made into a road, 25 metres wide on both sides of which it was decided to lay gardens. Hence the name Sadovoye (Garden) Ring.

The buildings along the Sadovoye Ring were varied. There were the small houses of the government clerks, the wooden houses of the artisans, the detached residences of the merchants and here and there the manor houses of the nobility. The houses were fronted by gardens and the roadway lined with a cobbled pavement. In the late 19th and early 20th centuries multi-storey blocks of flats began to appear here.

In 1937 the streets were widened to between 60 and 70 metres, according to the plan for the reconstruction of the capital, asphalted and made suitable for motorized transport. Building was begun on multi-storey blocks of flats and civic buildings, but it was not until after the war that this really got underway. Today the Sadovoye Ring is once more being reconstructed and made into a continuous motorway where eventually there will be no traffic lights, only underpasses and fly-overs.

I. FROM CRIMEAN SQUARE TO LERMONTOV SQUARE

Crimean Square

Crimean Square (Krymskaya Ploshchad) is situated on the left bank of the River Moskva right by the **Crimean Bridge** (Krymsky Most), which takes the Sadovoye Ring road across the river.

Built in 1938 by B. Konstantinov and A. Vlasov, the Crimean Bridge is the only suspension bridge spanning the River Moskva. It is held by two massive chains and a system of high metal pylons and is wide enough to take a three-lane highway.

The square and, consequently, the bridge derive their names from the ancient ford, which crossed the river here and which was once used by the Crimean Tartars in their incursions upon Moscow from the south.

That section of the Sadovoye Ring which runs from the Crimean Bridge to Kropotkin Street is called **Zubovsky Boulevard**. On the right-hand side of Zubovsky Boulevard (standing with your back to the Crimean Bridge) is one of the finest examples of early 19th century classical architecture in Moscow—the former **Supply Stores of the Moscow Garrison** (1832-35, designed by V. Stasov). The building is remarkable for the high level of artistry with which it is executed and, particularly the compact grandeur of its contours.

Both this building and that adjacent to it—a former prince's palace, which is now the **Moscow Institute of International Relations**—were the scenes of fighting during the 1917 Revolution. The cadets who had taken up a position here were maintaining continuous fire across Crimean Square and preventing the revolutionary units getting to the centre and the Kremlin. But on October 28 the workers' and soldiers' detachments managed to break through the resistance and there is a memorial plaque commemorating this event on the façade of the former Supply Stores.

Further along Zubovsky Boulevard and still on the right-hand side we come to a new building which has only very recently been opened. This houses the new offices of the **Novosti Press Agency** and the **Board of the USSR Union of Journalists** and in 1980 it was used as the press-centre for the 22nd Olympic Games in Moscow. It is equipped with press-boxes, simultaneous translation rooms, a TV studio and cinema, concert, conference and exhibition halls—in fact everything necessary for the press during that intensive period of activity.

Opposite the press-centre, on the left-hand side of Zubovsky Boulevard at No 17 stands another new building that was opened in 1977. This is Progress Publishers, the largest specialized publishers in the USSR. Here Soviet works are translated into many foreign languages and works of foreign authors from all over the world are translated into Russian. Progress Publishers— and you are reading one of their books now—publish approximately 1,000 different books a year on various subjects connected with the science and culture of the USSR.

On the ground floor of the building is a bookshop, which sells not only editions published by Progress, but translations of Russian works by other Soviet publishers as well as foreign literature.

Smolensk Square

Smolensk Square (Smolenskaya Ploshchad) as it stands today is one of the finest architectural ensembles on the Sadovoye Ring.

Here in 1951 the first of seven skyscrapers was built to house the **USSR Ministry of Foreign Affairs and the Ministry of Foreign Trade**. It was designed by V. Gelfreikh and A. Minkus and built by G. Limanovsky.

In the 1960s the square was enlarged and two multi-storey apartment blocks were put up. The ground floor of one contains the Ruslan, a men's clothing shop and the other an arts salon.

Finally, the whole ensemble of the square is completed by the two 21 storey blocks of the **Belgrade Hotel**. Set on the high ground on both sides of **Smolensk Street**, these twin towers form, as it were, gates opening on to Smolensk Square from the River Moskva.

The history of the square goes back some 200 years. After the earth rampart had been removed in the 18th century a market sprung up at the Smolensk Gates which continued in existence right to the early 20th century.

During the first Russian Revolution of 1905 Smolensk market was the scene of heavy fighting at the barricades and in October 1917 Red Guard units stationed here beat back the fierce attacks of the cadets. A memorial plaque at No 35 commemorates these events.

Tchaikovsky Street

The next section of the ring road, most of which has been rebuilt since the war, is called Tchaikovsky Street. On the right-hand side of the street, near Kalinin Avenue (Kalininsky Prospekt), the **Palace of Knowledge** (Dvorets Znany) is to be built. All-Union Znaniye (Knowledge) Society was formed for the purpose of disseminating information and exchanging experience about the latest developments in industry, building, transport, agriculture, the social sciences and the arts. This work is carried out in the form of lectures and seminars given by specialists and innovators in all the appropriate fields. The palace has four auditoria containing 1,500, 500, 300 and 150 seats, exhibition halls, reading rooms and a library. The Palace of Knowledge also houses society's executive organizations, a publishing house and the editorial offices of its periodicals.

On the same side of Tchaikovsky Street at the corner of **Bolshoi Devyatinsky Lane** at No 17 is the house where Griboyedov spent his childhood and youth. This old detached residence, built in the classical style, was badly damaged during the bombing in 1941 and restored after the war. It now has its original appearance and soon a museum to the great Russian writer will be opened here.

Further up on the same side, at No 25 another detached house contains a memorial plaque commemorating the fact that Fyodor Chalyapin once lived there. At the entrance to the building stands a marble bust of the great Russian singer.

At the end of Tchaikovsky Street on the right-hand side is a small two-storey building (No 46) built in the 18th century. The inscription on a plaque outside reads: "In 1872-73 Pyotr Ilyich Tchaikovsky lived in this house."

It was here that Tchaikovsky wrote his Second Symphony and the music to Ostrovsky's *The Snow Maiden.* "I shall remain,"

Tchaikovsky wrote to his sister, "an inveterate Muscovite to the end of my days."

In 1940 to mark the centenary of the great composer's birth, the street was renamed after him.

Insurrection Square

At the far end of Tchaikovsky Street you come out into Insurrection Square (Ploshchad Vosstaniya)—the "gates" of the Krasnaya Presnya district. The square was named in 1919 in memory of the revolutionary workers who fought at the barricades here in 1905 and 1917.

In the public garden which lies in front of the skyscraper, which houses apartments and shops, it is planned to build a monument to the armed insurrection of December 1905 and the heroic workers of the Presnya district.

Here in October 1917 Red Guard units fought stubbornly against the counter-revolutionaries who tried to launch an offensive against the nearby Byelorussian railway station. But supported by artillery fire the Red Guards broke through, took the square and moved on to the centre of the capital.

On the left-hand side of the square is an 18th century two-storey building set on a high pediment with a classical colonnade. Built in 1775 it was severely damaged in the fire of 1812 and later restored by Domenico Gilardi. Today it houses the **Institute for the Advanced Training of Doctors** and is the largest medical centre in the USSR, operating on a nationwide scale. Working in coordination with the finest clinics and hospitals in the country the institute carries out an extensive pedagogic and therapeutic programme.

Sadovaya-Kudrinskaya Street

Continuing along the Sadovoye Ring from Insurrection Square we come to Sadovaya-Kudrinskaya Street.

On the left are the railings of the Moscow Zoological Gardens. (The main entrance is at 1 Bolshaya Gruzinskaya Street), which was founded more than 100 years ago. The Zoo contains 3 thousand animals of 550 species from all over the world, most of which are kept in open enclosures. The comparatively small area occupied by the Zoo in the city centre (26 hectares) has long been too small and a new Zoo is planned to be built in the south-west district of the capital. A picturesque area of 150 hectares with lakes, gullies and woodland has been chosen as the new site and care has been taken to ensure that each species is provided with the closest approximation to its natural environment. In the new Zoo there will be more than 12 thousand animals of 2,500 species and it is expected to take up to 8 million visitors annually.

On the same side of the street, standing out clearly from among the other buildings is the high silver dome of the **Planetarium** (No 5), which was built in 1928 by M. Barshch and M. Sinyavsky. New equipment, however, was installed by the Karl Zeiss, Jena Company (GDR) in 1977 capable of reproducing such phenomena as the movement of the sun, planets and stars, solar and lunar eclipses, and the Aurora Borealis. Here viewers can see stellar landscapes which were formed thousands of years ago and those which will come into existence in hundreds of years time as well as the unseen side of the moon. The Planetarium runs a comprehensive programme of lectures.

At the entrance to a two-storey brick building on the opposite side of the road a metal plaque bears the inscription in old Russian lettering: "Dr. A. P. Chekhov." This is the **Chekhov House-Museum**. "I have special feelings about the house on Kudrinskaya Street," Chekhov wrote, "and these feelings have not paled with the years." Here he lived together with his family from 1886 to 1890, and here he wrote *The Steppe, A Dreary Story, Ivanov, The Proposal* and *The Bear*. It was while living in this house that he achieved the first major literary successes that changed the up-and-coming young writer, Antosha Chekhonte (as was his pseudonym), into the great Russian writer, Anton Chekhov. Many famous writers, composers and artists were guests here, but the house always remained "Dr. Chekhov's Surgery."

The museum was opened in 1954 to mark the 50th anniversary of Chekhov's death. The largest part of the exhibition is devoted to Chekhov's writings between 1890 and 1900 and Chekhov's creative contacts with the Art Theatre. The vast circulation of his books, which runs into millions of copies—many of which are on display here—in the languages of all the peoples of the USSR, demonstrate the feelings of the nation as a whole for this great writer.

Standing in its own vast grounds on the left-hand side of the road is the **Filatov Children's Clinic** (No 15), which is the largest pediatric centre in the country.

> One of the buildings in the hospital, a small detached house with a four columned Doric portico is among the few wooden structures that were left unharmed by the fire of 1812 and have been preserved to this day. The former residence of the poetess, Y. Rostopchina, it was frequently visited by Gogol, Turgenev and other famous writers.

At the junction between the Sadovoye Ring and Gorky Street (the former running through a tunnel below the latter) is **Mayakovsky Square**, for further details of which see Chapter *Gorky Street*.

Sadovaya-Samotechnaya Street

Passing under Gorky Street the Sadovoye Ring becomes first Sadovaya-Triumphalnaya Street, then Sadovaya-Karetnaya Street and then again Sadovaya-Samotechnaya Street.

Here in 1970 the new building of the **Central Puppet Theatre** was opened. The theatre has two studios: one with small chairs for children's performances and the other seating 500 for adults. Actually the pavement outside the theatre might be called the third studio, because here hundreds of people gather to watch the puppet clock.

> The huge face of the clock—42 sq. metres in area—is in the form of a fairy-tale house with twelve windows. Every hour the golden cock on the top wakes up, flaps its wings and crows. Immediately one of the windows opens and to the peal of the chimes a bear, a fox, a donkey, a hare and other characters from Russian fairy-tales appear. At midday all twelve puppets come out together and dance to the tune of a Russian folk song. Parents and children gather

round the theatre just before the clock strikes twelve waiting impatiently for the sound of the golden cock.

The theatre also contains a **puppet museum**, showing the history of the puppet theatre in Russia and the work of the various children's puppet theatres in the Soviet Union. The collection contains puppets and scenes from puppet performances from Ancient Greece and Rome, China, Tibet, Persia, Turkey, Japan, Burma and Europe. There are also puppets and models from the performances given by the Central Puppet Theatre.

Kolkhoz Square

Continuing along the Sadovoye Ring through Sadovaya-Sukharevskaya we come out into Kolkhoz Square (Kolkhoznaya Ploshchad).

Kolkhoz Square was formerly called Sukharev Square. Here stood the Sukharev Tower, which was built by Peter the Great in honour of Sukharev, a colonel who remained loyal to the young tsar during the revolt of the Streltsy (Tsar's body-guard). Here in 1701 Russia's first secular higher educational establishment was opened offering two courses in mathematics and navigation. Later the building was used as a water-tower, and finally in 1934 it was pulled down.

In December 1905 there was fierce fighting here in the square and in the neighbouring streets where barricades had been set up. In 1917 No 1/7, on the corner of Kolkhoz Square and Peace Avenue, housed the district branches of the Bolshevik Party, the Military Revolutionary Committee and the Red Guard Headquarters.

On the left-hand side of the square is a magnificent example of late 18th-early 19th century classical architecture, which today houses the **Sklifosovsky Moscow Municipal Research First Aid Institute** (No 3). Named after the founder of casualty services in Russia the institute is exclusively concerned with accident cases. The building has two curved wings with a semi-circular double colonnade surrounding a wide courtyard.

In 1794 the architect, Y. Nazarov, began work on the building of a huge palace for Count Sheremetyev. After the death of the count's wife, the actress, Praskovya Kovalyova-Zhemchugova, the palace was rebuilt as a charitable institution by the eminent Russian architect, G. Quarenghi. Later it became a hospital and in 1905 the hospital treated the wounded on the barricades. In March of the following year Lenin spoke at an illegal meeting of the Zamoskvorechye Committee of the RSDLP (Russian Social-Democratic Labour Party), which was held in one of the wings of the hospital. In 1920 Lenin came here twice to see how work was progressing on the restoration of the building and the demolition of the Sukharev Market.

Today the Sklifosovsky Institute is one of the largest centres of its kind in the country and includes within its network various sub-departments, city hospitals, first-aid posts and laboratories. Recently two new wings of the institute have been opened.

Sadovaya-Spasskaya Street

At 1 Sadovaya-Spasskaya Street, which is the continuation of the Sadovoye Ring, there is an interesting historical and architectural monument of the late 18th century built by V. Bazhenov. Here the eminent 18th century Russian educationalist and publisher, Nikolai Novikov, lived and worked for a period of ten years.

In the early 19th century the house became incorporated in the Spassky Barracks, which has several connections with the Russian national liberation and revolutionary movements. Here in 1828 the Russian poet, Alexander Polezhayev, who had previously been reduced to the ranks by Nicholas I for his poem *Sashka* which was written in praise of freedom, was confined to the underground casemate for disseminating the seditious poetry of Ryleyev. In 1905 there was a mutiny at the Spassky Barracks, when the soldiers refused to fire on the workers and in 1917 the infantry regiment stationed here came out on the side of the revolutionary workers.

At the end of the block where the stables of the Spassky Barracks used to stand are two 14-storey hotel blocks connected with the two-storey building of the bookshop.

On the corner of Sadovaya-Spasskaya and **Orlikov Lane** stands the **USSR Ministry of Agriculture** building, built by Shchusev in 1933 and one of the most interesting works of the constructivist period.

As you approach Lermontov Square (Lermontovskaya Ploshchad) at the end of Sadovaya-Spasskaya Street, be sure not to miss early 20th-century 8-storey building on the corner (No 19). It has connections with the history of rocketry in the Soviet Union, for here in the 1930s a small team of enthusiasts led by F. Tsander and S. Korolev, the future chief designer of all Soviet space-craft, worked on jet engines and the possibilities of space-flights.

Lermontov Square

The square was named after the great Russian poet in 1941 to mark the centenary of his death.

The local point of the square and the surrounding area is a twenty-four storey skyscraper with a three-tiered tower and side wings, which was built by A. Dushkin and B. Mezentsev as a largely administrative building. On either side of the tower there are apartment blocks.

Here on this spot in the early 19th century stood the two-storey stone house, where in 1814 Lermontov was born, but unfortunately the house itself has not been preserved.

In the public garden nearby there is a **monument to Lermontov** by Brodsky, which was unveiled in 1965. The sculptor has managed to capture in the erect stance of the poet high on his pedestal that rebelliousness of spirit and tragic fate of a genius that blossomed early and perished prematurely in the constraints of tsarist Russia.

The garden also contains another **statue**—the well-known figure of **"The Seasonal Worker"** as a representation of the Russian working man by the sculptor I. Shadr, whose work also appeared on the first Soviet coins in the form of the sower, symbolizing peace.

Red Square. Spasskaya Tower and St. Basil Cathedral

The Kremlin seen from the River Moskva
Red Square. Lenin Mausoleum

The Grave of the Unknown Soldier. The Eternal Flame

Lenin's Study in the Kremlin
The Palace of Facets

Monument to Lenin in the Kremlin

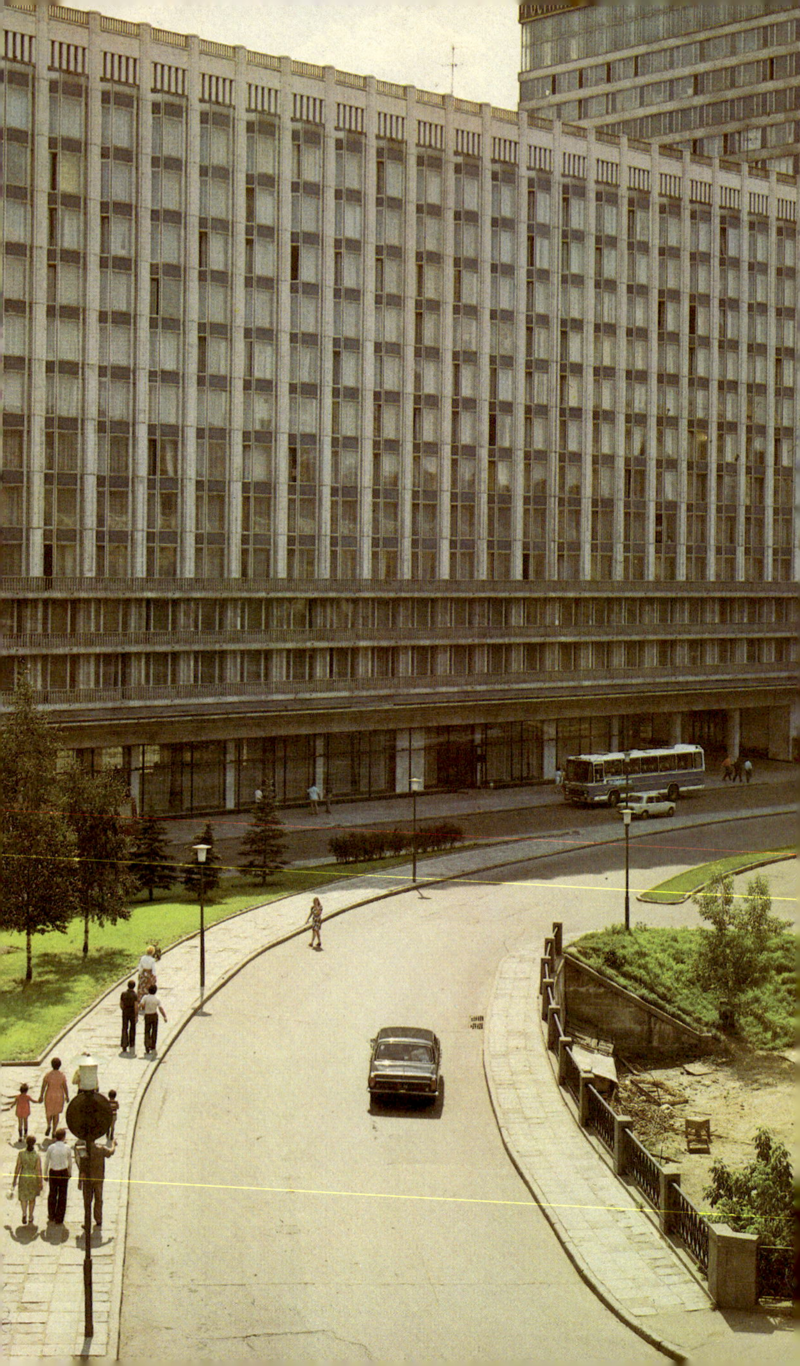

Rossia Hotel

**Sverdlov Square. The Bolshoi Theatre
The Pashkov House**

Friendship House

Novodevichy Monastery
Krutitsky Terem
Crimean Bridge

The clock outside the Puppet Theatre | View of the Maurice Thorez Embankment from the Kremlin

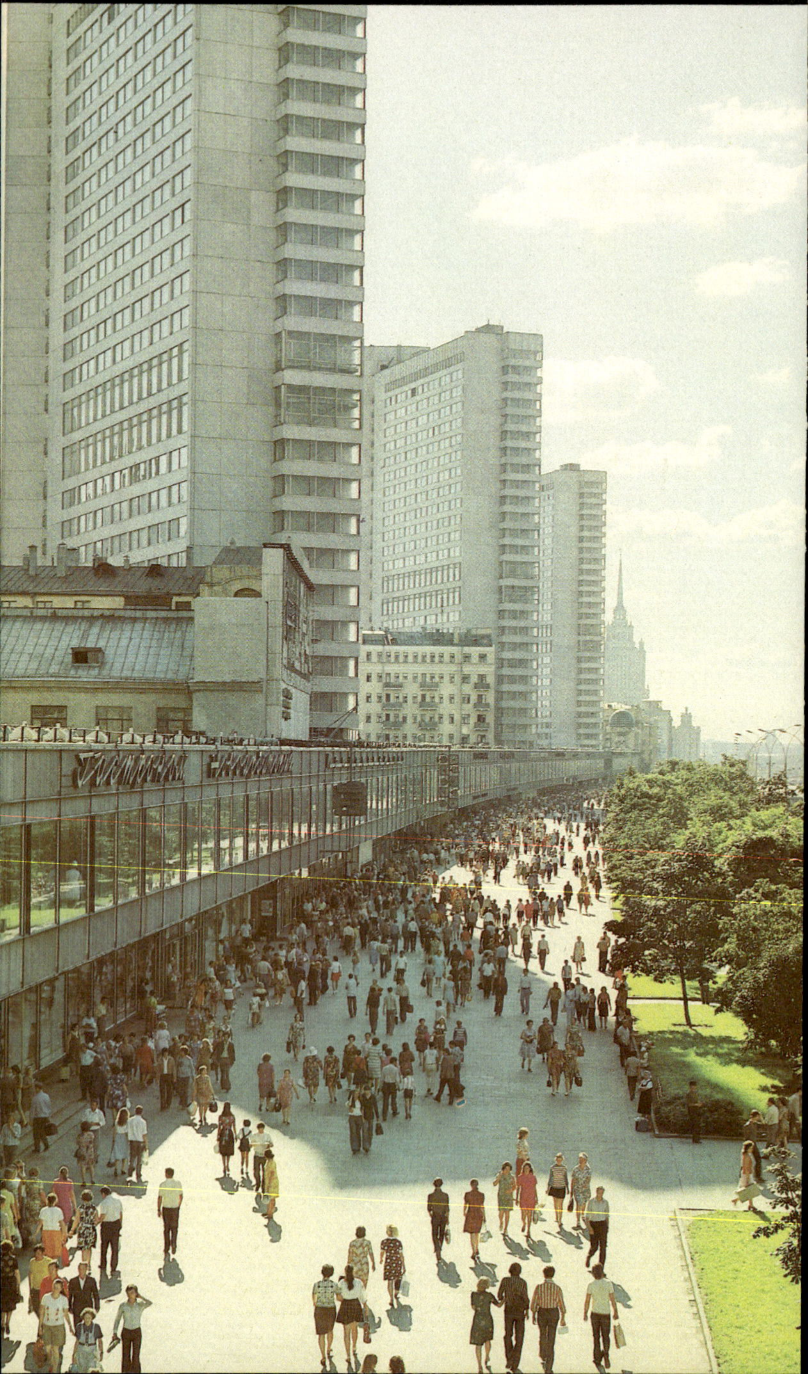

Kalinin Avenue

RSFSR House of Soviets
Monument to the Hero-City of Moscow on Kutuzov Avenue

The CMEA building

Triumphal Arch on Victory Square

SADOVOYE RING

Crimean Square–Lermontov Square

1. Crimean Bridge
2. Park Kultury Metro Station
3. Supply Stores of the Moscow Garrison (19th cent.)
4. Progress foreign languages bookshop
5. Belgrad Hotel
6. Smolenskaya Metro Station
7. Moscow Zoo
8. Planetarium
9. Chekhov House-Museum
10. Mayakovskaya Metro Station
11. Tchaikovsky Concert Hall
12. Monument to Mayakovsky
13. Central Puppet Theatre
14. Kolkhoznaya Metro Station
15. Skyscraper on Lermontov Square
16. Monument to Lermontov
17. Lermontovskaya Metro Station

Sadovo-Chernogryazskaya Street–Crimean Bridge

18. House of Volkov the Boyar (17th cent.)
19. Church of the Ascension (18th cent.)
20. House of the Razumovskys (early 19th cent.)
21. Kurskaya Metro Station
22. Kursk Railway Station
23. Urban Mansion (early 19th cent.)
24. Museum of Oriental Art
25. Taganskaya Metro Station
26. Bolshoi Krasnokholmsky Bridge
27. Maly Krasnokholmsky Bridge
28. Pavelets Railway Station
29. Lenin Funeral Train Museum
30. Paveletskaya Metro Station
31. Central Bakhrushin Theatrical Museum
32. Gorky Park of Culture and Rest
33. Exhibition Hall of the Union of Artists of the USSR
34. Oktyabrskaya Metro Station
35. Dobryninskaya Metro Station

GORKY STREET

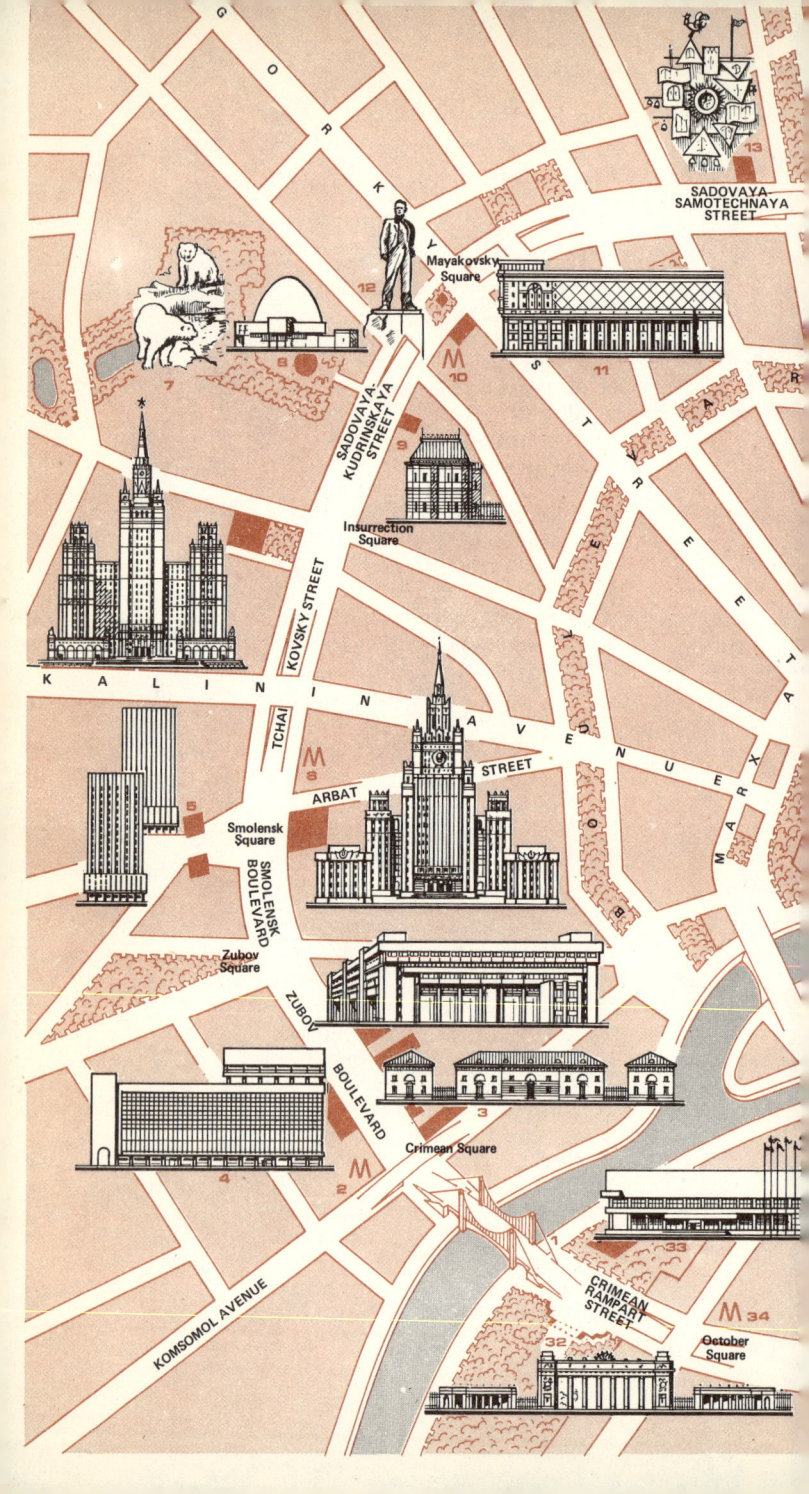

SADOVAYA
SAMOTECHNAYA
STREET

Mayakovsky
Square

SADOVAYA-KUDRINSKAYA STREET

Insurrection
Square

TCHAIKOVSKY STREET

KALININ AVENUE

ARBAT STREET

MARX AVENUE

Smolensk
Square

SMOLENSK BOULEVARD

Zubov
Square

ZUBOV BOULEVARD

Crimean Square

KOMSOMOL AVENUE

CRIMEAN
RAMPART
STREET

October
Square

PEACE AVENUE

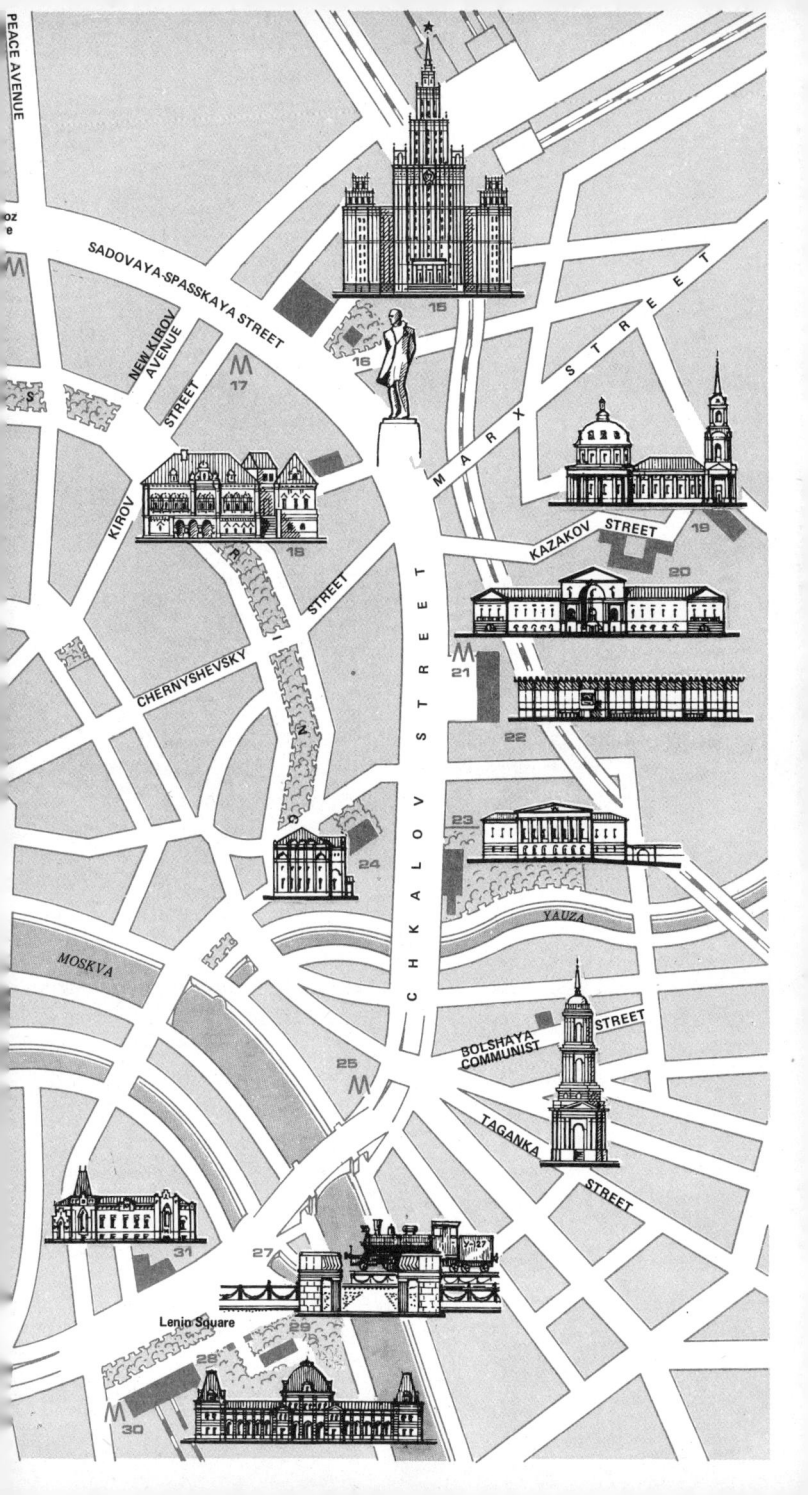

SADOVAYA-SPASSKAYA STREET

NEW KIROV AVENUE

KIROV STREET

17

15

16

M

18

19

KAZAKOV STREET

20

CHERNYSHEVSKY STREET

MARX STREET

21 M

22

23

24

YAUZA

MOSKVA

25 M

BOLSHAYA COMMUNIST STREET

TAGANKA STREET

CHKALOV STREET

31

27

Lenin Square

28 29

30 M

On the other side of the garden stands the **USSR Ministry of Railways** building. A plaque outside the building commemorates the fact that Felix Dzerzhinsky, a prominent figure in the Communist Party and the Soviet state worked here as People's Commissar for Railways from 1921 to 1924.

> The building itself was built in the 18th century as the Palace of State Reserves, but received its contemporary look in 1934 when it was restyled along constructivist lines by I. Fomin.

On the opposite side of Lermontov Square is the interesting façade of the **Lermontovskaya Metro Station** in the form of a giant shell, which was built in 1935 also by I. Fomin.

II. FROM SADOVAYA-CHERNOGRYAZSKAYA STREET TO CRIMEAN BRIDGE

Sadovaya-Chernogryazskaya Street

The name of this part of the Sadovoye Ring recalls the River Chernogryazka (Black-mud) which used to flow here. Most of the buildings were erected either just before the war or just after, but one or two pre-revolutionary blocks still remain.

In **Bolshoi Kharitonievsky Lane** (the first turning on the right) there is a fine example of a 17th-century Boyar's manor—**The House of Volkov the Boyar** (No 21).

> The façade of the building, in the style of traditional Russian wooden architecture with its steep roofs and its whitestone lintels set against a background of bright-red walls, gives the manor a very picturesque appearance. An outer stone staircase runs up to the first floor front and two stone lions guard its entrance. In 1727 the manor became the property of the Yusupovs, a family of rich Muscovite princes. In the early 18th century one small wing of the manor was occupied by the parents of Pushkin, who was at that time three years old. Here in the Yusupov garden the future poet, while still an infant, was taken for walks. In one of his verses he recalls that "I fre-

quently betook myself in secret to the magnificent gloom of that garden."

Today the building houses the **Presidium of the All-Union V. I. Lenin Academy of Agricultural Sciences**.

In the next street, **Furmanny Lane**, A. Vasnetsov, the well-known Russian artist, historian, archaeologist and expert on ancient Moscow lived and worked from 1903 to 1933. His flat has now been opened as a **memorial museum** (a branch of the Museum of the History and Reconstruction of Moscow). Here on display are many of his canvases, which with amazing authenticity recreate Moscow of the past.

Chkalov Street

The next section of the Sadovoye Ring is called Chkalov Street. It bears the name of Valery Chkalov, the famous Soviet test-pilot and commander of the crew which in 1937 made the world's first non-stop flight from the Soviet Union to the United States across the North Pole, thereby breaking the world's long-distance flying record.

Chkalov Street is the longest street on the Sadovoye Ring. In the not too distant past it was just a very narrow thoroughfare, lined haphazardly with old, half-dilapidated houses. But during the period of reconstruction it was expanded to almost twice its width and multi-storey buildings were put up along its entire length.

No 14-16 on the right-hand side bears four memorial plaques commemorating the fact that this was the home of Chkalov, S. Prokofiev, the world famous composer, S. Marshak, the well-known poet and one of the earliest Soviet children's writers, and K. Yuon, People's Artist of the USSR.

Off to the left of Chkalov Street is Kazakov Street, which was renamed in 1939 in honour of the 200th anniversary of the birth of the great Russian classical architect who adorned Moscow with more than 60 outstanding works, many of which you have already come across. One more of Kazakov's buildings is the **Church of the Ascension** with its impressive tiered bell-tower, which can be seen at the end of this street.

No 18 is also worth looking at. A unique example of late classicism, this former **House of the Razumovskys** (built in 1801-03 by Menelas) appears at first to be made of stone, but in fact its walls consist of huge oak beams jointed vertically together and covered with felt and plaster. The most attractive part of the house is the central arch at the main entrance, which opens on to a deep recess lined with ornamental statues.

Until recently the building housed the **Central Institute of Physical Culture** from which many national champions and world record holders have issued, but now the institute has moved to a new complex at Izmailovo.

Further along Chkalov Street on the left-hand side and set back some way from the road is the new **Kursk Station**. The old station was built in 1896 and it was from here in 1897 that Lenin left Moscow on his way to exile in Siberia and here again that he returned in 1900 when his period of exile was over.

In 1972 the new station was completed. The glass façade of this modern building, the "southern gates" of the capital, stretches a distance of 200 metres, and the area is almost twice that of the old square.

Continuing along Chkalov Street we come to a small building (No 53), which in spite of all the road widening and new building that has gone on here has been carefully preserved. A fine example of Moscow classicism, this building with eight-column portico (built by Gilardi in 1829-31) is one of the most beautiful and well preserved early 19th-century town manors in Moscow. Beyond the house a picturesque park with Empire style belvederes and a gently sloping staircase decorated with ornamental urns lead down to the Yauza River.

Taganka Square

Across the fly-over the Sadovoye Ring road runs through a tunnel which lies beneath Taganka Square (Taganskaya Ploshchad).

Until the 1960s this was one of the narrowest bottlenecks on the Sadovoye Ring and traffic was further hindered by the fact that the road here led up a steep incline. But in 1961 work was begun on the construction of a tunnel which now takes through traffic speedily and easily. From the Taganka Square the Sadovoye Ring continues across the **Bolshoi Krasnokholmsky Bridge**, which spans the River Moskva. Built in 1938 by V. Bakhurkin and V. Kokorin, the bridge, which is 725.5 metres long, crosses the river not at right angles but obliquely, which later helped town-planners to straighten the roadbed of Sadovoye Ring.

Crossing the drainage canal by the **Maly Krasnokholmsky Bridge** the Sadovoye Ring road enters the Zamoskvorechye. This was once the narrowest part of the ring, but here construction is going on to widen and improve the road with trees and parks. Many of the buildings here have been put up since the war, but the main alterations are still in the future for the reconstruction of this area is included in the General Plan for the development of the capital.

Lenin Square

The first part of this section of the ring road is Lenin Square (Leninskaya Ploshchad). It was here at the **Pavelets Station** in January 1924 that the funeral train from Gorki arrived bearing Lenin's body to Moscow. On the shoulders of his closest comrades and accompanied by a stream of mourners, Lenin's body was borne to the House of Trade Unions where it lay in state in the Hall of Columns. In the square by the station a **Funeral Train Museum** has been set up as a branch of the Central Lenin Museum. On display are both the funeral carriage and the engine. As a point of interest, the train itself has quite a history. In 1923 the workers at the Ryazan-Uralsk depot repaired the train during a Subbotnik and at an official meeting elected Lenin an honourary engine-driver. At that time the civil war had only just finished and the country was exerting all its efforts to cope with the terrible disruption that it had caused to the economy in general and transport in particular. In a letter to Lenin the workers wrote: "We workers have no doubt that you, Vladimir Ilyich, like an experienced engine-driver, will take us into a brighter future."

Lenin Square and Paveletsk Station are soon to undergo reconstruction. The square and the station are to be enlarged and a new hotel, post office and shopping centre to be built.

On the other side of the square in an old detached house on the corner of the ring road and **Bakhrushin Street** is the **Central Bakhrushin State Theatrical Museum** (No 31/12).

The museum was founded by A. Bakhrushin on the basis of his forty-years-old collection of theatrical items, which in 1913 he presented to the Academy of Sciences, since the Moscow City Duma had decided "not to accept Mr. Bakhrushin's gift, as even the enlightened countries of Europe had no such museum." Bakhrushin made only one condition, that the museum should always remain in Moscow. 1978 marked the 65th anniversary of its opening.

The museum today has more than 600 thousand exhibits reflecting the history of the theatre, opera and ballet in Russia. The collection includes a number of portraits of actors from Count Sheremetyev's serf theatre, which Bakhrushin came across at the Sukharev Market and which gave him the idea of starting the collection. There are also portraits of great actors by such famous artists as Kiprensky, Bryullov, Tropinin and Repin. The stage designs and costumes include work by Gonzago, the Vasnetsovs, Vrubel, Benois, Korovin, Serov, Roerich, Polenov, Kustodiev, Fedorovsky and Vilyams. There are more than 200 thousand photographs of Russian actors, models of stage designs, programmes, posters and sculptures.

The memorial collections include personal belongings and theatrical costumes of the greatest Russian actors and tape recordings of Chalyapin, Sobinov, Nezhdanova, Obukhova, Kachalov, Yermolova and many others. The museum library contains some 50 thousand volumes, including the rarest editions of 18th-century plays and books on the history of the theatre. The manuscript sections contain the valuable archives of many theatrical figures.

Dobrynin Square

The Sadovoye Ring road runs through a tunnel beneath Dobrynin Square (Dobryninskaya Ploshchad).

During the revolution the square was the scene of bitter fighting between the revolutionaries and the cossacks and dragoons. In 1918 the square was named in honour of Pyotr Dobrynin, a worker Bolshevik who commanded a unit of the Zamoskvorechye Red Guard and who died here in the fighting. A monument to Dobrynin stands outside the entrance to the Metro.

Like the other squares on the ring road, Dobrynin Square is a major road intersection. Here eight roads altogether meet, three of which lead to the centre and two link the square with the Warsaw Highway. The reconstruction of this area during the late 1960s has allowed through traffic below the square.

October Square

From the Dobrynin tunnel the ring road becomes Zhitnaya Street and enters a second tunnel running beneath October Square (Oktyabrskaya Ploshchad). October Square is the point at which Dimitrov Street from the north opens into Lenin Avenue, the main route to the south-west. (More detailed information on the square and on Lenin Avenue will be found in Chapter *The South-West*).

Crimean Rampart Street

From the October Square tunnel to the Crimean Bridge the ring road runs along Crimean Rampart (Krymsky Val). On the right-hand side of the street the buildings are mostly multi-storey flats built after the war, while on the left stand the wrought iron railings and colonnaded entrance to the **Gorky Park of Culture and Rest**.

>Opened in 1928 this was the first of the many parks of culture and rest in the Soviet Union. Over the past ten years the park has become a kind of open air club with musical evenings, concerts and

festivities of all kinds taking place there, including a permanent fairground. Lying along the bank of the River Moskva and covering an area of 110 hectares, the park is famed for its ponds, flower gardens, fountains and picturesque alleys with their ornamental sculptures. Recently a four-metre high monument to Gorky in forced bronze by N. Nikogosyan and R. Semerdzhiev was unveiled here.

The oldest part of the park (laid during the late 18th-early 19th centuries) is the famous **Neskuchny Gardens** (Pleasure Gardens) with its hillocks, groves and flowery glades.

In the Neskuchny Gardens the embankment is set on two levels joined by beautiful staircases. Two eight-columned belvederes, one of which was built by Kazakov in the late 18th century, stand on the bank of the river, and beyond them the granite stands of the water stadium reach down to the river.

Further along the Pushkin Embankment stands a huge amphitheatre, known as the Green Theatre— the largest open theatre in Moscow, seating 12 thousand. It stands on the site of an open-air theatre which was built in the 1830s and which used to perform to an audience of 1,500 people. Some of the great actors of the past like Shchepkin and Mochalov played here, and Pushkin also attended rehearsals here. Hence the embankment was named after him.

Today the whole park is undergoing reconstruction. It will be made something like two and a half times larger in area and stretch the whole way along the embankment to Leninskiye Gory Metro Station. All the 18th-century architectural monuments will also be restored.

Opposite the park, on the other side of Crimean Rampart, you can see once more the building of the Exhibition Hall of the USSR Union of Artists.

From here the Sadovoye Ring crosses the Crimean Bridge and you are back where you started at the beginning of this excursion.

LUZHNIKI

Volkhonka—The Pushkin Museum of Fine Arts. I. Metro-Builders Street—Komsomol Avenue—Lenin Stadium. II. Kropotkin Street—Bolshaya Pirogov Street

Volkhonka

If you continue the line of Marx Avenue in a south-westerly direction from Borovitskaya Square you come to one of the old streets of Moscow—Volkhonka. Here and in the neighbouring streets are some of Moscow's most famous museums.

At No 8 on the right stands a house, which at first may appear to be somewhat unprepossessing, but shouldn't be passed by lightly, for it is a former 17th-century boyar mansion with white-stone vaults. It has suffered somewhat over the centuries from rebuilding, but it is in the process of restoration to its original appearance.

The first street on the left is **Lenivka**, which leads down to the **Kremlin Embankment** (Kremlyovskaya Naberezhnaya), where a former 18th-century apartment block with a white colonnaded portico houses the **All-Union Book Chamber** (No 1/9). This establishment which has been in existence since 1917 receives a copy of every publication printed in the USSR. Already its collection is approaching 50 million. In order to accommodate the anticipated future collection, which by 2075 will amount to 400 million titles, a new building is being erected on Garibaldi Street in southwestern part of Moscow.

The Pushkin Museum of Fine Arts

Standing out from all the other buildings on Volkhonka with its huge portico, colonnades and staircase is the classical façade of the Pushkin Museum.

It was built in 1912 by R. Klein, who received for his work the title of academician. The museum was founded on the initiative and due to the tireless efforts of Professor I. Tsvetayev of Moscow University who organized a campaign to raise money for the building of the museum and the acquisition of exhibits.

The museum was opened on May 1912 with a collection consisting largely of Egyptian antiquities, Italian 14th-16th century icon painting and French 18th-19th century bronzes. Most of the sculpture consisted of plaster casts and there were only nine original paintings in the whole museum.

After the October Revolution the museum acquired many valuable collections of European painting and in 1924 the first four halls of the picture gallery were opened to the public.

Now, after the Hermitage in Leningrad the Pushkin Museum possesses the largest collection of world painting in the USSR with some three thousand paintings and 350 thousand drawings, etchings, sculptures and other *objets d'art*.

The museum has halls devoted to the art of Ancient Egypt, Babylon, Byzantium, Assyria, Persia and the Graeco-Roman world.

The picture gallery contains the works of the Italian Renaissance masters as well as paintings by the German, English, Spanish, Dutch and Flemish schools. The works of 17th-20th century French painters are particularly well featured.

Next to the museum at 4 **Marshal Shaposhnikov Street** is a detached residence built in the 1830s where today various exhibitions of engravings and sketches are put on by the museum. Here displays have been held of such masterpieces as the etchings of Rembrandt, drawings by Rubens, Poussin, Picasso, Van Gogh, Renoir and works by such Russian painters as Vrubel, Tropinin, Bryullov, Vereisky, Favorsky, Konashevich and others.

Exhibitions from the Pushkin Museum have been shown many times in Rome, Paris, London, Venice, Brussels, Tokyo and New York, while at the same time the Pushkin Museum systematically arranges exhibitions in Moscow of paintings from the picture galleries of the world as well as from private collections.

After the completion of restoration work on the neighbouring building, the former **Church of St. Antipios** (on the corner of Marshal Shaposhnikov Street and **Marx and Engels Street**) a second annexe to the museum will be opened. But here the main object of attention will be the church itself—a unique architectural monument, whose central nave (16th century) was one of the first structures in Russia with cross vaults and no columned supports. The rest of the building was added later at various times throughout the 18th century.

* * *

Nearby in an old manor house set back from the road amid leafy trees is the **K. Marx and F. Engels Museum** (5, Marx and Engels Street), which was opened in 1962. The museum possesses the largest collection in the world of relics connected with the life and work of the founders of scientific communism. These include manuscripts, editions of their works published in their lifetime, photographs of the two philosophers, their comrades, their kinsmen and friends, and historical documents. There are also drawings, pictures and engravings connected with the historical

Zubov Square

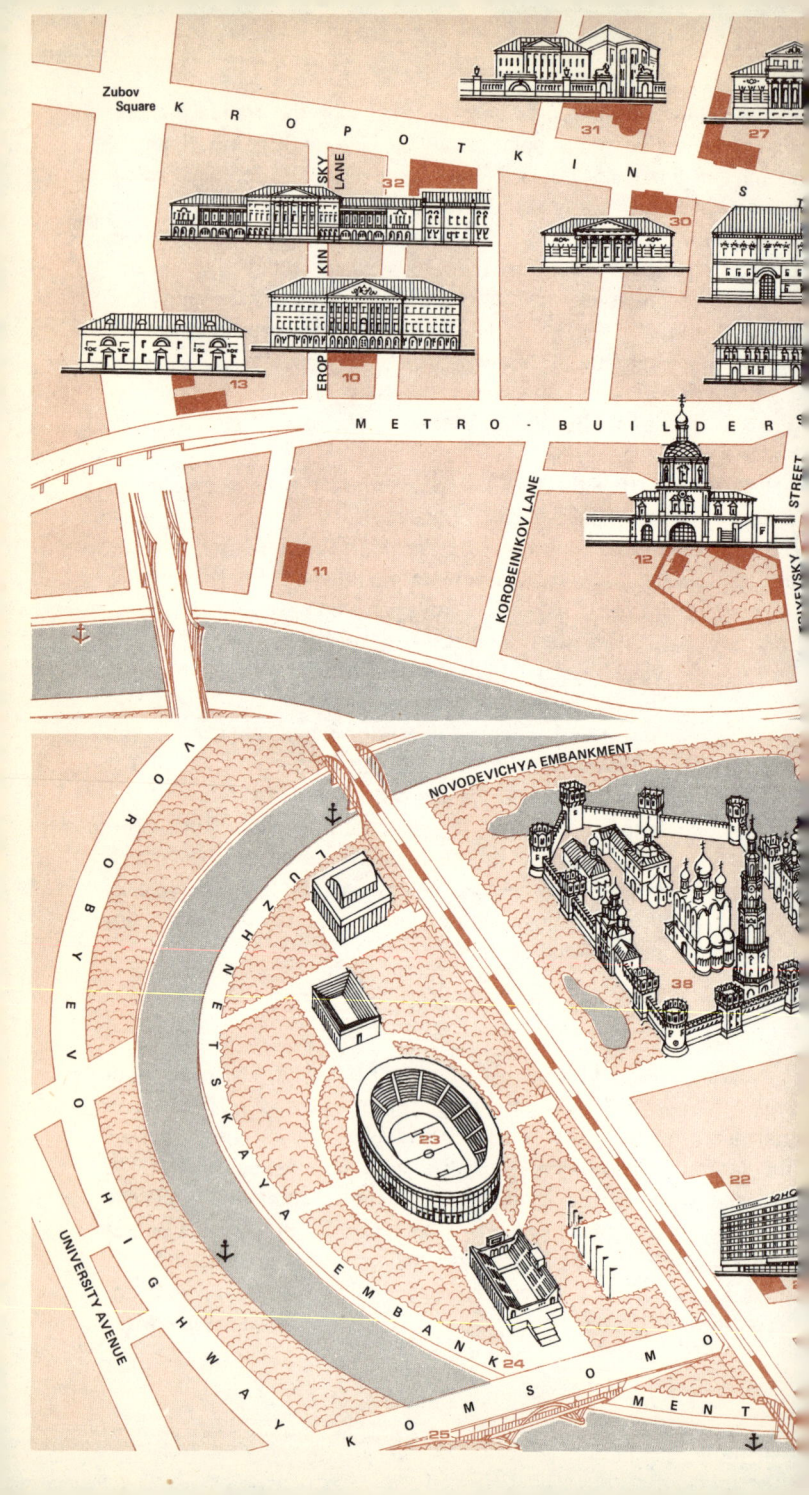

K R O P O T K I N S

METRO-BUILDER

KOROBEINIKOV LANE

EROPKIN SKY LANE

NOVODEVICHYA EMBANKMENT

LUZHNETSKAYA EMBANKMENT

VOROBYEVO HIGHWAY

UNIVERSITY AVENUE

KOMSOMO...MENT

Map labels

Kropotkin Square
FRUNZE STREET
ENGELS STREET
MARX AND
MARX AVENUE
VOLKHONKA ...EET
Borovitskaya Square
LENIVKA STREET
BERSENEVSKAYA EMBANKMENT
POGODIN STREET
PLYUSHCHIKHA STREET
BURDENKO STREET
BOLSHAYA PIROGOV STREET
LEV TOLSTOY STREET
...YOV STREET
...NZEE EMBANKMENT
PUSHKIN EMBANKMENT

2, 5, 6, 7, 9, 28, 4, 3, 8, 34, 33, 35, 36,37, 15, 13, 16, 14, 20, 18, 19, 17

TOWARDS LUZHNIKI

From Volkhonka

1. Biblioteka Imeni Lenina Metro Station
2. Pashkov's House
3. All-Union Book Chamber (18th cent.)
4. Pushkin Museum of Fine Arts
5. Engravings and Sketches. Branch of Pushkin Museum of Fine Arts
6. Church of St. Antipios (16th-18th cent.)
7. K. Marx and F. Engels Museum
8. Moskva Open-Air Swimming Pool
9. Kropotkinskaya Metro Station
10. Maurice Thorez Teachers' Training Institute of Foreign Languages
11. Chaika Swimming Pool
12. Convent of the Conception (16th cent.)
13. Supply Stores of the Moscow Garrison (19th cent.)
14. Church of St. Nicholas in Khamovniki (17th cent.)
15. Lev Tolstoy House-Museum
16. Former Cavalry Barracks
17. Board of the Union of Writers of the RSFSR (18th cent.)
18. Moscow School of Choreography
19. Building Exhibition (a branch of the Exhibition of Economic Achievement)
20. Frunzenskaya Metro Station
21. Yunost Hotel
22. Sportivnaya Metro Station
23. Lenin Stadium in Luzhniki
24. Luzhniki Bridge
25. Leninskiye Gory Metro Station

From Crimean Square

26. Soviet Peace Committee. Board of the Soviet Peace Fund
27. Pushkin Museum (19th cent.)
28. Monument to F. Engels
29. Town Manor House (17th cent.)
30. Lev Tolstoy Museum (19th cent.)
31. Scientists' Club
32. Academy of Fine Arts of the USSR; Academy's exhibition hall (19th cent.)
33. Monument to Lev Tolstoy
34. Pogodin's House (19th cent.)
35. Monument to Pirogov
36. Moscow Lenin Teachers' Training Institute
37. Darwin Museum
38. Novodevichy Convent (16th cent.); Novodevichye Cemetery

events that are so carefully studied in their works, as well as their personal effects and gifts received by the Museum from communist and workers' parties abroad and from friends of the USSR. One of the finest exhibits is the famous *Confessions*, which was presented to the museum by Marx's great-grand-son, the French artist and Communist, Frédéric Longuet.

> These *Confessions* were retained in the Marx family album and contain answers to questions that were put by Marx's daughter to all members of the family and guests of the house.
>
> "Your chief characteristic—Singleness of purpose.
>
> "Your idea of happiness—To fight."
>
> These are some of Marx's answers.

The museum shows the development of the ideas of Marxism-Leninism, their implementation in the practical work of the building of communism in the Soviet Union, in the world socialist system and the international communist and working-class movement in the world today.

> Returning to Volkhonka you can see nearby the Pushkin Museum the buildings of an old Muscovite **town manor house**, dating back to the 18th century (No 1/14). The main house, the outbuildings and the magnificent ornamental gates were designed by the architects S. Chevakinsky and I. Zherebtsov. Before the Revolution the manor housed the "Prince's Tavern", where Gorky, Repin and Surikov stayed. It was also in this house that the playwright, Alexander Ostrovsky spent the last days of his life.
>
> In the 1930s two additional floors were added to the manor and it now houses the **Institute of Philosophy** and the **Institute of Economics of the USSR Academy of Sciences**. Nearby at No 18 is the **Institute of Russian Language**.

On the left-hand side of Volkhonka you can see the **Moskva Open-Air Swimming Pool** (24 thousand cubic metres of water) set amid newly laid gardens. Here you can still swim in winter even during hard frosts, for the water is kept at a constant 28°C and the steam protects bathers from the cold. The pool is very popular in Moscow and used by something like 3 million people a year.

161

Volkhonka leads into **Kropotkin Square** (Kropotkinskaya Ploshchad) beyond which lies a labyrinth of quiet, winding side streets, which Herzen described in the last century as the "St. Germaine of Moscow".

From here we suggest two itineraries, both starting at Kropotkin Square.

I. METRO-BUILDERS STREET—KOMSOMOL AVENUE—CENTRAL LENIN STADIUM

Metro-Builders Street

Formerly Ostozhenka this street was renamed in 1935 in honour of the builders of the first line of the Moscow underground railway. After Komsomol Avenue was built in 1958, Metro-Builders Street (Metrostroyevskaya Ulitsa) became part of the new highway to the Lenin Stadium and Luzhniki and leading on further to the South-West.

Most of the buildings on Metro-Builders Street were put up at the turn of the century, when the noble manors were beginning to be replaced by multi-storey apartment blocks. Only in the middle sections of the street are there any late 18th-early 19th century buildings.

At No 38 there is a former nobles' mansion built in 1771 in the classical style. Today it houses the **Teachers' Training Institute of Foreign Languages,** which is named after Maurice Thorez, a prominent figure in the international communist and working-class movement. The institute has a **museum dedicated to Maurice Thorez** and outside there is a **monument** to the 5th division of the home guard which during the years of the Great Patriotic War was formed in this building. Nearby stands the new multi-storey institute block.

On the opposite side of the road is the small colonnaded house (No 37) which once belonged to Turgenev's mother, and where between 1840 and 1850 the writer himself often used to visit. The house is described in his story *Mumu.*

No 17/1 on the corner of **Dmitrievsky** and Metro-Builders Streets has a memorial plaque commemorating the revolutionary events which took place in this street: "Here in October 1917 fierce fighting took place between Red Guards of the Zamoskvorechye and Khamovniki districts and cadets, during which Pyotr Dobrynin, commander of the Red Guards was mortally wounded."

Another victim of street fighting was Lyusik Lyusinova, a girl student and one of the organizers of the Zamoskvorechye Youth League. Now a street not far from Dobrynin Square bears her name.

The oldest architectural monument on Metro-Builders Street is the **Convent of the Conception**, which was founded in 1523. The convent walls, the main entrance gates and the only remaining 17th-century building have been restored.

Metro-Builders Street crosses Crimean Square by a flyover where it becomes Komsomol Avenue.

Komsomol Avenue

The history of this district goes back to the 17th century, when it was the weavers' quarter. Here before the Revolution were humble wooden shacks which when the River Moskva flooded its banks became surrounded by swamps. The road was called Komsomol Avenue (Komsomolsky Prospekt) in 1958 to mark the 40th anniversary of the Komsomol, when the building of the road was completed.

The buildings on Komsomol Avenue and on **Frunze Embankment** (Frunzenskaya Naberezhnaya) which runs parallel with it have changed the district beyond all recognition. The embankment has been faced in granite, decorated with lawns and boulevards and is now one of the most beautiful parts of the city. All along Komsomol Avenue and in the neighbouring streets there are well-appointed apartment blocks, shops, schools and cinemas. Along the pavements there are limes and apple trees, which when they are in blossom turn the whole street into an enormous garden. The avenue is 80 metres wide.

The builders of the avenue have taken great care to preserve the monuments of architectural and historical value.

At the entrance to Frunze Embankment (No 10) there is an interesting building. It is a house, which according to the inscription on the façade was a home for workers erected by the Moscow City Soviet in 1923. This makes it one of the first houses to be built in Moscow after the Revolution. The house was later passed on to the workers of the 1st Model Printers at an official meeting and a report of that event describes the house as "the most beautiful building in the district," as indeed it was at the time.

At the entrance to Komsomol Avenue on the right-hand side is one of the most interesting monuments of old Moscow, the **Church of St. Nicholas in Khamovniki** (1679-1692), which is a fine example of Russian ornamental architecture. The red and green paintwork of the mouldings set on a background of white walls and the three rows of horseshoe-shaped *kokoshniks* give the church a specially decorative appearance, which is completed by the tented belfry with all its rich ornamentation. The church of St. Nicholas still continues to function.

Beyond the church we turn down **Lev Tolstoy Street** to look at No 21 where for 19 years (1882-1901) the great writer spent the winter months. The two-storey wooden house is protected by the state and contains the **Tolstoy House-Museum**. The buildings here have been restored and on the desk in Tolstoy's study you can see some of his manuscripts. It was here that he wrote *The Power of Darkness, The Kreutzer Sonata, The Fruits of Enlightenment, Father Sergius, The Living Corpse, Resurrection* and many others.

Returning to Komsomol Avenue, you can see on the right the squat buildings of the **former cavalry barracks** (Nos 18, 20, 22), built in 1807-1809, which have close connections with the history of the revolutionary movement. In 1817 when the royal court visited Moscow together with the guards units, the latter were quartered in a three storey house (No 13) opposite the barracks. Here in the rooms of Colonel Muravyov members of a secret society—the future Decembrists—gathered. These were the first Russian revolutionaries.

One hundred years later in October 1917 the infantry regiments stationed here hearkened to the call of the Bolsheviks and took active part in the fighting on the side of the revolution.

Today No 13, an example of 18th-century classicism, houses the **Board of the Union of Writers of the RSFSR**, while the old barracks have become the **Military Conductors' Faculty of the Moscow Conservatoire**.

Off to the left are three completely new streets—**Frunze 1st, 2nd and 3rd Streets**—which bear the name of Mikhail Frunze, a great general from the Civil War and one of the organizers of the Red Army.

An ensemble of buildings on 2nd Frunze Street, which were completed in 1968 and designed by V. Lebedev, A. Larin and S. Kuchanov, house the **Moscow School of Choreography** (No 5), which has been in existence for more than 200 years as a world famous school of ballet. The School of Choreography is in fact three schools combined in one: a music school, a choreographic school and an ordinary comprehensive school. All together there are places for 600 pupils, 300 of whom are borders. The school has its own theatre with seats for 450. Here future ballet dancers from all over the Soviet Union and abroad are trained. The building is designed to be fully functional, but at the same time to provide a pleasant creative atmosphere for working in.

Coming out onto Frunze Embankment by this street you can see the **Building Exhibition** (No 30) which is a **branch of the Exhibition of Economic Achievement**. Here some of the finest achievements in industrial and civic building in the USSR are displayed as well as the latest building materials and machinery. Visitors to the exhibition can learn about the most recent developments made by those who are building the new districts around Moscow, Leningrad and Kiev, new towns, like Togliatti and Naberezhniye Chelny, and the Baikal-Amur Railway.

Returning to Komsomol Avenue we come to the **Frunzenskaya Metro Station**, where soon the vast Palace of Youth is to be built out of funds provided by Muscovites from Communist Subbotniks. The palace is designed to have an auditorium seating 2,000, a Lenin Hall for official receptions and ceremonies, lecture theatres, exhibition and dance halls, clubs, a library and large rest rooms etc. Part of the palace will be given over to a museum devoted to the history of the Komsomol.

Further along Komsomol Avenue on the right is **Frunzensky Rampart Street**. Here at No 34 is the **Yunost Hotel**, a modest, compact building with tasteful interior decor, which was built in 1961 by Yu. Arndt. Here youth delegations from abroad usually stay when visiting Moscow.

The Lenin Stadium

Past the railway bridge Komsomol Avenue leads to the Lenin Stadium, the main sports stadium in Moscow. The stadium is situated in the Luzhniki bend of the River Moskva directly opposite the **Lenin Hills** (Leninskiye Gory) which rise up on the far bank of the river protecting the stadium from the south-westerly winds.

Until the mid-1950s the former settlement of Luzhniki was an area of marshy wasteland and wooden huts. But in 1955 work was begun on draining the area and raising it above the level of the river. Within a year or so an enormous sports complex was built here almost solely by the youth of Moscow. The complex covers an area of 187 hectares and includes more than 130 buildings for summer and winter sports including the Large Stadium (103,000), the Lesser Stadium (9,500), and a covered Sports Palace (14,000) with a transformable arena for ice-hockey or figure-skating. In all the complex has 24 sports halls, 10 football pitches and covered swimming and diving pools.

Outside the Large Stadium there is a monument to Lenin by M. Manizer, which was erected at the Soviet Pavilion in the World Fair in Brussels.

The whole complex is set in a picturesque park, which is a favourite spot for Muscovites during their spare time and at weekends. It was designed by A. Vlasov, I. Rogozhin, N. Ullas, A. Khryakov and built by V. Nasonov, V. Polikarpov and V. Reznikov who were awarded the Lenin Prize.

The Luzhniki Stadium was one of the main sites for the 1980 Olympic Games and it was here that the official opening and closing ceremonies were held. In the Large Stadium football, gymnastics and track-and-field events took place and in the Lesser Stadium (which is designed to be used all the year round) men's volleyball. Gymnastics and judo were held in the Sports Palace and water polo in the open swimming pool. One building which stands out from the rest for the originality of its design, which resembles the shell of a huge tortoise, is equipped with facilities for 12 different sports and has places for 3,000-4,000 spectators. The glass hall which appears light and delicate in structure, in fact supports a weight of many tons. The measurements of the main arena can be made to vary according to the type of event taking place. During the Olympic Games volleyball was played here.

From the Lenin Stadium Embankment you get an excellent view of the **Luzhniki Bridge**. Designed by K. Yakovlev and A. Susorov, and built by V. Andreyev and N. Rudometkin the bridge is in two tiers—the **Leninskiye Gory Metro Station** with its glass-fronted walls below and Komsomol Avenue above. The width of the river here is 198 metres, but the flyover stretches for more than a kilometre, making it the longest bridge in Moscow. From the bridge itself you have a wonderful view over the River Moskva and the Lenin Stadium.

On the other side of the bridge Komsomol Avenue becomes Vernadsky Avenue, which is covered in a subsequent chapter.

II. KROPOTKIN STREET—BOLSHAYA PIROGOV STREET

Kropotkin Street

Like many of the streets in Moscow, Kropotkin Street (Kropotkinskaya Ulitsa) is a veritable museum of Russian 18th and early 19th century architecture, and has been declared a protected area. Here you can see Moscow just as it was during the period of Russian classicism, though a number of buildings in the neighbouring side-streets are in the later Empire period. Kropotkin Street has many connections with the names of Pushkin and Griboyedov and their friends in the Decembrist movement.

The street itself has a long history. Here in the past was the grooms' quarter and the royal stables. In 1658 the street became known as Prechistenka (the street of the Immaculate Virgin), for it was along here that processions passed from the Kremlin to the Novodevichy Convent to worship at the Icon of the Immaculate Virgin. Gradually over the years the mews began to give way to the manor houses of the rich merchants. By the early 19th century Prechistenka was almost completely built up with part-wood, part-stone detached residences set in their own gardens. Each such manor occupied a whole block and stood apart from its neighbour across unpaved and unlighted streets.

By the late 19th century the larger mansions began to be replaced with large tenement buildings and only the Revolution was able to prevent this process from going too far and so preserve many fine architectural monuments that might otherwise have been destroyed.

At the entrance to the street there are two 17th century stone mansions, both are free from later additions, and have had their portals, roofs, lintels and other brick and whitestone ornamentation restored. They now house branches of the All-Union Book Chamber.

10 Kropotkin Street is known by millions of people as the offices of the **Soviet Peace Committee** and the **Board of the Soviet Peace Fund**. Every day the Fund receives contributions from enterprises, building concerns, collective farms, institutions, war and labour veterans, pensioners, students and schoolchildren and from supporters of peace abroad. It would be impossible to list all the help that has been provided by the Soviet Peace Fund. It includes such things as the building of medical centres for mothers and children in Africa and Asia, the provision of medicines, food and clothing for the developing countries and help for the children of Chilean political prisoners.

At No 12 stands a former urban manor house, built in 1814 on the site of an earlier one destroyed by the fire of 1812. This is the **Pushkin Museum** (not to be confused with the Pushkin Museum of Fine Arts on Volkhonka). Designed by A. Grigoryev the building is in the form of a single storey house placed on top of a high plinth which makes it stand out from all the other buildings on the street.

The museum of the great poet was opened here in June 1961 to commemorate the 162nd anniversary of his birth. The founding of the museum was a nationwide enterprise in which Muscovites played an important role by presenting a hitherto unknown bust of the poet by Opekushin together with manuscripts and numerous objects connected with his life.

On display in the museum are first editions of Pushkin's works together with letters, books and tape recordings of some of the greatest actors and actresses reading from his works. The museum holds literary recitals together with evenings where the public can meet famous Pushkin scholars and other cultural figures.

From the exhibition you get a good idea of what Pushkin's Moscow was like.

The detached Empire style residence at No 11 on the opposite side of the street with its enfilade of high reception rooms, ornamental frescoes and mouldings, built in 1822, is also by Grigoriev. In 1921 this building was opened as the **Tolstoy Museum.**

The museum contains something like one million manuscript sheets of Tolstoy's works together with archive materials, and has the only full collection of works on Tolstoy in the world. There are also 150 thousand volumes of his writings published in many languages throughout the world. The museum also possesses a collection of sculptures and portraits of Tolstoy, his family, friends and outstanding contemporaries executed by such artists as Repin, Kramskoy, Nesterov, Ghe and Merkurov. There are illustrations of his works and visitors can also have the chance to listen to a recording of Tolstoy's voice on a phonograph, presented to him by Thomas Edison, and now re-recorded on tape.

A little further along on the right-hand side is **Scientists' Club** (No 16). The house was built at the turn of the century, but in the 1930s it was extended and a large auditorium and other buildings added. At present a new wing is under construction which will contain a library, a reading room and a sports hall.

Beyond Scientists' Club on the same side of the street are two classical style buildings. No 20 is late 18th century and the former home of General A. Yermolov, a friend of the Decembrists and a hero of the war of 1812. The neighbouring house (No 22) is now occupied by the Moscow Directorate of Fire Services. This building has seen almost two centuries of Moscow's firemen, for the city's first fire department was housed here in the early 1800s.

In 1835 No 17a on the opposite side of the road belonged to Denis Davydov the poet who was a hero of the Patriotic War of 1812, and on whom Tolstoy based his character, Vasily Denisov in *War and Peace.*

Next to Davydov's House stands 18th century palatial building by Kazakov (No 19) whose façade stands out for the variety of its design: on either side of the six-columned portico are wide wings with suspended balconies and loggias. The neighbouring house (No 21) is also a fine example of early 19th century architecture. It houses the **Academy of Fine Arts of the USSR** and the **Academy's exhibition hall**, where regular exhibitions of Soviet and foreign artists are put on.

In the houses on Kropotkin Street and in the neighbouring streets many famous Decembrists like M. Orlov, A. Vyazemsky, I. Bibikov and I. Dolgoruky used to live, and at No 35 it is planned to open a museum to the Decembrists.

During the Civil War No 37 housed the People's Commissariat for War and it was here that operations reports coming directly from the front were forwarded to the Kremlin. Lenin visited the building in 1918.

Many famous figures from the world of culture also lived on Kropotkin Street. At No. 1 Vassily Surikov had his first Moscow flat, at No 10 Isaak Levitan lived in furnished rooms, at No 38 Valentin Serov painted his pictures and at No 39 Mikhail Vrubel created his famous works *Pan* and *The Swan Queen*.

Since 1921 the street has borne the name of Pyotr Kropotkin, the famous social activist, geographer and traveller.

Bolshaya Pirogov Street

Kropotkin Street leads into Zubovsky Square on the Sadovoye Ring the continuation of which is Bolshaya Pirogov Street.

Until the second half of the 19th century there was just a field here, called the Devichye Polye (Field of Virgins), which stretched to the walls of the Novodevichy Convent. It was the scene of carnivals and festivities with swings and roundabouts, circuses and bustling trade. People would come to these carnivals from all over the city.

But in the 1880s when this area became the site for the new university clinics, it gradually developed into a medical centre. Higher educational establishments were built here and during the summer and spring term the gardens in the Devichye Polye (at the entrance to Bolshaya Pirogov) look more like a lecture theatre with future doctors, teachers and chemists sitting hunched up on the benches over their books.

Here in the public garden on September 8, 1972, where Tolstoy during his lifetime liked to stroll, a solemn ceremony was held to unveil a **monument** to the great Russian writer.

Lenin said of Tolstoy: "What a rock, eh? What a giant of humanity!" The monument seems to be the physical representation of Lenin's figurative expression, for the figure of Tolstoy is hewn from a single granite slab. The sculptor, A. Portyanko and the two architects, V. Bogdanov and V. Sokolov spent more than 16 years on the work.

Almost the whole length of the block opposite one side of the triangular gardens is taken up by the façade of the **Frunze Military Academy**, one of the finest example of Soviet architecture, which was built in 1936 by L. Rudnev and V. Muntz. The Academy was founded in 1918 on Lenin's initiative and in 1924 the legendary Civil War commander, Mikhail Frunze, was appointed principal. Today a **monument to Frunze** stands opposite the entrance to the Academy building.

Many famous soldiers including Frunze himself attended the Academy. Today the names of men like Chapayev, Malinovsky, Rokossovsky, Biryuzov, Tolbukhin, Govorov and Meretskov are recorded on memorial plaques at the entrance to the building.

To the right-hand side of the triangular gardens runs **Plyushchikha Street**, where at No 64 on the corner stands the **club** of the nearby **Kauchuk Factory**—one of the first working men's clubs to be built in Moscow. It was built in 1927 by K. Melnikov in the "industrial" style which was fashionable at the time.

Further along this side of the gardens runs **Yelansky Street** (the former Clinic Street which was named after the clinic built here in the 1880s by K. Bykovsky). Here and continuing along the right-hand side of Bolshaya Pirogov Street is the **Sechenov Moscow Medical Institute** (2/16 Bolshaya Pirogovskaya Street), which is the oldest medical institute in the country. The sculptures and plaques here reflect the history of medicine in Russia. Before the main entrance there is a **monument to Pirogov** (1897), the great Russian doctor, who founded field-surgery and surgical anatomy. In the institute there are **monuments** to some of the leading figures in the Russian and Soviet medical sciences such as **Ivan Sechenov**, the materialist and natural scientist, who founded physiology in Russia, **Fyodor Erisman**, the founder of the school of Russian hygienists, **Nil Filatov**, the pediatrics expert, **Alexei Abrikosov**, the founder of the Soviet school of pathological anatomy, an Academician and a Hero of Socialist Labour.

In 1972 a **monument** in the form of the Red Cross emblem together with a sculptured group consisting of a wounded soldier and a nurse was erected here. The inscription on the monument reads: "To the Medical Services for their heroic endurance during the Great Patriotic War 1941-1945." The monument was designed by the sculptor L. Kerbel and architect B. Tkhor.

The institute also contains a hygiene museum.

Turning down **Abrikosov Lane** (Abrikosovsky Pereulok), which lies beyond the institute, you come out into **Pogodin Street** (Pogodinskaya Ulitsa), named after the famous historian and publicist, M. Pogodin. At his house (No 12), during the 1840s famous actors and writers frequently used to gather. Of the original manor only part of the garden, the outbuildings and a wooden house in the form of an old fashioned terem have remained. For a period of several years Gogol used to come and stay in this house, where he worked on his best known novel *Dead Souls* and the novel *Taras Bulba.* Here on May 9 it was the custom to celebrate the great writer's birthday and on one such occasion in 1840 Lermontov read his new poem *The Novice,* which was enthusiastically received by Gogol. The Pogodin cottage has now been fully restored and today it houses the regional **department of the Society for the Protection of Historical Monuments.**

To the left of Bolshaya Pirogov Street is **Malaya Pirogovskaya Street.** Here at No 1 is the **N. Pirogov Moscow Medical Institute,** the **Lenin Teachers' Training Institute** and the **Lomonosov Moscow Institute of Fine Chemical Technology.** The only Darwin museum in the world is also located on this street. Founded in 1907 the museum illustrates the Darwin theory of evolution and describes his work and discoveries. There are more than one hundred thousand exhibits including a fine collection of stuffed animals and birds, paintings, sculptures and picturesque reconstructions of extinct animals.

The building which houses the **Lenin Teachers' Training Institute** was built in 1910-12 by S. Solovyov as a higher educational establishment for women. The establishment itself was opened a little over one hundred years ago and was the first of its kind in tsarist Russia, where hitherto women had not been accepted into higher educational establishments. Today half the students in Moscow are women.

Between 1918 and 1921 Lenin made many speeches here. On July 26, 1918, for instance, he made a speech entitled "What the Soviet Constitution Will Mean to the Working Man" and again on August 28 of the same year he spoke here to the delegates of the 1st All-Russian Congress on Education in the auditorium, now called the Lenin Hall. On November 7, 1921 Lenin spoke at a meeting of workers, soldiers and youth of the Hamovniki District, on the forthcoming celebration of the anniversary of the October Revolution and twenty years later the educational institute, the oldest in the country was named after Lenin.

Returning to Bolshaya Pirogov, the whole block on the left is occupied by the building of the four central state archives. The oldest of these is the Archive of Ancient Enactments, which was founded by Peter the Great, and which contains millions of historical documents. The Archive of the October Revolution was built between 1936 and 1938 by A. Volkhonsky and is easily distinguished by its bas-relief band of revolutionary workers, soldiers and sailors. The other two buildings house the Archives of the Soviet Army and the National Economy.

Both Bolshaya and Malaya Pirogovskaya Streets run into **Tenth Anniversary of October Square**, near the former Novodevichy Convent.

The **Novodevichy Convent** was founded in the early 16th century to celebrate the 1514 victory over the Lithuanian Princes and the return of Smolensk to Russia. It was surrounded by a huge wall with 12 towers and used as a fortress guarding the approaches to the city.

The monastery itself is a unique 16th-17th century architectural ensemble, dominated by the huge five-cupola Smolensk Cathedral (1524-25) which was modelled on the Cathedral of the Dormition in the Kremlin. In the late 16th century the walls of the cathedral were ornamented with frescoes, reflecting episodes in the struggle for the creation of a centralized Russian State. In the 1680s Mikhailov and Andreyev together with a number of other master-carvers created one of the finest ornamental works of the period—

the multi-tiered, gilt carved iconostasis. The floor of the cathedral is made of cast-iron plates.

The most famous parts of the convent are the refectory, the belfry and the gate-house church which were all built in the 1680s. The decorative Moscow baroque style serves to harmonize the buildings with the abundance of whitestone ornamentation on the red-brick walls.

The elegant and unusually decorative belfry was erected in 1690 by Potapov. It is built in five octagonal tiers and crowned with a golden cupola.

In 1922 the convent became a branch of the State History Museum. Here you can see such works of art as the last paintings of Simon Ushakov and his pupil, Pavlov, frescoes on the Smolensk Cathedral by Yelizarov and Karpov and ancient ecclesiastical utensils.

Many of those who took part in the Patriotic War of 1812 and in the Decembrist uprising are buried here.

Next to the monastery is the **Novodevichye Cemetery**, where lie the bodies of prominent social and political figures and famous artists and scientists.

At the end of Bolshaya Pirogov Street you come out once more to the Lenin Stadium at Luzhniki.

KALININ AVENUE—ARBAT

Kalinin Avenue

The entrance to Kalinin Avenue (Kalininsky Prospekt) is immediately opposite the Troitskaya Tower of the Kremlin and from here it continues out in a westerly direction till it crosses the River Moskva and becomes Kutuzov Avenue, the first stage on the main highway to Minsk. The street is named after Mikhail Kalinin, a prominent figure in the Communist Party and Soviet state who for many years was President of the Presidium of the USSR Supreme Soviet.

Part of Kalinin Avenue (as far as Arbat Square) is one of the oldest streets in Moscow. Here in the 13th and 14th century lay the road to Great Novgorod and later to Smolensk.

The first house on the right (No 4, built by Bykovsky in 1900) was Gorky's home in 1905 and from here he actively participated in the events of the December armed insurrection in Moscow. His rooms were often visited by members of the Central Committee of the RSDLP, workers and members of the underground press. They became, in the words of one of the participants in the events of those times "a kind of support point for the insurrection. From here we armed the workers of the Schmidt factory and other fighting units."

On the left-hand side is the colonnaded main entrance to the Lenin Library and a wing containing scientific and reading rooms and the administrative block.

Off to the right along Kalinin Avenue are several sidestreets leading to Herzen Street, the first of which is **Granovsky Street,** named after a 19th century Russian historian. At the turn of the century a number of apartment blocks were built here.

No 3 has been the home of a number of prominent figures in the Communist Party and the Soviet state, as can be seen by the plaques outside. At No 2 the great Russian natural scientist, Kliment Timiryazev, who founded the Russian school of plant physiology and developed the contemporary theory of photosynthesis, lived from 1887 until his death in 1920. His flat has now been opened as a **memorial museum.**

The building directly opposite the entrance to Granovsky Street on the left-hand side of Kalinin Avenue (No 5) is an 18th century town manor built in 1787 by Kazakov. After the fire of 1812 the house was rebuilt, but the old staircases and late 18th-early 19th century frescoes remained. From 1920 to 1924 the building housed the Secretariat of the Central Committee of the Bolshevik Party, whose sessions were attended by Lenin. In 1957 the building was opened as the **Shchusev Museum of Architecture**, after the famous architect who was the founder and first curator of the museum. The museum illustrates the various stages of the development of Russian and Soviet architecture. Models, plans and photographs show the scale of housing, industrial, social and cultural development in the USSR, and you can see some of the finest architectural works in the country and learn about the various stages of postwar construction from the rebuilding after the destruction caused by the war to the latest building projects that are going up today.

In the courtyard of No 6 stands another example of the work of Bazhenov (1778). At the turn of the century it housed the Hunters' Club and for a short time after the Revolution, the Academy of the General Staff of the Red Army. On 19 April,

1919 Lenin spoke here at the first assembly of graduates from the Academy before their departure to the front.

The neighbouring house (No 8) with its corner half-rotunda, colonnade and arched balcony is of the same period as No 6 being built in 1780 by N. Lvov. This was formerly the home of Praskovya Zhemchugova-Kovaleva, the famous serf-actress and later the wife of Count Sheremetyev.

From 1923 to 1937 No 10 was the home of Bela Kun, a prominent figure in the Hungarian and international workers' movement, who was one of the founders of the Hungarian Communist Party and head of the Soviet Government in Hungary in 1919.

At the junction of Kalinin Avenue and **Semashko Street** a **monument to Kalinin** was unveiled in April 1978, (Y. Kutyrev, architect, B. Dyuzhev, sculptor) and it shows the figure of Kalinin in bronze on a pedestal of red polished granite.

A little further along at No 14 in a detached 20th century residence is the board of an organization which has more than 50 million members—the **Union of the Soviet Societies for Friendship and Cultural Relations with Foreign Countries**. The Union maintains permanent contacts with 7 thousand social, cultural, and scientific institutions and organizations in more than 120 countries.

The **House of Friendship with Foreign Countries** which occupies the neighbouring building is often called an international club of peace. This palace (No 16) which was built in the late 19th century by V. Mazyrin for A. Morozov, a millionaire textile manufacturer, stands out for its unusual pseudo-dramatic style. Here in the House of Friendship meetings take place between Soviet people and visitors from abroad. Members of the friendship societies hold celebrations to mark the national holidays in the various countries. Every year over 200 thousand take part in the various programmes arranged by the House of Friendship, such as exhibitions of painting, sculpture, photography and books, concerts and lectures, film reviews and literary discussions. Here Muscovites had the opportunity to meet such famous persons as the American painter, Rockwell Kent, the Danish cartoonist, Herluf Bidstrup, the English writer, Richard Aldington, the Chilean poet Pablo Neruda and many other progressive figures from the world of culture. The World Council of Peace gave the House of Friendship its honorary award for its "outstanding contribution to the strengthening of peace and friendship between nations."

In Arbat Square, on the left-hand side of Kalinin Avenue, where there are now public gardens there once stood a house which was destroyed during the bombing in 1941. This house was one of the places in Moscow associated with Lenin, for here in January 1894 at an illegal meeting of the democratic intelligentsia, which was held under the guise of a students' party Lenin delivered his first public speech in Moscow, which sharply criticized the liberal Narodniks and irrefutably argued the correctness of revolutionary Marxism. "He spoke with the boldness that was characteristic of him using all the weapons in his arsenal of knowledge and all the force of his conviction," wrote Lenin's sister, Anna Ulyanova-Yelizarova in her memoirs.

Arbat Square

Next on the left you come to Arbat Square (Arbatskaya Ploshchad), where the two **Arbatskaya underground stations** are located, one of which is the longest in Moscow, being 200 metres from escalator to escalator.

On the corner of **Frunze Street** and Arbat Square is an historical and architectural monument built by Camporessi in 1792, which, after the old wooden theatre had been destroyed in the fire of 1812, was used for various dramatic performances. In the late 19th century the building became the Alexander Military School, which during the 1917 Revolution became the seat of counter-revolution in Moscow. Here at the approaches to the school the Red Guards fought stubbornly and at last on November 2 succeeded in taking the building. During the Civil War this house became the headquarters of the Revolutionary Military Council of the Russian Republic.

In recent years Arbat Square has been considerably enlarged with a number of old houses being pulled down, a tunnel built and the huge **Communications House** which contains an automatic telephone exchange, a post-office, long-distance telephone communications and a telephone information service, erected. But there are still many changes ahead. A new House of Peace and Friendship is to be built here with a large hall for meetings and international forums and a monument is to be put up to "Peace and Friendship Between Nations" on the spot where a stone was solemnly laid in 1972 during the celebrations to mark the 50th anniversary of the founding of the Union of Soviet Socialist Republics.

Kalinin Avenue (continued)

Beyond Arbat Square Kalinin Avenue spreads out to become one of the major thoroughfares of the city. Where once there stood a mass of little side-streets leading into Arbat Street an attractive modern shopping centre has been built.

On the left-hand side of the street there are four twenty-six-storey administrative blocks which house various industrial ministries.

These tall blocks are connected by a two-storey structure which runs parallel with the main road all the way to its junction with the Sadovoye Ring in a continuous chain of glass-fronted windows. Here you will find a **flower shop**, a **photographer's** (the "Jupiter"), a **ladies' dress salon** and the **Charodeika hairdressers** as well as many other shops.

At the far end of this new block by the ring road is the **Arbat Restaurant** where in the evenings you can watch a variety show.

Along the right-hand side of Kalinin Avenue are five double twenty-four-storey apartment blocks which also have shops on their lower floors. There is a **perfumery** (the "Lilac"), a **jewelers**, the **Melodia record shop** and many others. Between the towers stands the largest bookshop in Europe, the famous **House of Books** (Dom Knigi). The shop is equipped with a conference hall where various exhibitions, including international displays of books, are held. A little further along is the Oktyabr Cinema, which has two studios and seats 3 thousand spectators. In the cinema concert hall you can watch performance by leading drama and variety companies and listen to concerts. The façade of the cinema is decorated with monumental wall-panels depicting themes from the Great October Socialist Revolution and multi-coloured stain-glass windows.

The whole architectural ensemble along both sides of Kalinin Avenue was designed by M. Posokhin (Chief Architect), M. Mndoyants, G. Makarevich, B. Tkhor, Sh. Airapetov, I. Pokrovsky,

MARX
GRANOVSKY STREET

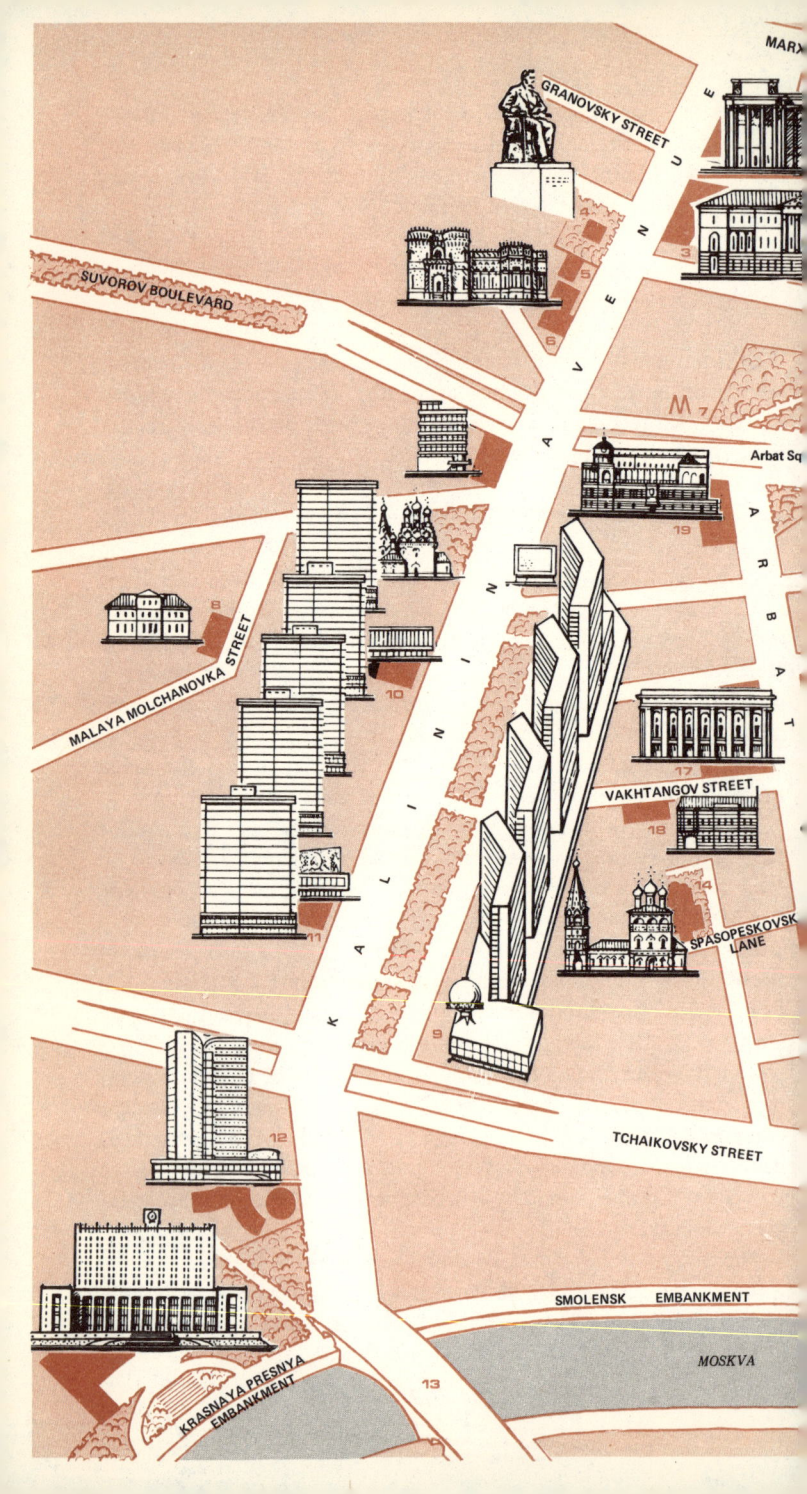

SUVOROV BOULEVARD

Arbat Sq

MALAYA MOLCHANOVKA STREET

KALININ AVENUE

ARBAT

VAKHTANGOV STREET

SPASOPESKOVSKY LANE

TCHAIKOVSKY STREET

SMOLENSK EMBANKMENT

MOSKVA

KRASNAYA PRESNYA EMBANKMENT

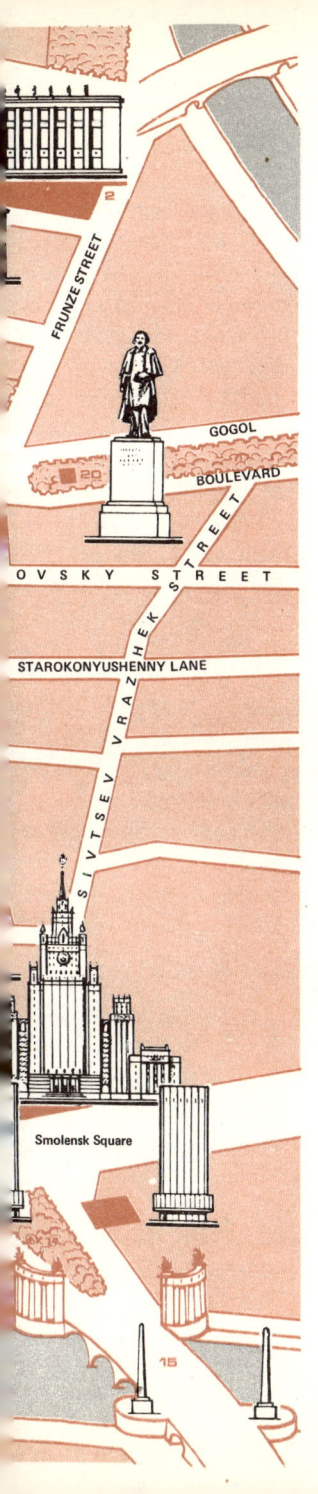

KALININ AVENUE—ARBAT

1. Biblioteka Imeni Lenina Metro Station
2. Lenin Library
3. Shchusev Museum of Architecture (18th cent.)
4. Monument to Kalinin
5. Union of the Soviet Societies for Friendship and Cultural Relations with Foreign Countries
6. House of Friendship with Foreign Countries
7. Arbatskaya Metro Station
8. Lermontov Flat-Museum
9. Arbat Restaurant
10. Dom Knigi Bookshop
11. Oktyabr Concert Hall, Oktyabr Cinema
12. CMEA building
13. Kalininsky Bridge
14. Church of the Saviour in Peski (17th cent.)
15. Borodinsky Bridge
16. Pushkin Flat-Museum
17. Vakhtangov Theatre
18. Skryabin Flat-Museum
19. Praga Restaurant
20. Monument to Gogol (Sculptor Tomsky)

Yu. Popov, A. Zaitsev, V. Nikolayev, and built by S. Shkolnikov, V. Sno and L. Gokhman, all of whom were awarded in 1966 the Grand Prix by the Centre of Architectural Research in Paris for their contributions to the development of town planning.

One of the side-streets leading off Kalinin Avenue near Arbat Square is **Malaya Molchanovka Street**, where lovers of Russian literature should not fail to miss a small single-storey building with a mezzanine floor. A memorial plaque of red porphyry on the façade of the building (No 2) informs the visitor that "From 1830 to 1832 the great Russian Poet Mikhail Yurievich Lermontov lived and worked in this house". Here in his student days the great poet worked on over a hundred of his poems and early dramas including the celebrated work, *The Demon*. Recently the house was restored and opened as the **Lermontov Flat-Museum**.

The third section of Kalinin Avenue lies beyond the Sadovoye Ring.

On the right-hand side, where the road rises stands the **Central Scientific Research Institute of Health Resorts and Physical Therapy**. Here a study is made of the therapeutic methods employed at health centres throughout the Soviet Union—in the Crimea, the Caucasus, Siberia, the Urals, Central Asia and Far East. Patients who attend the institute are able to make use of a fresh mineral water pumped directly from the earth the fount of which is situated inside the institute itself.

On the corner of Kalinin Avenue and **Krasnaya Presnya Embankment** facing a sharp bend in the River Moskva stand the two concrete and glass wings of the 105 metre high **Council for Mutual Economic Assistance (CMEA) building**. The main block of this huge building is connected to a second cylindrical block which contains a conference hall seating 1,000, a hotel, a library and a restaurant.

The CMEA is an international organization for economic cooperation between the socialist countries. Its members are: The People's Republic of Bulgaria, the Hungarian People's Republic, the Socialist Republic of Vietnam, The German Democratic Republic, the Republic of Cuba, the Mongolian People's Republic, the Polish People's Republic, the Socialist Republic of Romania, the Soviet Union and the Czechoslovak Socialist Republic. The Socialist Federative Republic of Yugoslavia participates in the work of a number of the CMEA bodies.

The work of the CMEA is directed towards coordinating the development plans of the member countries, strengthening cooperation and developing socialist economic integration. Examples of the fruitfulness of this cooperation may be seen in various projects like the "Druzhba" (Friendship) oil pipeline and such international systems as the "Mir" (Peace) energy network, the "Interkosmos" television network, the "Intermetal" organization as well as the experience gained by integrated long-term planning and national economic forecasting.

Sessions of the CMEA are held at the CMEA building on Kalinin Avenue, which also houses the executive Committee of the CMEA, legations from the member countries, the standing committees, the secretariat of the CMEA, the Institute of Standards and other bodies.

The CMEA buildings were a joint architectural project, in which the Soviet Union carried out the main construction work with the participation of Bulgaria, Hungary, Poland, Romania and Czechoslovakia. The complex was designed by M. Posokhin, A. Mndoyants and V. Svirsky and built by S. Shkolnikov and Yu. Ratsevich.

"A thing of beauty created by brotherhood" was the way the press described the CMEA building when it was first opened. Special marble and fine timber were brought in from Bulgaria and worked by Bulgarian specialists, the lighting came from the GDR, the lifts from Czechoslovakia and so on. The interior decor is executed with taste and variety making the CMEA ensemble altogether one of the most beautiful buildings in modern Moscow.

Kalinin Avenue leads on to **Kalinin Bridge** (Kalininsky Most) built in 1957 by M. Rudenko and S. Terekhin, and designed by K. Yakovlev and A. Susorov, which is 490 metres long and 43 metres wide. From the bridge you have a fine panoramic view of the two avenues—Kalinin and Kutuzov and the new embankments of the River Moskva. On Krasnaya Presnya Embankment your attention is immediately caught by the white marble façade of the recently built **House of Soviets of the RSFSR**, which is now the central offices of the Presidium of the Supreme Soviet of the RSFSR and the Council of Ministers of the RSFSR.

Looking left along Smolensk Embankment with its multi-storey buildings you can see the **Borodino Bridge** (Borodinsky Most). It was built in 1912 to mark the 100th anniversary of the battle of Borodino, which was the turning point in the war with Napoleon. The architect, R. Klein, and the engineer, N. Oskolkov decorated the bridge with semi-circular granite colonnades and with bronze mouldings and obelisks bearing the names of war heroes. In the early 1950s the bridge was widened and reconstructed.

The new section of Kalinin Avenue which is approximately one kilometre long and 90 metres wide, takes the main stream of traffic out from the centre of the city. It thereby frees the side-streets from congestion, and helps maintain them as a protected area. The largest of these is Arbat Street, which can be reached via **Smolensk Street** and **Smolensk Square** on the Sadovoye Ring.

Arbat Street

Arbat Street is one of the oldest streets in Moscow. The word *arbad* is of oriental derivation and means a suburb. As a result of the many fires and the subsequent rebuilding the street has changed its appearance many times, but today it is a typical street of old Moscow and has remained a favourite among the older inhabitants.

During the second half of the 18th century when most of the neighbouring streets were becoming a fashionable aristocratic area, Arbat Street was the only local shopping centre. Many of its shops have been preserved from those times.

Many great writers, artists and painters lived on Arbat Street and their houses have been carefully preserved.

In 1831 shortly after his marriage Alexander Pushkin spent several months in a flat on the first floor at No 53, his only flat in Moscow. Today it is a museum and the flat has been made to look like it did in Pushkin's time. This leads off the route to other places in the city associated with the great Russian poet's name—the houses he visited, the homes of his friends.

The neighbouring house, No 51, has connections with the poet Alexander Blok, who stayed here in May 1920 during his last visit to Moscow.

On the other side of the street in **Spasopeskovsky Lane** there is a 17th century monument—the ancient **Church of Our Saviour in Peski**. A painting by V. Polenov, entitled *A Moscow Side-Street* (Moskovsky Dvorik) in the Tretyakov Gallery, depicts this corner of old Moscow.

Theatre lovers will be well acquainted with the **Vakhtangov Theatre** (No 26) which stretches on to the pavement with its colonnaded portico. The contemporary themes of its plays, the high standards of production and its overall pleasant atmosphere make the theatre one of the most popular in Moscow. The theatre is named after Yevgeny Vakhtangov, the famous director who founded it in 1921. Many of the productions of this theatre have become Soviet classics: *Man with a Gun*, in which the character of Lenin was played on the stage by B. Shchukin for the first time, *Turandot* by Carlo Gozzi, *Irkutsk Story* by A. Arbuzov.

At No 11 **Vakhtangov Street** (on the left just before the theatre) the composer Skryabin spent his last years. His room was opened in 1922 as a **flat-museum** and contains manuscripts, portraits and letters from such people as Vladimir Stasov, Anatoly Lyadov, Alexander Glazunov and other friends which recreate the life and times of the composer. A tour round the museum is accompanied with recordings of his music and the museum also contains the apparatus by which Skryabin produced a colour accompaniment to his symphonic poem *Prometheus*.

The building opposite (No 12a) houses the **Shchukin Drama School** and the **Opera Studio of the Moscow Conservatoire**—a training theatre, where students from the senior courses—vocalists, musicians, directors and producers work on their first plays. The studio is a favourite among music lovers, for here you can often see the first performances of those who will one day become famous.

Lenin too spent some time in Arbat Street as a young man. In February 1897 after fourteen months' solitary confinement in a St. Petersburg prison, he spent a few days with his relatives in one of the side-streets off Arbat Street, from where he went off into exile in Siberia.

These little side-streets off the Arbat could tell much of the history of Russian culture.

For instance, on the right near Arbat Square is **Myaskovsky Street,** which is named after the famous Soviet composer. Here there are several buildings of interest. No 8, for example, was the meeting place of the well-known Stankevich circle during the 1830s, a progressive literary and philosophical group described by Herzen in his novel, *My Past and Thoughts*, and by Turgenev in *Rudin*. According to the famous revolutionary, philosopher and literary critic, Chernyshevsky, the Stankevich circle included "all those remarkable people whose names are part of our literary heritage". No 12 during the same period was the home of Sergei Aksakov, the famous writer, and organizer of the literary soirées known as "Aksakov Saturdays" which were attended by prominent critics, musicians and artists.

A memorial plaque outside No 27 informs the visitor that here was the home of the famous Russian sculptor Nikolai Andreyev, whose works you have already come across. Andreyev was given the opportunity of working in Lenin's study in the Kremlin where he made many sculptural studies and sketches. In 1920 he began working on the figure of Lenin and by the time of his death in 1932 had produced almost 100 sculptural studies, known as the Leniniana, which show the great philosopher and leader.

Returning to Arbat Street, you can see on the left the **Prague Restaurant,** famed for its Czech national cuisine. Ahead lies Arbat Square once more where this itinerary comes to an end.

KUTUZOV AVENUE—MOZHAISK HIGHWAY

*Kutuzov Avenue—The "Hero-City" obelisk—Panorama
of the Battle of Borodino—Mozhaisk Highway—Fili-Kuntsevo—
Davydkovo—Matveyevskoye—Rublyovo Highway—The
Sports Complex at Krylatskoye—Mozhaisk Highway
(continuation)—Borodino Field Museum-Reserve*

Kutuzov Avenue

Kutuzov Avenue (Kutuzovsky Prospekt) is the continuation of Kalinin Avenue on the other side of the River Moskva across the **Kalinin Bridge**. The building of the avenue was begun in the 1930s but it was not finally completed until the 1960s. It is now one of the most beautiful thoroughfares in the city. Kutuzov Avenue was named in 1957 after the famous Russian General, Mikhail Kutuzov (1745-1813), who commanded the Russian forces in the Patriotic War against Napoleon (1812-1813). The avenue

KRYLATSKOYE

FILI

BOLSHAYA FILI STREET

1812 YEAR STREET

BARKLAY STREET

Victory Square

RUBLYOVO HIGHWAY

KUNTSEVO

MARSHAL GRECHKO AVENUE

DAVYDKOVO STREET

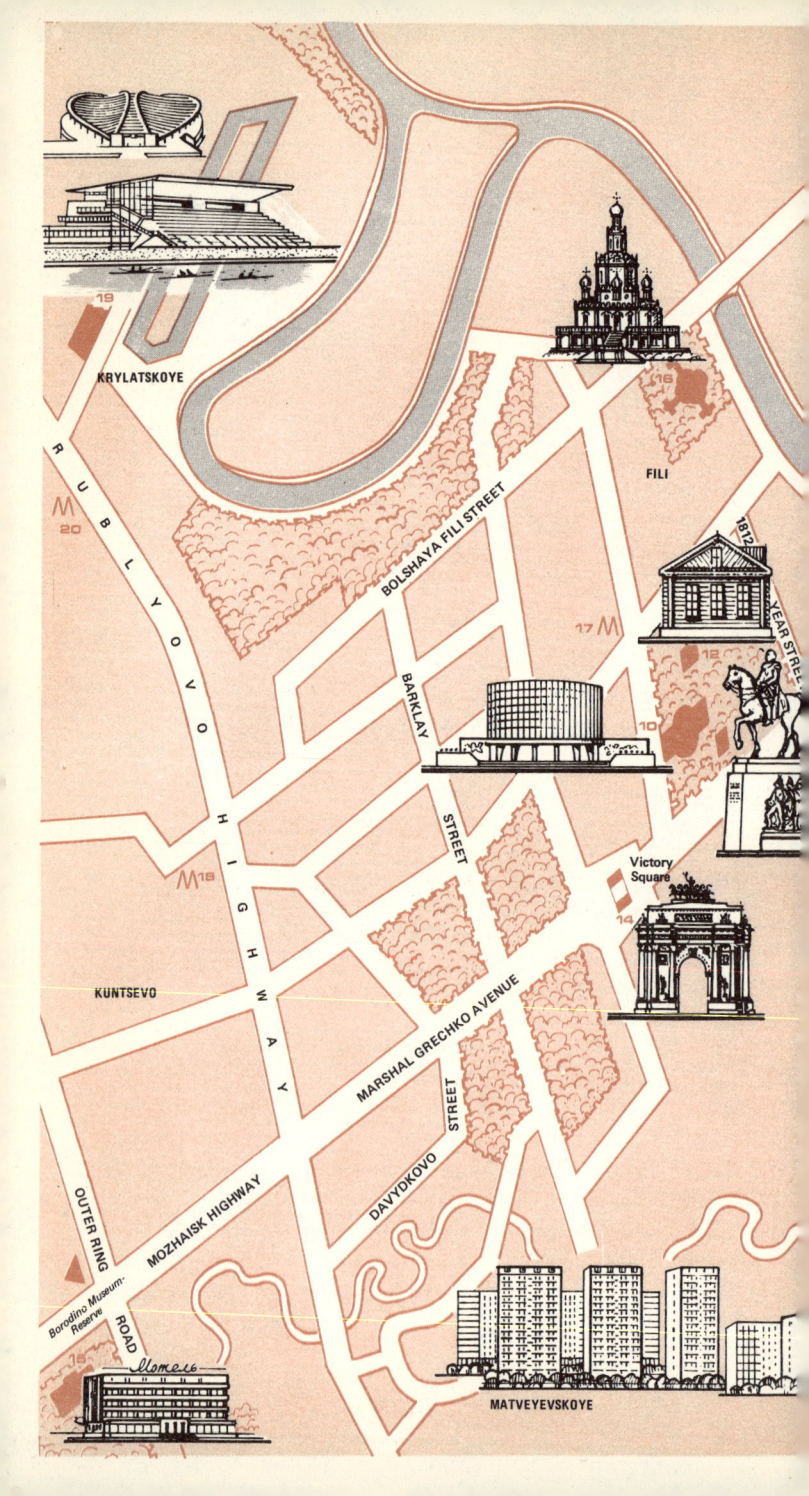

OUTER RING ROAD

MOZHAISK HIGHWAY

Borodino Museum-Reserve

Мотель

MATVEYEVSKOYE

KUTUZOV AVENUE–MOZHAISK HIGHWAY

1. Ukraina Hotel
2. Monument to Taras Shevchenko
3. "Soviet Russia" bookshop
4. Dom Igrushki toy shop
5. "Russian Souvenir" shop
6. Central Arts Salon of the USSR Arts Fund
7. Kiev Railway Station
8. Kievskaya Metro Station
9. "Moscow, Hero-City" Obelisk
10. Panorama Museum of the Battle of Borodino
11. Monument to Kutuzov
12. "Kutuzov's Izba" Cottage
13. Kutuzovskaya Metro Station
14. Triumphal Arch
15. Mozhaiskaya Motel
16. Church of Intercession in Fili (17th cent.)
17. Fili Metro Station
18. Kuntsevskaya Metro Station
19. Krylatskoye Sports Complex
20. Molodyozhnaya Metro Station

itself and the neighbouring districts contain many places made memorable by that war of national liberation, in which the Russian people fought against the Napoleonic armies.

At the entrance to the avenue on the right-hand side by the banks of the River Moskva stands the 29-storey **Ukraine Hotel** with its 170 metre high spire, which was built in 1956 by A. Mordvinov, V. Oltarzhevsky and V. Kalish. The hotel has 1,000 rooms, restaurants and a winter garden. At the top of the tower there is a glass-fronted rotunda giving a panoramic view of Moscow.

In the gardens in front of the hotel a **monument to Taras Shevchenko**, the great Ukrainian poet, artist and revolutionary democrat was erected in 1964. At the foot of the monument there always are flowers as a tribute of gratitude and love to the composer of the songs and verses, which ring out in dozens of languages across the whole of the USSR. The monument is the work of the Ukrainian sculptors, M. Gritsyuk, Yu. Sinkevich, and A. Fuzhenko.

The pedestal is inscribed with the prophetic words of the great poet addressed to his descendants:

> *And in the great new family,*
> *The family of the free,*
> *With softly spoken, kindly word,*
> *Pray, men, remember me.*

Both sides of Kutuzov Avenue are lined with multi-storey apartment blocks with shops on their ground floors. These include the large bookshop "Soviet Russia" (No 4/2), a shop selling plants (No 5/3), a toy shop (No 8) and a **"Russian Souvenir"** shop (No 9). On Ukrainian Boulevard, which leads off Kutuzov Avenue opposite the Ukraine Hotel is the **Central Arts Salon of the USSR Arts Fund** (No 6), where exhibitions are held and where you can buy original paintings, sculptures, ceramics, glassware, articles of wood, metal, amber, bone, carpets and decorative fabrics from all over the Soviet Union.

Further along Kutuzov Avenue, at the junction with **Bolshaya Dorogomilovskaya Street** incoming traffic enters a tunnel. Here in the 18th century stood one of the city's 18 customs posts. Bolshaya Dorogomilovskaya Street itself leads to **Kiev Station**, which links Moscow with many European capitals like Belgrade, Budapest, Bucharest, Prague, Sofia, as well as Kiev, Kishinev, Lvov,

Odessa and many other Soviet towns. The station was built between 1913 and 1917 by I. Rerberg and has recently undergone restoration work with its façades, frescoes and interior mouldings renewed.

In recent years Bolshaya Dorogomilovskaya Street and the streets adjoining the station square have been built up with multi-storey apartment blocks and building in this area is still in progress.

Kutuzov Avenue continues the line of the old road to Smolensk, which has since been called the Mozhaisk Highway and which has witnessed many historical events.

At the junction with Bolshaya Dorogomilovskaya Street there stands a huge silver-grey granite column crowned with a gold star. This obelisk bears the Order of Lenin and the text of the Ordinance of the Presidium of the Supreme Soviet awarding the city of Moscow the honorary title "Hero-City", the Order of Lenin and the Gold Star Medal to commemorate the 20th anniversary of the victory of the Soviet people in the Great Patriotic War of 1941-1945.

Around the obelisk stand three granite figures of a male and female worker and a soldier personifying the unity of the front and the rear during time of war, for it was by their hands that the victory was achieved over fascist Germany. The **obelisk** was unveiled on May 9, 1977 (sculptor A. Shcherbakov, architects G. Zakharov and Z. Chernysheva).

Nearby there are many buildings whose history is connected with the early war years. At No 4a, **Borodino 1st Street**, for example, is the Moscow Pharmaceutical School, where during the early days of the war the 6th regiment of the Kiev District (of Moscow) home-guard was formed, which was later to go all the way to Berlin. At No 6 Kutuzov Avenue the 4th Moscow Communist Division was formed, which was to be awarded for the liberation of Stanislav and Budapest. At Secondary School No 75 (10 **Poklonnaya Street**) the 23rd artillery division of the High Command was formed, which was later to distinguish itself in the liberation of Ternopol and the taking of Berlin.

Across the flyover which crosses the Moscow Circle Line Kutuzov Avenue rises up to the **Poklonnaya Gora**. In the olden days the traveller approaching Moscow had a panoramic view of the city from here. On September 14, 1812 Napoleon stopped here and waited for several hours to receive a deputation from the inhabitants of the city offering surrender. But

> *Elated by his victories,*
> *Napoleon waited here in vain*
> *For Moscow, kneeling at his feet,*
> *To tender him the Kremlin keys.*
> *But never did my Moscow deign*
> *To stoop with bended head in shame*
> *With gifts before the conqueror.*

Here today stands a memorial complex dedicated to the Patriotic War of 1812. It includes **"Kutuzov's Izba"** (Cottage), the peasant hut where in September 1812 Kutuzov held the famous council of war which decided the fate of Moscow. Here a museum was recently opened to the great soldier showing early 19th century arms and uniform, portraits of the heroes of the war who took part in the council of war, Kutuzov's personal effects and his manuscripts and orders and materials relating to his military career.

In 1962 a **Panorama Museum of the Battle of Borodino** was opened here to mark the 150th anniversary of the Patriotic War. A cylindrical building of glass and aluminium, designed by A. Korabelnikov, S. Kuchanov and A. Kuzmin and built by Yu. Avrutin contains a panoramic display of the Battle of Borodino, created in 1912 by the famous Russian artist, F. Rubo. Soviet artists under the direction of P. Korin and I. Yevstigneyev have carried out considerable restoration work on the giant canvas, which is 115 metres long and 15 metres high.

From the entrance hall of the museum you enter two small halls, where there are paintings, sculptures, engravings and drawings on themes from the war of 1812. Then you go upstairs to the viewers' gallery which stands in the centre of a huge circular hall and there, all around you, is the Battle of Borodino.

> On August 26, 1812 the Russian army under Kutuzov's command fought a tremendous battle against the numerically superior armies of Napoleon, the outcome of which changed the whole course of the war and brought about the collapse of Napoleon's plans. (See *Borodino Field Museum.*)

After its opening the Panorama soon became one of the most

popular attractions in Moscow and now more than a million people visit it every year.

On a stone parapet in front of the Panorama building there are a number of French cannons captured during the war of 1812, and on both sides of the entrance there are two huge mosaic panels by Talberg entitled *The People's Volunteer Corps and the Fire of Moscow* and *The Victory of the Russian Troops and the Flight of Napoleon.* The museum complex includes an obelisk set above the mass grave of 300 Russian soldiers who were killed in the war. In July 1973 a magnificent **monument** was unveiled, which stands on the right of the Panorama building and bears the inscription: "To Mikhail Illarionovich Kutuzov and the Glorious Sons of the Russian People who Were Victorious in the Patriotic War of 1812." The monument was built by sculptor N. Tomsky and architect L. Golubovsky.

One further monument of interest on Kutuzov Avenue related to the war of 1812 is the **Triumphal Arch.** The first Triumphal Arch was built in 1817 and made of wood. It was erected at the end of what is now Gorky Street at the Tver Gate, where a ceremonial welcome was held for the victorious Russian troops returning from the war. It was later replaced by a stone arch, an outstanding work by Bove, Vitali and Timofeyev, that was built between 1827 and 1834. In 1968 the arch was restored and rebuilt in the square at the end of Kutuzov Avenue at the Poklonnaya Gora which in 1975 was renamed **Victory Square** (Ploshchad Pobedy) to commemorate the 30th Anniversary of the victory of the Soviet people in the Great Patriotic War of 1941-1945. Here in 1941 stood the heavily fortified reserve defence line which bristled with anti-tank and anti-aircraft batteries. Today the square is surrounded by multi-storey apartment blocks built since the war. The square is particularly beautiful in spring when it is covered with a red carpet of tulips. In Victory Park on the nearby Poklonnaya Gora a sculptural and architectural ensemble will be erected to the immortal heroism and courage of the Soviet people in the years of the war with fascist Germany.

The Mozhaisk Highway

The section of the road from Victory Square to the Rublyovo Highway has been recently renamed **Marshal Grechko Avenue**. The remaining section as far as the outer ring road is the Mozhaisk Highway.

Many of the streets in this area are named after famous heroes from the war of 1812 like Bagration, Barclay de Tolly, Yermolov, Dorokhov and the partisans Denis Davydov, Vasilisa Kozhina and Gerasim Kurin. The streets in this neighbourhood also bear the names of Soviet heroes from the Great Patriotic War of 1941-1945. Besides Marshal Grechko Avenue there are also streets named after Marshal Tolbukhin, Marshal Nedyelin, Marshal Govorov, General Grishin, Colonel Polosukhin and Flying Officer Sviridov etc.

The Mozhaisk Highway has been widened and reconstructed. Where it joins the outer ring road there is the **Mozhaiskaya Hotel.**

All along the Mozhaisk Highway, where once stood villages and settlements there are now vast modern housing estates and other new buildings. Some of the most architecturally interesting of these are to be found at the junctions of the Mozhaisk Highway and 1812 Street, Minsk Street, and the Rublyovo and Aminyevskoye Highways.

Fili-Kuntsevo

This district, which stretches along the winding banks of the River Moskva is very picturesque indeed. The name of the locality is connected with the old villages which used to be here, whose history goes back five centuries.

In the 17th and 18th centuries Kuntsevo was owned by the noble family of the Naryshkins, whose estate covered a vast area. Today their 18th century manor house has been preserved as has the beautiful park on the steep bank of the River Moskva and the **Church of Intercession in Fili,** a magnificent architectural work, which stands near the **Fili Metro Station.**

The church was built in 1693 and is famous for its design and its whitestone ornamentation. It was one of the first works in the architectural style known as "Naryshkin Baroque". Inside are some remarkable works of Russian art: the multi-tiered carved gilt iconostasis, which rises right to the vaults, and the carved choir stalls. This church was visited many times by Peter the Great and one of the icons reproduces his portrait as a young man. The church has been restored and is now a branch of the Andrei Rublyov Museum.

During the Soviet period Kuntsevo has become a major industrial district, but it nevertheless remains one of the most attractive and picturesque parts of Moscow.

Here the town planners have contrived to combine the natural landscape of the area with original architectural compositions and have built new housing estates which are interestingly laid out and full of greenery, light and good air. At the same time the Metro line ensures a convenient and rapid link with the centre.

Davydkovo. Matveyevskoye

These two new housing estates are situated on the banks of the River Setun.

The Davydkovo Estate is intersected at its highest part by Marshal Grechko Avenue, which with its high-rise buildings makes an impressive silhouette.

The land slopes down from Marshal Grechko Avenue in a series of terraces where the buildings are set amid green trees and parkland. Thanks to this graded layout all the buildings here have a fine view over the wooden banks of the Setun and the neighbouring hills of Matveyevskoye.

Matveyevskoye was built 10-15 years ago and here the planners made optimum use of the natural landscape of hills and terraces formed by the two rivers Setun and Ramenka. The main street of this housing estate is a wide boulevard.

In the future the banks of the Setun are to be made into an area of rest and leisure for the inhabitants of Davydkovo and Matveyevskoye. A new main road will link the two districts and on the shores of an artificial lake there will be a park, beaches, boating stations and a sports complex.

Rublyovo Highway. The Krylatskoye Sports Complex

Off to the right of Mozhaisk Highway, not far from **Kuntsevo Metro Station**, runs the Rublyovo Highway leading to the new sports complex at **Krylatskoye**.

Here in 1973 a rowing canal was built which has been described by the Swiss President of the International Rowing Federation, Thomas Keller, as the finest canal of its kind in the world. Not only does it conform to the strict standards of international rowing, it has also been built with great architectural artistry.

The completion in 1980 of the second stage of the complex has turned Krylatskoye into a sports centre. At the 1980 Olympics it was the venue of the rowing regata, road and track bicycle races and the archery tournament. To accommodate these events new blocks have been built here containing sports gymnasiums, changing rooms, rest rooms, a conference hall and a solarium. As well as the covered stands by the rowing canal which seat 3,500, permanent and semi-permanent stands have been erected so as to extend the number of places to 21 thousand.

In a vast building large enough to accommodate two football pitches a covered track has been built for the sprinter-cyclists. The 2,000 square metres of cycle track is covered with a special type of wood, and the stands can take up to 6,000 spectators.

The complex can be used in winter for ski races and speedway.

To improve transport facilities to the sports centre a bridge has been built across the Moskva at Nizhniye Mnevniki and a new main road now connected Krylatskoye with the Leningrad Highway.

Borodino Field Museum

Borodino Field is situated 123 kilometres from Moscow on the Mozhaisk Highway. It can be reached by bus from the Shchelkovskaya Metro Station and by train from Byelorussian Railway Station.

For some 80 years the field on which the Battle of Borodino was fought has been opened to the public. Here you can learn about the events of the Patriotic War of 1812 and the course of the battle itself. The museum contains portraits of the soldiers, who distinguished themselves in battle, the uniform and equipment of the Russian and French armies and paintings illustrating the heroic exploits of the defenders of the Motherland.

On the field itself the remains of the earthwork fortifications have been preserved. On the hundredth anniversary of the battle 34 monuments were erected to the military units of the Russian army who heroically fought here. In the nearby village of Gorki there is a granite obelisk surmounted by a bronze eagle. This is the monument to Kutuzov.

Restoration specialists have drawn up a project for the detailed reconstruction of the locality so as to recreate it as it was on the day of the battle.

In 1941 Borodino once more became a field of battle. Here the Soviet Guards units repulsed tank attack by the invading forces. Today above the mass grave of the Soviet soldiers a marble obelisk has been erected in memory of their courage and heroism.

HERZEN STREET AND VOROVSKY STREET

*Herzen Street–Nikitskiye Gates Square–Kachalov
Street–Vorovsky Street*

Herzen Street and Vorovsky Street together with the neighbouring side-streets are another of the protected areas of old Moscow lying within the confines of the Sadovoye Ring. This district, which largely sprung up in the 16th and 17th centuries and which has retained much of its character, recalls in the names of its streets many of the events and names that are part of Russia's glorious history.

Herzen Street

Herzen Street was named in 1920 in honour of Alexander Herzen, the revolutionary thinker and writer, who was an active participant in the national liberation struggle of the Russian people. His name has occurred many times in the pages of this book, for Moscow greatfully preserves the memory of one of her finest sons.

In ancient times this was the road to Novgorod and here in the 16th century was the cooks' quarter, where those who prepared food for the royal household lived. Hence the names of many of the streets in this neighbourhood: Khlebny (bread), Skatertny (table cloth), Stolovy (dining table), Nozhevoy (knife) etc.

In the second half of the 18th century the district gradually became built up with large estates, some of which have still been preserved.

The first blocks on both sides of Herzen Street are taken up by the huge classical style buildings of the old Moscow University, which include now on the right-hand side two museums: the Anthropological Museum (18 Marx Avenue) and the Zoological Museum (6 Herzen Street).

The Anthropological Museum contains models of primeval man and displays illustrating the history of the evolution of the human race. There are also early tools and weapons, objects d'art and paintings, as well as pictures and models of typical ancient settlements made on the basis of excavations.

The Zoological Museum has been in existence for more than 200 years. Its collection of mammals, birds, amphibia, reptiles, fish and insects is unique, and the finest examples are displayed on the stands.

On the left-hand side of the block is the **University Humanities Department Club**. It is housed in what was formerly the university chapel (built in 1836 by Ye. Tyurin). Here in 1852 the body of the great Russian writer, Nikolai Gogol, lay in state. The neighbouring buildings (Nos 3 and 5, both 18th century) are also part of the university complex. The second building was built by Kazakov.

No 12 (entrance on Ogarev Street) was also built by Kazakov in the late 18th century. It is known as "Menshikov's Palace" and is a fine example of Moscow classicism. Recently this building underwent reconstruction.

The most famous institution on Herzen Street is the **Moscow State Conservatoire** (No 13) which has been **named after Tchaikovsky**. Besides Tchaikovsky himself, Taneyev, Ippolitov-Ivanov, Glier and Neuhaus all taught at one time here and the Conservatoire most famous pupils have included Rakhmaninov, Skryabin, Goldenweiser, Igumnov, Nezhdanova, Khachaturyan, Khrennikov, Richter, Oistrakh, Flier and many others. The conservatoire building is late 18th century, but it has been rebuilt several times, the present building being erected in 1901 by V. Zagorsky.

The most important events in the musical life of the Soviet Union take place in the **Great Hall of the Moscow Conservatoire**, which is one of the finest concert halls in the capital with seats for 2,000. Here world famous musicians perform as well as up-and-coming new stars. Since 1958, the International Tchaikovsky Competition for violinists, pianists, cellists and vocalists has been held here every four years and the winners have included such world-famous names as Van Cliburn, Tretyakov, Obraztsova, and Sinyavskaya.

In the **Lesser Hall of the Conservatoire**, which is situated in the left wing of the building, chamber music and organ recitals are held.

In 1954 a **monument to Tchaikovsky** by V. Mukhina, N. Zelenskaya and Z. Ivanova was erected outside the building and every spring the "Day of Songs" festival is officially opened with a concert of choral music given from the foot of the Tchaikovsky monument.

The reconstruction project for this protected area envisages setting up around the Conservatoire a whole musical library, music shops and permanent exhibitions in the ancient houses. The building of the former **Church of the Lesser Ascension** (early 18th century) which stands opposite the Conservatoire (No 18) will house the **State Collection of Musical Instruments**.

This collection contains more than 200 violins by Stradivari, Amati, Guarnieri, Montagnana, Guadagnini, Vuillaume, and the serf violin-maker Ivan Batov, who is called the "Russian Stradivari". There are also works by Soviet masters like Vitachek, Podgorny, Morozov, Frolov. The instruments are available for outstanding performers to use at concerts.

In some of the neighbouring houses the various faculties of the Conservatoire—theoretical, compositional, orchestral, fortepiano and vocal—will be accommodated, and in the nearby **Sredny Kislovsky Lane** (to the left of Herzen Street) the new opera studious will be built.

Also on the left, on the corner of Herzen Street and **Sobinov Lane** is a red-brick three-storey building with towers and a porch built in the late 19th century in immitation of the traditional Russian style. This is the **Mayakovsky Theatre** (No 18/19). This was one of the first drama theatres in Soviet Moscow. Founded in 1922, it was then called the Revolutionary Theatre. In 1954 the theatre was renamed after Mayakovsky, whose works together with those of Brecht, Pogodin, Vishnevsky and Arbuzov are part of the repertoire of the company. Outside the theatre is a memorial plaque to Nikolai Okhlopkov, People's Artist of the USSR, who for many years was in charge of the theatre. Also featured prominently in the repertoire of the theatre are Shakespeare *(Romeo and Juliette, Hamlet)*, Lope de Vega *(El Perro del Hortelano, La Fuente Ovejuna)* and Alexander Ostrovsky *(The Storm)*.

At 6 Sobinovsky Lane is the **State Institute of Theatrical Art**. It is named after the great Russian singer, Leonid Sobinov, who studied at the Music and Drama College of the Moscow Philharmonic Society where the Institute of Theatrical Art now stands. Here under the guidance of the greatest masters of the stage, directors, actors and theatre critics are trained. The Institute has produced about forty repertory groups of different nationalities, which formed the basis for the theatres in the Union and autonomous republics, which before the Revolution had no professional theatres of their own.

Probably more famous personages from the world of Soviet culture have lived in **Nezhdanova Street** (to the right of Herzen Street) than in any other street in Moscow. No 17 was the home of three famous actors from the Moscow Art Theatre, Vasili Kachalov, Ivan Moskvin and Leonid Leonidov, and the ballerina Yekaterina Geltser. At No 12 the famous director Meyerhold had his apartment and at No 7 lived Nikolai Golovanov, conductor of the Bolshoi Theatre, Fedor Fedorovsky, the stage designer, Nadezhda Obukhova, the singer and Ivan Shadr, the sculptor.

Apartment 9 of the same house (No 7) is now a **Memorial Museum to Antonina Nezhdanova**, the great

Russian singer after whom the street is named. Here the All-Union Theatrical Society arranges performances by well-known soloists and young players, and seminars are held and consultations given to amateur performers. A series of concerts from the Nezhdanova Museum are regularly televised.

No 8/10, which was built in 1956, is yet another of Moscow's musical centres—the **Union of Composers of the USSR** and **All-Union House of Composers**, with a concert hall seating 450 and various other rooms for social functions. On the wall outside is a memorial plaque with a bas-relief portrait of Dmitry Shostakovich, for here in apartment 23 from 1962 until his death in 1975 the composer lived and worked. In the study his archives have been preserved together with his desk and two pianos, and it is here that his friends and pupils come for the first performances of their new compositions.

At No 2 (Block A), on the corner of Nezhdanova Street and Herzen Street, the great Russian poet Sergei Esenin lived in 1924 and it was here that he created his verses on Lenin, his poem *Soviet Russia* and a number of other works.

Further along Herzen Street also on the right-hand side is **Stanislavsky Street**. Outside No 6 there is a memorial plaque with the following inscription: "Here Konstantin Sergeyevich Stanislavsky, the founder of the Moscow Art Theatre, lived and worked until his death on August 7, 1938." In 1940 the building was opened as the **Stanislavsky Museum** and here the visitor can learn about the life and work of the great theatrical innovator.

The low building on the opposite side of the street (No 7) with its porch, slender colonnaded gallery and small ornamental windows is a successful imitation of 17th century architecture. Today it houses the **Museum of Folk Art**.

> It contains examples of folk art from the 18th and 19th centuries and 17th-20th century handicrafts. Here you will see many interesting household utensils (spinning-wheels, jugs, birch baskets, all covered with fine ornamentation and painted scenes) and traditional folk costumes. There are examples of woven fabrics, folk embroidery, wood carving and painting, metal work, beautiful Palekh miniatures

that seem to radiate light, works by the artists of Mstera and Fedoskino, carvings from the peoples of the North, gold and silver inlays from Daghestan, brightly decorated ceramic toys and crockery from Gzhel, wooden toys from Zagorsk, lace from Vologda.

Stanislavsky Street also has connections with the revolutionary events of 1917. From here the White Guards tried to break through to Tver Street (now Gorky Street) and the Moscow Soviet building, and heavy fighting took place in this area. A memorial plaque on the entrance to No 18 commemorates the fact that here after the victory of the October Revolution were the offices of the Moscow Committee of the Bolshevik Party, where on September 25, 1919 a bomb was thrown by "left" Socialist-Revolutionaries, killing 12 Party members including the secretary, V. Zagorsky. The names of the dead are engraved on black marble and the plaque is surmounted by a bas-relief of a flag in red granite draped over the funeral urn.

A little further along Herzen Street and you come to the Boulevard Ring.

The house on the corner (No 23) is now a **cinema** showing repeat films, where you can see some of the finest past production of the Soviet and foreign screens.

Here in the 1830s at the apartment of Nikolai Ogarev, a friend and comrade of Herzen, a circle of students whose aim was the liberation of the people from autocracy and serfdom, used to meet.

"We were persuaded that out of this lecture-room would come the company which would follow in the footsteps of Pestel and Ryleyev, and that we should be in it"—recalled Herzen in his book *My Past and Thoughts.*

In 1905 the building once more became caught up with the revolutionary events, for it housed the printing press of the Moscow Committee of the RSDLP, which at that time was publishing a legal newspaper, *Borba* (the Struggle). The last issue of the paper which came out on December 6 of the same year published an appeal from the Moscow Soviet of Workers' Deputies and the Moscow Committee of the RSDLP "To All Workers, Soldiers and Citizens" for a general strike and an armed uprising.

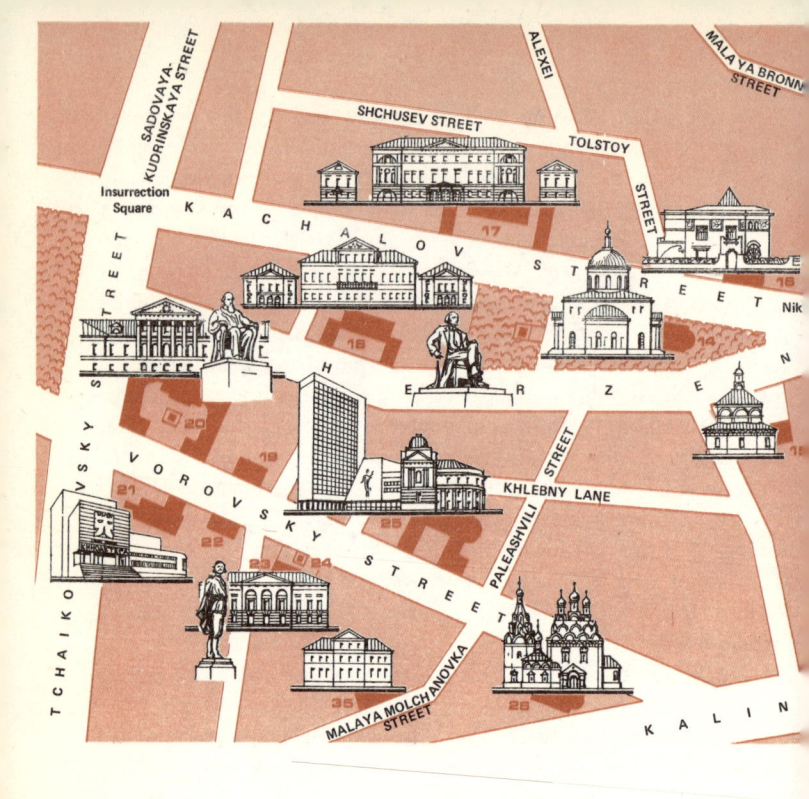

HERZEN AND VOROVSKY STREETS

1. Anthropological Museum
2. Zoological Museum
3. University Humanities Department Club
4. Menshikov's Palace (18th cent.)
5. Moscow Tchaikovsky State Conservatoire
6. Monument to Tchaikovsky
7. Mayakovsky Theatre
8. State Institute of Theatrical Art
9. Nezhdanova Flat-Museum
10. House of Composers
11. Stanislavsky House-Museum
12. Museum of Folk Art
13. Cinematheque
14. Church of the Greater Ascension (19th cent.)
15. Church of St. Theodore of Studious (early 17th cent.)
16. Gorky Flat-Museum
17. Urban Mansion (late 18th- early 19th cent.)
18. Central Writers' Club named after Fadeyev

19. USSR Writers' Union Board (18th cent.)

20. Monument to Lev Tolstoy

21. Film Actor Studio Theatre

22. Institute of Folk Art

23. Maxim Gorky Literary Museum

24. Monument to Gorky

25. Gnesins Musical and Educational Institute

26. Church of St. Simon the Stylite (17th cent.) Exhibition Hall of the Municipal Society for Nature Protection

27. Church of Ascension

28. Friendship House

29. Monument to Timiryazev

30. Central Exhibition Hall

31. Moscow State University

32. Monument to Herzen

33. Monument to Ogarev

34. Monument to Lomonosov

35. Lermontov Museum

In October 1917 the house was taken by counter-revolutionary forces, and became the scene of heavy fighting when Red Guard units advancing on two fronts from Insurrection Square and Tver Boulevard attacked the White stronghold. The fighting continued until November 2, when counter-revolutionary resistance was broken. These events are recalled in a memorial plaque on the façade of the cinema.

On the opposite side of the street is the new **TASS** building, designed by V. Yegerev, A. Shaikhet, B. Gurevich and G. Sirota. TASS (News Agency of the Soviet Union) is the central information organ of the Council of Ministers of the USSR. It communicates the official documents of the Soviet government and provides information for thousands of newspapers, radio and television stations throughout the Soviet Union and abroad.

Nikitskiye Gates Square

In recent years Nikitskiye Gates Square (Ploshchad Nikitskiye Vorota) has changed its appearance considerably. Now, thanks to the reconstruction that has gone on here, there is an excellent view of the **Church of the Greater Ascension**. In the late 17th century a stone church was built to replace the old wooden church that formerly stood here, but the present building was erected in the 1820s by F. Shestakov. Its strict lines and rotunda with a semi-circular cupola are typical of the transition from classicism to empire style. Among the notable events that have taken place here was marriage of Pushkin to Natalya Goncharova in 1831.

The church is now planned to be opened as a concert hall for the Osipov Folk Orchestra.

On the opposite side of the street is the low, squat **Church of St. Theodore of Studious** (early 17th cent.), which seems to have sunk into the ground with age. Here the parents of Field marshal Suvorov were buried and it is planned to turn the church into a memorial museum in honour of the great general.

But reconstruction work is still going on. Here will be the beginning of a new 10-kilometre highway, the Krasnaya Presnya Avenue.

Before continuing your walk along Herzen Street, we recommend you to have a look at Kachalov Street which runs from the Boulevard Ring to the Sadovoye Ring parallel with Herzen Street.

Kachalov Street

This street bears the name of one of the great actors from the Moscow Art Theatre, Vasily Kachalov, who lived here at No 22.

One of the most interesting houses on Kachalov Street is No 6, where Gorky lived and worked from 1931 to 1936. Here he wrote his epic novel, *The Life of Klim Samgin* as well as a number of plays, short stories and articles, carried on his work as chief editor of a number of publications and performed many other public functions. In this house Gorky received many famous personages from the international world of culture including Romain Rolland, George Bernard Shaw, Johannes Becher, Georges Sadoul, as well as young writers who were just beginning their careers.

Today the building is open to the public as the **Gorky flat-museum** and is a branch of the Gorky Literary Museum. The house itself is of some considerable interest architecturally. Built by F. Shekhtel it is considered one of the finest examples of early 20th century Art Nouveau and its external decor are equally original.

The museum receives some 50 thousand visitors annually.

The old stone wall with its enormous gates in front of No 12 immediately catches the eye. It is a late 18th century town manor which is today in an excellent state of preservation. Set well back from the road across a courtyard the manor house is connected with its annexes by means of an ornamental colonnade. Before the portico entrance stand two sculptured figures on low pedestals. These are the statues of Paris and Helen of Troy by an unknown Italian master of the period. Pushkin was frequently a guest in this house and here he wrote *Stanzas*, a poem devoted to the fates of the Decembrists, many of whom were his friends. The building now houses the **State Committee of the RSFSR for Publishing, Printing and Bookselling.**

Herzen Street (continued)

The section of Herzen Street that runs between the Boulevard Ring and the Sadovoye Ring is lined with two- and three-storey houses which for the most part recall the days of the nobles' estates and the rich mansions of late 18th-early 19th century.

> No 46, for example is a typical example of a late 18th-early 19th century urban mansion consisting of the manor house with two annexes, a walled courtyard and servants' quarters. Next door, where Nos 48 and 50 now stand, was once the town estate of the Goncharovs, the parents of Pushkin's wife.

At the end of the street on the left is the **Central Writers' Club** (No 53). This club, which is named after the famous Soviet writer Fadeyev, organizes discussions, exhibitions, meetings with readers, which are always of great interest in Moscow.

Herzen Street leads onto Insurrection Square, where you can turn left along the Sadovoye Ring and left again into Vorovsky Street.

Vorovsky Street

In 1924 this street was named after Vatslav Vorovsky, a prominent member of the Communist Party and a comrade of Lenin, a notable Soviet diplomat.

Vorovsky Street, which is about one kilometre in length, covers three centuries of Russian architecture. The many pages of *War and Peace* that are devoted to describing "the Countess Rostova's big house on the Povarskaya, so well known to all Moscow" have led students of literature to believe that No 52 was precisely the house Tolstoy had in mind. This fine ensemble built in 1787 is particularly important for the fact that it remains to this day almost unchanged. Today this building houses the **USSR Writers' Union Board** and in the centre of the courtyard stands a **monument to Lev Tolstoy** by G. Novokreshchenova erected in 1956. At No 48—a single-storey detached house with a mezzanine—the French writer Alexander Dumas stayed during his visit to Russia in the middle of the last century.

On the other side of the road is the **Film Actor Studio Theatre** (No 33) which was built in 1931-34 by the Vesnin brothers. Here actors whose experience has largely been confined to the screen have the opportunity of trying their talents on the stage. In one of the houses backing on to the yard of No 33 the great film director and People's Artist of the USSR, Vsevolod Pudovkin, who produced the world famous film, *Mother* as well as a number of other Soviet film classics, lived until his death in 1953.

The 19th century detached building at No 31 houses the **Institute of Folk Art**. Here objects of folk art are collected and studied and the exhibitions put on by the Institute are very popular at home and abroad.

One further example of a town manor is No 25 built in 1817-1819 in the Empire style by Gilardi. Today it houses the **Maxim Gorky Institute of World Literature** and the **Maxim Gorky Literary Museum**. In front of the building stands a **monument to** the young **Gorky**, the "stormy petrel" of the Revolution by Vera Mukhina.

Forty years have passed since the founding of the Gorky museum. It began as a small offshoot of the Institute of World Literature and today has the largest collection in the country of editions, documents, manuscripts and photographs relating to the work of the greatest of the proletarian writers.

On the opposite side of the road is a unique musical institute, founded through the enthusiasm and hard work of the Gnesin family, who were prominent figures in Russian culture before the Revolution. The institute was begun in the late 19th century as a musical school for adults and children. During the Soviet period it formed the base for a series of new musical institutes. No 30/36 which is decorated with columns and bas-reliefs of the great composers, was built during the Great Patriotic War as the **Gnesins Musical and Educational Institute**. The old building now houses two musical schools and a new 13-storey building has been erected for 1,200 young musicians, while the **concert hall of the institute** is one of the most popular in Moscow.

A **memorial museum to Yelena Gnesina**, a founder and director of the institute was opened in the flat.

The section of Vorovsky Street that runs down to Arbat Square was largely built up at the turn of the century. It was then fashionable to build detached villas decorated with ornamental mouldings, coloured mosaics, heraldic beasts, and all the other features of the Art Nouveau style. Buildings of this type can be seen in the neighbouring streets and today they are largely occupied by foreign embassies and legations, the permanent representatives of the Union republics and other organizations.

The building on the corner of Vorovsky Street and **Merzlyakovsky Lane** (No 8) is of interest, for here on November 21, 1905, the eve of the Revolution, the first Executive Committee of the Moscow Soviet was elected by workers' deputies.

On the corner of Vorovsky Street and Kalinin Avenue stands the only witness to the times when this street was first built—the 17th century **Church of St. Simeon the Stylite**. The church has been recently restored and now houses the **Exhibition Hall of the Municipal Society for Nature Protection**. There is a permanent **exhibition** here entitled **"Nature and Fantasy"** at which works of applied art by amateur artists from Moscow are displayed.

KRASNAYA PRESNYA–SEREBRYANY BOR

Barricades Street–Krasnaya Presnya Street–Bolshevik Street–Krasnaya Presnya Square–Krasnaya Presnya Embankment. International Exhibition Complex–Marshal Zhukov Avenue–Khoroshevo-Mnevniki–Serebryany Bor

This itinerary begins from Insurrection Square on the Sadovoye Ring, which you have already seen, and passes through the district of Krasnaya Presnya, which became legendary during the 1905 and the 1917 revolutions.

In 1905 Krasnaya Presnya was the centre of the armed uprising.

On December 7, 1905 in support of a decision by the Conference of Moscow Bolsheviks and the Moscow Soviet of Workers' Deputies to call a general strike which would develop into an armed uprising, all major factories in the city stopped work. By the following day more than 150 thousand workers had come out on strike and on December 9 the barricades went up. The heaviest fighting took place in what was then the Presnya district. For ten days the workers of Presnya withstood the onslaughts of the tsarist troops and for ten days Soviet power was proclaimed in the area. But the forces of the two sides were wholly unequal. On December 11 government troops began systematically shelling the Presnya district. The defenders displayed tremendous courage and performed great feats of heroism, but ammunition, food and medicines were running out. By December 17 the tsarist troops had the "Presnya Republic" completely surrounded making further resistance pointless. On December 19 at the request of the Moscow Committee of the RSDLP and the Moscow Soviet the insurrectionists left the barricades and began to break out of the encirclement.

It was during these heroic days of the first Russian Revolution that the Presnya district began to be called *Krasnaya* (Red). In October 1917 the workers of the district once again lived up to their high reputation. In 1922 the main street of the district was officially renamed Krasnaya Presnya.

Today the Krasnaya Presnya district has preserved many memories of those heroic days in its streets, buildings and monuments.

Barricades Street

Leading into Insurrection Square from the far side of the Sadovoye Ring is Barricades Street (Barrikadnaya Ulitsa, formerly Kudrinskaya), which was renamed in 1919 in honour of the fighting at the barricades that took place here in 1905. The bronze figure of one of the heroes of the Presnya barricades by A. Zelinsky stands high on a pedestal outside the **Krasnopresnenskaya Metro Station**, inside which there are bas-reliefs devoted to the events of 1905.

Krasnaya Presnya Street

Krasnaya Presnya Street is the continuation of Barricades Street and the main thoroughfare in the district.

If the revolutionary defender of 1905 who stands here on eternal watch could see Krasnaya Presnya Street as it is today, he would hardly recognize a single building. According to statistics before the Revolution there were in Presnya 378 wooden and 42 stone houses, 24 ponds, 18 vegetable gardens and 120 lamp-posts. Newspapers of the time described the region as a "universal cesspit".

Since the Revolution, however, a tremendous amount of construction work has gone on here: new broad streets have been built, modern apartment blocks erected and shops, schools, and medical centres provided. The whole area is surrounded with green parks.

According to the plan for the reconstruction of the city Krasnaya Presnya Street will become part of the new Krasnaya Presnya Avenue which will run from Nikitskiye Gates Square to Serebryany Bor—a favourite week-end resort on the banks of the River Moskva.

On the corner of Krasnaya Presnya and Bolshaya Gruzinskaya Streets is the main entrance to the Moscow Zoological Gardens (see Chapter *Sadovoye Ring*).

To the left of the Krasnopresnenskaya Metro Station is **Druzhinniki Street**. Situated here will be the All-Union Film Centre, a complex of buildings which include a research institute of cinematographic art, a Soviet cinema history museum, a lecture theatre and a cinema for showing repeat Soviet and foreign films.

At the end of Druzhinniki Street is the **Pavlik Morozov Children's Park**. The park stands on the former site of the Schmidt furniture factory. The owner, Nikolai Schmidt had become a revolutionary while a student at the university. He took active part in the 1905 insurrection providing material and financial aid to the workers against his own class. The authorities looked upon Schmidt's factory as a hotbed of sedition and in 1905 tsarist troops obliterated it with cannon fire. Schmidt himself was arrested and tortured to death in jail. Today one of the main streets in Krasnaya Presnya, Schmidt Passage (Shmitovsky Proyezd), bears his name and in 1971 a memorial of a granite cube with an inscription and a bas-relief portrait of Schmidt by G. Raspopov and V. Yudin was unveiled there.

The park has a District House of Culture for Children and a swimming pool. In the centre of the park there is a monument commemorating the events of 1905 in the form of a large slab of granite, which was placed here in 1920. It bears the inscription "December 1905 armed uprising in Presnya. December 1920". The park contains two other monuments, both to young national heroes—the Pioneer Pavlik Morozov and the Komsomol partizan, Zoya Kosmodemyanskaya.

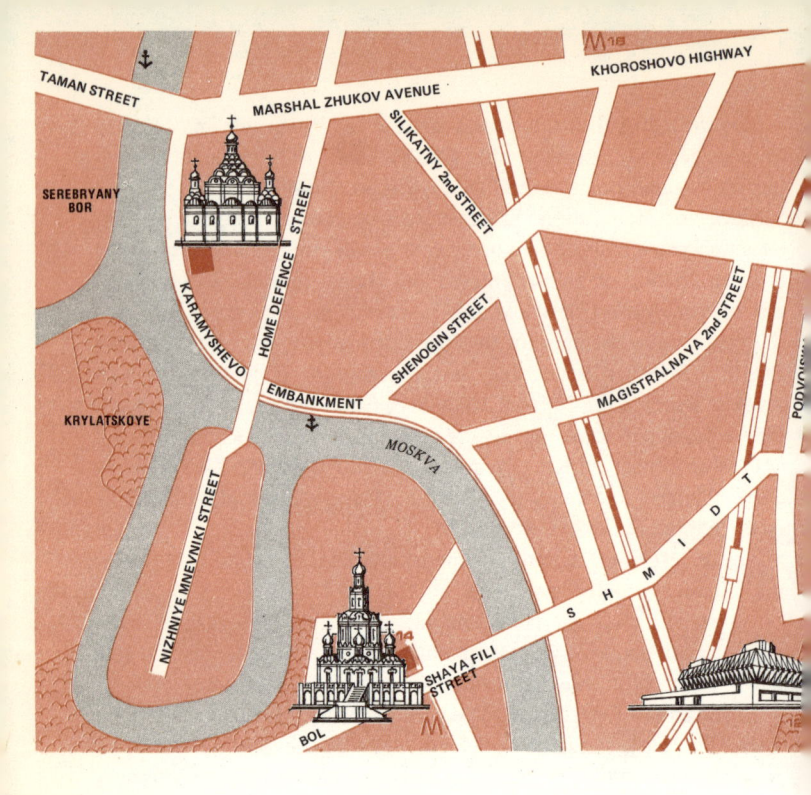

KRASNAYA PRESNYA—SEREBRYANY BOR

1. Krasnopresnenskaya Metro Station
2. Presnya Barricade Fighter. Sculpture
3. Barrikadnaya Metro Station
4. Moscow Zoo
5. Pavlik Morozov Children's Park
6. Krasnaya Presnya Museum, a branch of the Central Museum of the Revolution
7. Ulitsa 1905 Goda Metro Station
8. Sculpture, entitled "The Cobblestone—Weapon of the Proletariat"

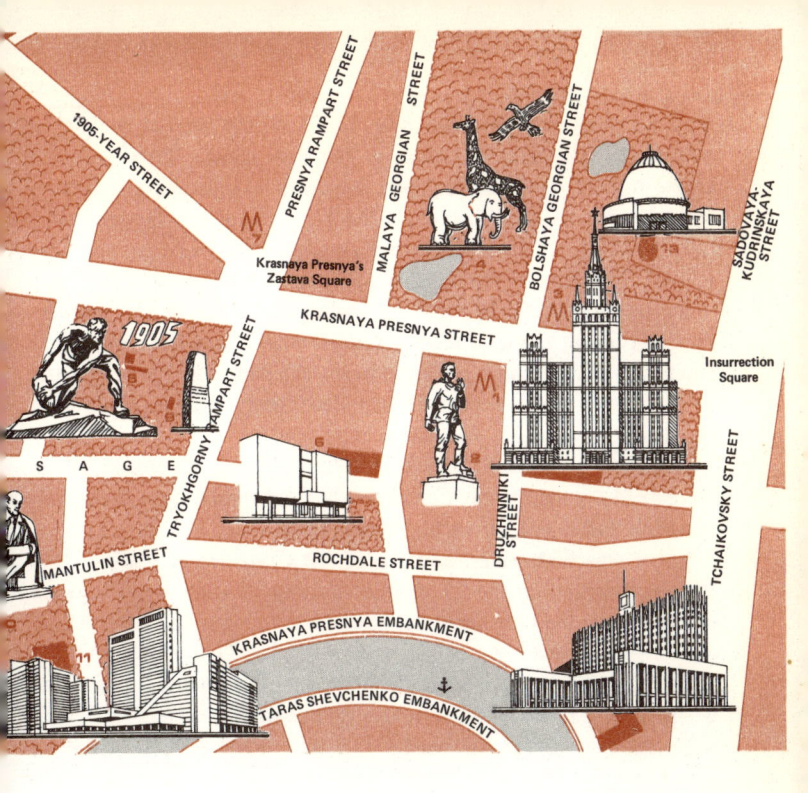

9. Obelisk to the Heroes of the Insurrection of December 1905
10. Monument to Lenin
11. International Trade Centre for Promoting Scientific, Technical and Commercial Links with Foreign Countries
12. International Exhibition Complex
13. Planetarium
14. Church of Intercession in Fili (17th cent.)
15. Begovaya Metro Station
16. Polezhayevskaya Metro Station

In neighbouring **Rochdelskaya Street** stands one of the oldest industrial enterprises **in Moscow, The Dzerzhinsky Tryokhgornaya textile factory** (founded in 1799), which is now the largest factory of its kind in the USSR. Here at the Tri Gory, one of the legendary hills of Moscow, the history of Krasnaya Presnya began and here in 1905 the flame of revolution in Russia was lit.

By the walls of the weaving block where the tsar's butchers shot a group of the defenders a funeral urn draped with a flag was placed in 1923. A marble plaque bears the names of the fallen and an inscription which begins: "Sleep, dear comrades, who first raised the flag of revolution. We will avenge you."

The factory canteen, where in 1905 thousands-strong meetings were held by the Presnya workers, has been rebuilt as the textile combine **Palace of Culture** (6 Tryokhgorny Val).

Lenin was highly appreciative of the contribution made by the Presnya workers in the December uprising. In 1906 he visited the places where the barricades had been erected and chatted to many of the participants. After the victory of the October Revolution when the Soviet government moved to Moscow Lenin met the workers of "Tryokhgorka" seven times and spoke at the factory canteen. Every year the workers of this plant symbolically elect Lenin to the Moscow Soviet, and thus he has remained their deputy for ever. The façade of the Palace of Culture is decorated with two large frescoes, one depicting the fighting at the barricades and the other devoted to the peace-time activities of the textile workers during the Soviet period.

Today the textile factory is equipped with the latest machinery and produces more than a billion metres of fabric annually.

Every third worker is engaged in some form of study or other, whether it be at technical colleges, institutes, the people's university or cultural societies. The pictorial art studios and some of the amateur arts groups of the Palace of Culture have been to Bulgaria, Poland and France.

One more street in the district whose name originates from the revolutionary days of 1905 is **Mantulin Street** (Mantulinskaya Ulitsa), which was named after Fyodor Mantulin who was shot by the tsarist troops for organizing a people's militia at the sugar refinery.

Bolshevik Street

Formerly Predtechensky Lane this street was renamed in honour of the regional party committee and Military Revolutionary Committee which in October 1917 had its headquarters here in a small wooden house (No 4), from where it controlled the Red Guard of the Presnya District.

Soon after the Revolution the house was opened as a museum dedicated to the events of 1905 and 1917 but recently a new building for the **Krasnaya Presnya Museum** was opened nearby as a **branch of the Central Museum of the Revolution**. The Museum contains important documents on the history of the revolution, models of the barricades, and paintings, sculptures, drawings, photos and portraits. The original house and a few other buildings in the area form a protected area and recreate Presnya as it was at the turn of the century with its cobbled street, wooden fences and oil lamps. The wooden huts are made up to resemble the old workers' hostels, where in a single room, separated only by curtains several families would be huddled together.

Krasnaya Presnya Square

Krasnaya Presnya Square stands at the far end of Krasnaya Presnya Street. On the left of the square are the **1905-Year Gardens** with their memorial ensemble, built in 1967 and dedicated to the memory of the heroes of the first Russian revolution. In the centre of the ensemble is the classical sculpture by I. Shadr, entitled **"The Cobblestone—Weapon of the Proletariat"**, which was finished in 1927 for the tenth anniversary of the Revolution. The bronze statue of the worker picking up a cobblestone with a look of grim determination on his face stands on a pedestal of grey granite. Behind the figure is a low granite wall which contains the inscription "The heroism of the Presnya workers was not in vain. Their sacrifices bore fruit. Lenin." The three-metre high granite **obelisk** in the centre of the garden was erected by workers of Presnya in 1920. It bears the inscription "To the Heroes of the Insurrection of December 1905".

At the end of the garden, near Schmidt Passage a **monument to Lenin** by B. Dyuzhev was unveiled in 1970. The bronze statue is surrounded by rose bushes which were planted here by Bulgarian workers from the Dimitrov district of Sofia in celebration of the centenary of Lenin's birth. A small marble plaque reads: "To Lenin, whose name is eternal, a hundred Bulgarian roses."

Krasnaya Presnya Square is undergoing reconstruction. New blocks have been built designed by M. Kruglov, B. Topaz and Yu. Khlebnikov for the **"Moskovskaya Pravda" Publishers** to contain a printing-house and the editorial offices of the central and regional newspapers.

Krasnaya Presnya Embankment

This is becoming the most beautiful part of Krasnaya Presnya. Until quite recently the only thing of interest here was the **Krasnaya Presnya Park of Culture and Rest**, which was built on the site of a former 18th century suburban estate with its picturesque ponds, islands and canals.

But in the 1970s the CMEA complex was erected here together with a number of apartment blocks, and in 1977 the **House of Soviets of the RSFSR** was built by a group of architects headed by D. Chechulin. The three-tier white marble building is set back from the embankment with its main façade facing the River Moskva. During your excursion along Kalinin and Kutuzov Avenue, you have already seen it.

Building is now nearing completion on the **International Trade Centre for Promoting Scientific, Technical and Commercial Links with Foreign Countries**. It was jointly designed and built by Soviet organizations and American companies and consists of a 22-storey building which will house the offices of firms and organizations permanently represented in Moscow. The complex also includes a multi-storey hotel with 625 suites for the representatives and their families, and a second hotel for businessmen on short-term visits. The buildings will be connected by a covered arcade and in the inner courtyard of the ten-storey hotel there will be a winter garden with fountains covered by a glass roof. The centre also includes a congress hall seating 2,000, a press-centre, a computer centre, salons for business meetings, a leisure complex with a cinema and exhibition halls, restaurants, cafés, cocktail-bars, a sports hall, a swimming pool and an underground car-park.

Krasnaya Presnya Park has been considerably extended. It now contains a new summer theatre, a restaurant, stadium and fairground.

Set in the park are the 16 pavilions of the **International Exhibition Complex**, in the building of which many countries have participated, including Bulgaria, Yugoslavia, West Germany, the United States, and Japan. Part of the complex was opened in 1976 and the rest in 1980.

The old district of Presnya, a former suburb of the city is now becoming a centre of international trade.

While the new Krasnaya Presnya Avenue is still under construction, you can continue your itinerary along.

Marshal Zhukov Avenue

Until recently Marshal Zhukov Avenue, which is now one of the main thoroughfares in the western part of the city, was a street with only low buildings along it. During the last two decades, however, a tremendous amount of construction has gone on here. On the left is one of the most verdant housing estates in the capital, **Khoroshevo-Mnevniki.**

At the intersection with **Home Defence Street** (Ulitsa Narodnovo Opolcheniya), the second major thoroughfare in the area, you will see a memorial park in honour of those who took part in the Battle of Moscow during the Great Patriotic War. In the centre of the garden is a monumental **sculptural group** by O. Kiryukhin and A. Yershov representing the heroes of the Volunteer Corps. The Avenue goes as far as Khoroshevo Hill and ends in an ensemble of 26-storey apartment blocks.

You are now approaching a picturesque island formed from a bend in the River Moskva and separated from the shore by a canal.

Serebryany Bor

Here in an area of some 150 hectares there are something like 40 thousand trees, many of which are at least 200 years old. The resinous smell of the pines and the cool river air attract crowds at this week-end resort with its beaches and boating stations.

In 1975 a **monumental triptych** was set up here in honour of the glorious 3rd Army, which in 1941 left for the front from here. The soldiers of the 3rd Army reached Berlin and raised the Flag of Victory over the Reichstag.

On the far side of the river, which can be reached by river ferry, and dominating the high bank, stands a fine example of Russian 17th century architecture— the baroque **Trinity Church** by Yakov Bukhvostov.

The perfection of its composition and the richness of its ornamentation make it fully comparable with the Church of Intercession in Fili. The architectural historian, M. Ilyin, described the Trinity Church as the "swan song of Ancient Russia".

Restoration work on the church has recently been finished with the brick and whitestone walls being refaced, the cupola regilded and the carved iconostasis renewed according to old drawings and measurements.

GORKY STREET

Gorky Street. Soviet Square–Pushkin Square. Museum of the Revolution–Mayakovsky Square–Byelorussian Station Square

Gorky Street

This road has long been considered the main thoroughfare of Moscow. Its transformation during the 1930s marked the beginning of the implementation of the first general plan for the Reconstruction of Moscow. Today it has many beautiful buildings with large shops, theatres and museums, restaurants and cafés. In summer its wide pavements are full of people shopping or simply strolling under the shady trees and on state holidays Gorky Street is one of the main routes for the parades on their way to Red Square.

In the 15th century the street, then known as Tver Street, led from the Kremlin to Tver (now Kalinin), and it was here that Muscovites began to build their first wooden houses. By the 17th century it had become a ceremonial street laid with whitestone along which the monarchs made their official entrances to Moscow.

When in the 18th century the capital was transferred to St. Petersburg Tver Street became the beginning of the road which linked the two largest cities in the country.

Gorky Street today is three kilometres long and contains four squares situated at the Moscow City Soviet building, at the intersection of the Boulevard Ring and the Sadovoye Ring and at the Byelorussian Railway Station. Tver Street was renamed Gorky Street in 1935.

The reconstruction work on the old street straightened, widened and improved it, adding new attractive buildings. The construction of the first section of the street from Marx Avenue to Soviet Square was one of the first attempts at creating a new design for the centre of the city. On the right-hand side of the road two seven-storey apartment blocks (Nos 4 and 6) designed by A. Mordvinov were built some distance back from the former line of the buildings. These buildings determined the new line for the whole street, which was subsequently built after many of the old and architecturally valueless buildings had been pulled down.

In order to preserve such valuable buildings as did remain, a means was devised for moving them back. Thus the four-storey building was moved back 50 metres and can now be seen in the courtyard of No 6. The 18th century building of the eye hospital "left" Gorky Street and was moved into Sadovskys Lane.

The high arch in the centre of No 4 is at the same time the entrance to **Georgievsky Lane.** Recently a modern adminstrative building was erected here to house the various departments of Gosplan (State Planning Committee) and other institutions. Behind it stand the 17th century **Chambers of the Boyars Troyekurov**, which were considered as fine as any terem building in the Kremlin.

Today the Chambers house the **Glinka Musical Museum**, which contains musical instruments from all over the world and from all ages. There are also autographed copies of the works of the great composers, a vast records library, and a collection of sketches used for the design of numerous stage presentations of musical works, as well as the costumes used in them. In the near future the Glinka Musical Museum is planned to be housed in a new purpose-built building.

The ground floor of No 4 is occupied by a number of shops. These include the **Podarki** gift shop, where you can buy examples of folk art from all over the Soviet Union and the **Kosmos** café, which serves forty different kinds of ice cream.

On the opposite side of the street (No 3) stands the 22-storey building of the **Intourist Hotel** (for 930) which was built in 1971 by V. Voskresensky, A. Boltinov and Yu. Sheverdyayev. Two of the restaurants in the hotel—the Russian Hall and the Starry Sky with its cabaret—have become very popular over the past few years. From here you have an excellent view over Red Square and the Kremlin.

The 19th century building at No 5 is the **Yermolova Theatre**, which was founded in 1937, and whose repertoire largely consists of modern plays.

Further up Gorky Street, still on the left-hand side, between **Belinsky Street** and **Ogarev Street** stands the monumental **Central Telegraph Building** (No 7) designed by I. Rerberg and built in 1927. It was one of the first civic buildings to be erected in Soviet times on Gorky Street.

The next two buildings on the same side of the road were both put up in 1949. The first is an apartment block with shops on the ground floor and the second is the **State Committee for Science and Technology.** The granite, which is used to face the plinth, is actually of German manufacture, being prepared on Hitler's orders for the erection of a victory monument in Moscow. After the Germans were defeated it was brought to Moscow and used as facing for buildings.

Further along still on the same side is the **Moscow City Soviet**, whose façade looks on to Soviet Square.

Soviet Square

The Moscow City Soviet building is a monument of historic and architectural value. Designed by M. Kazakov in 1782-1784, it was then the three-storey residence of the governor general of Moscow, and built from the brick that had been taken from the Bely Gorod Wall. Ten years later a small parade square was built in front of the house for ceremonial changing of the guard. In 1918 this square was renamed Soviet Square (Sovetskaya Ploshchad). In 1930 in **Stankevich Street** a new wing to the City Soviet building was added (designed by I. Fomin) and in 1938 the building itself was moved back 14 metres to widen the road and two new storeys were added. The original classical style façade of the building has been carefully preserved and the building now stands as the focal point of Soviet Square.

Many revolutionary events are connected with Soviet Square. In 1905 there were innumerable political meetings and demonstrations outside the governor general's residence. In March 1917 the building was taken over by the Moscow Soviet of Workers' Deputies and on October 25 when news came of the revolution in Petrograd the Bolsheviks chose it as the party centre for controlling the armed uprising. On the night of October 26 the Military Revolutionary Council took over the building and on the following day White Guards made the first attempt to get control of the square and the building. They launched their attack from three directions—Tver Street, what is now Herzen Street, and Pushkin Square. By the 28th the square was surrounded and cut off from the revolutionary suburbs.

The Bolsheviks therefore decided to leave the Military Revolutionary Council in the building and transfer the party committee to Zamoskvorechye. But on the next day Red Guard units succeeded in dislodging the counter-revolutionaries from their positions in what are now Pushkin Square and Mayakovsky Square and breaking through the blockade. Thus the Moscow Soviet building remained the headquarters of the revolution throughout the whole period.

After the Soviet government moved to Moscow, Lenin participated directly in the work of the Moscow Soviet and from 1918 until his death was a permanent deputy. Above the entrance on the second floor is a balcony from where Lenin several times addressed the workers and soldiers on their way to the front. In accordance with a resolution of the Plenum of the Moscow Soviet on February 7, 1924, Lenin has remained a permanent deputy and each time the Soviet holds its meetings, the deputy card No 1 is used in his name.

The Banner of the capital with its two Orders of Lenin, Gold Star Medal of a Hero-City and Order of the October Revolution is kept in the Moscow Soviet building.

Standing high on a granite pedestal is the **Monument to Yuri Dolgoruky**. The statue of the founder of Moscow, commissioned in 1947 for the eighth centenary of the capital, was finished in 1953 (sculptors S. Orlov, A. Antropov and N. Stamm).

Behind the statue at the rear of the square stand the **Central Party Archives of the Institute of Marxism-Leninism** (built in 1927 by S. Chernyshev). The Archives contain manuscript works of the founders of scientific communism, Marx, Engels and Lenin as well as documents relating to the history of the CPSU and the world communist and working-class movement.

The idea of collecting together the literary heritage of Marx and Engels, which includes their voluminous correspondence, was first put forward by Lenin. When the collection was begun it consisted of only eight original letters from Marx to his daughter Laura. Now the Archives contain the largest and fullest collection of originals and photocopies of the manuscript works of the founders of scientific communism. Furthermore this collection continues to grow as new additions are received from communist and workers' parties, progressive organizations and individuals throughout the world.

In front of the building stands a **monument to Lenin** by S. Merkurov (1938), one of the finest sculptural representations of the great philosopher and statesman. In 1977 a new building was added to the Archives, which opens on to Pushkin Street.

Opposite the Moscow Soviet building on the right-hand side of Gorky Street runs **Stoleshnikov Lane**, at the entrance to which stands the famous **Aragvi Restaurant** with its Georgian specialities.

The large building on the corner of Gorky Street and Soviet Square (No 8) was once the home of well-known Soviet writers— Demyan Byedny, Vyacheslav Shishkov and Ilya Ehrenburg. Now the ground floor of this building is taken up by **one of the largest book-shops** in the city, which has a constant turn-over of 25 thousand different books, albums, posters, paintings and postcards.

Next on the right beyond the bookshop is **Nemirovich-Danchenko Street**. Here at No 6 is the former Sever Hotel later renamed the Anglia where Pushkin on his return from exile stayed frequently from 1828 to 1832. A memorial plaque outside commemorates the meetings which took place here in 1829 between Pushkin and the great Polish poet, Adam Mickiewicz. Today the building houses the **Soviet Women's Committee** which represents millions of Soviet working women in the International Democratic Federation of Women. The committee is headed by the world's first woman-cosmonaut, Hero of the Soviet Union, Valentina Nikolayeva-Tereshkova.

The street was renamed in 1943 after Vladimir Nemirovich-Danchenko, who lived at No 5/7 and who together with Stanislavsky founded the Moscow Art Theatre. His former flat has been made into a **memorial museum**.

At 10 Gorky Street stands the **Tsentralnaya Hotel,** which was given over almost entirely to the Comintern Organization, and where many famous figures in the international communist and workers' movement, like Georgi Dimitrov, Klement Gottwald, Palmiro Togliatti, Maurice Thorez stayed on their visits to Moscow.

The restaurant of the Tsentralnaya serves chiefly Russian cuisine.

On the ground floor of this building is a baker's shop, which has sold bread for over a century being famous in pre-revolutionary Russia under the name of Filippov's Bakery. A memorial plaque on the wall outside commemorates the strike which took place here in 1905 when the Filippov bakers offered armed resistance to the police. There is also Beriozka jewelry shop in the building.

The abundance of groceries in the window at No 14 may suggest that the building is of no more than gastronomic interest. But here in the 1820s lived the Princess Volkonskaya, whose literary salon was frequently visited by such famous writers as Pushkin, Baratynsky, Mickiewicz, Vyazemsky, Zagoskin and Chaadayev. On December 26, 1826, Pushkin attended a farewell party here for Maria Volkonskaya, who was going to join her Decembrist husband in Siberian exile.

Later the building was converted into a luxurious food-store and is now Moscow's Gastronom No 1.

On the first floor above the shop is the **flat-museum of Nikolai Ostrovsky** the writer (not to be confused with Alexander Ostrovsky, the dramatist—*tr.*)

Nikolai Ostrovsky's life was short and heroic. After being badly wounded during the Civil War at the age of twenty, he lost first the use of his legs and then his sight. But being a man of indomitable will, he decided to write books on the youth of the twenties and what they had gone through during the war. As his sight progressively deteriorated he stopped writing and began to dictate the novel. The very writing of his two works, *How the Steel Was Tempered* and *Born of the Storm* was an heroic achievement in itself. The last of these two novels was written in this flat, which today contains an exhibition devoted to the life and works of Nikolai Ostrovsky and the patriotic movement among Soviet youth of different generations. Documents, letters and memoirs relate how Ostrovsky's books, which have been published in dozens of foreign languages, have helped young people all over the world face up to the difficulties of life like the heroes of the two novels.

On the corner of Gorky Street and Pushkin Square is the **All-Russia Theatrical Society** and the **Yablochkina Central Actors' Club** (No 16). The Moscow theatrical club has a youth section, a people's university of theatrical culture, and a theatre-lovers' club. Here meetings are held with great actors, which frequently become important theatrical events in themselves while the concerts given by the All-Russia Theatrical Society are broadcast on television across the whole country.

The opposite side of Gorky Street between Soviet and Pushkin squares is taken up by two huge buildings. Number 15 (nearer to Soviet Square) contains the **Druzhba bookshop**, where you can get literature from the socialist countries. The shop is visited daily by tens of thousands of people. Over one hundred libraries participate in the bookshop's work, including its chief advisor—the State Library of Foreign Literature.

At No 17 from 1945 to 1971 People's Artist of the USSR and Lenin Prize Winner, Sergei Konenkov, the sculptor, created his immortal works. His studio looks on to Tver Boulevard and now contains a **memorial studio-museum** where some of his finest works are on display.

The third floor of the same building contains the **museum-flat of Alexander Goldenweiser**, the great Soviet pianist. This museum is a branch of the Glinka Musical Museum.

Further up on the corner of Pushkin Square is the **Armenia** shop where you can buy famous Armenian brandies, cheeses, sweetmeats and national souvenirs.

Pushkin Square

Pushkin Square stands at the intersection of Gorky Street and the Boulevard Ring. The square with its ancient street lamps that stand round the bronze monument to the great poet and its huge clock—a favourite spot for lovers' meetings in Moscow—has a long history.

> The square was first laid in 1780 at the spot where formerly the Tver Gates Tower to the Bely Gorod had stood and where the road to Tver met the road to Dmitrov. It was then called Strastnaya Square after the Strastnoi Convent nearby. As Moscow grew the square, which had once marked the outskirts to the city, became now part of its centre, and the Tver Boulevard, which runs into it became one of the favourite promenades of the Muscovite nobility.

In 1880 a **Monument to Pushkin** financed by voluntary contributions was erected at the end of Tver Boulevard and the occasion of the unveiling became a national holiday. The monument by A. Opekushin, a simple yet elevated work, shows Pushkin as he was in real life. The pedestal is inscribed with lines from his poem *Monument*:

> *And long the people yet will honour me*
> *Because my lyre was tuned to loving-kindness*
> *And, in a cruel Age, I sang of Liberty*
> *And mercy begged of Justice in her blindness.*

For a long time Pushkin Square remained quite small without any systematic planning or treatment of its varied architecture. But in the 1930s the old unprepossessing buildings were pulled down and the square was increased to twice its original size. The buildings on the right-hand side were made two or three storeys higher, to match the large **"Izvestia" building** built in 1926 by G. Barkhin.

In 1949-50 a beautiful garden was laid in the centre of the square containing a pond and a number of fountains, and here the monument to Pushkin was brought from the Tver Boulevard.

On the far side of the square you can see the glass façade of the **Rossia cinema** and the broad staircase leading up to its entrance. It has a main hall seating 2,500 and two smaller halls for 200 each. Built in 1961 by Yu. Sheverdyayev, E. Gadzhinskaya, and D. Solopov, the cinema shows films from national and international film festivals.

Nearby the old *Izvestia* building a new block of offices housing the newspaper have recently gone up (architects: Yu. Sheverdyayev, V. Kilpe, A. Maslov, D. Solopov, and V. Utkin). But *Izvestia* is not the only newspaper to have its offices on Pushkin Square. At 16/2 Gorky Street are the offices of *Moscow News* which is printed in a number of foreign languages to inform readers abroad about life in the Soviet capital.

Further along at No 18 is an interesting building with original window-frames, mouldings, coloured mosaics and other features characteristic of Art Nouveau. This building once housed the printing works and flat of Ivan Sytin, the famous publisher and educationalist. After the Revolution it was made over to *Pravda* and a plaque on the wall outside is dedicated to the memory of Lenin's sister, Maria Ulyanova, who for many years worked as a secretary in the editorial offices of *Pravda*. The building is now the editorial offices of the Soviet trade-union newspaper *Trud*.

But work on the square has not yet finished. The new *Izvestia* building contains a vestibule entrance to the **Pushkinskaya Metro Station**. Here there is another tribute to the poet's memory as the whole decor of the underground station is based upon themes from Pushkin's poetry.

On the opposite side of the square a block of old buildings has been pulled down and replaced with beautiful flowerbeds, which are more in keeping with the square's new lay-out.

The next section of Gorky Street goes up to **Mayakovsky Square**. On the right-hand side stands the **Minsk Hotel**, built in

FOREST STREET

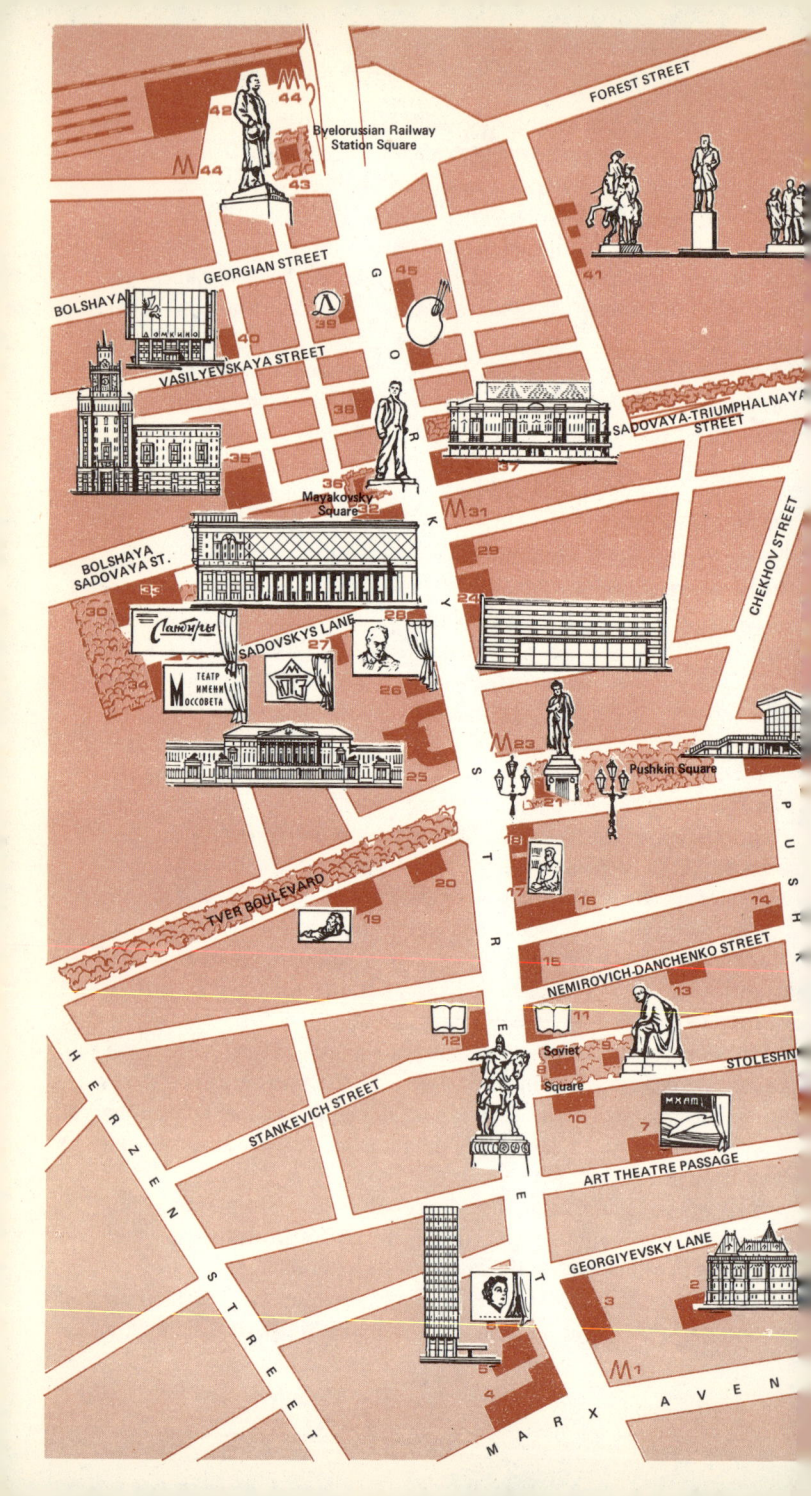

Byelorussian Railway
Station Square

GEORGIAN STREET

BOLSHAYA
VASILYEVSKAYA STREET

SADOVAYA-TRIUMPHALNAYA STREET

CHEKHOV STREET

Mayakovsky Square

BOLSHAYA
SADOVAYA ST.

SADOVSKYS LANE

Pushkin Square

TVER BOULEVARD

NEMIROVICH-DANCHENKO STREET

STANKEVICH STREET

Soviet Square

STOLESHN

ART THEATRE PASSAGE

HERZEN STREET

GEORGIYEVSKY LANE

PUSH

TREME

MARX AVEN

GORKY STREET

1. Prospekt Marksa Metro Station
2. Chambers of the Boyars Troyekurov
3. Podarki gift shop. Kosmos café
4. Natsional Hotel
5. Intourist Hotel
6. Yermolova Theatre
7. Moscow Art Theatre
8. Monument to Yuri Dolgoruky
9. Monument to Lenin
10. Aragvi Restaurant
11. Moskva bookshop
12. Druzhba bookshop
13. Soviet Women's Committee
14. Memorial museum to V. Nemirovich-Danchenko
15. Tsentralnaya Hotel
16. Gastronom No 1 (19th cent.)
17. Flat-Museum of Nikolai Ostrovsky
18. Yablochkina Central Actors' Club
19. Konenkov Studio-Museum. Flat-Museum of Alexander Goldenweiser
20. Armenia shop
21. Monument to Pushkin
22. Rossia Cinema
23. Pushkinskaya Metro Station
24. Minsk Hotel
25. Central Museum of the Revolution
26. Stanislavsky Drama Theatre
27. Theatre of the Young Spectator
28. Exhibition Hall of the Union of Artists
29. Baku Restaurant
30. Aquarium Gardens
31. Mayakovskaya Metro Station
32. Tchaikovsky Concert Hall. Intourist Cultural Centre
33. Moscow Satire Theatre
34. Mossoviet Theatre
35. Peking Hotel
36. Monument to Mayakovsky
37. Sofia Restaurant
38. Podarki gift store
39. House of Children's Books
40. Central Cinema House
41. Monument to A. Fadeyev
42. Byelorussian Railway Station
43. Monument to M. Gorky
44. Belorusskaya Metro Station
45. Exhibition Hall

1964, containing 400 rooms, a café and a restaurant, where you can try Byelorussian national dishes.

The left-hand side of the street is almost completely taken up with multi-storey apartment blocks, which are interrupted only at No 21—a smaller three-storey 18th century building with an eight-columned portico. The building is set back from the road and bounded by iron railings. At the gates there are stone lions and it is these same "lions at the gates" that Pushkin mentions in his poem *Eugene Onegin*, when describing the arrival of the heroine, Tatyana, in Moscow.

The house itself was built in 1780 and restored after the fire of 1812 by A. Menelas and from 1831 housed the English club, whose membership consisted of only the highest nobility. Since 1924 this building has housed the Central Museum of the Revolution.

Central Museum of the Revolution

This museum as its title suggests sets out in the form of documents and other factual material the whole history of the world's first socialist state. It covers the development of the Russian liberation movement from its earliest beginnings, the bourgeois democratic revolutions of 1905 and February 1917, the victory of the Great October Socialist Revolution in October 1917, the stages of building socialism in the USSR, the heroic years of the Great Patriotic War against fascism, the reconstruction of the national economy after the war, and the building of a developed socialist society in the Soviet Union.

As part of its illustrative material the museum includes works by many famous Russian artists and sculptors like I. Repin, V. Serov, B. Kustodiev, S. Konenkov, I. Brodsky, I. Grabar, K. Petrov-Vodkin, and K. Yuon. There are examples of the weapons used by the workers in defence of Soviet power, flags and banners of the revolutionary detachments, the first Soviet decrees on peace and land, the "Declaration of the Rights of the Peoples of Russia", the declaration and treaty on the formation of the Union of Soviet Socialist Republics and other documents of world-wide historical significance. In the half century since its formation more than 40 million visitors have been to this museum.

* * *

Next to the museum is the **Stanislavsky Drama Theatre** (No 23), founded in 1935 by the great theatrical innovator as a studio for operatic and dramatic art and later turned into a theatre and named after its founder. A memorial plaque commemorates the fact that Lenin delivered a speech here on November 20, 1918.

Further along on the left you come to **Sadovskys Lane**, which was named in honour of a family of Russian actors. Here at No 10 is the famous **Theatre of the Young Spectator** and on the opposite side is the eye hospital (which used to be on Gorky Street—see above). At 25 Gorky Street, where the hospital formerly stood, there is an apartment block built by A. Burov, whose façade is decorated with picturesque mouldings by Academician V. Favorsky, winner of the Lenin Prize. The ground floor of this building contains the **Exhibition Hall of the Union of Artists.**

No 27-29 contains a memorial plaque with a bas-relief portrait of Alexander Fadeyev, the famous Soviet writer and author of *The Rout*, *The Young Guard* and many other works. Here the writer lived during the last years of his life.

On the opposite side of the street is the **Baku Restaurant** famed for its Azerbaijanian national cuisine.

Mayakovsky Square

At Mayakovsky Square the Sadovoye Ring crosses Gorky Street by an underpass. The square, formerly named Triumph (Triumfalnaya) Square, has become part of the history of the first Russian revolution. On December 9, 1905 the first barricade was erected near the Aquarium Gardens (on the left-hand side of the square beyond the Satire Theatre). The dragoon guards of the tsar with artillery support attacked the barricade, but the workers courageously stood their ground and held the barricade until well into the night when a second barricade was erected. Barricades began to appear all along the ring road, at Tver, Bronnaya streets and neighbouring side-streets. The next day barricades had sprung up all over the city. Today a memorial plaque at the entrance to the Aquarium Gardens commemorates these first revolutionary battles of 1905.

The architectural façade of Mayakovsky Square was formed during the prewar and early postwar years. Like Sverdlov Square it forms another theatrical centre in the city, containing the **Tchaikovsky Concert Hall**, the Moscow Satire Theatre, and the Mossoviet Theatre. The first of these, the Tchaikovsky Concert Hall was built in 1938-1940 by D. Chechulin and K. Orlov and seats 1,650. Here symphonic concerts and organ recitals are given by the finest performers in the country and from abroad. Here in the Tchaikovsky Hall are the offices of the **Intourist Cultural Centre** (see *Practical Information*).

The **Moscow Satire Theatre** which is nearby is famed for its productions of witty comedies based on subjects taken from everyday life. The theatre was founded in 1924 and has worked in this building since 1965. The **Mossoviet Theatre,** which can seat 1,200 was also founded in 1924 and took over its present premises in the Aquarium Gardens in 1959. Famous Soviet actors who have worked here include N. Mordvinov, V. Maretskaya, L. Orlova, F. Ranevskaya, R. Plyatt and the director, Yu. Zavadsky.

On the opposite side of the square is the **Peking Hotel**, which was built in 1951 by D. Chechulin and next to it the **Moscow Architectural and Planning Directorate**, which controls all building in the city.

In summer 1958 the **monument to Mayakovsky** by A. Kibalnikov was erected. The poet stands as if he is reading his poetry to a crowded auditorium.

Mayakovsky Square has two restaurants—the **Sofia** and the **Peking**.

The next section of Gorky Street used to be called Tverskaya-Yamskaya, and the majority of the buildings here are late 19th and early 20th century tenements together with a few small trading establishments. During the 1930s and 1950s a few multi-storeyed houses went up here. The cranes once more appeared in the 1970s as the final stages of the reconstruction of this part of Gorky Street were completed. In late 1977 a nine-storey apartment block (No 37) was built on the left-hand side of Gorky Street. It was fronted with alternating arches and bay-windows (architects Z. Rosenfeld, V. Orlov and D. Alexeyev). The two lower floors with their huge front windows edged in gold metalic frames contain a café, a ladies' hairdressing salon and the **Podarki** gift shop.

Further along Gorky Street at No 46B there is an exhibition hall and arts salon. Of particular interest is the **House of Children's Books** (No 43), where some of the finest works of children's literature are on display at an exhibition that is continually being renewed and supplemented. Here young readers can get together with the writers and artists who produce their favourite books. The House organizes programmes of lectures and conducts a scientific study of the reading interests amongst children.

On the left of Gorky Street is **Vassilyevskaya Street**. Here right in front of you at No 13 is an original building designed in the form of a cube. Its plain, windowless, silver walls are somewhat reminiscent of a huge cinema screen. Built in 1968 it houses the Moscow cinema workers' club (chief architect Ye. Stamo). It is called the **Central Cinema House**. The club has an auditorium seating 1,200 and the foyer is decorated with works by the French artist Fernand Leger which were presented by his widow.

Further along to the right of Gorky Street you come to **Miusskaya Square** which can be reached by going down **Alexander Nevsky Lane**. Here you will see a building of some architectural interest, which was erected in 1960 by Yu. Sheverdyayev and K. Shekhoyan. This is the **House of Pioneers**, which besides accommodating various clubs and workshops has its own observatory, conservatory, swimming pool and ballet studio. In front of the House of Pioneers stands a **monument to Alexander Fadeyev** built in 1972 by V. Fedorov, sculptor, and M. Konstantinov and V. Fursov, architects. The composition depicts the writer himself, a favourite with young people in the USSR, surrounded by the heroes of his two famous novels, *The Rout* and *The Young Guard.*

Gorky Street ends at Byelorussian Station Square.

Byelorussian Railway Station Square

Byelorussian Station Square was laid on the site of the former Tver Gates in honour of the ceremonial home-coming of the Russian troops returning from Paris after the victory over Napoleon. But it was not until 1870 when the railway line linking Moscow with Smolensk was built here that Byelorussian Station Square took on its full significance for the city.

It was here that Moscow gave a ceremonial welcome to Captain Valery Chkalov and Captain Mikhail Gromov and the crews of their planes which in 1937 completed a non-stop flight from the USSR across the North Pole to the United States. Here too, in the same year, the city welcomed Ivan Papanin and the members of his legendary expedition to the North Pole over the drifting ice-flows of the Arctic Sea. But the greatest and most unforgettable welcome that ever took place at the Byelorussian Station was in 1945, when Muscovites came out to greet the victorious Soviet troops returning from the front at the end of the Great Patriotic War.

In the centre of the square in 1951 a bronze **monument** was unveiled **to Maxim Gorky**. The design for the monument was made by the great Russian sculptor Shadr and after his death completed by Vera Mukhina together with Z. Ivanova and N. Zelenskaya.

Work is still continuing on the reconstruction of this square. The old and decrepit houses around are being pulled down and the area of the square widened. A new block has been added to the Byelorussian Station increasing its overall area twofold. It now links Moscow with the western regions of the country as well as with Warsaw, Berlin, Vienna, Rome, Paris, London, Oslo and Stockholm.

THE LENINGRAD HIGHWAY

Leningrad Avenue–Leningrad Highway. The road to Sheremetyevo Airport–Khimki-Khovrino–Arkhangelskoye–Tchaikovsky Museum in Klin

Leningrad Avenue

Leningrad Avenue (Leningradsky Prospekt) is one of the most beautiful and spacious thoroughfares in the city. It is 120 metres across and has two avenues of trees dividing it down the centre and making it look like a long park.

Before the Revolution its entire length was in the suburbs of Moscow, and even as late as 1934, 158 of its 191 buildings were wooden. The multi-storeyed apartment blocks that now line the avenue were all built during the Soviet period.

On the right stands the huge glass and steel building of the **Watch Factory No 2**, which produces the famous "Slava" watch that is exported to over 70 countries.

A little further on to the right you come to **Pravda Street**, which was named back in the 1930s, when the **"Pravda" Complex**, the largest in the country, was located here. Built by P. Golosov, the building is noted for its architectural qualities—its neat and precise design and the simple ornamentation of its façades. Here *Pravda*—the central organ of the Communist Party of the Soviet Union—is published. Its first number appeared in Petrograd on April 22 (May 5), 1912 and May 5 is now celebrated in the USSR as Press Day.

The Pravda Publishing House also publishes a number of other newspapers such as *Komsomolskaya pravda, Pionerskaya pravda, Sovietskaya Rossia* and *Selskaya zhizn.* As a result of the continued expansion of these newspapers another twelve-storey building was built nearby in 1960s to accommodate the editorial offices and a number of new blocks were added to house the printing works.

Further along Leningrad Avenue on the other side of the street you come to **Begovaya Street**. Here another large square is to be built—part of the planned third ring road.

The **Sovetskaya Hotel** stands on this square (No 32). It was built in 1950 and included part of the famous pre-revolutionary out-of-town restaurant, the Yar. Today the hotel has a first class restaurant, while its **concert hall** features the **Romen theatre**, the only Gypsy resident theatre in the world. Performances by this theatrical group include Gypsy folk songs and dances and tell about the past and present life of the Gypsy people.

Opposite the hotel on the other side of Leningrad Avenue you can see huge wrought-iron gates on which are set two bronze groups showing Castor and Pollux which were made in the late 19th century by S. Volnukhin and K. Klodt. Beyond the gates is the **Skakovaya Lane,** which leads to the **Moscow Hippodrome**, the oldest racing track in the city. In 1955-56 the main building of the hippodrome was reconstructed according to a design by Academician I. Zholtovsky and the main entrance was placed on Begovaya Street. In the hippodrome stables there are some five hundred horses. Races take place on Wednesdays, Saturdays and Sundays.

Near the entrance to Skakovaya Lane is a six-storey apartment block (No 27) with pillars in reinforced concrete alternating with ornamental plant forms in fretted marble. The house was built in 1940 by A. Burov and B. Blokhin and the fretted marble ornaments designed by V. Favorsky.

On Begovaya Street there is a children's sports village called the **Young Pioneers Stadium,** which was built in 1952. It has places for 2,000 children and teenagers in its various sections and sports schools. Many later champions began their sporting careers here. The stadium has a cycle track, a sports ground for track-and-field events and a covered ice-rink with artificial ice.

Nearby the stadium in **Botkin 2nd Passage** stands the famous **Botkin Hospital**, which was founded in 1911 and bears the name of the eminent Russian doctor and progressive public figure, Sergei Botkin. On April 23, 1922 in block No 2 of this hospital Lenin was operated on for the removal of a bullet, after the attempt on his life, which was made on August 30, 1918.

Extensive work has been carried out on the Botkin Hospital, with all the old blocks being thoroughly modernized and new ones built. It is now the largest hospital in Moscow.

On the left-hand side of Leningrad Avenue there are several multi-storey apartment blocks, including one that is often referred to as the "House of Newlyweds" (No 33a) with a **Palace of Weddings** and a café on the ground floor.

On the other side of Leningrad Avenue and covering an area of some 40 hectares is the vast **Dynamo Stadium** complex—the first large-scale sports complex in Moscow, seating 60 thousand spectators. The original stadium was built in 1928 by B. Yofan and L. Cherikover. Before the national Spartakiad in 1979 and the Olympic Games in 1980, the stadium was reconstructed and thoroughly modernized. The stands and equipment were reorganized in the large arena, the small arena increased to accommodate 10,000 and two new blocks added to the training complex—one for gymnastics, hockey and figure skating and the other containing a universal sports hall, 115 metres long, 66 metres wide and 15 metres high with a football pitch, race track and courts for various summer sports.

Next to the stadium there is an old castle, girt with ancient stone walls and turrets (No 40). This is one of the finest examples of 18th century palatial architecture and in pre-revolutionary times was used by the royal family as an out-of-town residence, where they would rest according to tradition before entering Moscow. The **Petrovsky Palace** was built by the famous architect Kazakov between 1775 and 1782. Architecturally it combines the severe style of classicism with the ornamental style of old Russian building and the romantic features of Gothic. Particularly attractive is the white stone lattice patterns round the windows, arches, platbands, gates and towers. In 1812 Napoleon, retreating from the Kremlin during the fire, spent several days here.

For the last fifty years the palace has housed the **Zhukovsky Academy of Military Aviation**, whose famous graduates have included Artyom Mikoyan, Sergei Ilyushin and Alexander Yakovlev together with the cosmonauts Yuri Gagarin, German Titov, Andrian Nikolayev, Pavel Popovich, Valery Bykovsky, Valentina Nikolayeva-Tereshkova, Alexei Leonov, Pavel Belyaev and Vladimir Komarov.

Next to the Academy building there are **monuments to** the founder of space exploration, **Konstantin Tsiolkovsky** (by S. Merkurov) and the "father of Russian aviation", **Nikolai Zhukovsky** (by G. Neroda).

On the other side of Leningrad Avenue (No 37) stretching a distance of 280 metres is the **Moscow City Air Terminal,** which works twenty-four hours a day and is fully equipped to serve 3,000 people every hour. From here passengers are transported to the various airports around Moscow. The air terminal was opened on January 1, 1966 and was built and designed by D. Burdin, Yu. Rabayev, M. Artemyev, V. Klimov and V. Yakovlev.

Khodynskoye Field, which was the name given to the land on which the air terminal now stands has long been connected with aviation. Here at the turn of the century the first primitive flying apparatus was tested and later the Frunze Central Airodrome was built here.

During the October Revolution the troops stationed in the Khodynskoye Field Barracks took the side of the Bolsheviks and actively fought to assert Soviet power. On May 1, 1918 Lenin attended a parade here given by the military units of the Moscow garrison. Before the parade he inspected a hangar and various types of aircraft and chatted with the pilots. Today a dark-red granite plaque with a bronze bas-relief portrait of Lenin commemorates this and two other meetings between Lenin and soldiers and airmen of the Red Army on Khodynskoye Field.

In 1896 a disaster occurred in Khodynskoye Field. On May 18 during the coronation of Nikolai II, crowds gathered there at the celebrations organized by the government, during which more than two thousand people were crushed to death and over twice as many seriously injured through the criminal irresponsibility of the authorities. This tragedy left a deep imprint on the social life of the times.

Part of Khodynskoye Field is taken up by the **Central Army Sports Club** (designed by Yu. Krivushchenko), which has a sports palace seating 5,000, an inside swimming pool, tennis courts, a gymnazium equipped for heavy athletics and a training hall. Recently a covered sports arena seating 11,000 and containing two separate units—a football pitch and a stadium for track-and-field events was built here. During the 1980 Olympics the wrestling and fencing events were held here.

Thus taken all together the three stadiums here (the Dynamo Stadium, the Young Pioneers Stadium and the Central Army Sports Club) combine to make Leningrad Avenue renowned as a sports centre, which was naturally one of the focal points during the 1980 Olympics.

Further along the avenue is lined with multi-storey apartment blocks, administrative buildings and educational and scientific establishments.

On the right near the **Airport Metro Station** a new housing estate has been built.

Soon after the war a massive building programme was launched in the area adjacent to the **Sokol Metro Station** on the left of Leningrad Avenue. In ten years a major housing estate was built, with parks, green squares and gardens which has its own shops, cinemas and schools.

Some of the streets on this estate were named after prominent figures in the international communist and workers' movement who fought against fascism, like Walter Ulbricht, Gheorghiu-Dej, Salvador Allende and the famous Soviet agent, Richard Sorge.

At the end of Leningrad Avenue is the 27-storey tower of the All-Union Research and Design Institute (built by a group of architects headed by G. Yakovlev), which is named after S. Zhuk, the hydro-electric power station designer. The staff of this institute designed some of the largest hydro-electric power stations in the USSR including the Lenin Power Station and the 22nd Congress of the CPSU Power Station on the Volga as well as the Bratsk, Krasnoyarsk, Ust-Ilimsk, and Sayany-Shushenskoye hydro-electric complexes and has also worked on construction of power stations

LENINGRAD HIGHWAY

1. Sovetskaya Hotel. Romen Gypsy Theatre
2. Moscow Hippodrome
3. Young Pioneers Stadium
4. Dynamo Stadium
5. Petrovsky Palace (18th cent.)
6. Monument to Tsiolkovsky
7. Monument to Zhukovsky
8. Moscow City Air Terminal
9. Central Army Sports Club
10. Dynamo Metro Station
11. Airport Metro Station
12. Sokol Metro Station
13. Voikovskaya Metro Station
14. Monument to Volkov
15. Varshava Cinema
16. "Triumph of Victory" Monument
17. Northern River Port
18. Dynamo Water Stadium
19. Vodny Stadion Metro Station
20. Rechnoi Vokzal Metro Station
21. Monument to Peace and Friendship
22. Equestrian Centre
23. Central Popular-Science Film Studio
24. Multi-Purpose Sports Palace

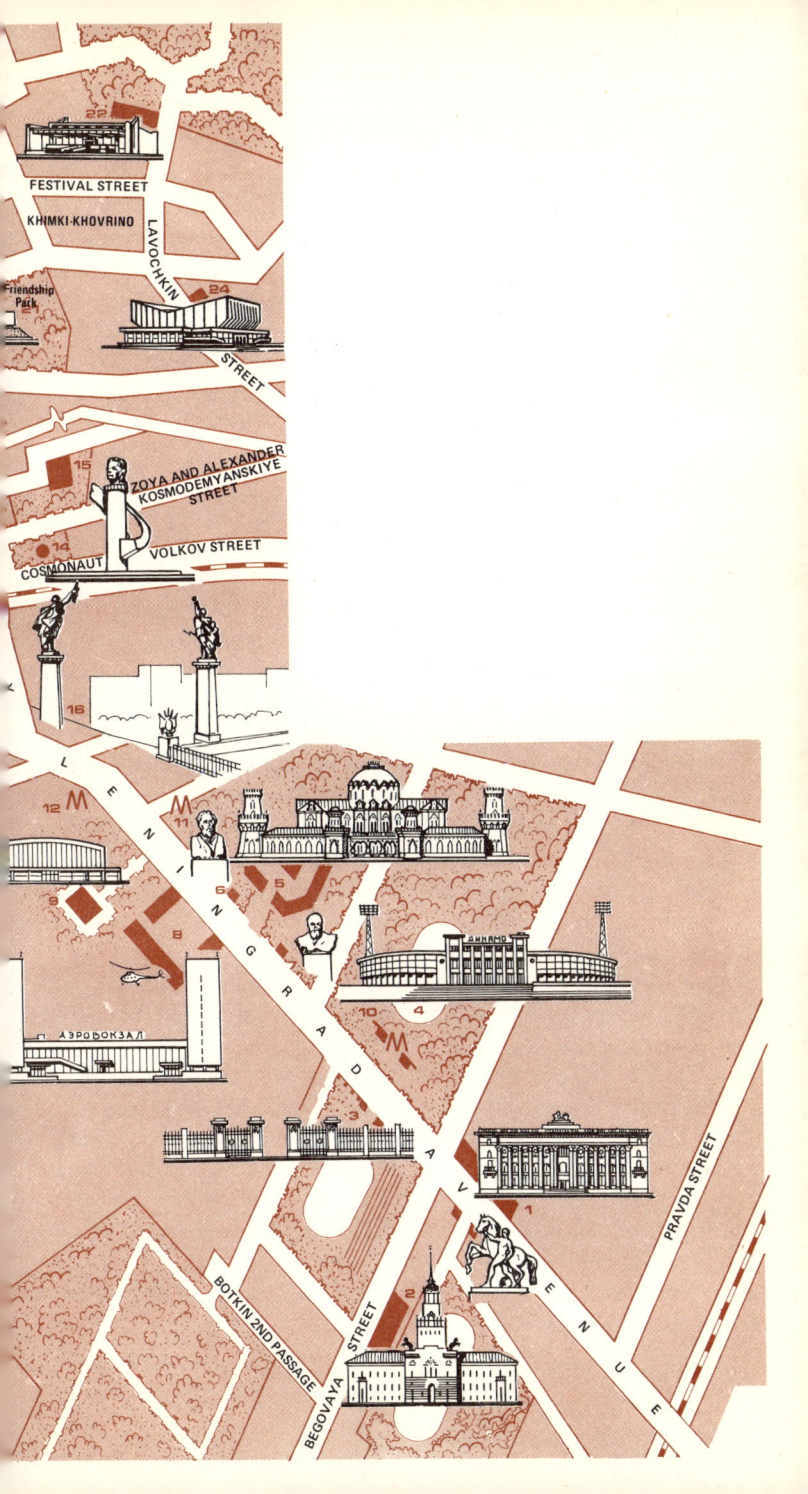

FESTIVAL STREET
KHIMKI-KHOVRINO
LAVOCHKIN STREET
Friendship Park
ZOYA AND ALEXANDER KOSMODEMYANSKIYE STREET
COSMONAUT VOLKOV STREET
АЭРОВОКЗАЛ
ДИНАМО
LENINGRAD AVENUE
BOTKIN 2ND PASSAGE
BEGOVAYA STREET
PRAVDA STREET

abroad. Beyond the institute building the road continues as the Leningrad Highway.

To the left is the **Volokolamsk Highway**, where in autumn 1941 the defenders of Moscow beat back the attacks of the fascist tanks from the very gates of the capital. Most distinguished in the fighting was the infantry division under General Panfilov, 28 of whose soldiers came under heavy fire from 50 enemy tanks without yielding an inch of ground. Almost all of them died the death of the brave, but they did their duty to their country and their deeds will never be forgotten. These soldiers, the *Panfilovtsy* as they are called have had books and even songs written about them.

The Leningrad Highway

This spacious modern motorway, which is ten times wider than the old Petersburg Highway links Moscow with **Sheremetyevo Airport**. That section of the Leningrad Highway that runs within the city limits has since the war been built up with multi-storey apartment buildings.

Near the **Voikovskaya Metro Station** you can see the **Varshava Cinema** (seating 1,400), where annual festivals of Polish films take place. Beyond the station the Leningrad Highway crosses the city circle line by means of an overpass at the entrance to which on ten-metre pedestals stand the figures of a Soviet soldier with his greatcoat slung over his shoulder and a girl-sniper. This **monument** is entitled the **"Triumph of Victory"** (sculptor, N. Tomsky). It recalls the dark days of autumn 1941 when units of the Soviet Army and divisions of the home guard formed from volunteers marched along the Leningrad Highway to the front.

On the right beyond the overpass you come to **Zoya and Alexander Kosmodemyanskys Street**, named after two young heroes of the Soviet Union. The tragic fate of Zoya Kosmodemyanskaya you have already read about. Alexander, her brother, was a member of a tank crew, who was killed at the front. On this street is the school which was attended by both brother and sister between 1933 and 1941.

From here to the city's outer limits the Leningrad Highway runs along the **Khimki Reservoir**, which lies on the left. Here in summer between the buildings and the green trees of the gardens you frequently catch sight of the blue surface of the water which is only disturbed by the leisurely motion of an occasional white motor launch or the creamy wake of a fast-moving hydrofoil.

On the banks of the Khimki Reservoir the **Dynamo Water Stadium** was built in 1938. Here before an amphitheatre seating 5,000 rowing, sailing and motor-boat races take place.

A little further along on the left and you come to the **Northern River Port** (built in 1936 by A. Rukhlyadev). The building with its open galleries, designed to look like decks resembles a huge ship. This resemblance is further increased by the 85 metre high mast, which can be seen from a long way off. On both sides of the building there are terraces with waiting-halls. The northern terrace contains a "Polar fountain" (by L. Kardashev) with white marble figures of bears and bronze flocks of ducks and wild-geese, while the southern terrace has a "Black Sea" fountain (by I. Yefimov) with the sculptured figures of dolphins.

The port building is set in a large park. A broad staircase leads down from the building to the quay.

The Northern River Port is the largest passenger embarkation point on the **Moscow Canal** which links the River Moskva with the Volga.

It is due to this canal that Moscow can rightfully claim to be a port for five seas—the Baltic, the Caspian, the White Sea, the Black Sea and the Sea of Azov. The canal solved the problem of providing water for the city. The level of the River Moskva rose considerably, making it once more navigable. Throughout the length of the canal there are a total of 11 locks by which ships are brought up from the level of the Volga to that of the River Moskva, five pumping stations, 8 hydroelectric power stations and more than 200 other constructions like weirs, bridges and tunnels. There are seven artificial reservoirs, some so big as to be called seas. Along their shores there are holiday resorts and boarding houses. The reservoirs that lie nearest to Moscow have become popular leisure spots, particularly for those who like sailing and motor-boating or hunting and fishing.

Opposite the River Port is the **Friendship Park**, the first trees of which were laid in 1957 by participants at the World Festival of Youth and Students which was held in Moscow. Should any of those who took part in planting this park chance to read this book, we take great pleasure in informing them that this former waste-land is now a beautiful park, which is carefully tended by the youth of Moscow as a monument to international friendship.

Recently an **ensemble of** two bronze **statues** entitled "Bread" and "Fertility" was erected here. The sculpture was the work of the famous Soviet sculptress, Vera Mukhina and completed after her death by her pupils N. Zelenskaya, Z. Ivanova and A. Sergeyev.

In autumn 1976 a **Monument to Peace and Friendship**—a gift from Budapest—was ceremonially unveiled at the entrance to the park. A similar monument stands in a park in Budapest. The monument consists of the statues of two women sit in a ten-metre stele as personifications of the two friendly nations. It bears the inscription: "The Eternal Friendship Between the Hungarian and Soviet People Is the Guarantee of Our Freedom and Peace." The monument was designed by the famous Soviet sculptor, Yevgeny Vuchetich and the Hungarian sculptor, K. Stróbl and built by the Hungarian sculptor B. Búza and the architect J. Zilachi.

Khimki-Khovrino

On the shores of the Khimki Reservoir lies one of the city's new districts—Khimki-Khovrino.

Building began here in 1961. Now over a territory measuring some 2,000 hectares there are some two million square metres of housing together with schools, clinics and shops etc.

Khimki-Khovrino combines the space and clean air of the countryside with all the comforts of town living. Thanks to a fast Metro line the journey to the centre of Moscow takes less than half an hour. The plans for the district won the Grand Prix at town-planning exhibition in Paris for their overall architectural design and their utilization of natural resources. The district has its own Palace of Culture, Palace of Pioneers, cinema and concert hall, multi-storey hotel and sports complexes.

The apartment blocks in this area are set far back from the streets and protected from the noise and dust of the roads by trees and gardens. The arrangement of the housing blocks is according to a system of free-planning with lawns, birch-groves, alleys, flower beds and children's playgrounds between the apartment buildings. Blocks of flats of 5, 9, 12, 14 and 16 storeys are placed together to form an attractive architectural ensemble. Most of the inhabitants of this district work near to their place of residence at the new industrial and transport enterprises which include an experimental jewelery's factory, a food factory, a bakery, a confectionary all of which are fully automated and meet the standards set for environmental protection.

A number of cultural and scientific establishments have been located in Khimki-Khovrino. These include the **Central Popular-Science Film Studio**, the **All-Union Extra-Mural Institute of Commerce** and a **Scientific and Technical Information Centre**. Work is still underway on the buildings for a number of research and design institutes and a **State Scientific and Technical Library** which will store 8 million volumes.

Recently two large sports stadiums were built here—the large and uniquely designed **Riding School on Dybenko Street** and the **Palace of Sports on Lavochkin Street,** which is equipped to handle 12 different sports and may also be used as a concert hall.

In 1974 a huge new bridge was built by which the Leningrad Highway crosses the Moscow Canal. From here two buildings can be seen among the woods on the right-hand side. These are recently built boarding houses for old people, which have been designed to provide all comforts for the elderly.

Arkhangelskoye

Arkhangelskoye is 27 kilometres along the Volokolamsk Highway and can be reached by taking a No 541 bus from the Sokol Metro Station.

The Arkhangelskoye museum estate, was the former home of Prince Yusupov and is a unique example of an 18th-19th century noble's country house built in the classical style. As such it was taken over by the state immediately after the October Revolution and later opened as a museum. The former owner was the director of the imperial theatres and the Hermitage in St. Petersburg and in his work of adding to the Hermitage collection, was not forgetful of his own possessions outside Moscow. Here in the palace he gathered together some of the finest paintings by Van Dyck, Boucher, Vigée-Lebrun, Tiepolo, Hubert Robert, as well as ancient statues, valuable furniture, mirrors, chandeliers, crystal and chinaware. The estate park descends in three picturesque terraces to the River Moskva. These terraces and staircases are decorated with ballustrades and marble statues. Along the alleys of the park there are elegant pavilions, belvederes and fountains. One of these alleys contains a bust of Pushkin in commemoration of his visit to the estate.

Arkhangelskoye was built by Yusupov's serfs, talented mastercraftsmen under the direction of the architect V. Strizhakov.

In the early 19th century the Arkhangelskoye Theatre was famed, for here the largest and best known company of serf actors used to perform. Now on the site of the former theatre an exhibition "The Serf Theatre of Arkhangelskoye" has been opened.

At the entrance to Arkhangelskoye there is a **restaurant** where you can try traditional Russian dishes.

Klin. House-Museum of Tchaikovsky

Klin is situated 90 kilometres along the Leningrad Highway and can be reached by train from the Leningrad Railway Station.

"I have become terribly attached to Klin and I myself am not sure why. I simply cannot imagine myself in another place... It must be the charm of the woods and the Russian countryside and the tranquility which I am coming to need more and more." These were the words of the great Russian composer Tchaikovsky, who departed from here in 1893 on his last journey to St. Petersburg.

In 1920 a society of friends of the memorial home of Tchaikovsky was formed.

During the war nazi troops took Klin and caused severe damage to the museum. After the liberation of the town the monuments were restored and on May 7, 1945 it was reopened for visitors. The house has been kept in the way it was during the composer's lifetime. In the drawing-room which was used as a study there are shelves of books and sheet music, and on a table the composer's last notes. In the centre stands a grand piano. Twice a year on the day of Tchaikovsky's birth and death, when celebrations are held in his honour, the finest Soviet and foreign musicians perform on his piano. In the bedroom a rustic birch table stands by the window. It was here that Tchaikovsky wrote his Sixth Symphony. At Klin Tchaikovsky wrote the music to the ballet *The Sleeping Beauty* and worked on the *Nutcraker* and his Fifth Symphony.

All the year round visitors come to Klin to pay their respects to the great composer, while winners of the International Tchaikovsky Competition which is held in Moscow consider it imperative to visit the house where Tchaikovsky lived.

TOWARDS DMITROV

*Pushkin Street–Chekhov Street–Kalyaev Street–
Novoslobodskaya Street–Butyrskaya Street–Dmitrov
Highway–Degunino-Beskudnikovo–Eastern Degunino*

This radial itinerary takes a number of streets which lie along the old trade route which went from Moscow via Dmitrov along the River Yakhroma to the Volga–the main waterway in Russia.

In the 14th century the inhabitants of Dmitrov who came to live in Moscow settled in a district which they called the Greater Dmitrov Settlement (Bolshaya Dmitrovskaya Sloboda) which stood at the entrance to the trade road in what is now Pushkin Street. Later, during the 16th century the Lesser Dmitrov Settlement (Malaya Dmitrovskaya Sloboda) sprang up behind the walls of the Bely Gorod in what is now Chekhov Street. Finally, during the 17th century when the nobility began to take over the centre, the inhabitants of these settlements moved out to form the New Dmitrov Settlement (Novaya Dmitrovskaya Sloboda) near where Kalyaev and Novoslobodskaya Streets now lie.

Pushkin Street

Until 1937 this street was called Bolshaya Dmitrovka, but it was renamed in honour of the centenary of the death of the great poet. The present appearance of the street with two rows of houses on either side is comparatively recent, for during the early 19th century the road had nothing on it but rich manor houses.

During the last century Pushkin Street became renowned for there is hardly a building here which is not connected one way or another with the theatrical history of Moscow. You only have to go as far as the first block and you will see the House of Trade Unions, which is one of the centres of the capital's concert life, while on the right you can see the rear of the Central Children's Theatre. (This used to be an ordinary apartment block but was converted into a theatre in the early 19th century.)

No 6 also a former manor house has now become a theatre. In 1888 S. Mamontov, a major industrialist and patron of the arts, who was friendly with many prominent artists of the time opened here nearby the imperial Bolshoi Theatre a private opera house which he ran as producer and director. It was here that Chaliapin made his debut and sang for several years and Rakhmaninov began as a conductor. After the Revolution the theatre was made a branch of the Bolshoi Theatre and in 1961 the building was given over to the **Moscow Operetta Theatre.** This is the largest theatre in the world (seating 2,000) exclusively engaged in the production of musical comedy.

Opposite the theatre in **Georgiyevsky Lane** is a low brick building in pseudo-Russian style. This was Moscow's first power station, which was opened in 1881, and which was used to provide electricity to the houses of the wealthy in the centre.

Further along Pushkin Street on the left runs **Art Theatre Passage** (Proyezd Khudozhestvennogo Teatra), a small street no more than one block long. Here at No 3 was the first home of the Moscow Art Theatre. The building was redesigned in 1902 by F. Shekhtel. Above the entrance there is a bas-relief by A. Golubkina together with Chekhov's Seagull, the emblem of the theatre. The theatre was founded in 1898 by the great theatrical innovators, Konstantin Stanislavsky and Vladimir Nemirovich-Danchenko. "We are trying to create the first theatre that is based on reason and morality and that is generally accessible to all. It is to this high ideal that we have devoted our whole lives,"–thus wrote Stanislavsky in those days. The "Stanislavsky Method" which is the generally accepted term for the system of acting techniques advocated by Stanislavsky still continues to exert a powerful influence on actors throughout the world. During the Soviet period the Moscow Art Theatre has done much to promote the building of a new society. The theatre is continually seeking out new means of creative expression, for its fundamental tradition is to be up-to-date.

On the corner of Pushkin Street and Art Theatre Passage is the **House of Educational Books**, a shop which specializes in literature for the teaching profession. At No 8, on the opposite side, is a late 18th century building, which from the mid-19th century housed the theatrical school of the Bolshoi Theatre. It is now the **Central Theatrical Library** and contains a vast collection of books on the history of the theatre, stage design, drama, as well as a unique collection of theatrical magazines and scenic painting.

On the corner of Pushkin Street and **Stoleshnikov Lane**, as was already mentioned in chapter *Gorky Street* stands the **Central Party Archives of the Institute of Marxism-Leninism** which is one of the few new buildings in this area.

> At the turn of the century No 15a was one of the centres of literary Moscow, for here a literary society, one of whose founder members was Chekhov, used to meet every Wednesday. This society was particularly active during the first years after the Revolution, organizing arts exhibitions and concerts. On November 6, 1918, the eve of the first anniversary of the October Revolution the literary society was visited by Lenin, who at the request of those present made a short speech on the significance of the Socialist Revolution.

Next door (No 17) is a former noble's mansion, which in 1938 was reconstructed as the **Stanislavsky and Nemirovich-Danchenko Opera and Ballet Theatre**. This theatre set itself the task of reforming the old opera and creating a new form of modern musical production. The theatre's repertoire now includes opera, ballet and musical comedy by Soviet and modern foreign composers as well as the works of the classical composers and it enjoys a high reputation abroad.

Moskvin Street, which runs off to the right of Pushkin Street is the site of yet another theatre, a **branch of the Moscow Art Theatre**, which was built by M. Chichagov in 1885 for a private theatre.

Finally, one more theatre is to be built on Pushkin Street—the new building of the Gypsy Theatre, the Romen.

Many of the houses in Pushkin Street also have theatrical connections. No 4, for instance, contains a memorial plaque with a portrait of the old Russian actress Alexandra Yablochkina, after whom Actors' Club on Gorky Street is named. For almost 80 years Yablochkina appeared on the stage of the Maly Theatre, giving the people the benefit of her outstanding talents.

This same building was also the home at various times of such famous artistes as Kachalov, Moskvin, Leonidov and Gorski, the famous ballet-master. No 14 was once the home of Ostuzhev, a famous actor from the Maly Theatre, whose performance of Othello and Uriel Acosta were unforgettable. At 5 **Nemirovich-Danchenko Street** (on the left-hand side of Pushkin Street near Moskvin Street) is the house where such famous actors and actresses of the Art Theatre as Olga Knipper-Chekhova, Mikhail Kedrov, Alla Tarasova and Vladimir Nemirovich-Danchenko spent the last days of their lives. 5/7 Art Theatre Passage was the home of Leonid Sobinov, a famous tenor from the Bolshoi Theatre and Nikolai Khmelev, the actor of the Art Theatre.

On the corner of Pushkin Street and Strastnoi Boulevard is a bright yellow building in the Empire style (No 39). Built in 1832 by D. Grigoriev, it once housed the **University Press**, one of the oldest

Street Map Labels

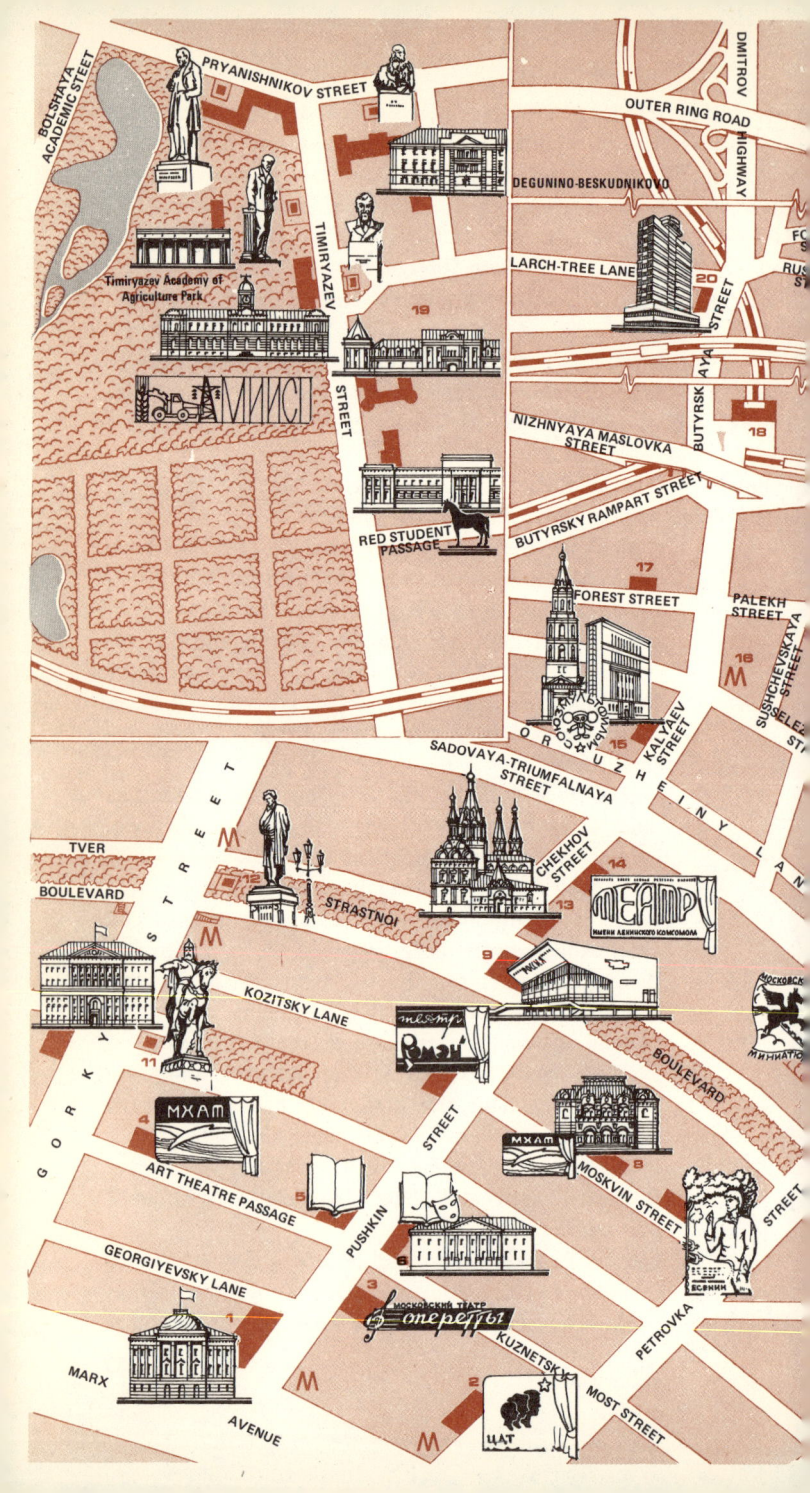

- BOLSHAYA ACADEMIC STEET
- PRYANISHNIKOV STREET
- TIMIRYAZEV STREET
- Timiryazev Academy of Agriculture Park
- МИИСП
- 19
- RED STUDENT PASSAGE
- DMITROV
- OUTER RING ROAD HIGHWAY
- DEGUNINO-BESKUDNIKOVO
- LARCH-TREE LANE
- 20
- BUTYRSKAYA STREET
- NIZHNYAYA MASLOVKA STREET
- BUTYRSKY RAMPART STREET
- 18
- FOREST STREET
- 17
- PALEKH STREET
- SUSHCHEVSKAYA STREET
- SELEZ... ST
- 16
- ORUZHEINY LANE
- KALYAEV STREET
- 15
- SADOVAYA-TRIUMFALNAYA STREET
- TVER BOULEVARD
- GORKY STREET
- STRASTNOI
- CHEKHOV STREET
- 14 ТЕАТР имени Ленинского Комсомола
- 13
- 12
- KOZITSKY LANE
- 9 МХАТ
- театр Ромэн
- BOULEVARD
- МОСКОВСК МИНИАТЮ
- 11
- МХАТ 4
- ART THEATRE PASSAGE
- 5
- PUSHKIN STREET
- МХАТ 8
- MOSKVIN STREET
- STREET
- GEORGIYEVSKY LANE
- 3
- Московский театр оперетты
- 1
- MARX AVENUE
- KUZNETSKY MOST STREET
- PETROVKA
- 2 ЦАТ

TOWARDS DMITROV

1. House of Trade Unions
2. Central Children's Theatre
3. Moscow Operetta Theatre
4. Moscow Art Theatre
5. House of Educational Books
6. Central Theatrical Library
7. Branch of the Moscow Art Theatre
8. Rossia Cinema
9. Theatre of Miniature
10. Monument to Dolgoruki
11. Monument to Pushkin
12. Church of the Nativity of the Virgin in Putinki (17th cent.)
13. Lenin Komsomol Theatre
14. Soyuzmultfilm Studios
15. Novoslobodskaya Metro Station
16. "Underground Press of the Central Committee of the RSDLP, 1905-1906", a branch of the Central Museum of the Revolution
17. Savyolovsky Railway Station
18. Timiryazev Academy of Agriculture, Liskun Livestock Museum, Horse-Breeding Museum, Williams Soil and Agronomy Museum. Garden Terrace and Grotto (18th cent.), Palace (19th cent.), Dendrological Park, monument to Timiryazev, monument to Pryanishnikov, monument to Williams, monument to Tursky, monument to Liskun

publishing houses in Russia. It was here that Gogol's novel *Dead Souls* was printed under the author's personal supervision as well as the works of Vassily Zhukovsky, Adam Mickiewicz, Sergei Aksakov and Ivan Turgenev.

Chekhov Street

Chekhov Street is the continuation of Pushkin Street beyond the Boulevard Ring. Since 1944 it has borne the name of the great Russian writer, Anton Chekhov, who lived here at the end of the last century.

At the entrance to the street stands one of the most interesting tent-roofed churches in Moscow, the mid-17th century **Church of the Nativity of the Virgin in Putinki**. The church was built at the Tver Gates of the Bely Gorod, where the road to Dmitrov began so as to bid farewell, as it were, to travellers leaving Moscow. The building itself bears witness to the great mastery of its unknown builders. Of exceptional elegance are the beautiful cupolas above which stands the tent-shaped belfry, while the walls and drums are rich in ornamentation.

6 Chekhov Street, next to the church, is the **Lenin Komsomol Theatre**. During the early years after the Revolution this building housed the lecture theatres of the Sverdlov Communist University, where in 1919 Lenin spoke many times. On October 2, 1920 at the Third All-Russia Congress of the Russian Young Communist League Lenin made a speech entitled "The Tasks of the Youth Leagues", which was to become the programme for the communist education of the younger generation in the Soviet Union.

> The building is of some architectural interest. Built in 1910 by I. Ivanov-Schitz, it combines the strict simplicity of classicism with the features of early 20th century Art Nouveau. Before the Revolution it housed the Merchants' Club and had its own concert hall, restaurant and hotel.

The Komsomol Theatre was founded in 1938 on the basis of the Theatre of Working Youth which had existed since 1927. As may be expected, it stages many plays about young people, and it is here that many young dramatists, actors and directors began their careers.

Opposite the theatre in 1976 a building was opened which with its embrasure windows resembles a castle. By utilizing old-time elements, the architect, V. Kilpe, harmoniously fitted this modern building in among the old houses.

Chekhov Street comes out on to the Sadovoye Ring, continuing on the far side as Kalyaev Street (Kalyayevskaya Ulitsa) and Novoslobodskaya Streets.

Kalyayev and Novoslobodskaya Streets

The first of these streets was renamed in 1919 after I. Kalyayev, the revolutionary who was executed by the tsarist government in 1905.

This street was not built up until the late 19th or early 20th century when two-storey houses began to go up, many of which have been preserved. According to the General Plan for the Development of Moscow, the street was widened and new apartment blocks and civic buildings erected. It is from here that the city's longest street, the future Timiryazev Avenue will begin its 19-kilometre journey to the outer ring road.

On the left-hand side at No 23 is the **Soyuzmultfilm Studios** which produces cartoons and other types of animated film that are enjoyed by adults as well as children. Some of the productions of these studios, like the cartoon series "Just You Wait!" are well known abroad.

No 18 is the *alma mater* of dentists— the **Moscow Medical Stomatological Institute**. In 1973 a **monument** (by A. Kostromitin) was unveiled in the main entrance to those surgeons who fought at the front and died during the war.

Novoslobodskaya Street is the continuation of Kalyaev Street. Here your attention is immediately attracted by the colonnade round the **Novoslobodskaya Metro Station**. Lovers of ornamental art should go down into the underground station itself and look at the 32 magnificent stain-glass windows by Pavel Korin, which are mounted on the station's columns. At present Novoslobodskaya is the only metro station on this radial highway, but a new line is planned to begin at Novoslobodskaya and run parallel with the Dmitrov Highway as far as the outer ring road.

Near Novoslobodskaya Station on **Red Proletarian Street** (Krasnoproletarskaya Ulitsa) is the **Krasny Proletary Printing House** (No 16/1). The printing house, which is one of the largest in the country, has contributed greatly to the country's heroic history. In 1905 the workers of this printing house formed an action unit, which took control of the local area during the armed uprising and brought help to their brothers in Presnya. At 21 **Sushchevskaya Street** is the **Molodaya Gvardia** (Young Guard) **Publishing House of the Central Committee of the Young Communist League**, which produces social, political, and popular science literature and fiction designed mainly for young people. The publishing house produces annually some 30 million books.

The publishing house was founded in 1922. One of its best known publications is the series entitled "Lives of Famous People", which was begun by Maxim Gorky and which now contains some 600 titles.

Further along on the left of Novoslobodskaya Street is **Forest Street** (Lesnaya Ulitsa), where No 55 (which is not very far along) is well worth a visit. Outside is a board with a very unusual sign: "Kalandadze, Wholesale Caucasian Fruit Dealers". The point is that here in the cellar of this former shop was the underground printing house that was set up during the first Russian revolution on Lenin's orders and the building is now the **"Underground Press of the Central Committee of the RSDLP, 1905-1906", a branch of the Central Museum of the Revolution.**

> Almost at the bottom of a two-metre well the revolutionaries dug a tunnel 142 cm by 50 cm and a small underground room to house the press. For long hours without light or fresh air they worked setting up the type and printing on a hand press the Bolshevik newspaper *Rabochy* (Worker). The press remained secret from the police, even though there was a police chief's residence opposite with a guard on continual duty.

Beyond Lesnaya Street Novoslobodskaya Street has been widened and built up with new houses. A few blocks further on you come to Savelovsky Railway Station, which was once outside the limits of the city itself. The square here is one of the most complex transport junctions in Moscow with traffic being organized on three levels.

Butyrskaya Street

Butyrskaya Street, which continues beyond the square has been built up with modern buildings and reconstruction work in this area is almost completed.

One hundred years ago the district was popular as a weekend and holiday resort and had its own railroad connecting it to the centre. It was here on this railway line that the famous Soviet writer, Konstantin Paustovsky, used to work as a young man. The line, still exists today, but it carries trams now instead of trains.

Towards the end of the last century a number of industrial enterprises began to spring up here and in 1905 the workers of this district took active part in the armed December uprising. Barricades were erected around Novoslobodskaya and Kalyaev Streets and fighting took place with the guards of the Butyrskaya prison.

During the Soviet period the old factories have been modernized and many new ones built.

From here the Dmitrov Highway begins, the main route to the north-west districts of the city.

Dmitrov Highway

According to the plan for the reconstruction of Moscow this highway will all become part of the new Timiryazev Avenue.

The roads leading off to the right here are mostly named after great writers like Rustaveli, Goncharov, Fonvizin etc. Among the older inhabitants of this district it is often called Butyrsky Farm. This name dates back to the old agricultural school that was founded here in 1823, and which after the Revolution became one of the oldest state farms in the country. On 22 October, 1921 Lenin, Kalinin, Krupskaya and Lenin's sister Maria Ulyanova visited this farm to watch the trials of an electric plough which had been developed in the Soviet Union. Today a memorial park with a monument to Lenin marks the spot where these trials took place.

From here on either side of the highway an enormous new housing estate has been built. Between 1971 and 1975 alone 600,000 square metres of housing were provided in this district. At the same time a number of scientific research institutes were built here.

Further along the road you come to the **Timiryazev Academy of Agriculture**, the centre of the agricultural sciences in the Soviet Union. The Academy itself was founded in 1865 and now has some 4 thousand students from all over the Soviet Union as well as from abroad studying at its various faculties.

The Academy is reached by a beautiful lane called **Larch Avenue** (Listvennichnaya Alleya), whose magnificent Siberian larches were planted in the middle of the last century. Behind the rows of trees stand the students' hostels, their club and a new sports complex which includes an indoor swimming pool and a riding manege. A stroll along the avenue with its bracing smell of pine has become a necessary ritual for students about to sit examinations.

The grounds of the Academy and the 18th-19th century buildings of which it was originally composed are a valuable architectural and historical monument. Here in the early 18th century Peter the Great built on what was then his grandfather's estate a livestock farm and personally planted the first trees here. In 1861 the estate was bought by the state and became the Petrovskaya Academy of Agriculture and Forestry.

To the 18th century belong the garden terrace in the park and the whitestone grotto as well as the farm building with four corner towers and the old byre (48 Timiryazev Street). The main administrative building is 19th century, being built in 1865 by Benois as are the wing and the two service annexes, one of which now contains the **Liskun Livestock Museum** (No 48). Other museums on Timiryazev Street include the **Horse-Breeding Museum** (No 44) and the **Williams Soil and Agronomy Museum** (No 55).

Part of the Academy grounds (covering an area of 38.5 hectares) is taken up by a dendrological park, which contains a unique collection of trees from Europe, Asia and America. The remaining 270 hectares are in fact a unique memorial, for here by tradition every student of the Academy plants his own tree. Among the ancient oaks and limes are trees planted by such famous scientists as the founder of Soviet agrochemistry D. Pryanishnikov, the soil scientist and founder of grassland crop rotation, V. Williams, and the forestry scientist, M. Tursky. In summer the heady fragrance of the limes of which there are many in this park, reaches far beyond the park itself. Konstantin Paustovsky has left us with this picture of the park in autumn:

"Ahead of us the park flamed in all the hues of autumn and everywhere was silence and tranquility. The tall limes and planes, interspersed with pale lemon aspen seemed to invite us to enter a land of beauty and peace. Yet here autumn herself in all her variety and colour had been bent to the will and talent of man, for this park had been laid by our botanists and landscape-gardeners."

In the grounds of the Academy there are monuments and memorial plaques to those famous scientists who taught or studied here. These include the founder of plant physiology, Kliment Timiryazev as well as D. Pryanishnikov, V. Williams, M. Tursky and the livestock specialist, F. Liskun.

But the Timiryazev Academy also has a glorious revolutionary tradition, for here in the 1890s one of the first Social-Democratic circles in Moscow sprang up. The Bolsheviks in the Academy took an active part in the 1905 Revolution and in the struggle for Soviet power in Moscow. A granite stele is inscribed with the names of those students, professors and lecturers who died at the front during the Great Patriotic War.

Degunino-Beskudnikovo

As it goes further towards the outer ring road the Dmitrov Highway passes through the two enormous estates of **Degunino-Beskudnikovo** and **East Degunino**, which have been built over the past 15 years, providing housing for 150 thousand inhabitants.

Degunino contains a number of important medical centres like the Hearing and Speech Restoration Centre, the Orthopedic Centre and Research Laboratories for Experimental and Clinical Eye Surgery of the Ministry of Health of the RSFSR.

Along the railway line which cuts through the district it is planned to build high embankments and plant them with trees. This is not only to give the district a more attractive appearance, but to serve as a sound barrier protecting the inhabitants from the noise of the trains. Near the Mark railway station the Dmitrov Highway passes below the fly-over which carries the outer ring road and leaves the capital.

PETROVKA STREET— KUZNETSKY MOST STREET

Petrovka Street–Kuznetsky Most Street–Pushechnaya Street–Zhdanov Street

The old streets which fan out northwards from Sverdlov Square and Marx Avenue in the direction of the Boulevard Ring form another of Moscow's protected areas. You will already have had some acquaintance with the streets included in this area when reading about the historical centre of Moscow.

The individuality of this particular corner of old Moscow reflects the changing epochs and styles and contains 33 monuments and ensembles of outstanding architectural importance.

The disposition of the streets here was determined in the 14th-15th centuries largely as a result of the sloping banks of the River Neglinnaya. Monastery fortresses were built on the higher spots to form part of the inner defence ring of the city and the radial streets which are now Petrovka and Zhdanov Street arose in place of the roads which linked the monasteries with the Kremlin and Kitaigorod. The usual process took place here in the 15th and 16th centuries whereby the artisans' quarters were ousted and replaced by the estates of the nobles and later in the 18th century the houses of the rich merchants began to be built here. Today this district with its lively narrow streets is full of exhibition salons, shops, restaurants and numerous buildings.

Petrovka

Petrovka Street runs parallel with Pushkin Street (see previous chapter). Together with Stoleshnikov Lane and Kuznetsky Most Petrovka Street has long been a popular shopping centre with crowds of people flooding its narrow pavements.

At the entrance to Petrovka, opposite the Bolshoi Theatre, stands a storey Gothic building built in 1906-1908 by R. Klein to house Russia's first department store. In 1922 it was reopened as the **Central Department Store** *(TsUM)* and in 1975 a new modern block was added to it which opens on to three streets—Petrovka, Kuznetsky Most and Neglinnaya Street. The old building underwent reconstruction and the store's area was increased some 2.5 times. It can now take up to 200 thousand shoppers daily. A little further along Petrovka is **Petrovsky Arcade** store, which was considered one of the biggest shops in old Moscow and is now part of *TsUM.*

Branching off to the left of Petrovka is **Stoleshnikov Lane** which leads into Gorky Street. Here a string of small shops—three or four to each of the early 19th-century houses there—the like of which are not to be found in any other Moscow street, line this narrow lane. The little sweet shop at 11 Stoleshnikov Lane has long been famed. Here on two 19th century stoves they still bake what are considered by the cognoscenti to be the finest pies and sweetmeats in Moscow, for which people come from all corners of the city to try. There are always long queues outside this shop for the old stoves can only bake 10 thousand pies a day.

As you leave Stoleshnikov Lane take a look at No 9, outside which there is a memorial plaque with a portrait of Vladimir Gilyarovsky, "uncrowned king of reporters" and commentator on the social life of Moscow. "I could more easily imagine Moscow without the Tsar Bell and the Tsar Cannon than without you," wrote the famous writer Kuprin in a letter to Gilyarovsky, who for the last 55 years of his life lived in Stoleshnikov Lane, maintaining it to be the centre of Moscow. Among his acquaintances were Tolstoy, Gorky, Chekhov, Repin, Levitan, Chaliapin, Mayakovsky and Yesenin.

Opposite the entrance to Stoleshnikov Lane on Petrovka you can see a house with a whitestone façade, vaulted entrance and ornamental wrought-iron lamps (No 16). This is now the shop **Russian Patterns** (Russkiye Uzory), and is run by the All-Russia Society for the Protection of Historical and Cultural Monuments. Here you can obtain interesting articles from all over the Russian Federation, including jewelry, bone and metal carving, enamel, semi-precious stones from the Urals, furs, ceramics, enamel and embroidery and lace work from Vologda.

On the right of the shop are two side-streets. The first, **Petrovskiye Linii**, is interesting for the fact that it forms a single architectural ensemble, built in the late 19th century according to a unified plan. It was originally designed as a private street, but later the owner made it over to the city. The whole of the right side of the street is taken up with the **Budapest Hotel** (No 2/18), whose restaurant serves Hungarian cuisine. Outside the hotel there is a memorial plaque commemorating the speeches made here by Lenin in 1918 and 1919 to meetings of the workers.

The next street is **Rakhmanov Lane**. Here in an old two-storey house at No 4 lived the great Russian critic, Vissarion Belinsky. No 3 in the same street housed the Moscow Labour Exchange in the years following the Revolution, which was finally closed in 1930 when unemployment was done away with in the Soviet Union. "The last unemployed worker in our country has found employment" was the announcement it made at the time thus marking the end of one of the worst vestiges of the pre-revolutionary past. Now typical job-ads begin with the word "Wanted..." The old labour exchange building is now occupied by the **USSR Ministry of Public Health**.

Beyond Stoleshnikov Lane Petrovka begins to noticeably alter its character. Shops become fewer and near the **Petrovskiye Gates** (where Petrovka crosses the Boulevard Ring) the street seems to return to the 17th and 18th centuries, when its life as a trading centre had not yet begun and it was simply a road leading to the Troitskiye Gates of the Kremlin. During high water the River Neglinnaya would flood its banks and so building took place only on the left-hand side of Petrovka. The only exception to this was the **Vysoko-Petrovsky Monastery** that stood on a hill on the right and so out of the reach of the flood waters.

This unique ensemble of ancient architecture (No 28) was founded in the 14th century and originally made of wood.

On the imperial command of Peter the Great in 1680s-1690s the monastery was rebuilt in stone. Above the triple-bayed arch of the main entrance—the Sacred Gates—rises a 40 metre high octagonal multi-tiered belfry. In the centre of the courtyard is the whitestone Church of Peter the Metropolitan, built by the Tsarina Natalya, mother of Peter the Great. The church is surrounded by open galleries with arcades and the household courtyard has an open arched gallery which connects the various buildings within it. The main church in the monastery is the **Bogolubskaya Church** which served as a family mausoleum for the Naryshkins, Peter the Great's maternal ancestors.

Restoration work has brought back the original unity and beauty to the monument. In the **Naryshkin Chambers** of the monastery there is the **State Museum of Literature** with an **18-19th Century Russian Literature Exhibition**.

The house opposite (No 25) was built in the late 18th century by Kazakov and is one of the finest examples of Russian classicism, and though it is only three storeys high appears monumental and very impressive. It now houses the **Rheumatic Research Institute of the USSR Academy of Medical Sciences**.

Petrovka continues beyond the Boulevard Ring as far as the **Hermitage Gardens**, one of the oldest public gardens in Moscow. The original layout of the gardens has been retained as well as the shady trees, the beautiful flower gardens, the concert hall and the summer theatre, which continue to attract crowds as they did in the past.

The Hermitage has become part of the theatrical history of the city. Here from 1898 to 1901 the Moscow Art Theatre gave its first performances. On March 2, 1900 Lenin saw Hauptmann's play *Fuhrmann Heuschel* and in a letter to his mother wrote: "They act well at the Moscow Art Theatre..."

> At the end of Petrovka near to the Zemlyanoi Val there stood in the 17th and early 18th centuries the crowded wooden shacks of the carters. Later when these craftsmen began to make carriages and coaches this part of the street began to be called **Carriage Street** (Karetny Ryad).

Running parallel to Karetny Ryad on the right is **Likhov Lane**, where at No 6 is the **Central Documentary Film Studios**, which produce newsreels covering all aspects of the life in the Soviet Union and whose reporters can be seen everywhere that important events are taking place. As well as newsreels the studios produce documentaries.

Kuznetsky Most Street, Pushechnaya and Zhdanov Streets

Kuznetsky Most Street begins opposite TsUM, near to the beginning of Petrovka. The incline by which it rises towards Dzerzhinsky Square was in the 15th-17th centuries called Kuznetsky Hill, for here the blacksmiths *(kuznetsy)* worked making cannons and bells for the nearby Cannon Foundary *(Pushechny Dvor)*. In these times the street crossed the River Neglinnaya by means of a bridge, and it is from this that the present day name of the street is derived, for Kuznetsky Most in Russian means Blacksmiths' Bridge.

During the 18th century when a decree from Catherine the Great permitted trading anywhere inside the city and not just in the special trading rows of the Kitaigorod, many particularly luxury shops sprung up here.

Kuznetsky Most Street has retained its influence over the world of fashion, for here at No 14 is the **All-Union House of Fashion**, where the finest designers in the country work.

> The House of Fashion moved into this building during the war and here as early as 1945 the first post-war fashion parade was held as a sign of a new

and happier life in a world of peace. The House of Fashion today sets new trends in design, which it demonstrates in the salon on the first floor, which can seat 250. Permanent exhibition is opened on the ground floor.

The TsUM department store new building faces Kuznetsky Most Street.

But above all today Kuznetsky Most is famed for its bookshops, which include the popular **Writers' Bookshop** and **Foreign Languages Bookshop** (No 18). Lovers of art will also be attracted to the art exhibitions that are permanently held at two exhibition halls in Kuznetsky Most Street—the **Moscow Artists' Club** (No 11) and the **Exhibition Hall of the Union of Artists of the USSR** (No 20).

Kuznetsky Most Street ends at **Vorovsky Square**, where outside No 21 which for many years housed the Ministry of Foreign Affairs stands a **monument to Vatslav Vorovsky**, built in 1924. Vorovsky was a famous Soviet diplomat who was killed in 1923 in Lausanne by an agent of a counter-revolutionary organization. The bronze statue by I. Katz, was placed on a pedestal of white marble, a gift from the workers of Italy.

Running parallel to Kuznetsky Most Street up what were once the banks of the Neglinnaya, but nearer to Marx Avenue, is **Pushechnaya Street**. Here until the early 19th century on the banks of the Neglinnaya stood the Cannon Foundary. But during the 1820s the street was rebuilt with stone houses, some of which still remain. Among the largest buildings in Pushechnaya Street is the **Berlin Hotel** (No 13) which was built at the turn of the century.

The whole block from here to Dzerzhinsky Square is taken up with the **Detsky Mir**, department store for children.

Opposite Detsky Mir is the **Central Club of Cultural Workers** (No 9). This club for the city's artists, musicians and painters has been in existence for over 50 years. Here concerts and cultural evenings are held as well as exhibitions and meetings with foreign personages from the world of culture. Outside there is a memorial plaque to commemorate the fact that in 1920 Lenin delivered two speeches here to the working people of Moscow. Also here in 1891 the drama group founded by Stanislavsky, which was eventually to become the Moscow Art Theatre held its first rehearsals.

Pushechnaya Street is crossed by a road which used to run from the Kremlin to the Rozhdestvensky Convent, which was built

Trubnaya Square

ROZHDESTVE
BOULEVAR

Русские узоры

RAKHMANOV LANE

STOLESHNIKOV LANE

KUZNETSKY

Турист

PUSHECHNAYA STREET

MARX AVENUE

PETROVKA–KUZNETSKY MOST

1. Bolshoi Theatre
2. Central Department Store (TsUM)
3. Petrovsky Arcade Store
4. Russian Patterns (Russkiye Uzory) Shop
5. Budapest Hotel
6. Vysoko-Petrovsky Monastery (17th cent.)
7-8. Naryshkin Chambers (17th cent.). Exhibition "18th-19th Century Russian Literature"
9. All-Union House of Fashion
10. Writers' Bookshop
11. Foreign Languages Bookshop
12. Moscow Artists' Club
13. Exhibition Hall of the Union of Artists of the USSR
14. Monument to Vatslav Vorovsky
15. Berlin Hotel
16. Detsky Mir department store for children
17. Central Club of Cultural Workers
18. Kuznetsky Most Metro Station
19. Moscow Municipal Excursion Bureau
20. Moscow Institute of Architecture
21. Architectors' Bookshop
22. Rozhdestvensky Convent (16th cent.)
23. Maly Theatre
24. Central Children's Theatre

in the late 14th century on the steep bank of the Neglinnaya. Formerly called the Rozhdestvenka, this street was renamed in 1948 **Zhdanov Street** after Andrei Zhdanov, a prominent figure in the Communist Party and the Soviet state.

Here in 1975 the new Kuznetsky Most Metro Station, was opened. It is as if the architects have once more bridged the River Neglinnaya, for it only takes a little imagination to see the bright marble-faced arches of the underground station as resembling the white arcade of a bridge.

The building opposite the station (No 5), which is about 150 years old now houses the **Moscow Municipal Excursion Bureau** which annually arranges trips around the city, the outlying regions and to more distant places for some 5 million people.

Beyond Kuznetsky Most Street is the **Institute of Architecture** (11 Zhdanov Street). It was built in 1778 by Kazakov to replace the old wooden houses that had previously stood here. In the late 1880s it housed the Moscow (formerly Stroganov) School of Industrial Art, the *alma mater* of many famous painters. A few years ago this institute was moved to a new building on the Volokolamsk Highway and the Moscow Institute of Architecture (founded in 1866) took over the premises. There is now a **bookshop** here selling literature on architecture.

The focal point of Zhdanov Street is the **Rozhdestvensky Convent** which was founded in 1386. The wooden buildings of the original monastery have not of course been preserved, but the single-cupola stone cathedral has and this now belongs among the oldest architectural monuments in Moscow. It was erected between 1501 and 1505 at the same time as the Cathedral of St. Michael the Archangel in the Kremlin. For many years the cathedral was without its helmet-shaped dome, but this has now been restored by Soviet specialists. The remainder of the monastery's buildings are 17th and 18th century.

Recently the Moscow City Soviet gave the monastery buildings to the Institute of Architecture and the students will carry on the restoration work as part of their studies, improving the grounds and converting this unique monument into a distinctive cultural centre.

NORTHERN RADIAL ROAD

Neglinnaya Street—Tsvetnoi Boulevard—Samotechny Boulevard—Commune Square—Academician Korolyov Street—Ostankino. Ostankino 1st Street—Central Botanical Gardens—Botanical Street—Altufyevo Highway—Otradnoye—Lianozovo—Bibirevo

There is as yet no "Northern Radial Road" on the map of Moscow. However, this thoroughfare is envisaged under the General Plan for the Development and Reconstruction of Moscow and parts of it—from Marx Avenue to the Ostankino Teletower and the stretch which runs amid the new housing estates to the outer ring road—have already been opened.

The Northern Radial Road is often called the "green" radial road, for it links together a chain of old and new boulevards. Thanks to this long green corridor the central regions of the city will be linked with Moscow's northern "oases"—Ostankino Park, the Botanical Gardens, the gardens and groves of the Exhibition of National Economic Achievement and the suburban woodlands. The Northern Radial Road is to begin at Neglinnaya Street.

Neglinnaya Street

About 200 years ago the River Neglinnaya which we have mentioned many times in describing the history of Moscow used to flow here.

The river crossed what is now Sverdlov Square, turned to the right at the Kitaigorod, skirted the Kremlin near the Bolshoi Kamenny Bridge and flowed into the Moskva. At high water or during the heavy rains, the Neglinnaya used to flood its banks and inundate the surrounding area. In the late 18th century the river bed was run through a canal, and in 1819 was finally covered over and taken underground. It was after this had been accomplished that the Kuznetsky Most (Kuznetsky Bridge) was pulled down and the neighbouring streets replanned. The road above the Neglinnaya was built up with two-storey houses. In the late 19th century Neglinnaya Street became one of the main shopping centres of the capital.

But the obstinate river continued to cause difficulties, occasionally breaking out on the surface and flooding the nearby streets. Now the problem has been finally solved, for a new wide conduit has been built to pipe the Neglinnaya right to the River Moskva.

At 12 Neglinnaya Street is the **State Bank of the USSR**, an interesting building in the renaissance style built by K. Bykovsky in the 1890s. During the Soviet period it became necessary to enlarge the premises of the bank and the central part of the building with its allegorical sculptures by Opekushin personifying farming, industry and trade had two large side annexes added by I. Zholtovsky.

Next door is an interesting relic of old Moscow—the **Sandunovskiye Baths,** which were also built in the 1890s and luxuriously decorated with moulded ceilings, gilt and marble. Even today lovers of the

Soviet Square. The Mossoviet building and the monument to Yuri Dolgoruky

Monument to Pushkin on Pushkin Square

Gorky Street

Central Museum of the Revolution
Northern River Port

Great Hall in the Moscow Conservatory
Gorki Leninskiye

"The Worker and the Collective Farm Woman"

The USSR Exhibition of Economic Achievement. Central avenue
Palace-Museum of Serf Art in Ostankino

Arkhangelskoye Estate-Museum. Interior of one of the halls

Ostankino Palace. Interior of one of the halls

The Tretyakov Gallery
New housing estate at Troparyovo

The Tretyakov Gallery
Lenin Avenue. Gagarin Square

Arkhangelskoye Estate-Museum, the park

Khromatron Factory
Church of the Resurrection in Kadashi

One of the buildings of the Olympic Sports Complex
Panorama of the Central Lenin Stadium at Luzhniki
View from the Lenin Hills

Universal Sports Hall at Luzhniki

Moscow University. Main building. Monument to Mikhail Lomonosov

Russian steam bath come here from all over the city. The name of the baths comes from the actor, Sandunov, to whom they belonged.

On the left-hand side of the street is a smallish building, decorated in bright eastern mosaics. This is the **Uzbekistan Restaurant** (No 29). Among the national dishes served here are the unforgettable *lagman* and *Uzbek pilau*. In the east they say that a poor man will not get rich by hearing the sound of money, nor a hungry man be full by smelling the aroma of food. In the same vein we say that the tourist will not know what *Uzbek pilau* or *lagman* are until he's tried them.

Towards its end Neglinnaya Street becomes a small boulevard leading into **Trubnaya Square**, which you have already come across in the chapter on the Boulevard Ring.

Tsvetnoi and Samotechny Boulevards

Both these boulevards lie above the River Neglinnaya. In the right-hand corner of Trubnaya Square, where it joins Tsvetnoi Boulevard is the **Central House of Political Knowledge** which is run by the **Moscow Regional and Moscow City Party Committees**. It is in fact a complex of buildings comprising an 8-storey administrative and educational block, a large library, a conference hall seating 2,000 and a number of other halls, auditoriums and studies. It will also have a cinema and concert hall combined which is at present being built on the other side of the road. Nearby a branch of the Maly Theatre is also under construction.

On the left-hand side of Tsvetnoi Boulevard are a number of buildings of interest: the **Mir Cinema**, equipped for three-screen projection and installed with stereophonic sound, which seats 1,220 (No 11); heavy athletics centre of "Trud" sports society; the indoor **Central Market** (No 15); and the **State Circus** (No 13), one of the oldest in the country. The Moscow Circus was opened in 1880, but the building was rebuilt during the Soviet period and now seats 2,100. Before the New Circus, as it is called, was built on Vernadsky Avenue (see Chapter *The South-West*), the Circus on Tsvetnoi Boulevard was the largest in the country.

On the opposite side of the street are the editorial offices of *Literaturnaya gazeta*, a popular weekly published by the Union of Writers of the USSR and the newspaper *Literaturnaya Rossia,* which is produced by the Union of Writers of the RSFSR (No 30).

With the development of the Northern Radial Road, Tsvetnoi Boulevard will be considerably widened and park benches, belvederes and decorative sculptures will be placed amid its avenue of trees.

Beyond the Sadovoye Ring fly-over at the far end of Tsvetnoi Boulevard is **Samotechny Boulevard** with its shady avenues of ancient oaks making it look more like a park than a city thoroughfare. In 1953 monuments were erected here in memory of two of Moscow's war heroes: a **bronze bust of** Flying Officer **V. Popkov**, Twice Hero of the Soviet Union and a **monument to Marshall of the Soviet Union Tolbukhin**, both by L. Kerbel.

At the end of Samotechny Boulevard on the right is a street that has been in existence since the 17th century. In 1927 it was renamed in honour of Vladimir Durov, the famous circus clown and animal trainer who was also known as a scholar and a public figure. No 4 contains a rather remarkable establishment—the **V. Durov Nook** set up in 1912 by Durov himself. It is a menagerie, a theatre and a museum all in one. Here 200 four-legged and winged circus artists are kept and trained. They give daily performances for children, which even include whole plays performed in a special Animals' Theatre. So popular are these shows that next to the old house a fine new circular building has recently been built with a high domed roof, which can seat 400 and is specially equipped with open-air cages and pools, etc. After Samotechny Boulevard is widened the Nook will be surrounded with greenery. The varied work of the Nook has the noble aim of encouraging children to love animals and nature.

Commune Square

Samotechny Boulevard leads into Commune Square (Ploshchad Kommuny), named in honour of the Paris Commune of 1871. The square is dominated by the **Soviet Army Theatre,** built in 1940 by

K. Alabyan and V. Simbirtsev and designed in the form of a five-pointed star with a colonnade running round its perimeter.

The Greater Hall of the theatre can accommodate 1,840 and the Lesser Hall about 500. Though its main repertoire is devoted to military and patriotic themes, the theatre also stages Russian and world classics as well as the works of Soviet and foreign modern dramatists.

In the garden in front of the theatre there is a monument to great Russian general Alexander Suvorov.

On the right-hand side of the square behind the old iron railings is a building which is almost 230 years old. In the mid-18th century this was the out-of-town manor of a member of the nobility set in spacious grounds. After the fire of 1812 its classical design was restored by Gilardi and Grigoriev, who gave it certain features of the Empire style making it more monumental in appearance. For the last 50 years it has housed the **Central House of the Soviet Army**. At the entrance stands a bust to Mikhail Frunze, after whom it is named. Here in the **Red Banner Hall** all important events in the life of the Soviet Army and Navy are celebrated and official evenings and concerts are held here.

> The **Gardens of the Central House of the Soviet Army** are among the most popular in Moscow. Shady avenues of trees, abundant verdure, beautiful flower beds and the arbours, pergolas and benches combine to produce an atmosphere of rest. The gardens have a theatre, an orchestral podium, courts for tennis, basketball and volleyball and a boating lake. The park entrance is decorated with a mosaic panel.

Next to the Central House of the Soviet Army is the **Soviet Army Museum** (No 2), designed by N. Gaigarov and built in 1965. Founded in 1919 the exhibition today comprises 25 halls and contains documents, photographs, militaria, paintings and dioramas on the past and present of the Soviet Army, which defends the peaceful life and labour of the Soviet people. In the memorial Hall of Victory stands the Victory Banner, which on April 30th, 1945 was raised above the Reichstag in Berlin. The courtyard contains exhibits of weaponry used by the Soviet Army in the past.

Nearby the museum is the **Military Artists Studio**, which is **named after Mitrofan Grekov**, a Soviet artist, famous for his battle paintings. It was built in 1969 by Yu. Krivushchenko and the façade is decorated with a monumental panel.

Behind the Soviet Army Theatre on **Dostoyevsky Street** (Nos 2, 4) two classical style buildings can be seen set amid rich greenery. The first used to be Mariinskaya Hospital for the poor and the second the Alexandrovsky Institute, a private school for the children of the petty bourgeoisie. Both buildings were built by Mikhailov and Gilardi.

The former Mariinskaya Hospital (No 2) is connected with the name of the great Russian writer Fyodor Dostoyevsky. It was here that his father worked as a junior doctor living in one of the hospital flats, where the author of *The Insulted and Humiliated, Crime and Punishment, The Karamazov Brothers* and other world famous classics was born on October 30, 1821 and spent his childhood and youth. The wing has now been opened as a memorial **museum to Dostoyevsky,** and in 1918 a **monument** to the writer built before the Revolution by Merkurov was erected in the courtyard.

Reconstruction work has altered, widened and straightened the streets beyond Commune Square, and this district of Moscow, which until only recently was considered a suburb of the city has been now built up with multi-storey apartment blocks. Here the Northern Radial Road passes through what was once called **Maryina Roshcha**, an area where for centuries the birch forests of the noble landowners had stood. In the late 19th century and early 20th century it became a warren of densely-packed side streets. Today it has once more been reborn. The low shacks that once littered the area have been pulled down and multi-storey apartment blocks built in their place. Between **Sheremetyev Street** and Peace Avenue a large park has been formed—one more splash of greenery on the Northern Radial Road—which recalls the original Maryina Roshcha. In the centre of the district there is an indoor stadium seating 45 thousand and a swimming pool. (See Chapter *Peace Avenue*)

Recently a large wide-screen **Tajikistan Cinema** (1,275 seats) was built on 14 Sheremetyev Street (architects: G. Vulfson and A. Solodukhin). Inside and out the building is covered with mosaic frescoes of smalt, while ceramics and ornamental vases in the traditional style comprise the theme of the interior decor. The walls of the foyer are decorated with scenes from Tajik classical literature.

Academician Korolyov Street, Ostankino 1st Street and Botanical Street

From here the **Ostankino Teletower** can be seen rising into the sky from where it stands on **Academician Korolyov Street**.

The ferro-concrete column of the tower is 385 metres high and is held in the ground by ten supports. Above the concrete section there is a 155-metre high TV aerial. The total weight of the tower is 55 thousand tons. In a strong gale the top of the tower will sway up to 4.25 metres from the vertical. The authors of this amazing feat of construction work were the engineers N. Nikitin, D. Burdin, Ye. Zlobin, M. Shkud and L. Shchipakin, all of whom were awarded Lenin Prizes.

Express lifts take you up to the observation floors. At levels 329, 331 and 334 m there is a circular **restaurant**, the **Seventh Heaven**, whose three tiers can accommodate 300. The restaurant itself slowly revolves so that without leaving your table you can admire a panoramic view of Moscow as it unfolds before you. The restaurant staff make every effort to ensure that their customers feel in their "seventh heaven". As it can be imagined, the number of those wanting to go to this restaurant is very high, so you are advised to book early through the service bureau at your hotel or the Central Bureau of Intourist (1, Gorky St.).

On the other side of Academician Korolyov Street (No 12) is the **Moscow Telecentre** shining with aluminium and glass. The architectural composition of this huge building (more than 1 million cubic metres in volume) is remarkable for its compactness, geometric precision and the way in which it fits organically into the landscape. It was designed by the architects L. Batalov, V. Zharov, Ya. Zakaryan, L. Solovyov, K. Shekhonyan and the engineer, L. Levenstein, all of whom were awarded the USSR State Prizes.

Moscow is the main television centre in the country and TV programmes from Ostankino are watched throughout the Soviet Union. Ostankino is also linked to the telecentres in a number of other countries by means of the Intervision and Eurovision networks.

In 1980 the Olympic section of the telecentre was opened to allow television broadcasts on 20 new channels and 100 new radio programmes. Altogether the Moscow Olympics were watched by some 2 billion viewers throughout the world.

Map Labels

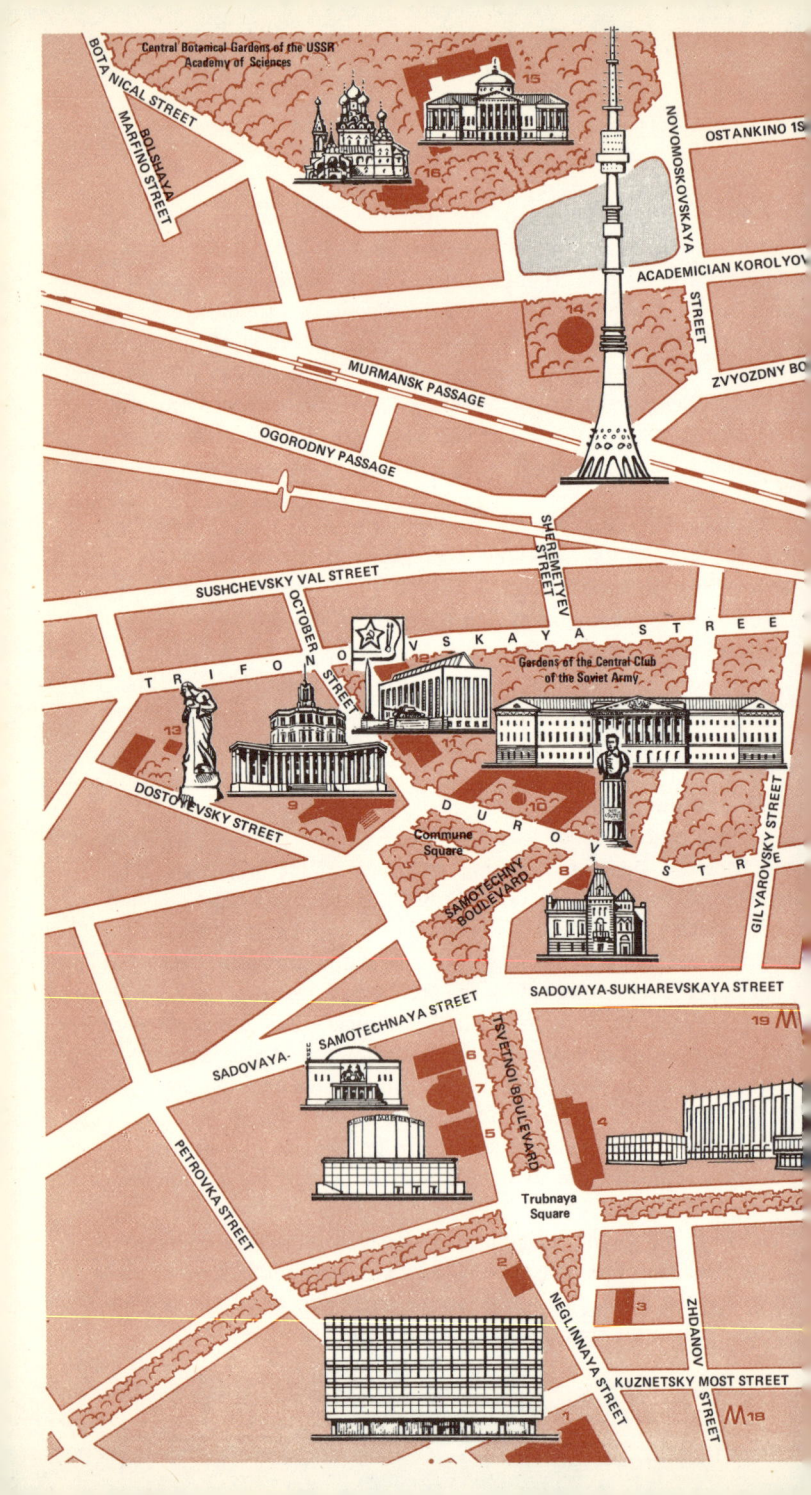

- Central Botanical Gardens of the USSR Academy of Sciences
- BOTANICAL STREET
- BOLSHAYA MARFINO STREET
- OSTANKINO ST
- NOVOMOSKOVSKAYA
- ACADEMICIAN KOROLYOV STREET
- ZVYOZDNY BO
- MURMANSK PASSAGE
- OGORODNY PASSAGE
- SHEREMETYEV STREET
- SUSHCHEVSKY VAL STREET
- TRIFONOVSKAYA STREET
- OCTOBER STREET
- Gardens of the Central Club of the Soviet Army
- DOSTOYEVSKY STREET
- DUROV STR
- GILYAROVSKY STREET
- Commune Square
- SAMOTECHNY BOULEVARD
- SADOVAYA-SUKHAREVSKAYA STREET
- SADOVAYA-SAMOTECHNAYA STREET
- TSVETNOI BOULEVARD
- 19 Ⓜ
- PETROVKA STREET
- Trubnaya Square
- NEGLINNAYA STREET
- ZHDANOV STREET
- KUZNETSKY MOST STREET
- Ⓜ 18

NORTHERN RADIAL ROAD
FROM NEGLINNAYA STREET TO COMMUNE SQUARE

1. Central Department Store (TsUM)
2. Uzbekistan Restaurant
3. Sandunovskiye Baths
4. Central House of Political Knowledge
5. Mir Cinema
6. Central Market
7. State Circus in Tsvetnoi Boulevard
8. Durov Nook
9. Soviet Army Theatre
10. Frunze Central House of the Soviet Army
11. Soviet Army Museum
12. Military Artists Studio named after Mitrofan Grekov
13. Dostoyevsky Flat-Museum

Towards Ostankino

14. Seventh Heaven Restaurant
15. Ostankino Museum of Serf Art (18th cent.)
16. Trinity Church (17th cent.)
17. Prospekt Mira Metro Station
18. Kuznetsky Most Metro Station
19. Kolkhoznaya Metro Station

Academician Korolyov Street, on the far side of which the Telecentre is situated, will become part of the city's fourth ring road. Here amid the green fields Ostankino's new town centre has been built with its various shops, hotels, sports stadiums, leisure centres and circus.

Not far from the ultra-modern television centre is an impressive example of 18th century architecture—the **Ostankino Estate** (Ostankino 1st Street), a fine example of Russian classicism. In 1790 the owner of the estate, Count Sheremetyev, who loved the theatre and who had his own troupe of serf actors, decided to build on one of his estates a private theatre. The result was this beautiful palace at Ostankino, built by his own serf architects A. Mironov, P. Argunov and G. Dikushin together with hundreds of unknown serf craftsmen. It was described by contemporaries as "exceeding everything in grandeur and magnificence that the most fertile imagination and the boldest artistic fantasy could ever conceive of". The building was finally completed in 1798.

Now the **Museum of Serf Art** (No 5), it stands in the old park by the side of a lake. Though built of wood the plaster finish is such that it gives the impression of stone. The main hall, called the Theatre Hall, is in the centre of the palace and connected by a gallery to the side wings. There are also a number of other ceremonial halls: the Egyptian banquet and concert hall, the Italian Reception Hall, the Crimson Dining Room, the Blue Hall and the Picture Gallery. Each room has its own distinctive decor, executed with great artistic mastery. Fine gilt wooden carving like lace decorates the portals and doors and covers the cornices, columns, walls and some of the furniture. Magnificent crystal chandeliers, the pride of Ostankino, hang from the multi-coloured ornamental ceilings. There are beautiful parquet floors, particularly in the Rotunda where they have been inlaid with pewter and mother of pearl. The paintings, sculpture, porcelain and engravings which decorate the palace constitute a valuable collection.

The Ostankino Theatre is known all over the world. The technical equipment used to produce various stage effects was indeed remarkable for the times. The floors, for instance, could be raised and lowered quickly and the auditorium together with the stage be converted into a dance hall. There were also various mechanisms for changing scenery and numerous ingenious devices thought up by Sheremetyev's serf craftsmen for different sound and lighting effects. Many of these have been preserved and are demonstrated to visitors. The theatre contains some fragments of the original decorations and scenery.

Sheremetyev's serf theatre consisted of 200 talented actors, singers, musicians and dancers. The star of the stage was the singer and actress, Praskovya Kovalyova-Zhemchugova, who was also a serf but who later became the wife of Count Sheremetyev. Praskovya Zhemchugova became almost a legend in her own lifetime and many of the historical and architectural monuments around Moscow (mentioned throughout the book) are connected with her name.

To the left of the palace-theatre stands the **Trinity Church**, built by the serf architect, Pavel Potekhin in 1688. This outstanding architectural work is complex in composition with its façades, entrance arches and lintels decorated in patterns of brick, whitestone and majolica.

The palace is set in a typically 18th century park with a symmetrical layout and its parterre bordered with marble busts and vases. Beyond this park there is a larger park with a number of ornamental lakes. Part of this now forms the **Botanical Gardens** (4 Botanical Street).

The Botanical Gardens were started in 1945. They cover an area of 360 hectares and contain some 20,000 species of plant life from all over the world. A huge hot-house, 5,000 square metres in area, has been built for the tropical and subtropical plants imported from Africa, South America, Australia and Polynesia.

The Botanical Gardens display flora from all the climatic zones of the Soviet Union. Here you can see plants from Central Asia side by side with liana and Amur grapes from the Far East and the three-metre high grass from Sakhalin and Kamchatka. Flora from the Caucasus Mountains can be seen growing together with Siberian silver fir, cedars and giant larches.

In the centre of the gardens is a 50 hectare forest reserve with birch, aspen, hazel and mountain ash, species which from time immemorial have grown around Moscow.

The pride of the Botanical Gardens is a huge rosarium with almost 20,000 plants of 2,500 varieties—a veritable sea of fragrant beauty. The roses here have been specially arranged so that there are flowers in bloom from early spring to late autumn.

The dendrological park covers 75 hectares and contains 2,000 species of tree and shrub.

There are unique exhibits in the Gardens like the blue American fir shoots grown from the seeds, which were given by the crew of the Apollo space craft to the crew of the Soyuz during their joint flight in outer space.

The staff of the Botanical Gardens carries out research work on the acclimatization and selection of plants. Every year they grow tens of thousands of seedlings for the parks and gardens of Moscow and other towns in the Soviet Union.

In the next few years a reservoir will be included in the gardens with several islands on which species of plant life from Japan will be planted. It is also planned to build an alpinarium and a number of climataria which reproduce the climatic conditions and natural landscapes of various hot zones such as jungles, savannahs, the dry and humid tropics and the oases of the West-Asiatic deserts. A glass underwater tunnel is to be built allowing visitors to admire the exotic plants that grow on the beds of rivers and seas.

These "distant regions" can be reached by the Moscow Metro new **station Botanichesky Sad** which will be opened on **Agriculture** (Selskokhozyaistvennaya) **Street** with its entrance facing directly on to the Gardens.

Altufyevo Highway—Otradnoye—Lianozovo—Bibirevo

To the north of the Botanical Street a 7-kilometre highway runs out to the outer ring road through a number of new housing estates of some 200,000 inhabitants.

The beginning of the highway—a half-kilometre fly-over spanning the Moscow circle line—was built in 1976.

Here lies the **Altufyevo Estate** with its lake, park and 18th century manor house. Further on to the left of the Altufyevo Highway are the large housing estates of Degunino and Beskudnikovo while to the right lies the new estate of **Otradnoye**, which when completed will have some 1.5 million square metres of housing space.

Otradnoye has a beautifully picturesque landscape, rich green gardens and three rivers running through it—the Chermyanka, the Yauza and the Likhoborka, where there are beaches and health and sports resorts. On the banks of the Likhoborka a park is soon to be opened.

The streets of Otradnoye are named after members of the Decembrist Movement, the first Russian revolutionaries who came from the nobility.

There are two more housing estates along the Altufyevo Highway: **Lianozovo** with its large park and 16-storey apartment blocks and the six residential districts of **Bibirevo** with 155,000 inhabitants in all. Here new Metro stations will be built together with a cinema for 2,500 and other necessary social amenities.

On the River Chermyanka it is planned to build a series of ornamental pools surrounded with greenery.

PEACE AVENUE

*Dzerzhinsky Street—Sretenka—Peace Avenue—The
Exhibition of National Economic Achievement—Babushkin—
Medvedkovo—Yaroslavl Highway—Abramtsevo—Zagorsk*

Peace Avenue (Prospekt Mira) runs from the city centre to the outlying north-eastern suburbs. This was once a part of the ancient road from Kiev and Smolensk to the towns of northern Russia. It was along this road that Prince Yuri Dolgoruky accompanied by a vast retinue was travelling from Vladimir to Kiev, when he stopped on the bank of the River Moskva and commanded a small fortress to be built, thus laying the foundations to the future city of Moscow.

Dzerzhinsky Street and Sretenka

Peace Avenue is reached via **Dzerzhinsky Street** and Sretenka. The street named after Felix Dzerzhinsky preserves the memory of many historical events, both of the recent and not so recent past.

At No 11 on the left-hand side Dzerzhinsky, Chairman of the All-Russia Special Commission for Combating Counter-revolution and Sabotage (Cheka), had his offices from 1918 to 1920 and here he was visited by Lenin. Next door (No 13) was the Cheka Club, where on November 7, 1918 Lenin spoke at a meeting held to celebrate the 1st Anniversary of the October Revolution.

The palatial mansion at No 14 on the other side is early 18th century. In 1812 it was owned by the Governor General of Moscow. One of the scenes in Tolstoy's *War and Peace*—during the fire of Moscow—takes place by this house. The building escaped the fire of 1812 and its façade has been preserved to the present day as a fine example of the work of Rastrelli.

At the end of the street on the left (No 19) is a 17th century monument—the **cathedral of the Sretensky Monastery,** founded in 1395 and recently restored. The cathedral contains a number of valuable frescoes, painted in 1707 and also recently restored.

Further along lies another of Moscow's oldest streets, **Sretenka**. Until the 16th century this was just a country road outside the city. In the early 16th century migrants from Pskov and Novgorod settled there. In the 17th century Sretenka was a lively thoroughfare and by the 18th century a prominent trading centre.

The narrow streets around Sretenka are of a type not found in any other part of the city. There are nine on one side of the main road and seven on the other. Almost every house in these sidestreets is separated by an alley from its neighbour and there are no front entrances at all, which suited the merchants who once owned them.

A few of the two- and three-storey 19th century merchants' houses with trading premises on their ground floors have also been preserved. These are now occupied by shops.

Peace Avenue

Sretenka enters the Sadovoye Ring at Kolkhoz Square, on the other side of which is Peace Avenue. Built in 1957 and named in honour of the World Festival of Youth and Students, which was held in Moscow in that year, it now stretches a total of 9 kilometres.

In the early 20th century it was a typical suburban street in a capitalist city, i.e. it contained a haphazard collection of rich merchants' houses, wooden shacks with little front gardens, barns, flats, inns, churches and shops.

In the mid-1930s the plans for the development of Moscow began by widening the street. In place of the front gardens pavements were built and the cobble stones were replaced with asphalt. The street became of particular importance in 1939 when the Exhibition of National Economic Achievement was opened. After the war work started on the building of the multi-storey apartment blocks which now line the street.

On the right-hand side of Peace Avenue there are several sights of historical and architectural interest. No 12, for instance, is the 17th century mansion where Yakov Brus, diplomat, soldier, scholar and comrade-in-arms of Peter the Great lived. In 1706 he was appointed to take charge of the printing of books in Russia and part of the house was made over for the printing press.

No 14 is an example of late 18th and early 19th century classical architecture. Here in 1894 on an underground press the second edition of Lenin's work, entitled *What the 'Friends of the People' Are and How They Fight the Social-Democrats* was published. The building is now the **Museum of the History of the Dzerzhinsky District**.

Next door (No 16) is a detached house built in 1770s by Bazhenov. In 1812 it was damaged by the fire, but later restored. In 1973 after complete restoration it was opened as a **Palace of Weddings**.

A memorial plaque hangs outside No 30 commemorating the fact that this was where the poet Valery Bryussov lived for many years and died in 1924. It is now the **Bryussov Flat-Museum** and stands in memory to the great Russian Soviet poet.

Further along on the same side is the **Moscow University Botanical Gardens**, the oldest botanical gardens in the country. Founded in 1706 by Peter the Great for growing medicinal herbs, it was known until 1805 as the "apothecary's garden". Now as the University Botanical Gardens it contains some 5,000 species of flora from all over the world and a large collection of palm trees in thirteen hothouses.

Here on the left-hand side of Peace Avenue is a large **sports complex**—an **indoor stadium** with a 126 × 91 metre arena. The stadium is equipped to cater for various sports like football, rugby, Russian hockey and track and field athletics. Part of the arena can be converted into an ice rink (112 × 72 m) for figure skating. But not only sports events can be held here. The stands can hold 45 thousand spectators which is three times as many as the Palace of Sports at Luzhniki. The stadium is also equipped for concerts, festivals, children's New Year parties, balls, and circus and stage performances. The stadium has a sliding acoustic curtain 152 metres long and 24 metres high, which can divide the arena into two and allow the simultaneous performance of two separate features. During the 1980 Olympics boxing and basketball were held here.

The complex also has a water sports hall, which has **two** large **swimming and diving pools** and a smaller one for children. These are set under an oval glass cover, the stands can seat 15,000 spectators.

Both the stadium and the water sports hall stand on a podium, which is reached by a number of attractive looking ramps and staircases. Also set on the podium are the training halls, medical centre, referees' rooms and various other rooms.

Now that many of the older buildings have been pulled down on Peace Avenue there is an excellent view of the **Church of the Metropolitan Philip** built by Kazakov between 1771 and 1788 which stands on **Gilyarovsky Street** (No 51). The classical architecture of this elegant circular church has preserved in the individual details and in the overall ornamentation many of the features of the baroque style which preceded it.

Further along Peace Avenue you come to **Trifonovskaya Street**, on your left. Here you can see the little **Church of St. Trifon on Naprudny** (No 38) one of the few ancient whitestone churches in Moscow that stand outside the Kremlin. This small 15th century building with its vaults, its triple laciniate finned arches and its remarkable belfry on two columns is quite unique in Moscow.

AGRICULTURE STREET

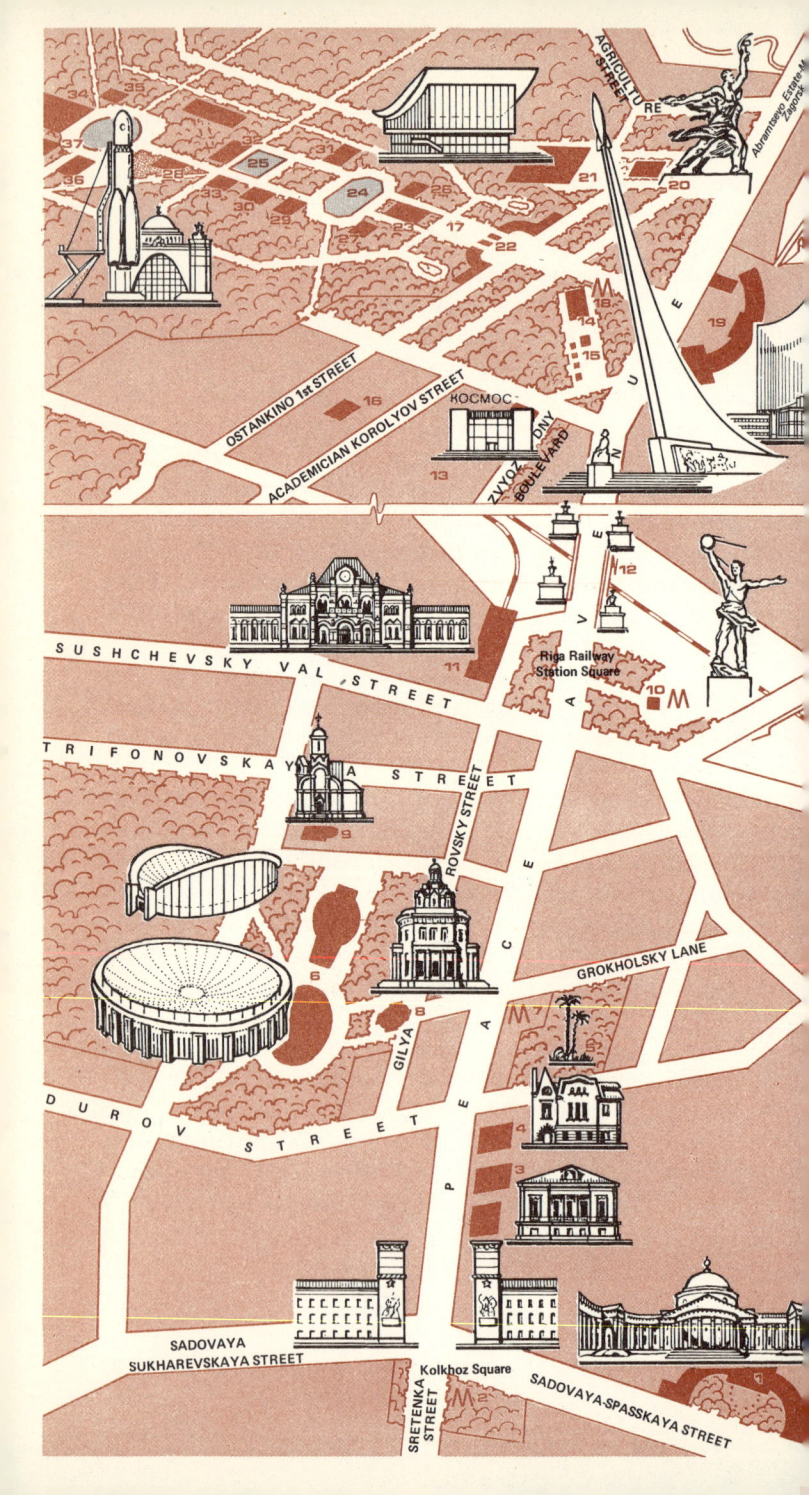

Abramtsevo Estate
Zagorsk

OSTANKINO 1st STREET

ACADEMICIAN KOROLYOV STREET

КОСМОС

ZVYOZDNY BOULEVARD

SUSHCHEVSKY VAL STREET

Riga Railway
Station Square

TRIFONOVSKAYA STREET

ROVSKY STREET

GILYA

GROKHOLSKY LANE

DUROV STREET

PEACE AVENUE

SADOVAYA
SUKHAREVSKAYA STREET

Kolkhoz Square

SRETENKA STREET

SADOVAYA-SPASSKAYA STREET

PEACE AVENUE–YAROSLAVL HIGHWAY TOWARDS VDNKH

1. Late 18th-early 19th century building
2. Kolkhoznaya Metro Station
3. Palace of Weddings (18th cent.)
4. Bryussov Flat-Museum
5. Moscow University Botanical Gardens
6. Sports complex—multi-purpose indoor stadium and swimming-pool
7. Prospekt Mira Metro Station
8. Church of the Metropolitan Philip (18th cent.)
9. Church of St. Trifon in Naprudnoye (15th cent.)
10. Rizhskaya Metro Station
11. Riga Railway Station
12. Krestovsky fly-over
13. Kosmos Cinema
14. Obelisk in honour of the Soviet cosmonauts. Cosmonautics Museum
15. Monument to Konstantin Tsiolkovsky. Cosmonauts' Avenue
16. Korolyov Memorial Museum
17. Exhibition of Economic Achievement (VDNKh)
18. VDNKh Metro Station
19. Kosmos Hotel
20. Sculpture "Worker and Collective Farmer"
21. Exhibition Pavilion at the VDNKh

EXHIBITION OF NATIONAL ECONOMIC ACHIEVEMENT

22. Main Entrance
23. Central Pavilion
24. "Friendship of the Peoples" Fountain
25. "Stone Flower" Fountain
26. Atomic Energy Pavilion
27. Education Pavilion
28. Mechanisation and Electrification of Agriculture Pavilion
29. Metallurgy Pavilion
30. Health Care in the USSR Pavilion
31. Culture Pavilion
32. Agriculture Pavilion
33. Radioelectronics Pavilion
34. Cosmos Pavilion
35. Electrification of the USSR Pavilion
36. Chemistry Pavilion
37. Transport Pavilion

Riga Railway Station Square

Riga Station which stands on Peace Avenue was built in 1899, and from here trains run to Riga, the capital of Soviet Latvia. The north wing of the station contains an exhibition of the history of rail transport in the USSR.

During the Soviet period the appearance of this station has changed beyond recognition. Between 1937 and 1940 the **Krestovsky fly-over** was built here to span the railway lines. In 1958 the **Rizhskaya Metro Station** was opened opposite the building of the main station. In front of the Metro station entrance is a sculpture symbolizing the launching of the world's first earth satellite, Sputnik, by the Soviet Union on October 4, 1957 (S. Kovner, sculptor and V. Kartsev, architect).

In 1975 a second **fly-over** was built to connect Peace Avenue with Sokolniki, the eastern district of Moscow.

Beyond Riga Station Square Peace Avenue follows the route of the former Yaroslavl Highway, which passed through what until recently were the suburbs of Moscow and where even as late as the 1930s there was not a single town house. Today the old suburban Moscow villages have been replaced with large modern housing estates.

Off to the left is **Godovikov Street**, along which run the blocks of one of the very first factories to be built during the Soviet period. This is the **Kalibr Factory**, which is now a major industrial enterprise turning out precise measuring and checking equipment. The factory is set amid green fields and flowers and here the workers have built a memorial Heroes' Avenue to honour those 700 workers from the factory who fought at the front during the Great Patriotic War. The bronze busts of five of them—I. Bochkov, S. Godovikov, I. Dokukin, D. Lebedev and V. Leonov all Heroes of the Soviet Union—have been set up in the avenue.

Beyond **Shcherbakovskaya Metro Station** Peace Avenue begins to go gently downwards. To the left on **Zvyozdny Boulevard** is the **Kosmos Cinema** (No 109) and ahead soaring up to the skies in a flash of silver is the 96-metre high **obelisk** of a space rocket, which was erected in 1964 **in honour of the Soviet cosmonauts**. The obelisk is made of silver titanium and the plinth on which it stands faced with granite and decorated with a bas-relief compositions on the theme of space exploration. Within the plinth there is a **Cosmonau-**

tics Museum. The obelisk was designed by M. Barshch, A. Kolchin, architects, and A. Faidysh, sculptor.

In front of the obelisk stands a **monument to Konstantin Tsiolkovsky**, the great Russian scientist and founder of space exploration.

On October 4, 1967 the tenth anniversary of the launching of the world's first artificial satellite by the Soviet Union, a special memorial known as the **Cosmonauts' Avenue** was opened. Here there are bronze busts of the pioneers of space flight: Yuri Gagarin, the first man in space, Valentina Nikolayeva-Tereshkova, the first woman-cosmonaut, Pavel Belyaev and Alexei Leonov, the first man to walk in space and Vladimir Komarov, who died heroically while on a space mission. At the entrance to the avenue, hewn from a granite slab, stands the bust of Academician Sergei Korolyov, chief designer of the first Soviet space craft. (The busts are by A. Faidysh, L. Kerbel, G. Postnikov and P. Bondarenko.)

Nearby on the corner of **Academician Korolyov Street** and **Ostankino 6th Lane** (No 2/28) a **Korolyov Memorial Museum** was opened in 1975 in the house where the great Soviet scientist lived. Here you can see Korolyov's study and look at photographs and other material relating to his work. There is also a film shown on Korolyov's life.

Beyond the space obelisk is the ceremonial arch, which stands at the main entrance to the Exhibition of National Economic Achievement.

Exhibition of National Economic Achievement

The Exhibition of National Economic Achievement is like a tour of the whole Soviet Union in miniature.

The exhibition covers an area of 280 hectares. The main pavilion—a three-tiered building 100 metres high with a flashing golden spire—was designed and built in 1953 by Ye. Stolyarov and Yu. Shchuko. It is on the list of architectural monuments protected by the state. The nine halls of this pavilion contain the main exhibits of the whole Exhibition. They show what the USSR has achieved in over six decades, the world historical significance of the October Revolution, the guiding and organizing role of the Communist Party and the selfless labour of the Soviet people in the building of communism.

Beyond the main pavilion lie 20 pavilions covering the various branches of socialist industry and transport together with a number of pavilions showing the development of agriculture. A special demonstration field, 22,000 square metres in area with stands for 2,000, has been built for the practical display of agricultural machinery.

The successes achieved by Soviet scientists can be seen in the Atomic Energy, Physics, Chemistry and Biology pavilions. Very popular among visitors is the Cosmos pavilion, in front of which stands a multi-stage launching pad carrying the famous spaceship Vostok, in which on April 12, 1961, Yuri Gagarin successfully completed the first manned space flight. The pavilion contains models of space stations and various other exhibits showing the achievements of Soviet rocketry and space exploration.

Culture and art in the USSR together with education, the health services, the press, radio, cinema and television are also covered in various pavilions.

There are more than 100,000 exhibits altogether showing the successes of the Union republics in all branches of the economy. Factories, power stations, mines, construction sites, transport departments, state farms, collective farms, research and design institutes, higher education establishments, schools, technical colleges and medical institutions all show their finest achievements.

Exhibitors are awarded a special medal (gold, silver or bronze), inscribed with the words "For National Economic Achievement". The work collectives receive a Certificate of Honour (1st, 2nd or 3rd class). In 1976 an All-Union Board of Honour bearing the names of the country's foremost work collectives was opened in the exhibition.

The main aim of the exhibition is to display the latest development in science, technology and culture and make available to the public the latest advances in scientific and technological thinking, which promote technical progress, raise productivity and help to fulfil and overfulfil the national economic plans. Every year the Exhibition of National Economic Achievement runs hundreds of smaller exhibitions, public demonstrations and seminars on important matters of economic and technological development.

But the Exhibition of National Economic Achievement is also an excellent place to spend one's leisure time. Here there are parks with trees and flowers, where it is wonderfully quiet, picturesque lakes with little islands reproducing the nature and appearance of the parks in the Union republics.

The exhibition is famed for its fountains. In Friendship Square, for instance, huge jets of water cascade down upon a golden sheaf of corn, the symbol of plenty, while fifteen women personifying the Union republics stand round in a circle. Another fountain, also in Friendship Square is called the "Stone Flower". Here a thousand jets of water set at different angles, make an indescribable play of colour as they spray a surface of semi-precious stones from the Urals, pouring out 1,200 litres of water per second. There is also an avenue of fountains running from the main entrance to the main pavilion.

There are cafes and restaurants here offering national dishes from the Union republics of the USSR, while amateur and professional entertainers from all over the country perform on indoor and outdoor theatres.

There are various forms of transport facilitating access to all parts of the exhibition, including electric trams and mini-buses. In winter there are sleigh rides for the children.

* * *

Peace Avenue skirts the south-eastern boundary of the exhibition. Here opposite the **VDNKh Metro Station** stands 27-storey building with a concave façade. This is the **Kosmos Hotel** for 3,500, which contains a hall of congresses (seating 1,000), 7 meeting halls, banquet chambers, restaurants, buffets, bars, a swimming pool, saunas, tenpin bowling and an underground parking lot.

The hotel was built by the French company SEFRI and Yugoslavian firm Komgrap under contract to Intourist and meets the highest standards of comfort. The project was designed by the Soviet architects, V. Andreyev and T. Zaikin and the plans drawn up by the French architects.

On the same side of Peace Avenue in the grounds of the old Alexeyevskoye village, which formerly belonged to the tsars stands a five-cupola **17th-century church**, the only building of the palace to have been preserved.

Further along Peace Avenue in front of the north entrance to the exhibition stands the classic composition, entitled **"Worker and Collective Farm Woman"** by Vera Mukhina, one of the masterpieces of Soviet pictorial art. Despite its vast size (some 25 metres) the sculpture seems light and full of dynamic energy. This was the first statue to be made in stainless, chrome-nickel band steel. It was shown at the 1937 Paris World Fair where it made a considerable impression. Press reports at the time said that the sculpture was a visible expression of the grandeur of the new socialist system.

Behind the monument is the largest building in the whole exhibition—the former Soviet pavilion at the Expo-67, in Montreal. Designed by M. Posokhin, A. Mndoyants and B. Tkhor the pavilion was brought from Canada to Moscow after the exhibition and is now one of the new sites of the city. The pavilion is 30,000 square metres in area and designed for major industrial exhibitions.

Further along Peace Avenue crosses the River Yauza by the **Rostokinsky Bridge**. Here in the depression that lies on the right you can see the old aqueduct, built almost 200 years ago. It is 356 metres long and with its 15 metres high supports, making it the largest stone bridge in Russia of its day. It now carries a pipeline.

Beyond the **Severyanin Railway Station**, which it crosses by means of a broad overpass, Peace Avenue becomes the **Yaroslavl Highway**. On the right-hand side from here to the outer ring road lie huge housing estates.

Babushkin and Medvedkovo

As you enter the district of Babushkin, which lies along the Yaroslavl Highway you can see the **Moscow Civil Engineering Institute**, which is easily recognizable from the round building which houses semi-circular lecture theatres and the 23-storey block. The complex also contains teaching blocks, student hostels and gymnazia.

The main street is named after M. Babushkin (1893-1938), the Arctic pilot who took part in rescue operations to save members of the expeditions on the airship *Italia* and the icebreaker *Chelyuskin* and the landing of the first floating Polar station on the North Pole. Between the Yaroslavl Highway and Babushkin Street, a number of research institutes and a printing technical college have been built.

Everything in this estate is new, and that includes the **New Drama Theatre** which is making a name for itself far beyond the confines of Medvedkovo and Babushkin.

The northern districts of Moscow contain many parks and here within the city limits lies a natural tract of forest that has been made into a **game reserve**. It is called **Elk Island** and runs in a long wedge between the Yaroslavl and the Shchelkovo Highway reaching as far as Sokolniki. Its overall area, including the region which stretches beyond the outer ring road amounts to some 11,000 hectares. Here the countryside has been preserved just as it was centuries ago.

The reserve is divided into three zones. The outer zone, which lies nearest to the housing estates is designed chiefly for leisure. Here you can go for walks through the woods, or sit with a book on a park bench. At the entrance to the zone (on the outer ring road near the village of Abramtsevo) there is a museum of environmental protection, environmental research centre with laboratories, a dendrological park, enclosure for wild animals and an excursion bureau.

The second zone is largely there to protect the inner zone, and here walking is only permitted along special routes.

The third zone has central, northern and eastern sectors. Here nature is left entirely to itself and protected from any interference by man. There are over two hundred species of animals and birds including dappled deer, wild boar, wild goat, and of course the king of the forest, the elk.

Visitors are allowed here only accompanied by a guide. There are special routes with observation hides and paths through the marshes so that tourists can see the wild life around them without disturbing the animals. Not only is hunting and felling forbidden but mushroom, flower and berry picking as well.

In 1978 the northern district of the capital was brought nearer the centre with the extension of the metro line eight kilometres from the VDNKh Metro Station and the opening of a number of new **stations, Botanichesky Sad, Sviblovo, Babushkinskaya, and Medvedkovo.**

Abramtsevo

60 kilometres along the Yaroslavl Highway. Trains from Yaroslavl Station

The estate of Abramtsevo, which is now a memorial museum, has twice been a centre of Russian cultural life. In the mid-19th century, when the estate belonged to the famous Russian writer Sergei Aksakov it was frequently visited by such personages as Turgenev, Tyutchev, Gogol and the actor, Shchepkin. After Aksakov's death in 1859, the estate was left empty, but in 1870 it received a new owner, the rich industrialist and patron of the arts, S. Mamontov. For many years a number of famous Russian artists and cultural figures like Repin, Serov, Surikov, Levitan, the Korovin brothers, Nesterov, Vrubel, Chaliapin, Stanislavsky, Yermolova, and Fedotova lived and worked here.

A small church was built here in the old Russian style which was designed by Polenov and Vasnetsov and ornamented by Repin, Polenov and Antokolsky. A fairytale "Cottage on chicken legs" was also built here designed by Vasnetsov. Many of the artists' works are on show in the museum including a number of interesting coloured majolica by Vrubel. The museum also contains memorial halls to Aksakov and Gogol.

Zagorsk

71 kilometres along the Yaroslavl Highway. Reached by bus from the city bus station and by train from the Yaroslavl Station

The Monastery of the Trinity and St. Sergius at Zagorsk is one of the most outstanding examples of old Russian architecture. The origins of the monastery date back to 1340 when it was an important fortress on the outer approaches to Moscow. It was prominent in many of the battles against the Tartar-Mongol invaders and from 1608 to 1610 withstood a 16-month siege by Polish and Lithuanian troops.

In the 16th-17th century the monastery was a major cultural centre where icon-painters, scribes, wood-carvers and other craftsmen worked.

In 1920 the monastery was opened as a museum. Moscow Theological Academy and the Theological College continue to function there.

As an architectural ensemble the monastery has no equal, being a harmonious combination of 14th-18th century styles. There is the whitestone **Trinity Church** (1432), the **Church of the Holy Spirit** (1477), the **Cathedral of the Dormition** (1559-1585), the **Hospital** (1637), the **Refectory** (1686-1692) and the fortress walls and watchtowers (1540-1550). The unique collection of icons includes works by Andrei Rublyov, and other 14th and 15th century masters.

Since the Revolution the small town of Zagorsk has been built up with a number of major enterprises and scientific and educational establishments. There is also a unique **Toy Museum** with a collection of Russian toys from ancient times to the present day.

Not far from Zagorsk is the village of Bogorodskoye famed for its wood carving.

The route to Zagorsk passes the **Russkaya Skazka** (Russian Fairytale) **Restaurant**, which motorists are well advised to try.

THE ROAD TO THE NORTH-EAST

Kirov Street–Komsomol Square–Krasnoprudnaya and Rusakov Streets–Sokolniki Square–Sokolniki Park–Stromynka and Bolshaya Cherkizovo Streets–Shchelkovo Highway. Golyanovo

The centre of Moscow is connected to its north-eastern districts by a lively thoroughfare, which begins at Kirov Street, between Dzerzhinsky and Komsomol Squares.

Kirov Street

Kirov Street is one of the main streets in the centre. It was renamed in 1935 in honour of Sergei Kirov, a prominent figure in the Communist Party and the Soviet state. The historical and architectural monuments of various epochs that are found on Kirov Street have made it one more of the city's protected areas.

Its former name, Myasnitskaya (Butchers' Street) goes back to the 16th century, when the quarter was full of butchers' shops and slaughter-houses.

During the 17th and 18th centuries nobles' houses, monastery hostels and churches began to be built here. Most of these buildings, which were wooden, were destroyed in the fire of 1812, after which they were replaced with one- and two-storey stone buildings. Later, in the late 19th century, the street became the business centre of capitalist Moscow, with banks, offices, shops and apartment buildings being put up here.

The early 18th century detached house at No 7, which was built by serf craftsmen, is one of the few buildings not destroyed by the fire of 1812. During the early 19th century it was the home of A. Chertkov, marshall of the nobility, connoisseur of Russian history, poetry and music and owner of a unique library of ancient books. Many writers and artists used to attend his literary soirées and Pushkin is known to have used his library and Gogol to have recited chapters of his *Dead Souls* here.

Today the building is occupied by the **Znaniye Society House of Scientific and Technical Information**. Here specialists in all fields give lectures on the latest advances in scientific and technological thinking, exchange experience with their colleagues and hold consultations.

The 18th century building at 4 **Krivokolenny Lane** (on the right of Kirov Street) was the home of the poet D. Venevitinov. Here on October 12, 1826 after his return from exile Pushkin read his new tragedy, *Boris Godunov* to a gathering of friends.

On the opposite side of Kirov Street is **Markhlevsky Street**, named after the Polish revolutionary and Communist. The ten-storey building at No 5 was built in 1904 to house the **Central Telephone Exchange** and was then one of the tallest buildings in Moscow.

In October 1917 the Telephone Exchange and Central Post Office (26A Kirov Street) were important strategic objectives. The fierce fighting that went on for possession of the buildings has produced some of the most heroic and glorious pages in the annals of the revolution.

Further along Kirov Street on the left-hand side is a building known as the **"Yushkov House"** (No 21), which is one of the few remaining works of the great architect, V. Bazhenov. The house was built in the late 1780s for a rich noble family. In 1844 the Moscow Arts Society acquired the building and opened up a school of painting, sculpture and architecture. The school's most famous pupils and teachers included Savrasov, Perov, Levitan, Shishkin and Serov. It was here in 1872 that the first exhibition was held of the Peredvizhniki School of painting, whose work was characterized by its realistic and democratic trends.

In 1918 the establishment was renamed the Higher Arts and Technical Workshop, and many now famous Soviet artists, sculptors and architects graduated from it. On February 25, 1921 the workshop was visited by Lenin and Krupskaya. Lenin spent three hours chatting to the students about art and literature. He asked them how they were getting on, looked at their work and answered their questions. According to Krupskaya, Lenin used to recall with great pleasure his meeting with the lively and enthusiastic students from the workshop. Later it became the **Surikov Moscow Arts Institute** and was moved to new premises.

For many years the house was practically hidden from view by the old buildings around it, but these have recently been pulled down and a public garden laid, which reaches as far as Turgenev Square. The old building has now been restored to its original appearance. A monument to the great Russian writer, Ivan Turgenev, is to be erected in Turgenev Square.

On the opposite side of Kirov Street (No 26A) is the **Central Post Office.** The building was designed and built in 1912 by O. Muntz and D. Novikov with the Vesnin brothers helping with the design of the façade. As compared with many early 20th century buildings, which are largely characterized by their motley styles, the Central Post Office is remarkable for its purity of line and strict proportions.

The part of Kirov Street which lies beyond the Boulevard Ring contains architectural monuments of both the past and the present.

The row of houses on the left-hand side (Nos 33-37) is comprised of early 19th century mansions built by Bove, who designed the Bolshoi Theatre and many other buildings in Moscow which you have already seen.

Further along at No 39 is one of Moscow's first "glass" houses, the work of the great French architect, Le Corbusier. The building which stretches along the whole block was built between 1929 and 1936 with the help of the Soviet architect, N. Kolli, and is one of the most interesting civic buildings of the period. Today it houses the **Central Statistics Board**. One of its façades looks out on to Kirov Street and the other on to the future New Kirov Avenue, which was included in the city's development plans as early as the 1930s.

A little further along at No 43 stands an 18th century manor house behind iron railings, built by the famous architect, F. Camporessi.

On the opposite side there are two more relics of the past. The first is a 17th century house concealed in the courtyard of a modern block of flats (No 40), and the second (No 42), built by Kazakov between 1797 and 1802, is a fine example of late 18th century Russian classicism. The central section with its elegant portico is set right back while the two side wings come forward to the line of the street and are connected by high railings so as to form an inner courtyard. Here in the winter of 1823-24 the great Russian writer, Griboyedov worked on his classic comedy, *Woe from Wit*, while staying with a friend who owned the house.

The building is now occupied by the **Central Institute for Scientific Research in Health Education,** whose work is concerned with one of the main branches of the Soviet health service.

The neighbouring side-street was renamed in 1960 in honour of **Griboyedov**, whose **monument** stands at the intersection of Kirov Street and the Boulevard Ring.

Kirov Street also has connections with Pushkin, for it was here that many of his friends lived.

At the end of Kirov Street near the Sadovoye Ring a building resembling a huge glass cube was recently built. This is the **Main Computer Centre of Gosplan** (No 45). Next door stands an administrative building, which was built in 1927 by B. Velikhovsky and is now occupied by the **RSFSR Ministry of Trade**. The main façades of both these buildings, like the Le Corbusier's house look on to the New Kirov Avenue.

The building of the New Kirov Avenue is one of the largest construction works in the centre of the city. Its first section starts at Dzerzhinsky Square and runs to the left of Kirov Street as far as Turgenev Square. From here it will run to Komsomol Square. On this section of the Avenue an impressive architectural composition is at present under construction. It will consist of three large, bright buildings, resting on a single four-storey, granite-faced stylobate and taking up almost the whole of the left-hand side of the street. These premises are to be occupied by a number of international banks: the **Vneshtorgbank of the USSR**, founded in 1924 and having more than 1,200 correspondents throughout the world, the **International Investment Bank**, founded in 1970 and the **International Bank of Economic Cooperation**, founded in 1963.

The whole project has been designed by a group of architects headed by D. Burdin, V. Nesterov and V. Talkovsky.

The side façade of the **USSR Ministry of Agriculture** built by Shchusev in 1933 and the 26-storey **Leningradskaya Hotel**, built in the 1950s by L. Polyakov and A. Boretsky will look onto the right side of the Avenue. All along the new Avenue spaces will be left between the buildings allowing visual access to Kirov Street. In this way the old architectural monuments will become an organic part of the new highway.

Komsomol Square

Komsomol Square (Komsomolskaya Ploshchad), or "Three Stations Square", as it is often called, is the city's main railway junction and is named in honour of the Komsomol members who built the first line of the Moscow Metro. The three stations here are Leningrad Station, Yaroslavl Station and Kazan Station.

Leningrad Station has recently undergone reconstruction. The old central section (K. Tom, 1851) has been extended with the addition of two side-wings containing modern passenger halls. This has resulted in an almost twofold increase in the overall area of the station.

Leningrad Station is also a building of historical and revolutionary interest. Here on the morning of October 25, 1917 the first report was received by railway telegraph of the beginning of the Great October Socialist Revolution. As soon as it was relayed to the Moscow Committee of the Party, the order was given for the Red Guard railway workers to take possession of the station. Here again on

March 11, 1918 the Central Committee of the Communist Party and the Soviet Government headed by Lenin arrived from Petrograd to take up their quarters in the new capital.

Yaroslavl Station was built in 1902 by F. Shekhtel and is the starting point for the Trans-Siberian Railway. The building itself is a stylized reproduction of an old Russian terem with its walls decorated in coloured tiles. In 1965-67 the building underwent reconstruction and enlargement. Its picturesque façade was left untouched, but a two-storey glass building was built on to the back near the platforms. In front of the station a **monument to Lenin** by A. Kibalnikov was unveiled in 1967.

Between these two stations stands the **Komsomolskaya Metro Station**, which is crowned with a helmet-shaped silver cupola surmounted by a spire with a five-pointed star. The splendour and magnificence of the underground hall with its high vaults supported by 68 dark-red marble columns and its grandiose mosaic ceiling panels by P. Korin give the impression more of a palace than a Metro station. The station was designed by A. Shchusev, V. Kokorin and A. Zabolotnaya.

Also on this side of the square is a new building, the **International Post Office** (No 1A).

Almost the whole of the opposite side of Komsomol Square is taken up by **Kazan Station**, a remarkable architectural work by A. Shchusev. Building was begun on the station in 1913, and was finished in 1926. The architect has employed many of the techniques from traditional 17th century Russian architecture, particularly the use of whitestone moulding on a red façade. The building is surmounted by a multi-tiered tower. The internal decor makes extensive use of paintings and moulding, the best examples of which are to be found in the restaurant where the ceiling is covered with paintings by the well-known artist, Lansere. The station itself has also been enlarged in recent years.

A little further along on the same side of the square and almost exactly opposite the Yaroslavl Station is the **Railway Workers' House of Culture** (No 4). Its various amateur arts groups frequently tour the USSR and abroad.

Reconstruction work on Komsomol Square continues. The three railway stations are joined by underpasses, the traffic is to be channelled underground, and the square laid open to pedestrians only.

Krasnoprudnaya and Rusakov Streets

Both these streets continue the north-eastern highway.

In the mid-18th century **Krasnoprudnaya Street** was the scene of various popular festivities. But after the stations were opened here, small insalubrious houses began to be built. It was not until the 1930s when the reconstruction of the city began that decent blocks of flats were put up and a Metro line opened. A particularly extensive construction programme was undertaken here in the 1970s under the ninth and tenth five-year plans. A large shopping centre is under construction here and further along Krasnoprudnaya Street a 22-storey tower-block erected for the "Express" railway ticket office.

Rusakov Street (Rusakovskaya Ulitsa) was named in honour of I. Rusakov, the Bolshevik doctor, who was one of the organizers of the Soviet health service.

At the point where Rusakov Street becomes **Stromynka Street** work is underway on the construction of **Sokolniki Square**. Here an interesting architectural ensemble is being built. It will include the Intourist Hotel (accommodating 2,000), another hotel (for 1,500) and a large concert hall. On the other sides of the square there will be four groups of 16-storey apartment blocks with shops, cafés and various community service enterprises. Opening on to the central part of the square is a broad avenue of trees with fountains, flower beds and sculptural works. This avenue leads to the new palace of sport and Sokolniki Park of Culture and Rest.

Sokolniki Park

The park is almost 600 hectares in area. The name "Sokolniki", which means Falcon Park, derives from the time when the tsars used to come here with their falcons to hunt foxes and hares.

Tolstoy, Chekhov and Levitan have been inspired with the beauty of this park. Here before the Revolution the workers of Moscow used to hold illegal meetings and revolutionary gatherings.

Lenin visited Sokolniki on a number of occasions to speak at meetings and in the winter of 1918-1919 visited Krupskaya, who was convalescing at a Boarding School here after an illness. In

January 1919 Lenin attended a children's new year party, which was held at the school.

> All round the park there are forests. Its layout is designed like a fan with radial paths running out from the centre. Of particular note is the rosarium containing some 30,000 bushes of a hundred different types. The air around Sokolniki is fresh and bracing. In summer you can go for pleasant woodland strolls and in winter the park is full of ski-tracks and ice-rinks.

For almost 20 years now international exhibitions have been held at Sokolniki Park, the first of which was the USA exhibition in 1959 and the original pavilion from this exhibition still remains. Since the International Exhibition Complex is being built at Krasnaya Presnya, the pavilions at Sokolniki will be rearranged for the recreation of visitors.

Not far from the main entrance to the park at 16 **Sokolniki Rampart Street** (Sokolnichesky Val) there is yet one more new sports complex, the **Sokolniki Palace of Sports**. This huge hall with glass walls as high as a six-storey house has been designed for volleyball, basketball, hockey, figure skating and other sports. The stands can accommodate 11,000 and there are all the required facilities for training athletes as well as for the press, radio and television.

Stromynka and Bolshaya Cherkizovo Streets

At the entrance to **Stromynka** on the right is one of the first five workers' clubs to be built in Moscow, the **Rusakov House of Culture** (No 10), built by K. Melnikov in the late 1920s in the "industrial" style which was popular at the time. Standing next to it is a bright spacious pavilion, through the transparent walls of which a large sports hall (132 × 36 m) can be seen with a running track. This is the **Winter Athletics Stadium**, which is **named after the Znamensky brothers**, famous Soviet sportsmen.

Stromynka ends at the bridge across the Yauza. Here on either side run the granite walls of the **Rusakov** and **Preobrazhensky Embankments**, built up with blocks of flats. Before the Revolution the area beyond the river belonged to the tsars' village of Preobrazhenskoye.

THE ROAD TO THE NORTH-EAST
KIROV STREET–SOKOLNIKI

1. Znaniye Society House of Scientific and Technical Information (18th cent.)
2. Yushkov House (18th cent.)
3. Monument to Griboyedov
4. Urban Mansion (early 19th cent.)
5. Urban Mansion (18th cent.)
6. Leningradskaya Hotel
7. Kirovskaya Metro Station
8. Turgenevskaya Metro Station
9. Komsomolskaya Metro Station
10. Leningrad Railway Station
11. Yaroslavl Railway Station
12. Kazan Railway Station
13. Railway Workers' House of Culture
14. Sokolniki Palace of Sports
15. Krasnoselskaya Metro Station
16. Sokolniki Metro Station

ROSTOKINSKY PASSAGE

YAUZA

STROMYNKA STREET

BOGORODSKOYE HIGHWAY

Sokolniki Park

Sokolniki Square

RUSAKOV

SOKOLNIKI RAMPART STREET

STREET

KALANCHEVSKAYA

NEW KIROV AVENUE

SPASSKAYA STREET

STREET

PRUDNAYA STREET

KRASNO

Komsomol Square

ЦДКЖ

Lermontov Square

NOVORYAZANSKAYA STREET

NOVAYA

BASMANNAYA STREET

SADOVAYA-CHERNOGRYAZSKAYA STREET

Stromynka Street—Shchyolkovo Highway

17. Rusakov House of Culture
18. Winter Athletics Stadium named after the Znamensky brothers
19. State Republican Young People's Library
20. Preobrazhenskaya Ploshchad Metro Station
21. Lokomotiv Stadium
22. Sports Complex of the Central Institute of Physical Culture
23. Shchyolkovskaya Metro Station
24. Exhibition Hall of the USSR Union of Artists
25. Bus Terminal
26. Sofia Cinema
27. Lermontovskaya Metro Station
28. Monument to Lermontov
29. Monument to Dzerzhinsky
30. Monument to Krupskaya
31. Church of St. Michail the Archangel (Menshikov Tower)

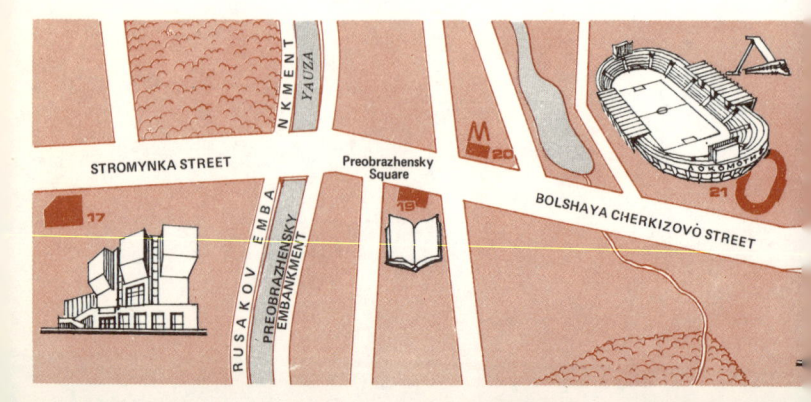

In 1657 the Tsar Alexei Mikhailovich built a wooden palace here in which he spent the summer months with his family and hunted in the neighbouring woods. His son, the future Tsar Peter the Great, used to play soldiers here and on the banks of the Yauza built a "toy" fortress with a genuine earth rampart, walls and towers.

On the far side of the bridge is **Preobrazhensky Square**, the central square in this large district, from which **Bolshaya Cherkizovo Street** runs through what was once the village of Cherkizovo. During the last 15 years the small houses with their little gardens and fences which once littered the area have been replaced by blocks of modern flats and tall civic buildings which stand on either side of the new highway. The new buildings include the **State Republican Young People's Library** (No 4), the **Sevastopol Cinema** (No 93), by the side of the Cherkizovo Lake and new **Lokomotiv Stadium** (No 125A) which can seat 40 thousand. Also by the side of the lake is a 17th century church.

Shchelkovo Highway

Until recently this was just a narrow country lane. Now beyond the overpass across the railway line it runs to the outer ring road as a modern dual carriageway with an avenue of trees down its centre. On both sides of the highway there are massive construction projects underway.

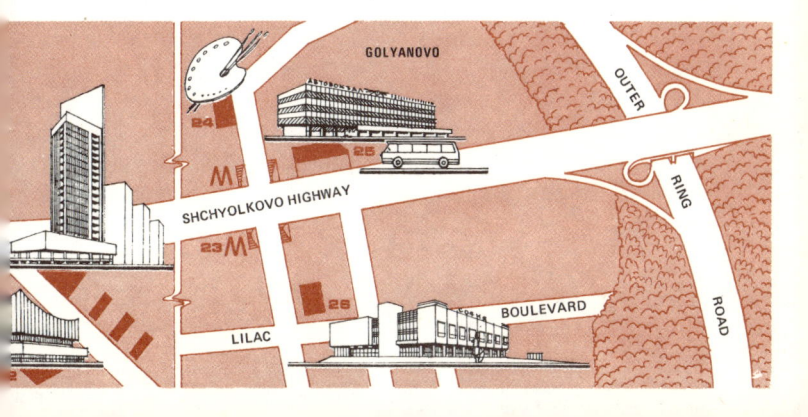

On the right, where the highway branches off to **Lilac Boulevard** (Sirenevy Bulvar) is the huge 28-hectare **sports complex of the Central Institute of Physical Culture** (Izmailovsky Park Metro Station), which was built by a group of architects headed by B. Iofan. This impressive architectural composition, which includes a track-and-field stadium, gymnazia and administrative buildings stretches half a kilometre along Lilac Boulevard. The sports complex contains 16 training gyms, a universal sports hall with stands for 5,000, a heavy athletics stadium, training rinks for hockey and figure skating, and indoor swimming and diving pools. There are also lecture theatres, a library with a reading-room, assembly hall and laboratories, as well as football fields, tennis courts, and other sports grounds. The complex was one of the Olympic centres in Moscow.

Over the last ten years a new housing estate, **Golyanovo**, has sprung up on the left-hand side of the Shchelkovo Highway. Its north-easterly position relative to the city centre has determined the names of its new streets, which are called after north-eastern regions of the Soviet Union such as Amur, Tagil, Baikal, Altai, Ussuri, and Kamchatka. Already more than 100,000 people live here. On **Urals Street** (Uralskaya Ulitsa), the main street in the district, the **Exhibition Hall of the Union of Artists of the USSR** (No 6), which is second only to the Manege in the city centre, has recently been opened.

The **Shchelkovskaya Metro Station**, which has been built on the Shchelkovo Highway, is 23 minutes from the centre. Nearby there is also a **bus terminal** and the **Sofia Cinema** (1,600 seats) on 31 Sirenevy Boulevard.

Golyanovo takes great pride in the forest reserve which lies immediately to its north. This is "Elk Island". (See Chapter *Peace Avenue*.)

Not far from the city's outer ring road you may suddenly catch sight of the glass walls of a building which looks like a fairy-tale palace. But this palace was built for a 20th century muse, the television. It is in fact the **Khromatron Factory**, which produces cathode ray tubes for colour television sets. With no smoking chimneys and no noise coming from the benches, the factory is a model of modern industrial design and high quality production methods.

THE ROAD TO IZMAILOVO

Bogdan Khmelnitsky Street–Chernyshevsky Street–Karl Marx Street–Novaya Basmannaya Street–Spartak Street–Bakunin Street–Bauman Street–Lefortovo–Izmailovo

Bogdan Khmelnitsky and Chernyshevsky Streets

This part of Moscow is one of the largest protected areas in the city. The very layout of the streets here with their twists and turns and ups and downs, determined by the geography of the district, is in itself a fine example of early Russian town planning. The buildings here span many centuries. There are 16th and 17th century houses, old churches, mansions, the two-storey merchants' shops of 19th century Moscow, rebuilt after the fire of 1812, and the relatively large office blocks of the late 19th and early 20th centuries. The considerable restoration work that is

311

being carried out here, is aimed not only at the preservation of individual buildings, but of whole streets in their historical setting.

In the 17th century **Bogdan Khmelnitsky Street** was called Maroseika or street of the Ukrainians *(Malorossy)*, for here there was a Ukrainian hostel, at which the hetmans' representatives used to stay. The liberation struggle of the Ukrainian people against Poland in 1648-54 for reunification with Russia was led by the Hetman Bogdan Khmelnitsky and in 1954 the street was renamed after him to mark the 300th anniversary of the reunification treaty.

The first house on the left is the only building on the street from the Soviet period. It was built in the 1920s and now houses the **Central Committee of the All-Union Leninist Young Communist League** (Komsomol). (You will have seen this building from Dzerzhinsky Square and New Square.)

On the left-hand side of the street stands the 17th century **Church of St. Nicholas in Blinniki** (No 5), which has been recently restored.

On **Bolshoi Komsomol Lane** which runs off to the left in the direction of Kirov Street is a three-storey building on the corner (No 11). This was built in the mid-18th century as a development of the single-storey 17th century **Ukrainian Hostel.**

One more monument of architectural interest is No 17. This late 18th-early 19th century house once belonged to P. Rumyantsev-Zadunaisky, a prominent field marshal, and later to his son, N. Rumyantsev, whose book collection formed the basis of the Rumyantsev Museum and library, which is now the Lenin Library. The building of the house was a joint project of two great Russian architects, Bazhenov and Kazakov, with the former designing the plans and the latter carrying out the building and interior decor. Unfortunately during the late 19th century the house was partially rebuilt. Today it houses the **Byelorussian SSR Legation.**

To the right of Bogdan Khmelnitsky Street is a warren of side-streets, all included in the protected area. The first of these, **Arkhipov Street,** was renamed in 1962 in honour of Arkhipov, the well-known realist painter, who lived at No 4 (Kazakov, 18th century). Here at No 8 is the **Moscow Choral Synagogue**.

4 Petroverigsky Lane, the next side-street on the right, once belonged to I. Turgenev, the chancellor of the University of Moscow and later to the Botkins, a family of social progressives. Many of the greatest figures of Russian 19th century culture, like Belinsky, Gogol, Herzen, Ogarev, Ostrovsky, Nekrasov, Turgenev and Tolstoy, at one time or another visited this house. It now houses the **Moscow Council for Tourism.**

The neighbouring buildings are taken up by the **Meditsina Publishing House** (No 6/8) and the **Institute of Cardiology** (No 10), which is named after the famous specialist, Professor A. Myasnikov. In 1973 a **monument** to this great doctor (sculptor M. Olenin) was erected at the entrance to the institute.

Further along is **Starosadsky Lane**, where on the corner with Bogdan Khmelnitsky Street stands the recently restored **Church of Sts. Cosmas and Damian** (1795) by Kazakov. The church is in the form of an elegant rotunda with smooth, plane walls. On the left of Starosadsky Lane there is a late 18th-early 19th century mansion (No 5) consisting of a central block, two wings and a north block.

The 19th century building at No 7 is the **Diafilm Studios**, which annually produce some 20 million black and white and coloured slides, including slides on literature, the arts and other visual aids for colleges and schools as well as fairy-tales for children.

No 9 is the **State Historical Library**, which has some two and a half million volumes.

Running downhill from Starosadsky Lane is **Zabelin Street**, renamed in 1961 after a famous connoisseur of the history, archeology and life of Moscow. On its higher side, which is called the Ivanovskaya Hill, stands the **Ivanovsky Convent** (No 4), which was founded in 16th century. During the 17th and 18th centuries the convent was used as a secret prison, where famous prisoners of state were held. The preserved to date several monastery buildings replaced the original ones in 1861-1878.

Armenian Lane (Armyansky Pereulok). Here in the late 18th century house at No 11 was the family home of Fyodor Tyutchev, great Russian poet, where he spent his childhood and university years.

The name of the street derives from the Armenian colony which settled here in the 18th century. The house with the large courtyard, several wings and surrounded by railings (No 2) was built in the early 19th century by the Lazarevs, who founded here the Armenian College and the Institute of Oriental Languages. In the courtyard there is a monument to the Lazarevs. Today the building is occupied by the **Armenian SSR Legation**, the **Oriental Literature Publishing House** and the **Institute of Oriental Studies of the Academy of Sciences of the USSR.**

Beyond Armenian Lane Bogdan Khmelnitsky Street becomes **Chernyshevsky Street**, which was renamed in 1940 after the great Russian revolutionary democrat, literary critic, writer and materialist philosopher, Nikolai Chernyshevsky to mark the 50th anniversary of his death.

Here among the buildings of the more distant past there are quite a number of early 19th century two-storey buildings, which were built when the street began to acquire a commercial character. The ground floors of these buildings, which were formerly occupied by merchant stalls, are now the premises of small shops, cafes, repair shops and boutiques etc.

Off to the right on **Kolpachny Lane** is the 17th century house of the hetman, Ivan Mazepa (No 10) and various other 17th and 18th century buildings (courtyard of No 6). Since 1941 No 5, an early 20th century building, has been the offices of the **Moscow Committee of the Komsomol**, and it was from here in that same year that many of the city's sons and daughters set out for the front at the outbreak of the Great Patriotic War. Today Komsomol members depart from here to work on important construction projects. The city branch of the Komsomol has already won three state awards. The Moscow Committee Roll of Honour that is kept here includes the names of the hero-cosmonauts.

Kolpachny Lane leads into **Podkopayevsky Lane**. Here at No 5/2 is one of the oldest stone civic buildings outside the Kremlin—the **House of the Boyars Shuisky** (16th-17th century). Also leading off Kolpachny Lane is **Khokhlovsky Lane**, where settlers from the Ukraine built the **Trinity Church in Khokhly** (1696). It is brightly ornamented in coloured tiles, the work of the Byelorussian master, Stepan Polubes.

Higher up the lane is the **large stone 17th century house** (No 7) that once belonged to the prominent diplomat, Ye. Ukraintsev. He has gone down in history as the man who brought Pushkin's ancestor, Ibrahim Hannibal, to Russia from Ethiopia. In the late 19th century the house was bought by P. Yurgenson, the owner of the largest musical publishers in Russia. Yurgenson published the majority of the works of Tchaikovsky and the great composer often had occasion to visit this house.

Back on Chernyshevsky Street beyond the Boulevard Ring is a mid-18th century building, which with its bright azure walls and white ornamental moulding, its colonnaded porticos and sculptural embellishments, and its windows of various shapes and sizes immediately catches the attention. This is a remarkable example of Russian baroque created by an unknown architect.

Also noteworthy here is the former **Church of the Resurrection in Barashi** (No 26) with its magnificent ornamentation. The name of the church is derived from the word meaning "tent-maker", for here from the 15th to the 17th century lived the tsar's tent-makers. The church was built in 1734.

At the intersection of Chernyshevsky Street and the Sadovoye Ring **Novorossiisk** twin-studio **Cinema** was opened in 1977. It is set in a small garden and has been made to fit in with the older buildings surrounding it.

Karl Marx Street, Novaya Basmannaya Street, Spartak Street, Bakunin Street

These streets lying beyond the Sadovoye Ring form the next part of the itinerary.

In the 17th century this region was known as the German settlement and was largely inhabited by immigrants. During his youth Peter the Great frequently visited the area and later moved the royal residence here. The tsar was soon followed by the nobility and the area soon began to develop as the new aristocratic region of Moscow with all the prominent noblemen and generals building their palatial mansions here. These were later succeeded by the rich merchants and factory-owners. By the late 19th century various industrial enterprises had begun to spring up along the Yauza bringing with them the inevitable hovels and shacks of a typically 19th century workers' district.

In recent years a lot of building has been going on in this area with new high-rise blocks replacing the older buildings. But great care has been taken to preserve all monuments of architectural and historical value, especially those connected with the Revolution.

On the corner of **Karl Marx Street** and **Gorokhovsky Lane** there is a late 18th-early 19th century **mansion** and a **17th century house** (No 6). Next door, at No 3, stands another early 19th century **mansion**, of which the main structure and part of the old railings have been preserved. Opposite at No 4 is the former mansion of I. Demidov, the Urals mine-owner, which was built in the late 18th century by Kazakov in the style of Russian classicism. In the 1960s restoration work was carried out on the magnificent interior decor of the "Golden Rooms" as they are called which were designed by Kazakov and ornamented by serf goldsmiths.

The building now houses the **Institute of Geodesic Engineering, Aerial Photography and Cartography.** The institute has two other blocks also on this street—a 17-storey student hostel and a large laboratory wing. The institute also occupies another interesting historical building on Karl Marx Street (No 23), which once belonged to I. Muravyov-Apostol, the father of the Decembrist Muravyov-Apostol brothers. Wooden buildings like this once lined the whole street in the 18th century, but this is one of the few that has remained.

Opposite the entrance to Gorokhovsky Lane, on the other side of Karl Marx Street is a group of **16th-18th century** buildings that once formed a **town manor** (No 15). The grounds of the manor and the neighbouring gardens were joined together in the 1920s to form what is now the **Bauman Gardens.** Today the gardens have been enlarged and a concert hall and a number of other buildings built here.

Further along is the 18th century **Church of Nikita the Martyr** (No 16), which was built by D. Ukhtomsky and includes part of the earlier 17th century church.

Off to the left lies **Novaya Basmannaya Street**, which is included in the protected area as one of the few streets in Moscow that is entirely built in the same style, in this case late 18th-early 19th century Russian classicism. In the 17th century this area was part of huge monasterial grounds, but at the end of the century Peter the Great built an estate here for the officers of his new regiments and travelled by this road from the Kremlin to Preobrazhenskoye village.

The town manor with its well-preserved main buildings and annexes (No 26) is the work of Kazakov. Since 1873 it has housed the **Basmannaya Hospital**, the premises of which have been significantly extended in the Soviet period.

The small house with the classical style portico on the opposite side of the street (No 27A) once belonged to the family of Sofia Perovskaya, the Russian revolutionary and one of the founders of the "Narodnaya Volya" (People's Will) organization.

No 19 is the offices of the **Khudozhestvennaya Literatura** (Fiction) **Publishing House**, which publishes the works of writers from the Soviet Republics and from abroad. Each year it puts out 400 different titles with a total circulation of 100 million copies.

On the same side of the road is the building of the former **Church of Sts. Peter and Paul** (No 11), built between 1705 and 1717 and designed by Peter the Great himself (the architect is thought to be I. Zarudny). The bell tower was built in 1740-1744. The forged railings which encircle the church are particularly fine.

Nos 4 and 6 are part of a **town manor** built in the late 18th century by Kazakov. Here the original façade of the central building with its six-columned portico has remained almost intact.

At the intersection of Karl Marx Street and Novaya Basmannaya Street is a small square that still bears the name Razgulyai. Facing on to the square is a large stone house with a monumental classical portico, which was built by Kazakov in the late 18th century. This is the former residence of the famous archaeologist and bibliophile, Count A. Musin-Pushkin, who discovered and subsequently published that magnificent work of Old Russian literature *The Lay of Igor's Host*.

From here Karl Marx Street becomes **Spartak Street** (Spartakovskaya Ulitsa), where reconstruction work is nearing its completion. It is now wider, brighter and more elegant, and far more shops have been built here. On the left-hand side there are a number of late 18th-early 19th century houses (Nos 3, 7, 9, 11). Beyond these stands the largest church in Moscow—the **Cathedral of the Epiphany**, (No 15) built by Ye. Tyurin between 1837 and 1845 on the basis of the original 18th century church. Tyurin's intention, it was claimed, was to build a church similar to St. Peter's in Rome, but with a five-cupola top. Among the items of interest inside the church is the registry book which contains an entry on the birth of Pushkin.

A little further along and you come to **Bauman Square**. Here in 1931 a **monument** was erected **to Nikolai Bauman**, a professional revolutionary and prominent member of the Communist party, who helped organize the distribution of Lenin's revolutionary paper, *Iskra*. On October 18, 1905, Bauman was traitorously shot by a police agent while leading a demonstration of several thousand workers to the Taganka Prison in order to set free political prisoners. The bronze statue is set on a granite pedestal, which contains bas-reliefs depicting episodes from Bauman's short but heroic life. The monument was designed and built by B. Korolyov.

At the end of the street is **Moscow Puppet Theatre** (No 26) which is very popular among young Muscovites.

Spartak Street leads into **Bakunin Street**, named in honour of the Russian revolutionary, Mikhail Bakunin, who participated in many of the revolutionary events that took place in 19th century Europe. Today 12- and 16-storey blocks of modern flats and offices have replaced the old wooden buildings that used to be here. The 17th century **Church of Intercession in Rubtsovo** has been recently restored and made over to the **RSFSR State Chamber Music Choir** as a rehearsal hall.

Bauman Street and Lefortovo

Bauman Street turns off to the Yauza at the point where Spartak Street becomes Bakunin Street. A memorial plaque outside No 60 marks the place where Bauman was shot.

The street used to be the main road of the old German settlement, which was divided by a network of side-streets into blocks of small wooden houses with little gardens, high above which were the huge Lefortovo Palace on the same bank of the Yauza and the Golovin's Palace on the opposite bank. That at least is how the area was depicted on an early 18th century engraving.

Today the Yauza embankments—Golovin, Rubtsovo, and Lefortovo—are faced with granite and built up with multi-storey blocks of flats and offices. Bauman Street is being widened with many of the old buildings that have remained from the pre-revolutionary factories and workshops being pulled down, and new apartment blocks built, the factories themselves being moved out into the industrial estates, which lie right outside the residential areas. Here clean, new, noise-free and smokeless factories are being built.

The old German settlement today is now one of the city's centres of learning with several higher education establishments being located here. Among the oldest institutes in Lefortovo is the **Central Aerodynamics Institute**, which was founded soon after the Revolution by Nikolai Zhukovsky, the "father of Russian aviation" and his pupil, Chaplygin, according to a project approved by Lenin. It was here that the first Soviet aircraft were designed. At No 17 **Radio Street** at the bottom of Bauman Street is the **Zhukovsky Memorial Museum.** A memorial plaque outside the house on the corner of Radio Street and the **Tupolev Embankment** commemorates the fact that the great aircraft designer, Andrei Tupolev, who built the famous TU airliners worked here for many years.

On Bauman Street there is a monument of great significance for lover of Russian literature. On the façade of the school building is a plaque which reads: "Here stood the house, in which on May 26 (June 6), 1799 Alexander Pushkin was born." In front of the school is a **bronze bust** of the poet by Ye. Belashova.

Despite all the changes that have taken place here, the layout of the original German settlement, curving as it does around the Yauza, has been partially preserved as have a number of the original buildings. One of these is a detached 17th century brick house with curved whitestone columns at its corners and a wooden mansard. This is the "House of Anna Mons" (6 Starokirochny Lane). It is connected with the romantic story of the love affair between Peter the Great and the beautiful daughter of a German wine trader, Anna Mons.

Bauman Street ends near **Lefortovo Embankment** with **Bauman 2nd Street** and **Lefortovo Square** running to the left of it.

Bauman 2nd Street, on which there are two palaces, is also part of the protected area.

Lefortovo can be considered Peter the Great's first attempt at town planning, an art which he was later to develop to the full in the building of Petersburg, the city on the Neva.

The building of the **Lefortovo Palace** (No 3), which was a gift from the tsar to Admiral of the Russian Fleet, Franz Lefort, was designed by D. Aksamitov who made a successful combination of early 17th century architectural motives and the new elements of the classical style. The palace itself faces the Yauza. In front of it lies a large park with a lake and a canal which is continued on the far side of the river.

Building was begun in 1697 and completed in 1699. For many years it was the main residence of Peter the Great. Here he received diplomats, held banquets and receptions and put on theatrical performances.

In 1707 Peter the Great gave the Lefortovo Palace to his favourite Alexander Menshikov, who in 1708 surrounded the parade ground with stone buildings, whose ground floors were open arcades. This was the building of a new kind, the like of which Moscow had never seen before. Unfortunately during the 19th century the arches were covered with an outer layer of stone but the entrance arch to the palace has remained.

The palace today houses the Sound Archives as well as one of the most ancient archives in Russia, the Archives of Military History, which have been in existence since 1819.

Restoration work on the palace is still in progress.

Alongside the Lefortovo Palace a second palace was built around 1740 for a member of the Russian nobility. It is set in a park with ornamental grottos, lakes and fountains. The building was altered twice by Quarengi and in the late 18th century became the **tsar palace.** It was badly damaged in the fire of 1812 and rebuilt in 1827-1830 by Gilardi in the Empire style. In the attic of the main building there is a group of sculptural figures by Vitali.

Today the building (No 5) houses **Moscow Technical Institute** founded in 1832 and now named after N. Bauman. The teaching staff and students have included such famous engineers as Nikolai Zhukovsky, Andrei Tupolev and Sergei Korolyov.

The institute also has glorious revolutionary traditions. Here one of the first Marxist circles in Moscow sprang up and during the revolutionary events of 1905 the college was the Bolshevik centre in Moscow, for it was here that the Moscow Committee of the Party and its Military and Technical Bureau worked. In the assembly hall of the institute the working people of Moscow bid farewell to

Nikolai Bauman and it was from here that the two hundred thousand strong funeral procession set out.

During the Soviet period the original palace has had additional blocks built for the teaching rooms, laboratories, student hostels and a House of Culture.

The **Lefortovo Bridge** (Lefortovsky Most) was built in the 18th century to connect the Lefortovo Palace on one side with the Golovin's Palace on the other. Unfortunately, as a result of rebuilding and fires the latter has not remained. But you can see the large **Golovin Park**, which once surrounded the palace and which today still remains as a fine example of 18th century landscape gardening. As you go in the direction of the park along **Krasnokazarmyennaya Street**, which begins immediately beyond the Lefortovo Bridge, you can see what has been left of the old Golovin Palace (No 1) as well as the building of the Military Academy (No 2), built by Bove in the early 19th century.

The façade of the **Catherine's Palace** which is one of the largest 18th century buildings in Moscow (about 200 metres in length) faces on to the avenues of trees in the park. The palace was built by Antonio Rinaldi, Giacomo Quarengi and Francesco Camporessi. Quarengi built the magnificent loggia with its 16 Corinthian columns of natural stone which adorns the main façade.

The north-east edge of the park is skirted by **Hospital Street** (Gospitalnaya Ulitsa). Here stands the **Military Hospital** (1 Hospital Square), founded by Peter the Great in 1706, where the first Russian school of surgery was formed together with an "apothecary's garden" for growing medicinal herbs. The wooden buildings of Peter's time have long since been burnt down, and the central building you see today was built between 1797 and 1802 by V. Yegotov. The other buildings in Hospital Street were built in 1838 and the oldest building in the area which is located on the Yauza Embankment dates back to 1736.

To the right runs **Soldiers' Street** (Soldatskaya Ulitsa) where the soldiers of the Lefortovo Regiment used to be billeted. The tent-shaped church that stands at the entrance to the street is the **Church of Sts. Peter and Paul** built by Peter the Great in 1711 (No 4).

The old **Vedenskoye Cemetery** (formerly the German Cemetery), which is reached via **Hospital Rampart Street**, contains the graves of the Vasnetsov brothers, the artists, Prishvin and Seifullina, the

Map Labels

- BOLSHOY KOMSOMOL LANE
- ARMENIAN LANE
- CHISTOPRUDNY BOULEVARD
- BOGDAN KHMELNITSKY STREET
- CHERNYSHE...
- ARKHIPOV STREET
- PETROVERIGSKY LANE
- STAROSADSKY LANE
- KOLPACHNY LANE
- NOVAYA BASMANNAYA STREET
- BAKUNIN STREET
- SPARTAK STREET
- BA...MANSKY STREET
- RUSAKO...
- RADIO STREET
- LEFORTOVO EMBANKMENT
- YAUZA
- GOLOVIN EMBANKMENT
- RED BARRACKS STREET
- SOLDIERS STREET

ТУРИСТ

Bauman Gardens

KARL MARX STREET

CHKALOV STREET

GOR OKHOVSKY LANE

STREET

12

11

Театр Гоголя

15 M

M 31
Semyonovskaya Square

33

35

STREET IZMAILOVO HIGHWAY

M 32

MAY 1 STREET

Izmailovo Park

M 34

THE ROAD TO IZMAILOVO
BOGDAN KHMELNITSKY STREET–BAKUNIN STREET

1. Church of St. Nicholas in Blinniky (17th cent.)
2. Moscow Choral Synagogue
3. Moscow Council for Tourism
4. Church of Sts. Cosmas and Damian (18th cent.)
5. Diafilm Studios (early 19th cent.)
6. State Historical Library
7. Ivanovsky Convent (18th cent.)
8. House of the Boyars Shuisky (16th-17th cent.)
9. Trinity Church in Khokhli (17th cent.)
10. Palacial building (18th cent.)
11. Church of the Ressurrection in Barashi (18th cent.)
12. Novorossiisk Cinema
13. Institute of Geodesic Engineering, Aerial Photography and Cartography (18th-19th cent.)
14. Church of Nikita the Martyr (17th-18th cent.)
15. Kurskaya Metro Station
16. Khudozhestvennaya Literatura Publishing House
17. Church of Sts. Peter and Paul (18th cent.)
18. Cathedral of the Epiphany (19th cent.)
19. Moscow Puppet Theatre
20. Monument to Nikolai Bauman
21. Church of Intercession in Rubtsovo (17th cent.)

Lefortovo–Izmailovo

22. Baumanskaya Metro Station
23. Baumansky Market
24. Zhukovsky Scientific and Memorial Museum
25. Lefortovo Palace (17th cent.)
26. Moscow Bauman Technical Institute (17th-19th cent.)
27. Lefortovo Bridge
28. Catherine's Palace (18th cent.)
29. Church of Sts. Peter and Paul (18th cent.)
30. Palace of Water Sports
31. Elektrozavodskaya Metro Station
32. Semyonovskaya Metro Station
33. Izmailovsky Park Metro Station
34. Olympic Hotel Complex
35. Izmailovskaya Metro Station
36. Housing Estate of Izmailovo, 18th century, (bridge-tower, hunter's lodge, Church of Intercession)

writers and Gaaz, a well-known Russian doctor. Here too are buried the French pilots from the Normandy-Niemen Squadron, who died fighting fascism during the Second World War.

Izmailovo

Hospital Rampart Street ends at the junction between **Bolshaya Semyonovskaya Street, Izmailovo Highway** and **Semyonovskaya Square**, above which rise the tower of the **Main Computer Centre of the Central Statistics Board**. It contains a single computer system used by all the socialist countries and it is here that information on the national economy is processed.

The Izmailovo Highway leads to another of the city's Olympic zones. The **Palace of Water Sports** (27 Mironov Street) has existed for over 25 years. Now the complex has been reconstructed with an additional ten pools added (making a total of 15), some of which are international class 50-metre pools. For health purposes some of the pools are filled with water, which is very similar to sea water and which comes up through special holes one and a half kilometres deep.

Near the **Izmailovsky Park Metro Station** is the **Olympic Hotel Complex**, which can accommodate 10,000, and comprises five 30-storey buildings, with restaurants, a cinema and concert hall, dancing halls and an underground car park.

From the windows of the hotels there is a panoramic view of the vast Izmailovo park, which occupies an area of more than 1,500 hectares.

In the 17th century Izmailovo was a suburban royal estate. Here Peter the Great spent his childhood, sailing on the Izmailovsky Lake and on the Yauza in a homemade boat, which has gone down in history as the "father of the Russian navy". It was here too that Peter's young regiments which later became the first Russian regular army used to march.

Near the Olympic complex is the old Izmailovo estate set on an artificial island 34 hectares in area. The original wooden palace has not remained, but thanks to many years of restoration work which has only just been completed, ten old buildings have been restored to their former splendour. These include the palace gates, the bridge-tower, a number of houses, the hunter's lodge and the apiary. The unique **Church of Intercession** with its picturesque ornamental roofs designed like barrels, poppies and sheaves of corn and its central cupola which is as high as a five-storey house is particularly impressive. The church is now used as a concert hall. On the island you can also see early 18th century redoubts built by Peter.

Almost half the area of the forest-park is taken up with the **Izmailovo Park of Culture and Rest**, which was opened in the 1930s. The beautiful countryside here attracts millions of Muscovites, especially since you can get to Izmailovo from Revolution Square in 14 minutes by Metro. The park has recently had additions and improvements made to it. In summer there are five open theatres where professional actors and amateur arts groups perform. There are also a summer theatre, two cinemas, a circus, billiard halls, a sports village, a children's village, a slot-machine pavilion and a funfair. Izmailovo is also a favourite place for horse riding and in winter its snowy slopes are filled with skiers.

But Izmailovo's greatest beauty are its pine forest, groves of trees, woodland glades, and lakes where you can hear the song of the nightingale and feel yourself in the depths of the Russian countryside.

Beyond the park's northern boundary between the **Izmailovo Avenue** and the **Shchelkovo Highway** lies the huge **housing estate of Izmailovo**, building on which began immediately after the war. The district has a precise geometrical layout with Pervomaiskayas and Izmailovskayas Streets running from west to east, being intersected by 16 Park Streets running from north to south. The blocks of flats here are in different styles and show the way in which building changed and improved in Moscow during the postwar years.

SOLYANKA–ZAYAUZYE–ENTHUSIASTS HIGHWAY

Solyanka Street–Zayauzye. International Street, Upper Radishchev Street, Volodarsky Street– Ulyanov Street. Andrei Rublyov Museum of Old Russian Art–Ilyich Square–Enthusiasts Highway– Perovo, Ivanovskoye, South Izmailovo

This itinerary runs to the eastern boundaries of Moscow. From here the road continues to the ancient Russian towns of Vladimir and Suzdal.

Solyanka Street

This street has existed since the 14th century, but its name dates back to the 17th-18th centuries when here stood the royal salt factory which had the monopoly of the salt trade. Today a huge early 20th century apartment block (No 1) stands on the site of the old factory.

The monumental architectural ensemble in the Empire style with its eight columned portico and small central dome which stands on the right-hand side of the street is one of the finest works of Gilardi and Grigoryev, built in the early 19th century. The moulded bas-reliefs and friezes round the façade are by Vitali. Today the building houses the **USSR Academy of Medical Sciences**. The Academy controls 40 research institutes. It also organizes joint research projects between its own institutes and those abroad.

Set well back from its iron railings and reached by an avenue of limes is the former Children's Home. This major 18th century building in civic Moscow (built between 1764 and 1770 by K. Blank) was designed to care for 8,000 children of the poor. But so bad were the conditions in which the children lived that the institution used to be called the "death factory".

Today the old street is being widened and improved. New buildings are going up but the valuable architectural monuments of the past are being restored.

Solyanka once led to the Yauza Gates of the Bely Gorod. An idea of what it looked like at those times can be got from **Yauza Street** (Yauzskaya Ulitsa), which is no more than a block in length. Here the buildings have been preserved on the right-hand side only. On the left in front of the three bridges—the Bolshoi Ustyinsky across the River Moskva, the Maly Ustyinsky and the Astakhov across the Yauza—are a small square and gardens.

The **Astakhov Bridge** (Astakhovsky Most) replaced the old Yauza Bridge and was named in honour of I. Astakhov, one of the heroes of the revolution. A granite memorial plaque beneath his portrait bears the inscription: "Here on February 28, 1917 during a workers' demonstration Comrade Astakhov, a fitter at the Guzhon (now Hammer and Sickle factory) was brutally murdered by a police agent."

To the right of the bridge near the tall building on the Kotelnicheskaya Embankment the Yauza flows into the River Moskva. Here at the intersection of the ancient waterways and highways lies yet another **protected area**—the **Zayauzye**.

The Zayauzye

The five centuries of architectural monuments concentrated in this relatively small area and the twisting and turning streets that cover the sides of Taganka Hill have made the Zayauzye into a veritable open air museum.

Leading up from Astakhov Bridge is **International Street**. Here from the 15th to the 17th centuries lay the Blacksmiths' Quarter. During the 18th century the craftsmen began to be eased out by the merchants and industrialists. A typical building from this time can be seen at No 9-11, which was built for Batashev, the factory owner. Behind the richly ornamented gates and fretted railings which face on to the street is a large courtyard at the back of which stands the building with its portico and elegant side-wings. The house was built by R. Kazakov and M. Kiselnikov. In 1812 during the Napoleonic invasion Marshal Murat took up residence here and in 1876 the building was taken over by the **Yauza Hospital.**

International Street becomes **Upper Radishchev Street**. Here is the **Church of St. Nicholas in Taganka** (No 20), built by Osip Startsev in the late 17th century. To the right along the crest of the high bank of the River Moskva runs **Volodarsky Street**, where there are several unique architectural monuments. The first of these is the **Church of the Dormition in Gonchary** (No 29), a small red and white church with five bright blue cupolas covered with golden stars. The church was built in 1654 and the bell-tower added later in 1790. The façade of the refectory is finished in coloured tiles, the work of the Byelorussian master, Stepan Polubes.

Further down is a late 18th-early 19th century **urban mansion** (No 16), the gate columns of which have retained the features of 17th century Moscow baroque. Recent discoveries have turned up 17th century chambers within the main grounds. The buildings have been restored and are now occupied by the **House of Scientific Atheism**.

Another late 18th century **town manor** (No 12) is of interest for the fact that it was built by two great Russian architects, Bazhenov and Kazakov. At 6 Volodarsky street is yet another of the few ancient 16th century stone churches outside the Kremlin, the **Church of St. Nikita beyond the Yauza.**

Ulyanov Street — Ilyich Square

The Zayauzye is bounded to the north by **Ulyanov Street**, named in 1919 in honour of Lenin, who was born Vladimir Ilyich Ulyanov. It continues in the same direction as Solyanka running from Astakhov Bridge to Ilyich Square.

The first large building on Ulyanov Street is the **Foreign Languages Library** (1972) which stands on the bank of the Yauza. The 16-storey building contains books in 132 languages—the finest productions on the international book market. In addition the library receives copies of more than 5,000 periodicals from 92 countries and has book-exchange facilities with libraries, publishing houses, universities and institutes in 85 countries. The library has a particularly large collection of books on history, linguistics, literary criticism and classical and modern literature from all over the world. The Shakespearian collection alone numbers some 6,000 volumes. The reading-rooms can accommodate over 700. The library organizes evenings of foreign literature and culture, which enjoy great popularity in Moscow.

Almost all the rest of the buildings in this part of the street are late 18th-early 19th century. Of particular interest is the **Church of St. Simeon the Stylite** (No 10), built by Kazakov in 1798 in the form of an elegant two-tier rotunda with a dome and a four columned portico. There is also an early 19th century **town manor** (No 16).

Ulyanov Street passes beneath the Sadovoye Ring fly-over and rises uphill. Here at the end of the street on the left is a section of old 18th and 19th century Moscow which has survived intact and which now comes under state protection. At No 49, for instance, there are the fine azure-blue walls of a mid-18th century **manor house** with their decorative baroque ornamentation and prominent brick lintels. The neighbouring house (No 51) is 17th century. Here the old whitestone chamber and reception rooms on the first floor have been restored as have the façade and the front courtyard with its iron railings. The next two buildings (Nos 53 and 55) were once the homes of wealthy merchants and with their classical pediments, moulded ornamentation on façades and gates typify the building that took place in Moscow after the fire of 1812. This group of buildings also includes the **Church of the Metropolitan Alexei** on the other side of the road, which together with its beautiful three-tier bell-tower is considered by the Russian art historian, Igor Grabar, to be among the finest works of mid-18th century Moscow architecture.

You now come out into **Pryamikov Square** (formerly Andronyevskaya), which since 1919 has borne the name of N. Pryamikov, one of the active participants in both the 1905 and the 1917 revolutions, who was killed in 1918 in a skirmish with bandits.

Along the far side of the square on the high bank of the Yauza is the **Andronikov Monastery,** a unique architectural ensemble. The monastery was founded in 1360 as a fortress on the eastern approaches to Moscow. Here in 1380 the citizens of Moscow came out to welcome Dmitry Donskoi on his return after the victory at Kulikovo Field, which not only meant defeat for Mamai Khan and his hordes, but marked the beginning of the end of the Golden Horde and the liberation of the Russian and other peoples from the Mongol-Tartar yoke. Here in the monastery the soldiers who fell in the battle of Kulikovo are buried.

In the 14th century the monastery had a small wooden church with monks' cells and was surrounded by wooden walls. But in the about 1420s the Church of the Saviour was built in the monastery out of whitestone and this is now the oldest example of stone architecture in Moscow. Here during the late 14th and early 15th century the famous Russian icon painter, Andrei Rublyov, lived, worked and was buried. His icons and paintings are among the greatest works of art in the world. Towards the end of his life Rublyov painted the walls of the Church of the Saviour, but by the 17th century these had all been destroyed.

In the 1960s the Andronikov Monastery became the **Andrei Rublyov Museum of Old Russian Art,** devoted to Russian early and late medieval art and culture. The original appearance of the monastery has been restored. The Church of the Saviour bears witness to the high degree of craftsmanship in its unknown builders, for it shows an external compactness of form and purity of line and an internally interesting treatment of space with graded rising vaults.

Another ancient monument of considerable interest is the single-column Refectory (1504), which was built like the Palace of Facets in the Kremlin.

The other buildings include the late 17th-early 18th century three-tier church of the Archangel and the living quarters, walls, towers and main gates of the same period.

In 1967 a **monument to Andrei Rublyov** by V. Lenskaya, sculptor, and E. Yavorsky, architect, was erected in Pryamikov Square in front of the monastery.

From here we continue down **Tulin Street** towards **Ilyich Square**, formerly known as Rogozhskaya Zastava. This was one of the old workers' centres of Moscow and visited by Lenin on many occasions. On the eve of the 50th anniversary of the Great October Socialist Revolution a **monument to Lenin** (G. Iokubonis, sculptor, V. Chekanauskas and V. Belozersky, architects) was erected here.

In recent years Ilyich Square has been considerably widened. The old buildings have been demolished and replaced by 18- and 24-storey apartment blocks, large office buildings, places for entertainment and leisure, a big shopping centre and a public garden. Among the new buildings going up here is the House of Folk Arts and Crafts, which includes a folk art museum and a research institute of folk art. The square is to become a centre for the city's eastern planning zone.

Enthusiasts Highway

This 11-kilometre modern motorway runs straight as an arrow from Ilyich Square to the outer ring road. Before the Revolution this was the infamous Vladimir Road along which for several centuries Russian revolutionaries had marched to prison and exile in Siberia.

About one hundred years ago factories began to be built here and the whole area soon became one of Moscow's major industrial districts with its own vast marshalling yard, warehouses and the inevitable hovels of the workers. By 1905 it had become one of the revolutionary proletarian centres of Moscow and in January of that year in answer to the "Bloody Sunday" massacre in St. Petersburg when the soldiers fired on a peaceful demonstration the workers of the Guzhon (now Hammer and Sickle) factory went on strike.

In December 1905 barricades went up all over the district, and workers from the Guzhon factory took part in the fighting on the barricades at Presnya and the Sadovoye Ring. Again in October 1917 the workers from this area were active in the revolutionary battles.

Almost immediately after the Revolution the district began to change its appearance. The pitiful wooden huts of the workers that were without even the most elementary conveniences or any kind of greenery were pulled down in the 1920s and replaced with a new workers' estate consisting of 24 large blocks of flats with trees and gardens, children's playgrounds, a school and a clinic.

Today Enthusiasts Highway is lined with new housing estates with their gardens, broad streets, shops, cinemas, clubs and blocks of research institutes.

The old factories have changed beyond recognition and many new ones have been built. These new factory buildings are very modern in design and equipped with all the latest technology.

Immediately beyond Ilyich Square at the entrance to Enthusiasts Highway stands the giant **Hammer and Sickle Factory,** the front façade of which is 600 metres long. The huge edifice nearby is also part of the factory as is the elegant glass and steel building. The factory produces various types of quality steel, rolled steel and other metals.

Alongside the factory blocks is the **Hammer and Sickle Palace of Culture** (11/15 Volochayevskaya St.), whose amateur ballet company, which is formed entirely from factory workers, has been awarded the title "People's Ballet".

On the right is **Voitovich Street,** named after Vasily Voitovich, a hammerer who organized a detachment of the Red Guard and fell in the fighting in 1917. The factory where he worked is also named after him.

Further along on the right-hand side is the **Kompressor Factory Palace of Culture** (No 110/2) which is well known for its amateur opera group, drama company and choir. In the factory club there is a museum showing the development of the plant from a small, semi-handicraft workshop to a modern industrial enterprise. A memorial plaque outside the factory (on 5 Enthusiasts 2nd Street) states that "Here at the Kompressor Factory in the dark days of

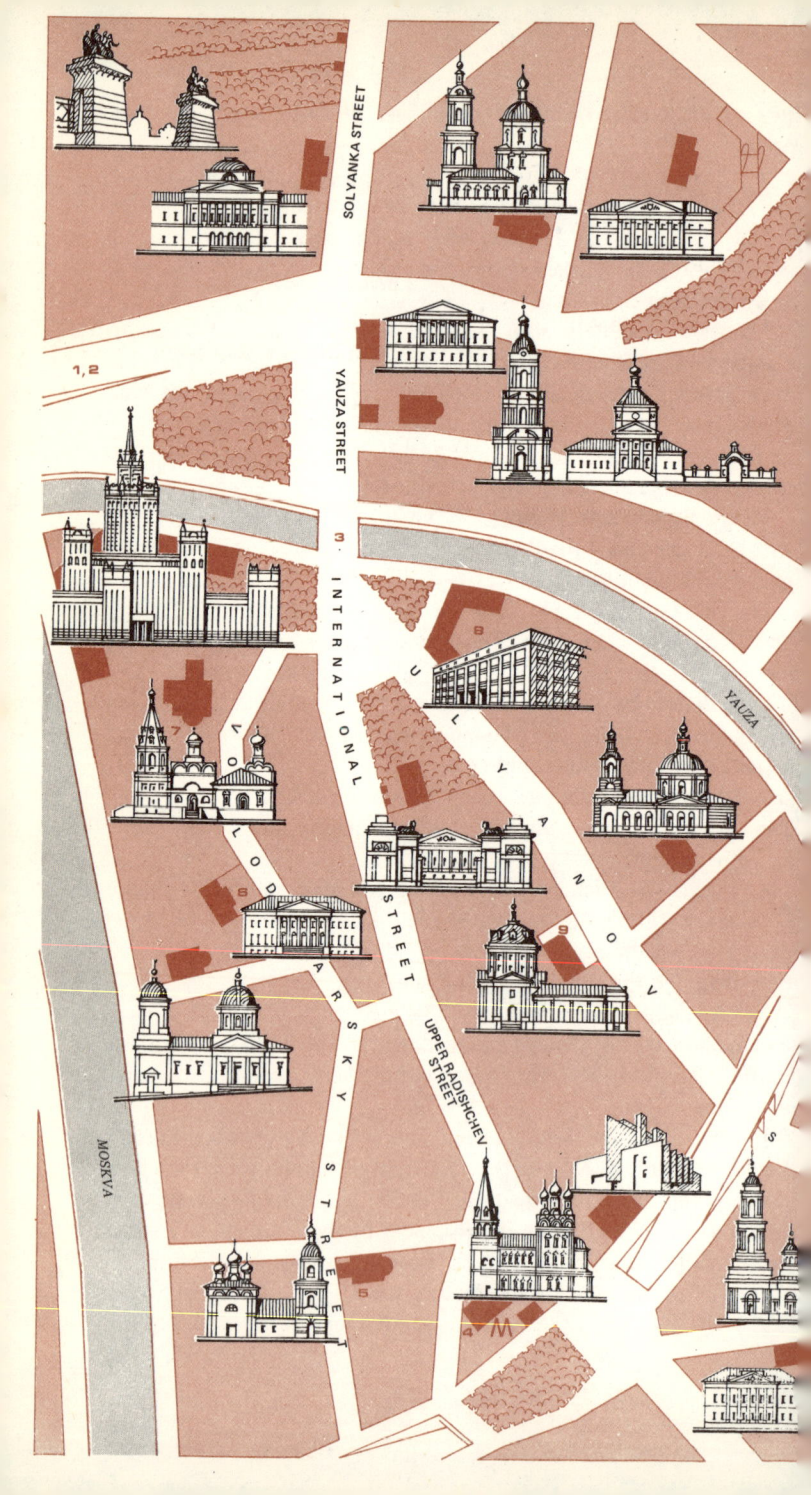

SOLYANKA STREET

YAUZA STREET

INTERNATIONAL STREET

ULYANOV

YAUZA

VOLODARSKY STREET

UPPER RADISHCHEV STREET

MOSKVA

1, 2

3

4

5

7

8

9

SOLYANKA STREET—ZAYAUZYE

1. Bolshoi Ustinsky Bridge
2. Maly Ustinsky Bridge
3. Astakhov Bridge
4. Church of St. Nicholas in Taganka (17th cent.)
5. Church of the Dormition in Gonchary (17th-18th cent.)
6. Urban Mansion (late 18th-early 19th cent.)
7. Church of St. Nikita beyond the Yauza (17th-18th cent.)
8. Foreign Languages Library
9. Church of St. Simeon the Stylite (18th cent.)
10. Church of the Metropolitan Alexei (18th cent.)
11. Andrei Rublyov Museum of Old Russian Art (former Andronikov Monastery, 14th cent.)
12. Monument to Andrei Rublyov
13. Monument to Lenin

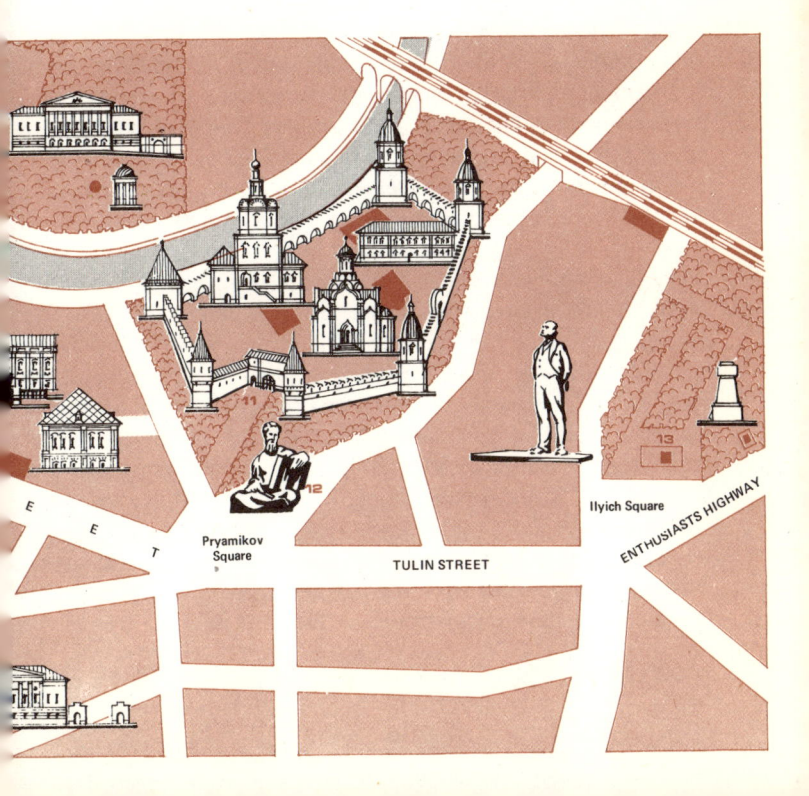

the Great Patriotic War the famous 'Katyusha' jet mortars were made which inflicted so much damage on the enemy."

Today the Kompressor Factory produces fridges and freezer equipment to international standards, and its products are known in many countries.

The new modern apartment blocks were built in this area for the workers of the Kompressor Factory.

On the left beyond the fly-over you can see the brick locosheds of the **Moscow Marshalling Yards**. On April 12 and May 10, 1919 the first Communist Subbotniks were held here at which without pay the workers mended railway engines that were so essential to the new Soviet Republic. Lenin warmly supported this initiative and in his work *A Great Beginning* he wrote: "The Communist subbotnik organised by the workers of the Moscow-Kazan Railway is one of the cells of the new, socialist society...".

This initiative, that was begun by the workers of Moscow in 1919 and described by Lenin as a great beginning has become part of the country's labour tradition. Every year on the Saturday in April that precedes Lenin's birthday tens of millions of people throughout the country including workers, office employees, schoolchildren, students and even pensioners, take part in a Communist Subbotnik in which they do a day's unpaid work. The proceeds of this labour go towards building kindergartens, sports stadiums, hospitals and various other establishments. The Marshalling Yard now has **"A Great Beginning" Museum** (8 Burakov Street).

For several kilometres beyond the circle line Enthusiasts Highway runs through the spacious green tracts of Izmailovo Park.

On the right-hand side a new district, **Perovo**, has been built with an administrative and social centre. The centre of Perovo has been planned as a parterre type park. It now includes a concert hall, several large shops, apartment blocks, a restaurant and cafés etc. Here around the streets and squares of Perovo you can see many works of the leading Moscow sculptors. In the central square there are mosaic steles depicting the most important events in the history of the Soviet Union. In 1979 the new **Perovo Metro Station** was opened.

In building the new blocks of flats and offices, the town planners have taken care to preserve the monuments of the past. Recently restoration work was completed on the **Church of the Icon of the**

Mother of God "The Sign" (1705) near Zelyony Avenue with its elegant cupola.

Near the outer ring road two more large housing estates, **Ivanovskoye** and **South Izmailovo**, have been recently built on either side of Enthusiasts Highway.

Work was begun on Ivanovskoye (on the right of Enthusiasts Highway) in 1972 and is now nearing completion. The estate is made up of three smaller residential districts with some 60,000 inhabitants. Bold use has been made of the natural landscape. At the intersection of the two main roads stands a two-storey complex of buildings which include a cinema, a department store, a restaurant, a library and a community services bureau.

Lying adjacent to Ivanovskoye is the Terletsky forest-park, which is part of an 17th-18th century estate. Here amid the ancient groves of trees and picturesque lakes, the pride of the district, there is now a recreation area with a stadium, swimming pool, beaches and facilities for boating. A broad pedestrian esplanade runs from the park to the district centre.

South Izmailovo, on the left of Enthusiasts Highway, has about 35,000 inhabitants. It wasn't until 1976 that the first streets appeared in the area but now there are 12- and 14-storey tower blocks planned in an original layout.

Such then are the "Eastern Gates" of Moscow in 1980. They stand a long way from that stone pillar in Ilyich Square (the former Rogozhskaya Zastava) which used to greet travellers at the eastern approaches to the city with the words: "Moscow. 2 Versts. 1783."

THE SOUTH-EAST

*Taganka Square. I. Taganka Street–Nizhegorodskaya
Street–Ryazan Avenue. Veshnyaki-Vladychino–
Kuskovo Estate-Museum–Vykhino.
II. Marxists Street–Krestyanskaya Zastava
Square–Vorontsov Street–Volgograd Avenue–
New Kuzminki–Kuzminki Park*

Taganka Square

Taganka Square (Taganskaya Ploshchad) is an important road junction. From here two main thoroughfares, Ryazan Avenue and Volgograd Avenue, run to the south-eastern districts of the city.

In the 15th century this area was inhabited by trivet makers (hence the name of the square which derives from the Russian word *tagan* meaning trivet), who produced their wares for the royal guards. In the late 18th-early 19th centuries when the artisans were being replaced by the merchants, Taganka became the centre of the bread trade. Architectural monuments of that time—stone and wooden detached houses in the Empire style—are still to be seen on Bolshaya Communist Street (Nos 2A, 4, 11, 13, 20).

Taganka Square also played its part in the revolutionary struggle of the Moscow proletariat. In 1905 meetings and demonstrations were held here and the workers had frequent skirmishes with the soldiers defending the local police station. In December of that same year barricades went up in the square. In October 1917 the district Soviet, the Military Revolutionary Committee and the headquarters of the Rogozhsky District Red Guard were located on Bolshaya Communist Street.

Taganka Square is undergoing reconstruction with its boundaries being extended. According to the development plans the southeastern side will be bounded by an architectural ensemble and in the centre of the square there will be gardens with fountains. Under the square a spacious hall is to be built with exits to all ten roads that meet here and platforms on three Metro stations.

Among the first reconstruction projects on the square was the **Taganka Theatre of Drama and Comedy** (76 Chkalov Street) which was rebuilt and extended. This new theatre—it celebrated its 15 anniversary in 1979—has acquired tremendous popularity through its new approaches to stage direction and its new treatment of modern and classical works.

I. TAGANKA STREET — RYAZAN AVENUE

Taganka Street

Taganka Street is almost one kilometre long. Before the Revolution it was a workers' district lined with small wooden houses, but today there are absolutely no traces left of these times. All along the street and around it there are modern blocks of flats.

Off to the left is **Comrades' Lane** (Tovarishchesky Pereulok), where in a new building at No 30 is the Moscow **State Art Institute** (Surikov Institute), recently moved from Kirov Street.

A memorial plaque outside 34 Taganka Street informs the visitor that here in July 1941 a division of the people's home guard was organized; it later formed the nucleus of that army division which was to perform so many splendid feats and reach Berlin.

Taganka Street leads into **Abelman Zastava Square**, named after N. Abelman, a Bolshevik who was killed here in 1918 while helping to put down a Left Socialist-Revolutionary uprising. Around the square there is an architectural ensemble consisting of 12-storey brick apartment blocks on protruding stylobates, which house shops, community services bureaux and a restaurant. Included in the overall composition of the square will be also flower beds, tree-lined avenues of the **Zhdanov Park of Culture and Rest** and an architectural monument, the **Pokrovsky Monastery**, after which the square used to be named. The monastery complex, which contains 17th, 18th and 19th century buildings will be used after restoration work is completed as concert and exhibition halls.

Nizhegorodskaya Street

Nizhegorodskaya Street runs from Abelman Zastava Square to Ryazan Avenue. On the right is the **Moscow Meat-Packing Factory**, where Hero of the Soviet Union, Victor Talalikhin worked until the outbreak of war. In August 1941 while defending Moscow during an air attack, Talalikhin was the first pilot in the history of aviation to ram an enemy plane during a night air-raid. Neighbouring **Talalikhin Street** is named after him.

On the other side of Nizhegorodskaya Street are a number of major industrial enterprises. These include the **50th Anniversary of the Establishment of Soviet Power Automated Plant.** In 1976 this factory built new premises for its Palace of Culture, where according to long established traditions the Mayakovsky Theatre stages its premières. The factory has had long and friendly contacts with the Mayakovsky Theatre which opened a branch theatre in the Palace.

Ryazan Avenue

Ryazan Avenue begins on the far side of the railway line. It is a broad highway that was built only some 15 years ago. On the left at its beginning are a number of industrial enterprises, some of which have only recently been built. There are also many new apartment blocks here built especially for the workers at these factories. In a relatively brief space of time Ryazan Avenue has been built up with new estates with their schools, clinics, shops and film theatres.

In 1974 two new bridges were built to take traffic on the Avenue across the Ryazan and Gorky railway lines.

Lazar Papernik Street, named after sniper-scout and Hero of the Soviet Union, leads to the fly-over on the left. Here begins a quiet green street called **May Day Alley** (Alleya Pervoi Mayovki), where in 1895 hundreds of Moscow workers gathered together to celebrate International Workers' Solidarity Day—May 1. Revolutionary speeches were made, songs sung and verses read. When the meeting was over the workers returned openly marching under the red flag. This event which demonstrated the extent to which the proletarian movement had developed in Russia was so important that Georgy Plekhanov, one of the first Russian Marxist theoreticians wrote about it in a letter to F. Engels. A monument is soon to be erected on Ryazan Avenue in memory of this May Day meeting.

To the right of Ryazan Avenue lies the new estate of **Veshnyaki-Vladychino**, which has a population of about 150 thousand. Building here has not yet finished. Around the central square, for instance, a number of new buildings are going up. One of these is the **Entuziast Cinema**, which is far more than just a cinema, for as well as a main hall seating 1,000, there is a dance hall, a smaller cinema studio, and a café. In the centre of the square is a **sculptural composition** entitled "The Builders" by O. Kiryukhin, sculptor, and V. Lebedev and I. Voskresensky, architects, which is dedicated to the builders of Moscow. The monument shows the bronze figures of the builders themselves while all around the results of their labour can be seen in the buildings of new Moscow.

Off to the left of Ryazan Avenue and running in the direction of **Novogireyevo**, another large **housing estate**, is **Youth Street** (Ulitsa Yunosti) which passes right alongside the **18th century museum-estate of Kuskovo**.

Kuskovo was the out of town estate of Count P. Sheremetyev, who owned 150,000 serfs. It was known to contemporaries as the Moscow Versailles. This late 18th century architectural ensemble is one of the few remaining estates built in the style of early classicism by the serf architects A. Mironov, F. Argunov and G. Dikushin and hundreds of thousands of serf craftsmen.

In the centre of the estate by the banks of a lake is the wooden building of the manor house set on a whitestone plinth. Two ramps lead up to the entrance which is covered with a colonnaded portico. Here it is worth while pausing on the balustrade before you enter the building and looking back. A beautiful landscape spreads out before you—the smooth surface of the lake, the canal running from its far bank into the woods and beyond it the avenues of trees and wide open spaces.

The manor house is beautifully decorated inside. The suite of rooms, which are decorated with carving and ornamental mouldings, covered with damask and woven carpets and full of period furniture, end in a large White Dance Hall. The windows of the hall look on to a rectangular park with ornamental flower beds, belvederes, whimsical fountains and white-marble statues. Also of interest in the park are the conservatory, the Dutch House, the Hermitage, the Italian House, containing a small exhibition and the Grotto.

Kuskovo Park has recently been made into a museum of landscape gardening. It has been widened and parts of the old scenic park have been restored according to the original plans. The whole estate is now declared a museum area.

In the house itself you can see a collection from the **State Museum of Ceramics** which contains examples of ancient pottery, glazing majolica and Russian, West-European and Eastern porcelain and glass.

Ryazan Avenue goes to the outer ring road and the large estate of **Vykhino**, which stretches over an area of 500 hectares on the right. At Vykhino the **Moscow Institute of Management** has a whole complex of buildings with teaching rooms, laboratories, hostels, a club and a large sports village.

THE SOUTH-EAST

1. Taganskaya Metro Station
2. Taganka Theatre of Drama and Comedy
3. Moscow Surikov Art Institute
4. Pokrovsky Monastery (17th-19th cent.)
5. Entuziast Cinema
6. Ryazansky Prospekt Metro Station
7. Zhdanovskaya Station
8. Kuskovo Estate Museum, 18th cent. (palacial building, pavilions, State Ceramics Museum)
9. Proletarskaya Metro Station
10. First Ball-Bearing Plant Palace of Culture
11. Sports Complex of the Lenin Komsomol Auto Works
12. Volgogradsky Prospekt Metro Station
13. Tekstilshchiki Metro Station
14. Monument to Yesenin
15. Estate of Lyublino (18th-19th cent.)
16. Kuzminki Metro Station
17. Estate of Kuzminki, 18th century (ponds, Green Star garden, pavilions)

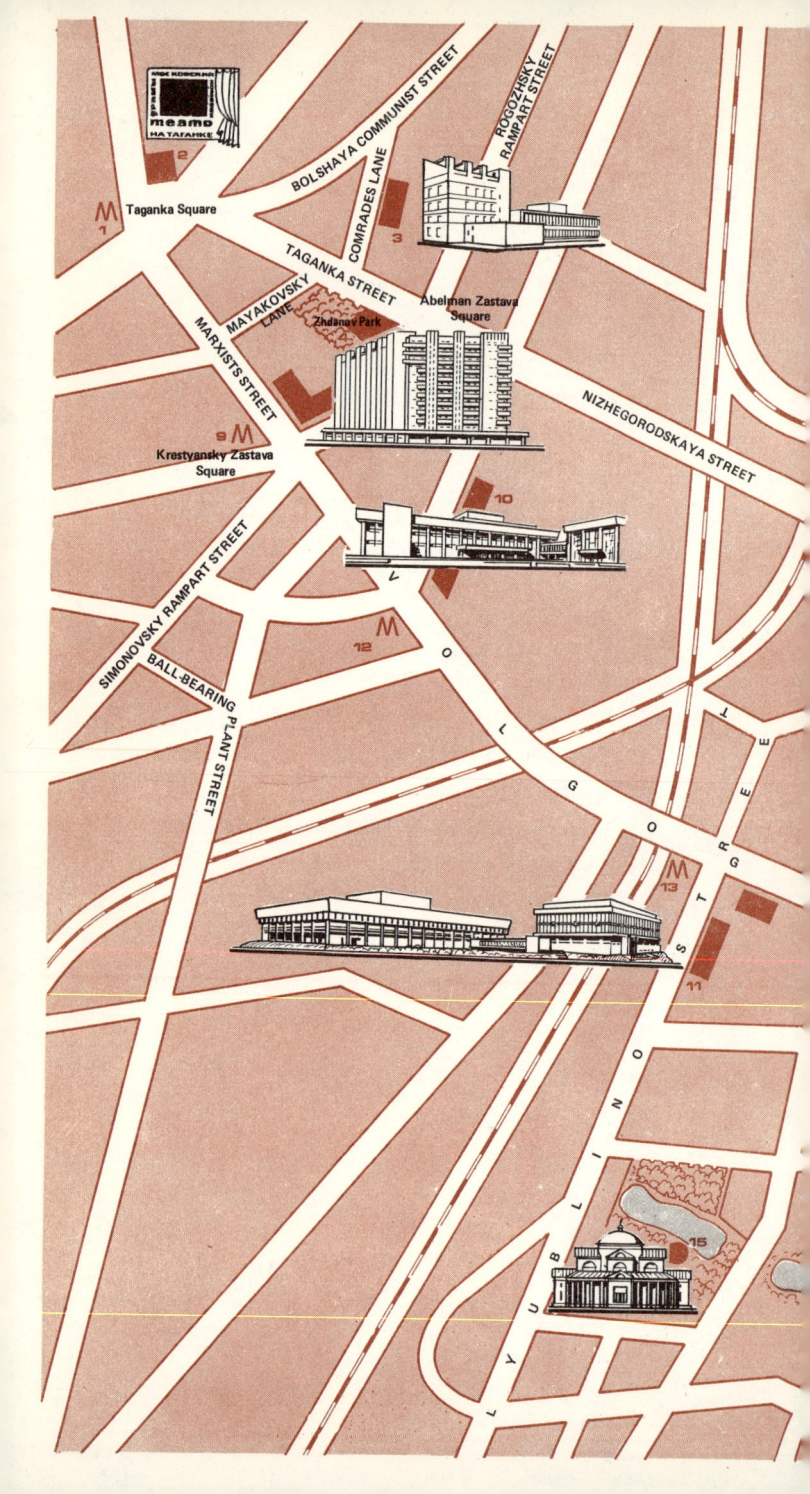

- Taganka Square
- BOLSHAYA COMMUNIST STREET
- COMRADES LANE
- ROGOZHSKY RAMPART STREET
- TAGANKA STREET
- MAYAKOVSKY LANE
- Zhdanov Park
- Abelman Zastava Square
- MARXISTS STREET
- Krestyansky Zastava Square
- NIZHEGORODSKAYA STREET
- SIMONOVSKY RAMPART STREET
- BALL-BEARING PLANT STREET
- VOLGOGRAD STREET
- LYUBLINO STREET

PEROVO NOVOGIREYEVO

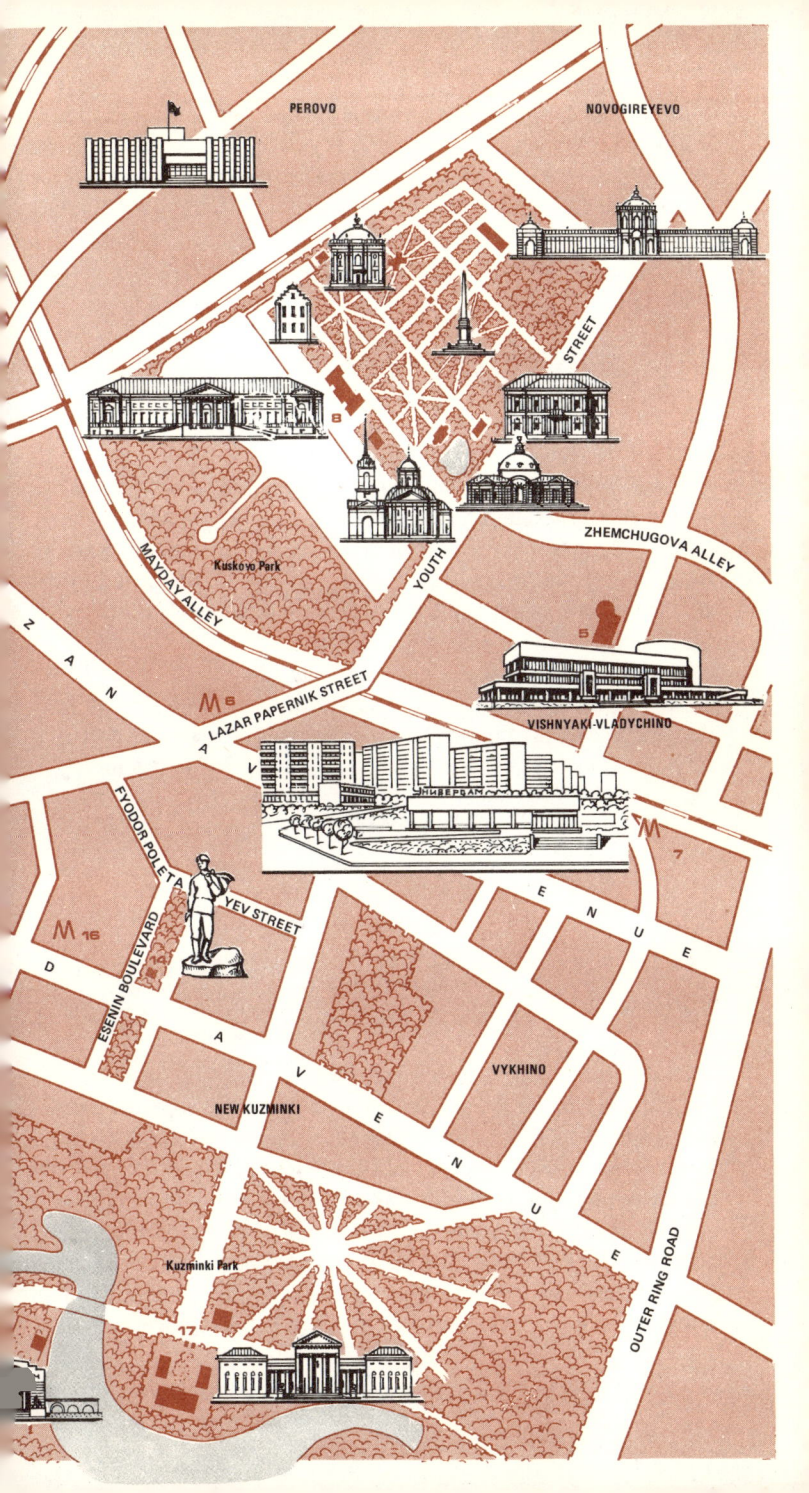

STREET

MAYDAY ALLEY

Kuskovo Park

YOUTH

ZHEMCHUGOVA ALLEY

LAZAR PAPERNIK STREET

VISHNYAKI-VLADYCHINO

FYODOR POLETAYEV STREET

ESENIN BOULEVARD

AVENUE

VYKHINO

NEW KUZMINKI

OUTER RING ROAD

Kuzminki Park

At the end of Ryazan Avenue is the **Zhdanovskaya Metro Station**, the last on the line which is connected directly with the railway station of the same name, making it a short walk from the Metro to the electric train. From here it is a very quick journey to Bykovo Airport, and only 20-25 minutes from the city centre.

Returning to Taganka Square we take the second south-eastern itinerary.

II. MARXISTS STREET – VOLGOGRAD AVENUE

Marxists Street and Vorontsov Street

These two streets run parallel from Taganka Square to Krestyanskaya Zastáva Square–the beginning of Volgograd Avenue. These streets have changed their appearance many times throughout the centuries. In 1812 all the wooden houses were burned to the ground and were later replaced with stone buildings, motley shops, small factories and handicraft workshops.

At 13/15 Mayakovsky Lane (near **Marxists Street**) is the house where the great Soviet poet, Vladimir Mayakovsky lived in 1926. Perhaps it was his impressions gleaned from the nearby workers' estate of Dubrovsky that suggested to him the following lines:

> *I see–*
> > *where garbage lies rotting today,*
> *where only the bare earth spreads out–*
> *fathoms deep I see,*
> > *from under it*
> *the Commune's*
> > *huge houses*
> > > *sprout.*

This street, which until recently was narrow and crooked, has been cleared of all its old delapidated buildings, straightened out and widened to almost three times its original size. The left-hand side of Marxists Street is lined with 16-storey houses made of standardised units. Here the planners and builders have created a number of different architectural ensembles, all well-designed and attractive in appearance. The façades are decorated with ornamental floral panels and the balconies and loggias edged with silver aluminium which combine to give the buildings a distinctive appearance.

Between Marxists and **Vorontsov** Streets is the **1st State Clock Factory** started in 1930. This factory insued the Soviet clock and watch industry and its products are now known throughout the world. In the 1960s and 1970s a number of new blocks were added. A palace of culture and sport is being built, which besides a cinema hall and several club rooms has a number of sports halls and a swimming pool.

Krestyanskaya Zastava Square (formerly Spasskaya Square) is also being rebuilt. Architecturally, its focal point is a 1,000 room hotel and a large public garden. Here a monument is to be erected to commemorate the exploits of the Soviet people in the battle of Stalingrad. An overpass will connect Marxists Street with Volgograd Avenue. Underground pedestrian passageways are planned with exits on to several streets and a multi-storey car park for 2,200 cars.

Volgograd Avenue

Volgograd Avenue runs 11.7 kilometres from Krestyanskaya Zastava Square to the outer ring road. "When you go beyond Spasskaya Zastava, you are coming into a different world," declared a Moscow newspaper in 1911. "Here in this dismal furrowed plane where the soil is arid and the atmosphere polluted live a race of people who have long forgotten the meaning of fresh air."

Looking at Volgograd Avenue as it is today with its high bright buildings, shop windows, trees, pavements, cinemas, cafés, clubs and stadiums this is very hard to imagine.

The new highway was built in the mid-1960s. It was named in honour of the Hero City, Volgograd to commemorate the great battle of the Volga in 1942-1943, which ended in the encirclement and defeat of the fascist German troops at Stalingrad (now Volgograd), thereby constituting a radical turning point in the course of the Second World War.

In recent years rapid development has taken place on Volgograd Avenue and adjacent areas, and the road, one of the longest radial highways in the city, has been completely rebuilt.

On the right at the entrance to the avenue is the workers' estate of Dubrovsky, mentioned earlier. Built during the 1920s this was one of the first Soviet workers' estates and its 25 five-storey blocks of flats are now the oldest in the district. But new buildings continue to go up. Recently the **1st Ball-Bearing Plant Palace of Culture**—an elegant building with an attractive façade—was built by Yu. Raninsky, P. Kamensky and Yu. Yurov. It has a cinema seating 500 and a theatre with places for 1,200.

The actual factory is in **Ball-Bearing Plant Street** (Sharikopodshipnikovskaya Street), which is in itself an historical monument, for here once stood a rubbish dump that was famous throughout old Moscow. During the 1930s a factory was built on the site of the old dump, which subsequently freed the USSR from the necessity to import ball-bearings. Today the factory exports to dozens of different countries.

Another large factory, the **Lenin Komsomol Auto Works** is located near the **Volgogradsky Prospekt Metro Station**. Here they manufacture the Moskvich motor car.

At the **Tekstilshchiki Metro Station**, Volgograd Avenue crosses **Lyublino Street**, an avenue of green limes. During the 1950s a housing estate was built here and in the ten adjacent streets for workers in the nearby factories and today Lyublino Street is almost entirely inhabited by workers from the Auto Works.

The Auto Works itself has recently been enlarged with the building of a major sports complex, which includes a large stadium with stands for 10,000, several football pitches, a running track, various courts and a two-storey Palace of Sport with a track-and-field area of 3,500 square metres, a swimming pool and various sports and training halls.

All this, which is designed for the inhabitants of the district, is conveniently placed near where they live and work. It is hardly surprising, therefore, that more than 60 per cent of the Auto Works employees are members of the sports club "Moskvich" and take part in the Spartakiads.

Nearby the sports centre is the **Auto Works Palace of Culture.**

A little further along Lyublino Street is a beautiful park with a lake. This is the late 18th century **estate of Lyublino**, which was once famous for its serf theatre. The old theatre and drama school buildings have been preserved as have the former stables, the conservatory and a number of other buildings. The house which has a very picturesque colonnaded gallery along its façade stands on the shores of the lake. Built by I. Yegotov, the whole ensemble is a valuable historic and architectural monument. On the opposite shore of the lake a **Palace of Pioneers and Schoolchildren** with its own theatre, sports halls and swimming pool has been built.

The last **Metro Station** on Volgograd Avenue is **Kuzminki**. Off to the left in the direction of Ryazan Avenue lies **Noviye Kuzminki**, one of the first really large housing estates to have been built in the south-east of Moscow.

Naturally the buildings that have gone up in recent years here are more attractive and interesting to look at than the older buildings. Most of these are 12, 14 and 16 storeys high, but at the intersection of Volgograd Avenue and **Yesenin Boulevard** there are two experimental 17-storey ferro-concrete apartment blocks that have recently been built. As a result of new technology this type of apartment block can be built at the rate of one floor per day.

In the centre of Yesenin Boulevard, almost on the road to his native Ryazan, stands the bronze figure of the great Soviet poet, Sergei Yesenin. The **monument** which is set in a grove of young birch trees by a small pond was erected in 1972 (sculptor V. Tsigal; architects S. Vakhtangov, Yu. Yurov).

Yesenin Boulevard leads to **Fyodor Poletayev Street**, which was named after a Russian soldier of legendary courage, who fought against fascism in the Italian Resistance, and was made both Hero of the Soviet Union and National Hero of Italy.

On the right-hand side of the road is **Kuzminki Park**, which contains the former **estate of Kuzminki** with its unique examples of the art of landscape gardening, which were created in the early 19th century by Gilardi and, presumably, Grigoryev.

> According to the USSR Academy of Sciences *History of Russian Art*, Gilardi has achieved "a remarkable organic link between the creation of the human hand and the works of nature. One gets the impression that not only wood, stone, plaster and iron were his building materials, but that he also made equal use of the sun, the air, the water and the verdure."
>
> The layout of the central part of the estate is subjected to the strict symmetry of Russian classicism. The courtyard is surrounded with wrought-iron railings, which include whitestone pillars ornamented with sculptured lions. In front of the gates there are four tall iron street lamps decorated with winged gryphons.

The positioning of the outbuildings, grottos, bridges and weirs along the meandering banks of the lake reflects the romantic style of the early 19th century. They are designed to become part of the landscape and can be seen to advantage from different angles all over the estate. Lying also along the shores of the lake is a white colonnade of propylaea and the famous Riding Stables, a masterpiece of early 19th century park architecture.

Kuzminki is also famous for its many examples of the fine craft of iron working, which were produced by Russian masters in the Urals.

Considerable restoration work is still in progress on the 18th and 19th century architectural masterpieces at Kuzminki and the original system of weirs and canals in the park is being restored as is the 18th century garden with its 12 radial paths, which is known as the Green Star.

Kuzminki estate is now there to be enjoyed by the people. An exhibition hall is planned in a classical style outbuilding, together with a library in the Orange Cottage and a museum in the Weir House. The Egyptian Pavilion, built by A. Voronikhin will be there for the use of chess players and concerts will once more be held in the Music Pavilion.

PROLETARIAN AVENUE—KASHIRA HIGHWAY

Bolshiye Kamenshchiki Street—Simonovsky Rampart Street—Bicycle-Plant Street—Lenin Village Street—Auto-Works Street—Nagatino—Proletarian Avenue—Kolomenskoye Museum Reserve—Kashira Highway—Proletarian Avenue (continued). Tsaritsyno—Lenino-Dachnoye, Biryulevo-Zagorye, Orekhovo-Borisovo—Kashira Highway (continued)—Gorki Leninskiye

Proletarian Avenue is one of Moscow's newest radial highways. It was built in the 1960s to connect the large housing estates of south Moscow with the centre.

Bolshiye Kamenshchiki Street

From Taganka Square Proletarian Avenue is reached via Bolshiye Kamenshchiki Street, which is now 60 metres wide and runs across what was during the 17th century the stone-masons' *(kamenshchiki)* quarter. It was these who built the **New Monastery**

of the Saviour, (10 Krestyanskaya Square). Founded in 1462 and built to protect the Kolomna Road, this monastery was the southernmost tip of the horseshoe of fortified monasteries that defended the city. The 15th century buildings, however, have not been preserved, and the monastery as it stands today is basically 17th century. The 78-metre bell-tower by Ivan Zherebtsov, which surmounts the main entrance, was begun in 1759 and took 30 years to build. It commanded a view over the whole south-east part of the city. Today the monastery houses the **All-Union Restoration Studios.**

Beyond the New Monastery of the Saviour on small hills *(krutitsy),* the former **Metropolitan's residence** is located here (4 Krutitsky 1st Lane), which is considered a masterpiece of old Russian architecture.

Standing on the crest of the hill the buildings look from the distance like a stage backdrop. Of particular interest is the Krutitsky Teremok, built by the great architect, Osip Startsev, and set over the gallery. Its walls, cornices, panels and the columns along its windows are all faced in coloured tiles and covered with interwoven patterns of trees, leaves and flowers. It is considered that here the Russian art of monumental ceramics reached its apogee. The Krutitsky ensemble is 17th century, but it was based on the buildings of a smaller and much older monastery. During restoration work 15th century whitestone masonry and the outline of ancient windows were discovered. The vault of the refectory has already been restored to its original 15th century appearance and coloured tiles are being made to replace those that have been lost from the façade of the Teremok.

Part of the Krutitsky ensemble has been made over to the **Moscow branch of the All-Russia Society for the Protection of Historical and Cultural Monuments** as an exhibition site.

Simonovsky Rampart Street, Bicycle-Plant Street

Your itinerary continues down Simonovsky Rampart Street and Bicycle-Plant Street (Velozavodskaya Ulitsa). Here you pass through one of the city's major industrial districts, which grew up during the second half of the 19th century. At the end of Bicycle-Plant Street on the right is **Lenin Village Street** (formerly Simonovskaya Sloboda) on which stands the **Dynamo Electrical Engineering Factory** (No 26).

The Bolshevik party organization at the factory was founded in 1903 and was one of the oldest in Russia. In December 1905 the workers of this and other factories in the Simonovskaya Sloboda district formed a "Simonovskaya Republic" and detachments of workers fought from the barricades and from the monastery bell-tower to prevent tsarist troops from penetrating their territory. It was only after crack units from Petersburg were brought in that the "Republic" was finally overthrown.

In October 1917 Red Guards from the Simonovsky district together with units from the Rogozhsky district took the Simonovsky powder-magazine and the Krutitsky barracks and later fought in the battle for the Kremlin.

The Dynamo Factory today is an advanced industrial enterprise. Two new shops have recently been built and installed with the latest technology. The production of electric locos, electric engines and other electrical equipment has risen considerably and the factory now exports to 40 countries and accounts for a sizeable proportion of the home market.

On **Eastern Street** (Vostochnaya Ulitsa) which runs from Bicycle-Plant Street to Lenin Village Street, stands the **Simonov Monastery** (No 4), also a former fortress. The monastery was founded in 1379, but destroyed by fire in the early 17th century. All that remained was the 16th century Corner Tower by Fyodor Kon. The Smithy and the Salt Towers, the wall between them and the gates are all mid-17th century.

Nearby is the **Stadium** and **Palace of Culture of the Likhachov Automobile Works**. Built between 1930 and 1934 by the famous Vesnin brothers, the palace is one of the finest examples of early Soviet architecture. The outer appearance of the building with its two attractive façades (the theatre façade looking on to the river and the club façade) is designed to emphasize its importance and social character. The Palace of Culture has an auditorium seating 1,200, a library, a concert hall and a lecture theatre as well as premises in which exhibitions can be held. Much interest is taken in the factory's amateur arts groups, and the factory drama group has been awarded the title of People's Theatre. One wing of the building is given over entirely to children.

Auto Works Street

Further along Bicycle-Plant Street on the right is Auto Works Street (Avtozavodskaya Ulitsa) both the origins and name of which derive from the **Likhachov Automobile Works** (No 23), the first automobile plant in the USSR.

The famous ZIL lorries produced here are known in many countries of the world. "One of the finest machine-building enterprises in the country," was how Leonid Brezhnev described the factory, when writing in the guest-book during a meeting with factory workers on April 30, 1976.

The present auto works were begun on the site of a previous enterprise, that was before the Revolution an assembly workshop for the spares were imported from abroad. In 1924, to mark the 7th anniversary of the October Revolution, the first ten Soviet one-and-a-half-ton lorries came off the production line and were ceremonially driven through Red Square.

During the years of the first five-year plans the factory became a major automobile works. A vast production combine, the Mosavto-ZIL, was formed with branches in several cities. It now produces lorries, tip-up lorries, buses and cars, and is beginning the production of new, increased capacity lorries.

Employees at the ZIL works have flats, kindergartens and nurseries, sanatoria and holiday hotels built for them by the factory. In the last five years alone some 38 thousand employees and their families have been provided with new accommodation by the factory. In 1976 17 thousand children attended factory kindergartens and nurseries and went to Pioneer camps while 22 thousand employees went on reduced-price holidays either to sanatoria or on excursions around the USSR and abroad.

Proletarian Avenue

In August 1970 the first section of the new Proletarian Avenue (3.6 km from the intersection with Auto Works Street through the **housing estate of Nagatino**) was opened for traffic. This was the culmination of a whole series of complex engineering projects. First the old channel of the Moskva was closed with two dams, then the river was rechanneled through a canal 3.5 km long and 170 m wide. This had the effect of checking the spring flood which for centuries had turned many kilometres of river bank into permanent marshland. An 800-metre fly-over carrying a motorway and a Metro line was then built to span the channel. At the intersection of Trofimov Street an overpass was added to carry the street across both the new avenue and the railway line, and a number of underground pedestrian passageways were built. During construction work enough earth was taken out of the ground to fill a goods train stretching from one end of the USSR to the other.

The engineers and designers who worked on the Nagatino project were awarded the USSR State Prize in 1976.

This whole area, which was once a water meadow has now become a vast estate, which will contain something like 150 thousand square metres of housing. Along the **Nagatino Embankment** a distinctive architectural ensemble is to be created. Above the granite sides of the embankment runs a wide boulevard behind which will stand six major housing complexes comprising blocks of flats of various heights which will give the whole ensemble an impressive silhouette. Between the buildings there are beautiful views on to the river.

One of the new buildings here is the 22-storey **Research Institute of Automobile Technology**.

The large island that has been formed in the river by the digging of the new canal is being converted into a **park** to be named in honour of **the 60th anniversary of the October Revolution** and thousands of trees have already been planted here. At the eastern end of the island a number of sporting facilities will be provided and on the banks of the lake there will be a children's play centre with sports grounds, a Palace of Pioneers and a music school.

On the banks of the Moskva is the **Southern River Port**, the largest in Moscow. Its 17 berths can receive vessels of up to 2,000 tons. On the opposite bank a new building for the river terminal is planned.

Beyond the river Proletarian Avenue approaches the lands of

what was once the "Tsar's Village" and is now the **Kolomenskoye Museum Reserve** (16th-17th century). Located on the southern approaches to the city Kolomenskoye was the scene of many battles in the struggle of the Russian people against the Tartar yoke. Kolomenskoye too played its role in later history. In 1606, for instance, Ivan Bolotnikov, leader of the first peasant revolution in Russia, made his camp here, from which he laid siege to the city for five weeks. In 1662 the participants of the Moscow rebellion that has gone down in history as the Copper Revolt came here to ask the tsar to lower taxes, a request that was met with bloody reprisals against the insurrectionists. The Kolomenskoye Museum contains materials relating to these and other episodes in Russian history.

Within the Kolomenskoye reserve you can see the first tent-shaped stone church in Russia, which was built in 1530-1532 by a great architect whose name has long since been forgotten. For more than four centuries the **Church of the Ascension** has delighted the eye with its beauty and magnificence. The famous 19th century French composer, Hector Berlioz, wrote: "I have seen much in my life that I have admired and been astounded at, but the past, the ancient past of Russia which has left its imprint on this village, was for me something most miraculous. Here before my gaze stood the beauty of perfection and I gasped in awe. Here in the mysterious silence, amid the harmonious beauty of the finished form, I beheld an architecture of a new kind. I beheld man soaring on high. And I stood amazed."

The Church of the Ascension at Kolomenskoye possesses one of the remarkable features of Russian architecture—it rises from the steep bank of the River Moskva and seems to blend in organically with its surroundings as if it were always part of the natural landscape.

Kolomenskoye contains a number of 17th century buildings, including a number of interesting wooden structures from ancient Russia—the 17th century brewery and a small house once belonging to Peter the Great (1702) brought from Arkhangelsk. There is an exhibition of Russian tiles, castings, wood and metal carving and

17th century icons. The museum is set in a 16th-19th century park, which contains magnificent oaks, several centuries old. Included in the Kolomenskoye museum reserve is the former court **village of Dyakovo**. Standing loftily on the high slope of the River Moskva is the **Church of John the Baptist.** It is believed that the church was built by Barma, one of the architects who built St. Basil's Cathedral in Red Square.

Here on the banks of the river the remains of an ancient township have been found. Excavations have discovered traces of 10th-12th century Slavonic culture together with flint arrow heads and other weapons from the 5th century B.C. At Dyakovo the archaeological and ethnographical sections of the Kolomenskoye Museum will be opened and there will be a display showing peasant life in a 19th century suburban Moscow village, as well as objects of folk art, etc.

Kashira Highway

Near Dyakovo Proletarian Avenue crosses the Kashira Highway, one of the oldest southbound roads in Moscow. Kashira Highway begins at its junction with Warsaw Highway (see next chapter).

Kashira Highway and Proletarian Avenue are the main thoroughfares running through the Krasnogvardeisky district, largest district in the city. In recent years a tremendous amount of building work has gone on here with housing estates, industrial enterprises, scientific and educational establishments and social and cultural buildings being built.

Kashira Highway is now a broad arterial road carrying non-stop streams of traffic across fly-overs and through underpasses into the centre of the city. The road runs 13,5 km within the city boundaries and is the main route to **Domodedovo Airport**.

Stretching along both sides of the highway near the **Kashirskaya Metro Station** is the **All-Union Cancer Research Centre**, the largest institute of its kind in the world. The centre includes clinics, research laboratories, polyclinics and hospital accommodation for long-stay patients. The wings of the centre are linked by underground passageways and there is a hotel for Soviet and foreign specialists visiting the centre.

The Cancer Research Centre was built largely from funds raised during Leninist Subbotniks. Treatment at this first class institute, which is installed with all the latest medical equipment and facilities, is, like in all other medical centres in the USSR, absolutely free of charge.

Also along the Kashira Highway is the 17-storey building of the somatic hospital with 1,200 beds, which was opened in 1976 and nearby work is still in progress on the new Research Institute and Clinic of Dietetics.

Proletarian Avenue (continued)

Beyond Kashira Highway Proletarian Avenue leads out to the new estate of **Lenino-Dachnoye**, which already numbers some 100,000 inhabitants. A new shopping and community centre is being built here and 12-, 14- and 16-storey houses continue to go up. A children's park is being laid with its own Palace of Pioneers and Schoolchildren, cinema, music school, funfair and sports grounds.

Lying between Proletarian Avenue and Kashira Highway is the famous late 18th century estate of **Tsaritsyno**.

In 1775 Catherine the Great acquired the estate in order "to live near Moscow like a simple landowner", and the famous architect, Bazhenov was commissioned to build an out-of-town residence. Making extensive use of the techniques of Old Russian architecture, Bazhenov created a large palace and park ensemble. With impeccable taste he arranged the main buildings and pavilions, the ornamental arches and galleries, the bridges across the gulleys, the artificial ruins, the lakes with islands, the jetties and the summer-houses. The buildings are of red brick ornamented with white-stone lattice and set amid the greenery of a huge park. But in 1785, when Catherine arrived at Tsaritsyno to look at the almost complete palace, it did not meet with her approval and Bazhenov was disgraced and the palace pulled down.

Kazakov was commissioned to build a new palace, but he decided to retain the initial idea of Bazhenov, his master. After Catherine's death the palace and the whole estate were left unfinished. Today you can see the huge park, the chain of lakes with their ornamental bridges, the half-destroyed building of the palace, the refectory, joined on to the palace by a vaulted gallery, the opera house and one or two other buildings.

Despite the fact that it was never completed, the ensemble at Tsaritsyno is an excellent example of the great art of its two creators and remains as a masterpiece of Russian classical architecture.

Recently Tsaritsyno was made over to the USSR Academy of Fine Arts, who are to carry out restoration work on this unique monument of Russian classical architecture and landscape-gardening.

Tsaritsyno park is to be enlarged and made into a leisure zone for the whole of the south-east of the city. In the Lesser Palace a museum is to be opened.

In 1977 the last section of Proletarian Avenue was begun. Here it runs through the new estates of Birulyovo-Zagorye and Orekhovo-Borisovo which stretch out to the outer ring road.

Birulyovo-Zagorye lies to the right of Proletarian Avenue. Lying nearby are Tsaritsyno park, the vast plantations and dendrological park of the **Moscow Zonal Institute of Horticulture**, the air here is bracing and filled with the heady aroma. Building here is confined to 9-, 12- and 16-storey apartment blocks within the estate itself and 20-storey building along Proletarian Avenue. Already 500 thousand square metres of housing space, nurseries, schools, cinemas and shops have been built here.

Orekhovo-Borisovo lies to the left of Proletarian Avenue and on both sides of Kashira Highway. Orekhovo-Borisovo itself is a large plateau lying above the neighbouring valleys. To the north and north-east it is bounded by the River Moskva and to the south-east by the outer ring road. The region is full of woodland areas and lakes. In the reign of Boris Godunov three whitestone dams were built here to form a cascade of lakes. All told the Borisovo and Tsaritsyno lakes which lie near them cover an area of some 80 hectares. In summer their green indulating banks, their golden beaches and the smooth surface of their waters give you the impression that you are not in the town but at one of the southern seaside resorts. A holiday resort is at present being built round the lakes.

Running at right angles to Proletarian Avenue are a number of green pedestrian boulevards which in the not too distant future will connect the estates with the residential area centre and new Metro stations.

Orekhovo-Borisovo received its first new inhabitants in 1974, and by 1980 there were 3.6 million square metres of housing space built here. It is in essence a new town with a population of some 300,000.

All are guaranteed work according to their individual occupations, schools for their children and facilities for spending their leisure hours as they please—and all these amenities are situated only a stone's throw from their place of residence. Orekhovo-Borisovo is a colourful district with each apartment block decorated with its own colour and finished in ceramic tiles and long-lasting enamel.

You can see Orekhovo-Borisovo as you travel along Kashira Highway from the Kashirskaya Metro Station. Along the road you will also notice the **Moskvorechye Palace of Culture** which has a concert hall seating 800 and the buildings of the **Moscow Physical Engineering Institute** with its teaching blocks, laboratories and computer centre, which has some 10,000 students. Student hostels are also being built here together with a sports stadium, a swimming pool, an indoor riding school and tennis courts.

On your return you can travel again by Metro from the Kashirskaya Metro Station, a journey of 17 minutes to the centre (Sverdlov Square).

Gorki Leninskiye.
Lenin's House-Museum

Lenin's House-Museum lies 37 km along the Kashira Highway and can be reached by a No 513 bus from Revolution Square, or by train to Leninskaya Station from Paveletsky Station

...Running through a forest of firs the road turns sharply to reveal a bright colonnaded house set amid tall trees. It was here that Lenin spent his last days.

PROLETARIAN AVENUE–KASHIRA HIGHWAY

1. Novospassky Monastery (18th cent.)
2. Krutitsky Ensemble (15th-17th cent.)
3. Proletarskaya Metro Station
4. Avtozavodskaya Metro Station
5. Simonov Monastery (16th-17th cent.)
6. Palace of Culture of the Likhachov Works
7. Kolomenskaya Metro Station
8. Nagatino fly-over
9. Southern River Port
10-12. Kolomenskoye Museum Reserve, 16th century
10. Church of the Ascension
11. Peter the Great's cottage
12. Church of John the Baptist
13. Kashirskaya Metro Station
14. Moskvorechye Palace of Culture
15-17. Estate of Tsaritsyno (18th cent.)
15. Grand Palace
16. Khlebny (Bread) House
17. Opera Theatre
18. Gorki Leninskiye

Taganka Square

BOLSHIYE KAMENSHCHIKI STREET

VORONTSOVSKAYA STREET

KRASNOKHOLMS EMBANKMENT

Peasants Square

VOLGOGRAD

KAYA

SIMONOVSKY RAMPART

BALL BEARING PLANT STREET

VILLAGE STREET

BICYCLE-PLANT STREET

LENIN AUTO WORKS STREET

PROLETARIAN AVENUE

60th Anniversary of the October Revolution Park

MOSKVA

NAGATINO EMBANKMENT

NAGATINO STREET

KOLOMENSKOYE

KASHIRA HIGHWAY

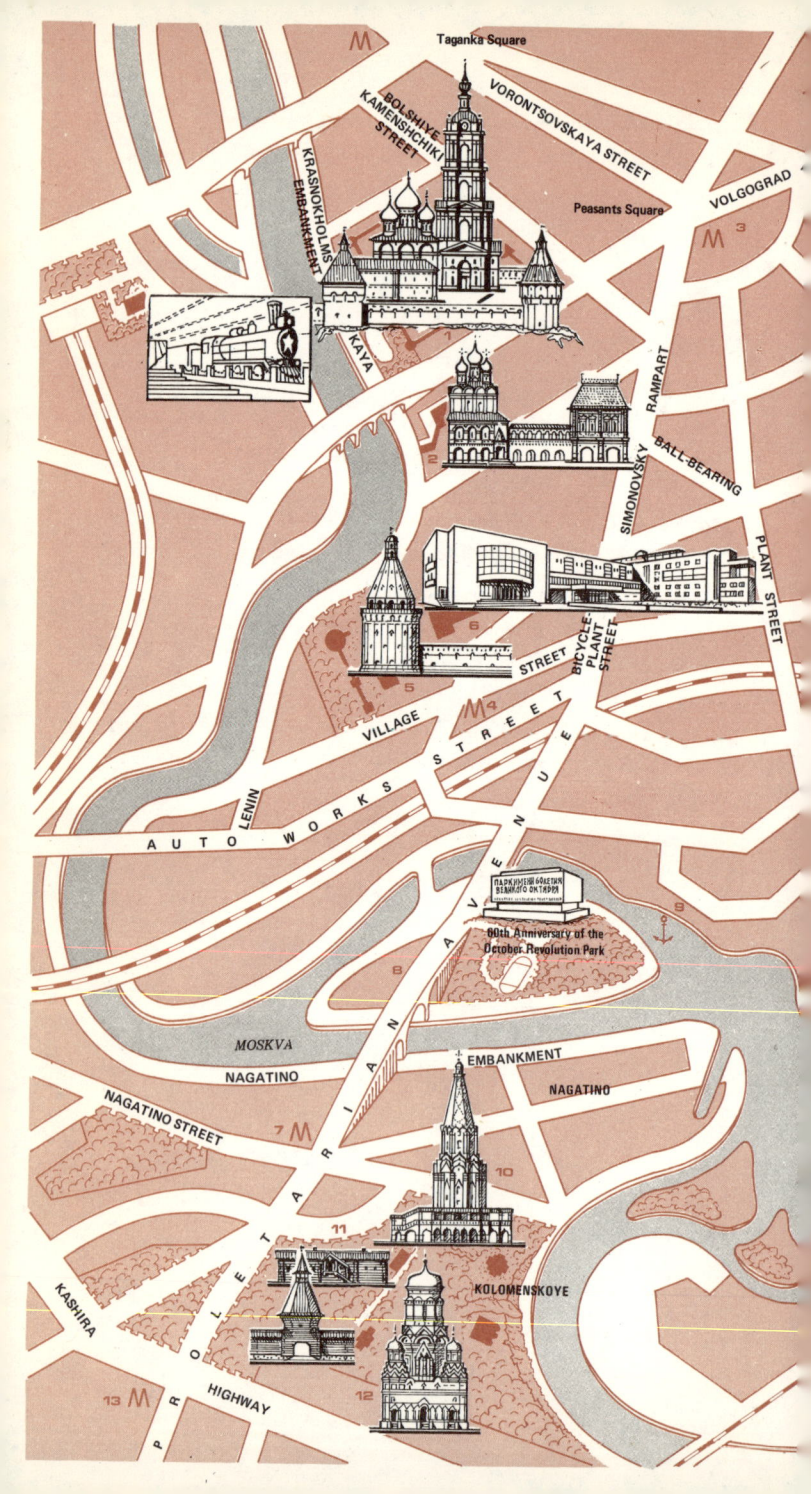

Moskvorechye

Tsaritsyno

BAZHENOV STREET

BORISOVO POOLS

SHIPILOVSKAYA STREET

BELOV BOULEVARD

OREKHOVY BOULEVARD
OREKHOVO-BORISOVO
YASENEVO STREET

Gorki Leninskiye and Domodedovo Airport

OUTER RING ROAD

KASHIRA HIGHWAY

PROLETARSKY AVENUE

KASHIRA

GORKI-LENINSKIYE

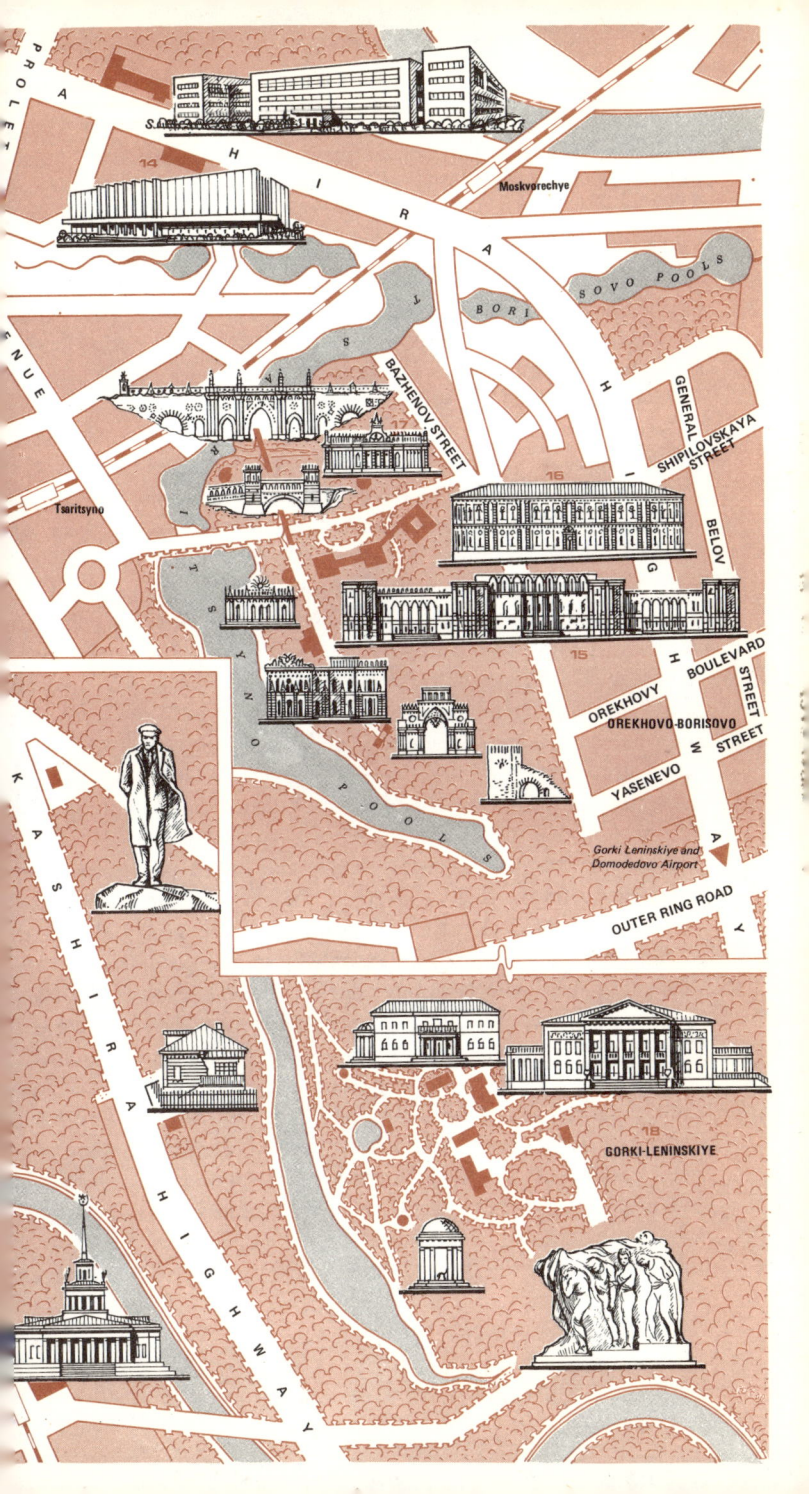

The wounds he had received during the attempt on his life in 1918 combined with the constant pressure of work seriously undermined Lenin's health. His doctors ordered him to rest up from time to time in the countryside and on September 25, 1918 Lenin came here to Gorki for the first time. He liked the large park on the high bank of the Pakhra and the beautiful countryside around. Lenin often visited Gorki when he was free, and in May 1923, when his illness took a turn for the worse, came to live here permanently. In summer Lenin and his family lived in the main building and in winter they moved into the side-wing.

But Lenin did not stop working here. He was constantly visited by members of the Council of People's Commissars and the Party Central Committee. Here he gave instructions on various party and state matters and travelled to Moscow to attend sessions of the Central Committee, and the Council of Labour and Defence. At Gorki Lenin worked on the problems of building a new society, examined questions relating to the international working-class and communist movement and wrote a number of articles and books, including *The Proletarian Revolution and the Renegade Kautsky* and *Left-Wing Communism—An Infantile Disorder.* Here too Lenin received such famous persons as Romain Rolland, Martin-Andersen Nexö, Henri Barbusse.

On the 25th anniversary of Lenin's death Gorki was opened as a museum.

In respectful silence visitors enter the house and ascend the staircase to the first floor. Here is the room where Lenin lived and died. On the desk are a number of books, including the volume of Jack London containing the story "Love of Life", which Krupskaya was reading to Lenin two days before his death. Among his modest furniture only one ornamental item stands out—a carved chair given to Lenin by the workers of Ferghana. On the southern veranda where Lenin liked to rest stands his small table and wicker chair. In a round arbour above the lake he used to sit during his walks and admire the beautiful view. He was particularly fond of a small bench—a simple board on two posts—placed beneath the fir and lime trees. Here when his doctors would let him he would work for long hours in the fresh air...

Millions of people from all over the world have come here to honour the memory of a man, who in the words of Henri Barbusse had done more for people than any other man.

The estate has now been turned into a state historical reserve, which includes the memorial park.

The memorial area includes the main buildings of the estate. Restoration work is to be carried out on the house of the peasant Shulgin, where on January 9, 1921 Lenin addressed a meeting of peasants with a speech on the country's international and internal position, and the school which he visited here.

The landscape of the estate, which has naturally undergone many changes over the years, is to be renewed. The ponds and lakes are to be cleaned and all extraneous buildings removed from the estate. It has been decided to build a museum building, which will house documents, manuscripts and other materials relating to Lenin's work at Gorki, then Lenin's house will be restored to its original state.

THE ROUTE SOUTH

Lyusinova Street—Greater Tula Street—Greater Serpukhov Street—Pavlovskaya Street—Danilovsky Rampart Street—Warsaw Highway—Zyuzino—Chertanovo—Northern Chertanovo

Lyusinova, Greater Tula, Greater Serpukhov and Pavlovskaya Streets

Lyusinova Street, which later becomes Greater Tula Street (Bolshaya Tulskaya Ulitsa), begins at Dobrynin Square (Dobryninskaya Ploshchad) on the Sadovoye Ring Road, and connects Bolshaya Ordynka, the main thoroughfare through the Zamoskvorechye with the Warsaw Highway. Both streets have been widened and the old dilapidated houses of pre-revolutionary times pulled down to make way for new multi-storey apartment blocks set amid flower gardens.

Lyusinova Street is named after Lyusik Lisinova, a student from the Commercial Institute (now the Plekhanov Institute of National Economics) which was located on Stremyanny Lane at the beginning of Greater Serpukhov Street. In 1912 the revolutionary students of the Commercial Institute formed a Bolshevik Party organization and carried out active work among the proletariat of the Zamoskvorechye. Lyusik Lisinova was one of the organizers of the Third International Young Worker's League. On November 1, 1917 she was killed in the fighting on Ostozhenka (now Metro-Builders Street).

Greater Serpukhov Street (Bolshaya Serpukhovskaya Ulitsa), which also runs from Dobrynin Square (to the left of Lyusinova Street) takes its name from the ancient road that once led to the town of Serpukhov and is known to have existed since the 14th century. Buildings began to appear here in the late 17th century and one of them was the **Church of the Ascension at the Serpukhov Gates** (No 24), which was built between 1698 and 1709 and later (1763) recast in the baroque style.

On Greater Serpukhov Street stands a complex of buildings which go to form the **Institute of Surgery of the USSR Academy of Medical Sciences** (No 27). At the entrance stands a **monument to** the institute's founder, **A. Vishnevsky**, by the prominent Soviet sculptor, Sergei Konenkov. Recently a new 17-storey research and clinical wing was opened and the architects who designed it—V. Voskresensky, T. Drozdova and L. Kiriltsev were awarded the RSFSR State Prize.

To the left of Greater Serpukhov Street is **Pavlovskaya Street** on which stands the **Vladimir Ilyich Electrical Engineering Factory**. In October 1917 the workers of the factory were among the first to form armed detachments.

Lenin visited this factory many times. On May 11, 1918 he attended a solemn ceremony held in one of the factory buildings, in which the officers and men of the new Red Army took the oath of loyalty to the revolution. Lenin stood in the first rank and together with the Red Army men pronounced the words of the oath: "I swear by the first call of the Workers' and Peasants' government to defend the Soviet Republic... and not to spare myself or my very life in the struggle for socialism."

It was here too, outside the factory that on August 30, 1918 an attempt was made on the life of Lenin. There now stands a granite slab put up by the workers of the factory, which bears the inscription: "Let the oppressed peoples of the whole world know that here on this spot a bullet fired by capitalist counter-revolutionaries tried to cut short the life and work of the leader of the international proletariat, Vladimir Ilyich Lenin." In the public gardens nearby there is a **monument to Lenin**, unveiled on November 1, 1967 on the eve of the 50th anniversary of the October Revolution (V. Topuridze, sculptor, and K. Topuridze, architect).

In 1977 the factory celebrated the 55th anniversary of its receiving the name of Vladimir Ilyich. It is now a major enterprise producing sophisticated electrical equipment.

At the end of Pavlovskaya Street is the **Pavlovskaya Hospital.** Set in the midst of a large park, which is surrounded by old railings, the building is approached via a double gate over which stand ornamental stone lions. The hospital's first premises, which were made of wood, were built in 1760. But between 1801 and 1807 Kazakov built the main stone block and the fence. In the 1820s the two side-wings were added by Gilardi and Grigoryev, who also built the two annexes and the round pavilion in the park.

Opposite the hospital, along the left-hand side of Greater Serpukhov Street are the relatively low buildings of the former **Alexandrovskiye barracks**. In both 1905 and 1917 the regiments who were stationed here under arms joined the Red Guard factory units at the appeal of the workers.

Pavlovskaya Street leads into **Danilovsky Rampart Street** (Danilovsky Val), where you can see at No 22 the buildings of the **former Danilovsky Monastery** (circa 1272). Many times this monastery-fortress drove off the incursions of the Tartar hordes. All that remains today of the monastery are the walls, six 17th century towers and a few earlier buildings.

In recent years much new construction has gone on in this district with houses, civic buildings, industrial enterprises, cultural establishments and research institutes. These include the **Pravda Cinema** on Lyusinova Street, seating 1,200, the **Vladimir Ilyich Factory House of Culture** on Pavlovskaya Street, the **Ministry of Higher and Secondary Specialised Education** between Lyusinova and Mytnaya Streets and the new building of the **State Mint** on Danilovsky Rampart Street.

Warsaw Highway

The Warsaw Highway (Varshavskoye Shosse) begins beyond the Greater Tula Street and the fly-over and rises along the right bank of the River Moskva. Over the last 15 to 20 years the narrow country lane that once ran here has been transformed into a wide tree-lined avenue. It is one of the city's main radial thoroughfares linking the centre with the new districts in the southern part of Moscow and going on past the outer ring road to Kharkov, Simferopol and other towns of the South.

The beginning of the Warsaw Highway is one of Moscow's old industrial districts. Today all the older factories have been renovated and many new ones have been built.

From the highway you get a fine view over Nagatino, the Nagatino Bridge across the Moskva and Proletarian Avenue, running straight as an arrow.

The **Varshavskaya Metro Station** marks the beginning of one more of the city's picturesque housing estates, **Zyuzino**. To the right of the highway run the streets and avenues of this district, which are mostly named after southern cities, like Simferopol, Balaklava, and Sebastopol, etc. Zyuzino is one of the greenest districts in the city and has a population of some 70,000.

Beyond Zyuzino lies the largest estate to be built in Moscow in recent years—**Chertanovo**, covering an area of 2,000 hectares. The first inhabitants moved in here in 1969 and their number has now risen to 300,000 living in more than 4 million square metres of housing space.

The architectural layout of Chertanovo is based on elongated 9-storey buildings interspersed with 12-, 14- and 16-storey tower blocks. This type of arrangement can also be found in other parts of Moscow, but in Chertanovo with its complex natural landscape, they create a unique silhouette. The blocks and towers rise easily up the hillsides and down to the ponds, making way for the islands of greenery.

The apartment blocks occupy the right-hand side of the highway and are separated from the roads by boulevards with ponds, which protect the inhabitants from noise and dust.

Chertanovo lies adjacent to the **Bitsevo Forest-Park** (1,100 hectares), where in summer 1979 a new equestrian sports complex was open for the USSR National Spartakiad. The new complex

BOLSHAYA SERPUKHOV STREET

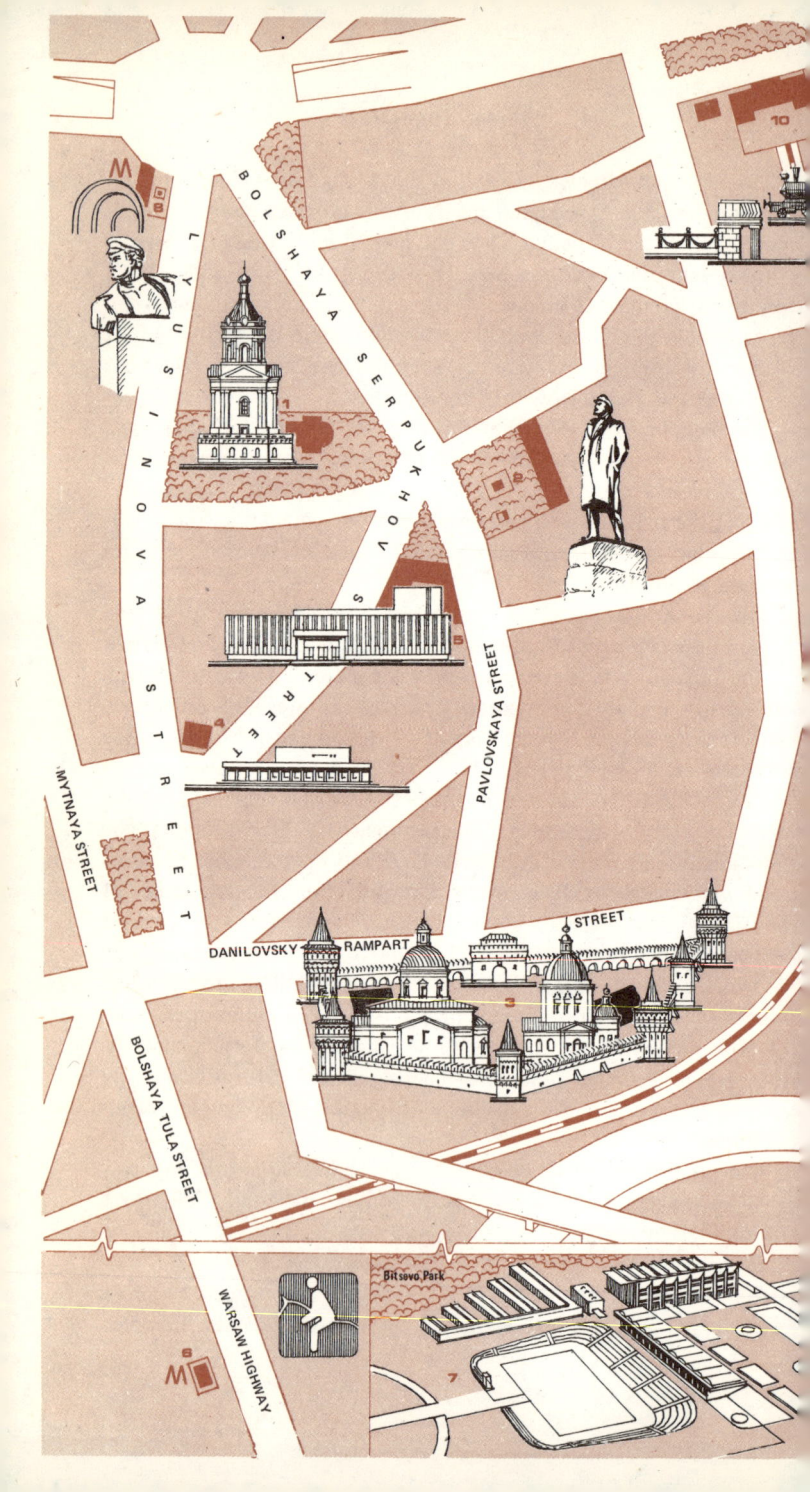

LYUSINOVA STREET

MYTNAYA STREET

PAVLOVSKAYA STREET

DANILOVSKY RAMPART STREET

BOLSHAYA TULA STREET

WARSAW HIGHWAY

Bitsevo Park

THE ROUTE SOUTH

1. Church of the Ascension at the Serpukhov Gates (17th-18th cent.)
2. Monument to Lenin
3. Danilovsky Monastery (17th cent.)
4. Pravda Cinema
5. Vladimir Ilyich Factory House of Culture
6. Varshavskaya Metro Station
7. Trade Union Equestrian Centre in Bitsevo Park
8. Monument to Dobrynin
9. Lenin Funeral Train Museum
10. Pavelets Railway Station

includes the original building of the indoor manege with stands for 8,000, an outdoor manege, a competition field surrounded by three stands designed to accommodate a total of 12,000 spectators, and 1,800 m steeple-chase track, stables, a veterinary centre, a hotel, cafés and facilities for training the pentathlon. Since the 1980 Olympics the equestrian centre has been given over to the equestrian and pentathlon sports school.

The 7.5 km section of the Warsaw Highway that runs through Chertanovo has been designed as the centre of the capital's southern development zone. On both sides of the highway there are shops, hotels, cinemas, exhibition halls, restaurants and cafés, etc. A children's theatre is also under construction here. In Chertanovo there are also a number of administrative institutions, research and design institutes and educational establishments together with a few factories on the industrial estate to the left of the highway. Most of the workers at these factories live in Chertanovo.

In Chertanovo you can see the Moscow of the future, in the form of the new experimental housing estate of Northern Chertanovo (20 thousand inhabitants).

Northern Chertanovo is bordered by **Balaklava Avenue** in the north, **Chertanovo Street** in the east, **Sumy Street** in the south and the **Bitsevo Park** in the west. The estate is formed from two fan-shaped terraces, the upper, which is larger, having apartment blocks, the lower containing civic buildings. A picturesque esplanade lies between the two terraces and below it there is a motorway with drive-ins branching away to each house. The apartment blocks consist of elongated 12- and 16-storey buildings interspersed with 21- and 25-storey tower blocks. Each block is an original architectural composition looking quite different from the rest. The ground floors of these blocks are made over to the various house clubs and equipped with cinema halls, libraries, reading rooms, dance halls, rooms devoted to different hobbies and interests, workshops of various kinds and service bureaux which fulfil a variety of requests. The flats have spacious kitchens and halls and are equipped with automatic electric stoves and a pneumatic waste-disposal and anti-dust system.

Here at Northern Chertanovo you can see the practical application of all the latest developments in architectural and engineering design and town planning. There are new types of apartment block and other buildings providing social amenities, which are in line with the requirements of the future and the need to turn Moscow into a model communist city.

At present there are only two Metro stations on the Warsaw Highway—Varshavskaya and Kakhovskaya—but construction is underway on a 14-kilometre line from Dobrynin Square to the outer ring road which will run along the Warsaw Highway.

THE SOUTH-WEST

I. Lenin Avenue–Gagarin Square–60th Anniversary of October Revolution Street–Trade Unions Street–Noviye Cheryomushki–Konkovo-Derevlyovo–Belyaevo-Bogorodskoye–Tyoply Stan–Lenin Avenue (continued). II. Vernadsky Avenue–Moscow State University–Troparyovo

The South-West was the first of the large housing estates that now surround Moscow to be built. Here on the wide expanse of high ground, famous for its fresh and bracing air, building of the new estate was begun in 1952. It was to be larger in area and have more inhabitants than the whole of pre-revolutionary Moscow, and be serviced by two metro lines. **Moscow State University, named after Lomonosov,** which covers an area of 167 hectares was to be the architectural centre of the South-West. The university was built on the main town-planning axis of new Moscow, whose centre was the Kremlin and Red Square. Early building in the south-west district, which was done at a time when the architects and builders were only beginning to approach the tasks of town planning, tends to be a little monotonous. It is not until the 60s and 70s that the architecture becomes more interesting and modern in design. In certain areas—Troparyovo, Noviye Cheryomushki, and parts of Lenin Avenue and Vernadsky Avenue—building still continues.

We would recommend two itineraries to cover the main South-Western districts.

I. **Lenin Avenue**

Entering Moscow by **Vnukovo Airport** you come to the city via Lenin Avenue (Leninsky Prospekt)—a wide, straight and modern thoroughfare. It is along this road that all the city's notable visitors are given a ceremonial welcome by the people of Moscow.

With the exception of a few buildings, architectural monuments of the 18th and early 19th centuries, the whole avenue has been built up during the Soviet period. One of the longest roads in Moscow, it stretches 14 kilometres from **October Square** on the Sadovoye Ring to the outer ring road.

> Here once stood the Kaluga Gates on the Zemlyanoy Rampart, which used to encircle Moscow and from here the road ran to Kaluga, a road that had witnessed much history in the struggle of the Russian people against the Tartars, the Polish interventionists and the Napoleonic invaders.

October Square (Oktyabrskaya Ploshchad) has undergone radical reconstruction. In the centre of the square a monument has been erected to the October Revolution commemorating the fact that in October 1917 this square was the centre of the revolutionary struggle of the Zamoskvorechye workers. A magnificent architectural ensemble is at present being built here.

Reconstruction work on the first stage of Lenin Avenue was begun in 1939 with the building of 11 multi-storey apartment blocks. Building was resumed after the war and continues to this day. At the entrance to the street on the right is the 12-storey **Institute of Steel and Alloys**, built in 1972-73 by I. Gomelina, O. Shustikova and D. Ulyanitsky. This is the first of the many scientific buildings on Lenin Avenue, which include the USSR Academy of Sciences building and 30 other major scientific institutes, some of which like the institutes of physics, energetics, high pressure physics, physical chemistry, plant physiology, cardiac and vascular surgery, paleontology, metallurgy and genetics are famous throughout the world.

On the left-hand side of the street is a very modern building (No 9) which seems to be made up of three multi-storey towers. Built in 1969 by Ya. Belopolsky, Ye. Kozlova, and Yu. Tikhonov it houses the **Committee of Standards, Weights and Measures.**

A number of valuable 18th and 19th century monuments have remained on Lenin Avenue, including two exceptionally fine examples of Russian classicism which form part of the **Pirogov Clinical Hospital** complex. At No 10 there is one of Kazakov's finest works (built between 1798 and 1801) and No 8 was built by Bove between 1828 and 1833. The Pirogov Hospital includes the **Bakulev Institute of Cardiac and Vascular Surgery**, where in 1948 Academician A. Bakulev performed the first ever heart operation in the USSR.

Off to the left runs **Donskoy 1st Passage** (Pervy Donskoy Proyezd) through which you can get to the **Donskoy Monastery**, which lies behind its red-brick walls in Donskaya Square (No 1). The monastery was founded in 1591 on the spot where the Russian troops encamped before going out to fight the hordes of Kazi Girei-Khan. The Old (sometimes known as the Lesser) Church is late 16th century, but the walls with their 12 towers are late 17th and early 18th century. It was then that the New (or Greater) five-cupola Church in the style of Russian baroque was erected. In the church you can see a 17th century six-tier carved iconostasis together with mural paintings by Bazhenov.

In 1934 the former monastery was made into an architectural museum and it is now a branch of the **Shchusev Museum of Architecture**. The main display is held in the New Church. Here you can see original drawings, building plans, blue-prints and models of many architectural works by major Russian architects of the past. These include a wooden model of the Great Kremlin Palace, which was designed by Bazhenov. The building was never completed and all that remains now is this magnificent model made by the great architect himself.

The old cemetery of the Donskoy Monastery has existed since the 16th century. Here lie the graves of a number of famous people including the 18th century writers M. Kheraskov and A. Sumarokov, the philosopher and poet, a friend of the Decembrists, P. Chaadayev, the poet V. Maikov, the architect O. Bove, the historian V. Klyuchevsky, the artist V. Perov, the founder of Russian aviation, N. Zhukovsky and the heroes of the Patriotic War of 1812.

Nearby in neighbouring Shabolovka Street is the 165-metre aerial of the first Soviet radio broadcasting station, built in 1921 by V. Shukhov. Until 1971 it was still used for television broadcasting.

On the right-hand side of the avenue between two multi-storey apartment blocks are the huge columns of what was once the entrance to the **Neskuchny Palace** (No 14).

The Neskuchny Palace is a valuable architectural and historical monument. It was built in the 1750s for the mine-owner, Demidov, who laid out fine terraces along the banks of the River Moskva and astonished all Moscow by creating a botanical garden, which received the name Neskuchny (Leisure). In the late 18th century the palace and its grounds passed into the hands of Count Orlov, a favourite of Catherine the Great. He organized luxurious festivities here, inviting hundreds of guests whom he entertained with fireworks and other amusements, even going to the extent of organizing mock battles on the River Moskva.

In 1830 the palace was rebuilt by Ye. Tyurin. The building now has the characteristics of the Russian classical period. On the entrance pylons there are two sculptural groups, the work of the famous 19th century sculptor, Vitali, and in the courtyard in front of the palace there is a fountain which is also Vitali's work.

Since 1934 the building has housed the **Presidium of the USSR Academy of Sciences**, which in 1974 celebrated its 250th anniversary. The history of the Academy is the story of discovery in all branches of human knowledge. The Presidium of the Academy of Sciences supervises the research work into all the major fields of knowledge that is being carried out by the various academies in the Union republics.

The USSR Academy of Sciences consists of four sections: physical and mathematical sciences; chemical, technological and biological sciences; soil sciences; and social sciences. These are then divided into another 16 subdepartments, each including the most important research institutes and scientific councils in the country that deal with the particular topics covered by the subdepartment.

The Academy of Sciences organizes the work of Soviet scholars and directs the scientific research towards fulfilling the tasks of communist construction. It coordinates the work of the academies of sciences of the Union republics, holds sessions, scientific congresses and meetings for the discussion of relevant scientific problems, develops international scientific contacts and participates in the work of 150 international scientific organizations. More than 900 Soviet scientists are elected honorary members of numerous foreign academies of science and scientific societies.

Around the palace there are several buildings in the classical style which are part of the original ensemble. Within the Neskuchny Gardens, where they become part of the Gorky Park of Culture and Rest is a stone three-arched bridge.

Very soon the Presidium of the Academy of Sciences is to leave its present premises and move to new quarters in a complex of buildings occupying 20,000 sq m by the River Moskva near Gagarin Square.

Gagarin Square

The reconstruction work which began here before the war made this one of the largest squares in Moscow. Formerly known as Kaluga Zastava Square, it was renamed on April 12, 1968 in honour of Hero of the Soviet Union Yuri Gagarin, the first man in space.

As you approach the square from the South-West, you are confronted by a ceremonial semicircle formed by two 8-storey buildings with towers at their corners. Built in 1940 it marked then the entrance to the city.

There is a beautiful view from the square over the estates of the South-West. To the right of Lenin Avenue you can see the **Vorobyovo Highway**, running along the bank of the river and to the right **60th Anniversary of the October Revolution Street.**

60th Anniversary of the October Revolution Street—Trade Unions Street

60th Anniversary of the October Revolution Street (Ulitsa Shestidesyatiletiya Oktyabrya) which later becomes Trade Unions Street (Profsoyuznaya Ulitsa) is the central thoroughfare of the Noviye Cheryomushki district.

The name Cheryomushki, which means "bird-cherry trees", was chosen for many of the new housing estates that were built all over the Soviet Union after the war, and there are many towns now which have their own Cheryomushki district. The district of Noviye Cheryomushki in Moscow, which was the first of these to be so called derives its name from the 16th century estate that once stood here and which was famous for its white bird-cherry trees. But Noviye (New) Cheryomushki is concerned to preserve its past and the late 18th-early 19th century noble's **estate of Cheryomushki** (Bolshaya Cheryomushkinskaya Street, Nos 90, 91) has been fully restored.

The buildings that line 60th Anniversary of the October Revolution Street and Trade Unions Street which run 12 kilometres to the outer ring road, present a history of the gradual development and improvement of Moscow's architectural façade.

Not so long ago at the intersection of Trade Unions Street and **Krasikov Street** was a dusty quarry. This has now disappeared and in its place stands a group of new academic institute buildings, central place among which belongs to the **Institute of Scientific Information on the Social Sciences**, a building of strict but expressive architectural lines. In front of this building is a pool with fountains, above which a ramp leads to the main entrance on the first floor. The two lower floors of the building are occupied by a book depository containing 7 million volumes while the upper floors contain reading rooms, offices, and a conference hall. The building was designed by Ya. Belopolsky, Ye. Vulykh and A. Misozhnikov.

Nearby is the four-storey building of the **Central Scientific Medical Library** and the tall **Economics and Mathematics Centre** (by L. Pavlov and G. Delembovskaya).

The main town centre of the whole South-West planning zone will be located in the square formed at the intersection of Trade Unions Street and **Garibaldi Street** near the **Noviye Cheryomushki Metro Station**. The complex landscape here makes it possible to form an interesting architectural ensemble set on various levels amid the greenery. The inhabitants of the South-West district and there are already more than one million of them will have here a cultural centre with a music theatre, a large exhibition hall and a twin-studio cinema. The indoor sports hall here will be bigger than the Palace of Sports at Luzhniki, being able to accommodate 25,000 spectators.

The central part of the composition will be raised on high ground and consist of four 26-storey hotels, an apartment block of the same height, shops, restaurants and other social and cultural establishments. It is also planned to build here new premises for the All-Union Book Chamber.

Further along Trade Unions Street and in the adjacent streets there are a number of other modern buildings housing various research and design institutes. There is also the **Krugozor Toy Factory** which produces a wide range of toys from talking dolls to remote control cars.

The 15-storey building resembling a huge cube which you can see near the **Kaluzhskaya Metro Station**, houses the Moscow **Central State Archives** with their millions of historical documents.

The next **metro station** along is **Belyaevo**. Nearby in part of the grounds of an old estate stands the late 17th century **Trinity Church**, which is beautifully decorated with whitestone carving.

Beyond Belyaevo Metro Station on both sides of Trade Unions Street lie the new **housing estates of Konkovo-Derevlyovo and Belyaevo-Bogorodskoye** with their 140 thousand inhabitants.

Here between Trade Unions Street and Lenin Avenue is the huge complex of the **Pirogov Moscow Medical Institute**, which comprises a 23-storey hospital with 3,000 beds, 13 clinics, a teaching laboratory with accommodation for up to 8,400 students, a children's hospital with 1,000 beds, 2 research institutes, a sports centre and a library. The whole complex is surrounded by an old park.

Further along Trade Unions Street becomes **Kaluga Highway**, which rises up towards Tyoply Stan, the highest point in Moscow (200 m above sea level and 80 m above the River Moskva).

Here at the outer ring road is the large estate of **Tyoply Stan** consisting of 9 residential areas and covering a total of 350 hectares between Trade Unions Street, Kaluga Highway and Lenin Avenue. In designing the estate the architects have carefully noted the features of the natural landscape. The apartment blocks are arranged in terraces to form a huge amphitheatre encircled by a green belt of forest park, where a holiday resort is being built for the inhabitants of the whole of the South-West. It is here that the new Moscow Zoo is to be built.

Each residential area in the Tyoply Stan estate has its own unique appearance. Compositions are formed from 12- and 16-storey buildings. Along Lenin Avenue there is a group of 23-storey apartment blocks and along Trade Unions Street a large shopping centre is under construction.

Between the residential areas there are pedestrian boulevards. The whole estate is designed for 140-150 thousand inhabitants.

Here in this area the new buildings for the Friendship University, named after Patrice Lumumba, are in the process of completion (its present site is further along Lenin Avenue). Other academic institutes to be housed here in new buildings include the Academy of Pedagogical Sciences, the Pushkin Institute of Russian Language and the Geological Expeditionary Institute.

Lenin Avenue (continued)

The building of this section of Lenin Avenue was begun in 1957. The bands of green lawns and flower-beds divide the road into four thoroughfares and serve to protect the residential quarters from the noise and dust of the traffic. The ground floors of these apartment blocks are mostly taken up with shops, restaurants and cafés.

On the left-hand side of Lenin Avenue are the buildings of the **research institutes of the USSR Academy of Sciences**, built between 1940 and 1950 in the style of classical architecture.

On the right is the multi-storey **Sputnik Hotel** (No 38) and further along on a plot of green land set back from the line of the other buildings stands a building (architect A. Vlasov, 1939) made up of several wings which houses the offices of the **All-Union Central Council of Trade Unions** and the central committees of the trade union branches (No 42).

The Soviet trade unions together with the other public organizations take part in the running of the affairs of state and society and in decision-making on matters of political, economic, social and cultural significance. Through the initiative and active participation of the trade unions a number of Soviet laws have been passed including the law on pensions, the law on restricting the working day, and the regulations regarding procedure in labour disputes. The trade unions run scientific and technical societies, the All-Union Society of Inventors and Rationalizers, people's universities, clubs, palaces and houses of culture, libraries, publishing houses, newspapers and magazines. The trade unions have their own sanatoria, holiday homes, boarding houses as well as voluntary sports societies and a network of sports schools, stadiums, swimming pools and sports halls. Soviet trade unions cooperate with the World Federation of Trade Unions and have contacts with trade unions in 115 countries. Altogether Soviet trade unions have a membership of 106 million.

Off to the right of Lenin Avenue is **University Avenue** (Universitetsky Prospekt) which leads up to the Moscow State University buildings. This avenue is lined with silver birch trees and carpeted with flower-beds, making it a beautiful spot for a pleasant stroll in summer.

> The next main road to intersect Lenin Avenue is **Lomonosov Avenue** on the right of which stand the first buildings to go up when construction of the South-West district began in 1952. They consist of two multi-storey apartment blocks with the **Progress Cinema** between them. The 10- and 14-storey blocks opposite by Ya. Belopolsky and Ye. Stamo, 1953-1956 are reserved for lecturers at Moscow University.
>
> To the left of Lenin Avenue the continuation of Lomonosov Avenue runs down to **Vavilov Street**. Here at the intersection of these two roads stands the very popular **Cheryomushki Market.**

In 1960 Lenin Avenue ended in a group of buildings at the entrance to **Kravchenko Street**. Since then the avenue has been extended several kilometres to the outer ring road. On the left a row of 19-storey apartment blocks has been built and 16-storey buildings on the right. Crossing Lenin Avenue beyond these is **26 Baku Commissars Street.**

Here at the intersection of the two roads is a **monument** to the leaders of the Azerbaijan proletariat, who died in the struggle for Soviet power.

The red granite column of the monument contains the portraits of four of these heroes: Shahumyan, Dzhaparidze, Azizbekov, and Fioletov. The monument was a gift to the Gagarin District of Moscow from the 26 Baku Commissars District of the City of Baku (sculptor I. Zeinalov).

Here also at the intersection of Lenin Avenue and 26 Baku Commissars Street is the recently opened **Central Tourist House**—a 34-storey hotel for 1,300. Another block contains all the necessary facilities for tourists including restaurants, cafés, a large cinema and concert hall, a sports hall, a swimming pool, a library and service bureaux where you can select various itineraries and watch tourists' amateur films.

On the opposite side of Lenin Avenue beyond the intersection with **Miklukho-Maklai Street** building is nearing completion on the new **Patrice Lumumba Friendship University**. The university has six faculties—agriculture, physics and mathematics and natural sciences, medicine, engineering, economics and law, history and philology. There are more than 6 thousand students here from 96 countries. The university also has a preparatory faculty. Education, medical care and board at the students' hostels are free of charge, and students are provided with grants. The Friendship University is a member of the International Association of Universities.

Beyond the intersection of Lenin Avenue and Vernadsky Avenue lies the new estate of **Troparyovo** with its beautifully designed apartment blocks.

II. Vernadsky Avenue

Vernadsky Avenue (Prospekt Vernadskovo) begins from Vorobyovo Highway as the continuation of Komsomol Avenue (see Chapter *Luzhniki*).

The avenue was named after Vladimir Vernadsky, a famous Soviet scholar, who founded the sciences of geochemistry, biogeochemistry and radiogeology. The **Vernadsky Institute of Geochemistry and Analytical Chemistry** was one of the first buildings to go up here. The reliefs on the façade of the building are the work of Sergei Konenkov.

Near the Institute of Geochemistry stands the **Moscow Municipal Palace of Pioneers and Schoolchildren**, which was built in 1960-62.

It consists of eight small buildings connected by passageways. The glass walls of the palace let in the light and form a link between the interior decor and the outside landscape. Both internal and external façades of the Palace are decorated with monumental paintings. At the main entrance stands the **bronze figure of Malchish-Kibalchish** (Nipper Pipper) by sculptor V. Frolov and architect V. Kubasov, the hero of a well-known novel by Arkady Gaidar.

Gaidar was a famous Soviet writer whose heroes are loved by Soviet children. The young boy, Malchish-Kibalchish, whose figure stands here in the Palace of Moscow Pioneers is one of his best known characters.

To give you some idea of the work of this remarkable organization let us quote a few statistics. More than 15,000 children attend the 850 circles run by the Palace of Pioneers and there are a further 10,000 girls and boys who are permanent members of 14 clubs.

The Palace has 450 rooms including laboratories, workshops, TV studios, a cinema hall, photographic studios and rooms for painting, sculpture, music and ballet. There are also halls for official meetings and ceremonies including the Lenin Hall, the International Hall, a concert hall seating 1,000, a winter garden, a pioneers' theatre, a planetarium, observatory and exhibition rooms.

The Palace of Pioneers has a sports centre comprising a stadium with stands for 7,000, a swimming pool and an indoor gym, as well as gardens, allotments and apiaries for young naturalists and a lake for water sports.

The whole ensemble of the Palace of Pioneers was designed by a group of young architects: V. Yegerev, V. Kubasov, F. Novikov, B. Palui, I. Pokrovsky and M. Khazhakyan and built by young Muscovites.

Not far from the Palace of Pioneers on the Lenin Hills is the 22-storey **Orlyonok Hotel** (15 Vorobyevskoye Highway), which is designed to accommodate 1,860 young visitors to the capital. Further along Vernadsky Avenue you come to a building of rather original design. This is the **Children's Musical Theatre** (No 5), the only one of its kind in the world. The main hall seats 1,250 and there is a concert hall for 300. The stage in the large hall is so designed that it surrounds the audience, making them as it were, participants in the action. The building was designed by A. Velikanov, V. Krasilnikov and V. Orlov.

The theatre performs pantomimes and symphony concerts, written specially with young audiences in mind. Since the theatre has opened it has become very popular.

Near the **Universitet Metro Station** the **new circus** building was opened in 1971. This huge round brightly lit building is 100 metres in diameter and can be seen from far away. It can seat 3,400 and the interior makes a truly impressive sight. The entrances are placed 4 metres higher than the level of the ring so that on entering the audience have an immediate view of the whole panorama of the circus: the brightly carpeted ring, the rows of seats, the cinema screen which encircles the whole hall and the tall silver dome. The ring floor can be changed without interrupting the circus programme and replaced by an ice-rink or a manege or filled with water to a depth of 2.8 metres. The new circus can produce all kinds of lighting and water effects including fountains, waterfalls and even a rainstorm. It is impossible to describe all the wonders of the new circus, you must see them for yourself. The circus was designed by Ya. Belopolsky, Ye. Vulykh, S. Feoktistov, V. Khavin and A. Sudakov.

To the right of Vernadsky Avenue lies the grandiose ensemble of the **Moscow State University**.

The original Moscow University was opened in 1756 largely through the efforts of Mikhail Lomonosov. It was the first university in Russia. In 1776 the university began to publish the first public newspaper in Russia, the *Moskovskiye Vedomosti*. The university printing house played an important role in the development of education in Russia (the building of the printing house you will have seen in your excursion along Pushkin Street (see Chapter *Towards Dmitrov*). According to the poet P. Vyazemsky, a friend of Pushkin, "Russia learned to speak, read and write Russian from the books and magazines published in Moscow". Moscow University has produced a veritable constellation of great names in science and culture, including such men as Pirogov, the great Russian surgeon, scholar and public figure, Ushinsky who made an incomparable contribution to the study of pedagogics in Russia, Chebyshev, the famous engineer and mathematician, and such great figures in the world of culture as Radishchev, Griboyedov, Lermontov, Belinsky, Herzen, Ogarev, Tyutchev, Alexander Ostrovsky and Chekhov. The lecturers at the University included such famous scholars as Sechenov, Botkin, Timiryazev, Zhukovsky, Vernadsky, and Granovsky.

THE SOUTH-WEST

LENIN AVENUE

1. Varshava Hotel
2. Donskoy Monastery (16th-18th cent.)
3. Oktyabrskaya Metro Station
4. Shabolovskaya Metro Station
5. Leninsky Prospekt Metro Station
   60th Anniversary of the October Revolution Street—Trade Unions Street
6. Cheryomushki Estate (18th-19th cent.)
7. Akademicheskaya Metro Station
8. Noviye Cheryomushki Metro Station
9. Kaluzhskaya Metro Station
10. Belyaevo Metro Station
11. Trinity Church (17th cent.)
12. Profsoyuznaya Metro Station

Lenin Avenue (continued)— Vernadsky Avenue

13. Sputnik Hotel
14. Moskva Department Store
15. Progress Cinema
16. Cheryomushki Market
17. Central Tourist House
18. Patrice Lumumba Friendship University
19. Moscow Municipal Palace of Pioneers and Schoolchildren
20. Orlyonok Hotel
21. Children's Musical Theatre
22. New Circus building in Vernadsky Avenue
23. Universitet Metro Station
24. Leninskiye Gory Metro Station
25. Moscow State University
26. "The First Komsomol Members" monument
27. University Botanical Gardens
28. Monument to Lomonosov
29. Observation ground
30. Prospekt Vernadskovo Metro Station
31. Zvyozdny Cinema
32. Druzhba Hotel
33. Yugo-Zapadnaya Metro Station
34. Church in Troparyovo (17th century)
35. Olympic Village

RAMENKA

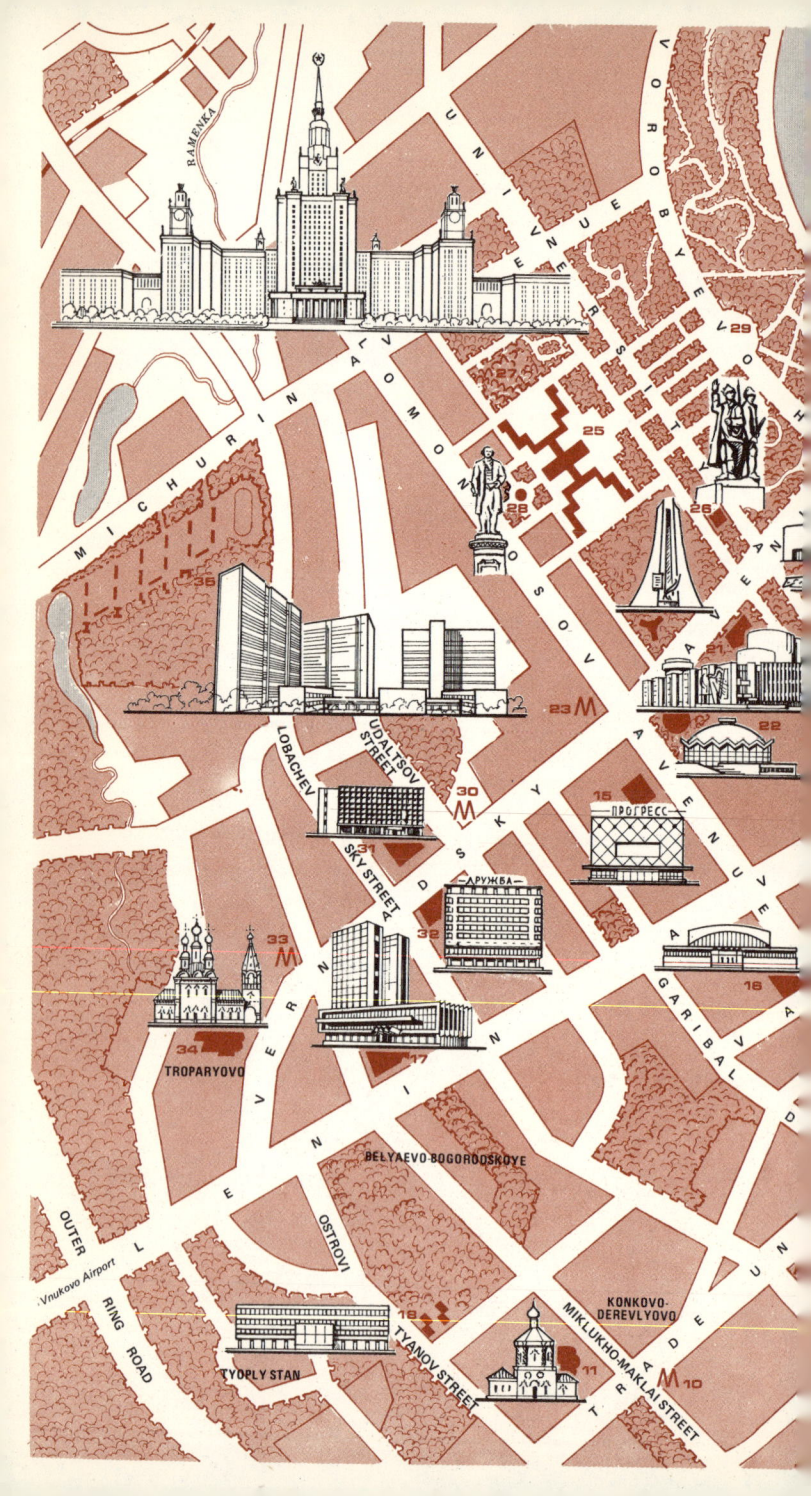

MICHURIN AVENUE

LOMONOSOV AVENUE

UNIVERSITY

VOROBYEVO

LOBACHEV STREET

UDALTSOV STREET

SKY STREET

LENINSKY AVENUE

GARIBAL...

ПРОГРЕСС

ДРУЖБА

TROPARYOVO

BELYAEVO-BOGORODSKOYE

OSTROVI

OUTER RING ROAD

Vnukovo Airport

TYOPLY STAN

TYANOV STREET

KONKOVO-DEREVLYOVO

MIKLUKHO-MAKLAI STREET

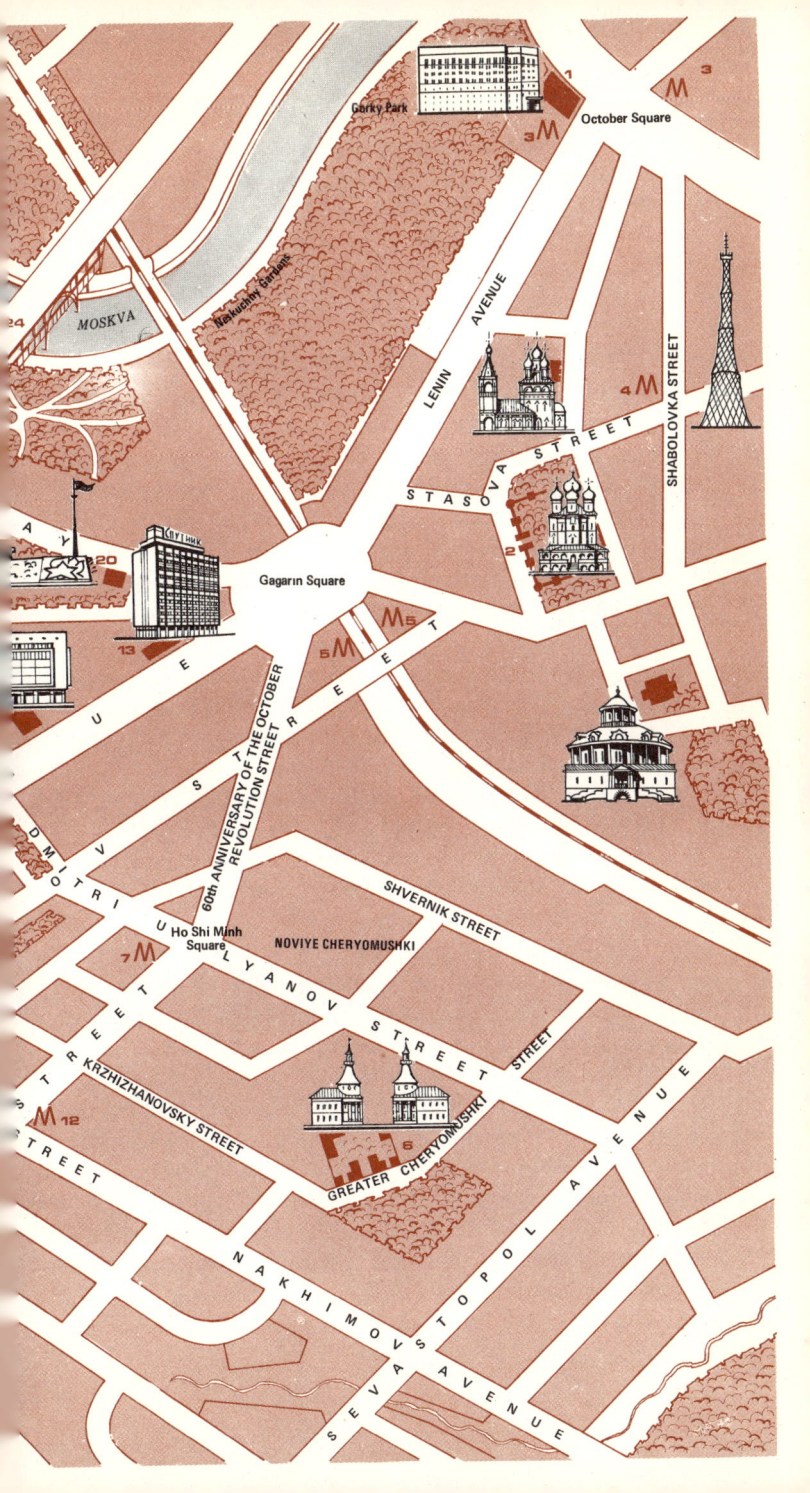

MOSKVA
Gorky Park
Neskuchny Sad park
October Square
LENIN AVENUE
SHABOLOVKA STREET
STASOVA STREET
Gagarin Square
60th ANNIVERSARY OF THE OCTOBER REVOLUTION STREET
SHVERNIK STREET
Ho Shi Minh Square
NOVIYE CHERYOMUSHKI
ULYANOV STREET
KRZHIZHANOVSKY STREET
GREATER CHERYOMUSHKI STREET
DMITRI ULYANOV STREET
NAKHIMOV AVENUE
SEVASTOPOL AVENUE

Moscow State University today (it was named after Lomonosov in 1940) is the largest higher educational institution in the Soviet Union, and one of the centres of world science. Some 30 thousand students study in its 17 faculties and these include 2,500 students from 105 foreign countries. Today the university runs several scientific institutions, museums and scientific societies and has its own publishing house producing journals, bulletins and collections of learned articles.

The life of students at Moscow State University, like that of all the Soviet students, is closely linked with the life of the country. During their vacations they can be found working on building sites, at power stations, in factories and on such major construction projects as the Baikal-Amur Railway. The students have special "working terms" as they are called in which they can learn various practical skills and in some cases entire manual occupations if they so wish. For this work they are paid. Many of the work teams are international and students from Moscow can work with their fellow students from abroad.

The main university building on the Lenin Hills can be approached from University Avenue. There is a four-metre high monument entitled **"The First Komsomol Members"** made out of forged bronze (sculptor Yu. Nyeroda, architect Ye. Stamo).

Work on the university buildings was begun in 1949 according to a project designed by L. Rudnev, S. Chernyshev, P. Abrosimov and A. Khryakov, and on September 1, 1953 the auditoria were first opened. In the space of five years 27 major and 20 subsidiary wings had been built with 50 thousand different rooms including 1,000 fully equipped laboratories, a main library with reading rooms, museums, a hall seating 1,500, a House of Culture with a hall seating 730, administrative offices for the various faculties and departments and 6,200 rooms for students coming to Moscow from all over the USSR and abroad.

The main teaching block is a 36-storey tower which stands facing the River Moskva, in front of which there is an enormous square with flower beds and a pond. In front of the building stands a **monument to Lomonosov** by Nikolai Tomsky. On the far side of the square on the crest of the Lenin Hills there is a large terrace with a polished red-granite ballustrade. From here you have a beautiful view over the entire city with the Lenin Stadium and the golden cupolas of the Novodevichy Convent in the foreground and the sulhouettes of the Kremlin towers and the skyscrapers on the horizon.

To the left of the university lie the **University Botanical Gardens** (47 hectares), the most interesting feature of which is the alpinarium with its artificially created mountain rivers and waterfalls, and where thousands of species of plant life from the Altai Mountains, the Caucasus, the Crimea, Central Asia and the Far East grow.

In the University park, which lies along Vernadsky Avenue there is a teaching observatory and behind it the University sports village. Further along is the 11-storey humanities building, which was completed in 1970. Its auditoria, laboratories and studies cover an area of almost 41 thousand square metres. Adjacent to it are two large sports halls.

The building on Vernadsky Avenue are all modern in design and arranged into various architectural ensembles. Just beyond Kravchenko Street for example is an attractive ensemble of ten-storey buildings, dominated by the 26-storey tower block of a new university hostel (accommodating 2,700 students), which can be seen reflected in the mirror like surface of the large pond outside it. Further up the avenue are 16-storey blocks placed in a row to emphasize the straightness of the road.

On the right-hand side of Vernadsky Avenue is the **50th Anniversary of the Great October Socialist Revolution Park.** In November 1967 thousands of Muscovites gathered here, on what was then just a wasteland to lay a memorial park in honour of the fiftieth anniversary of the Soviet power. In the centre of the park 50 fifty-year-old oak trees were planted. These were encircled by 15 lawns in honour of the 15 Union republics and in each one similar fifty-year-old trees were planted. From that time the park has grown in size until now it covers some 80 hectares and is one of the favourite spots for the inhabitants of the South-West.

Beyond the park is the **Olympic Village** (nearest **Metro station** is the **Yugo-Zapadnaya**). Here 16-storey blocks of flats, an administrative building, various sports buildings, a cultural and entertainment centre with its own concert hall and two cinemas and a shopping centre were made available for the 12,000 participants in the 1980 Moscow Olympics. The whole village is set out on picturesque terraces, with green glades, artificial ponds, fountains and open staircases ornamented with sculptures.

The Olympic Village was built so as to guarantee the sportsmen comfortable living conditions during their stay in Moscow. After the Games all 225 thousand square metres of living space were made over to the new inhabitants of the South-West district.

Returning to Vernadsky Avenue we find on the left-hand side beyond the **Prospekt Vernadskovo Metro Station** the 15-storey **Druzhba Hotel** (1969). The hotel offers Russian cuisine and has an observation platform into an excellent view over the South-West districts of Moscow. Opposite is the twin-studio **Zvyozdny Cinema** (seating 1,400). The group of buildings going up alongside house the **Centrosoyus,** the head offices of the USSR consumers' cooperative, and a member of the Invernational Cooperative Alliance. The 10-storey block will be mainly administrative with receptions, official meetings, conferences and exhibitions being held here; the second building will be a recreational centre with two large halls, a library and rooms for various clubs and sporting activities.

Further along at the **Yugo-Zapadnaya Metro Station** Vernadsky Avenue turns to the left and joins Lenin Avenue. In the picturesque undulating countryside that lies between these two avenues building is nearing completion on the new **housing estate of Troparyovo** (50,000 inhabitants). Troparyovo was one of the first estates in Moscow where the building of non-standardized apartment blocks out of standardized sectional units was tried out in practice. The distinctive arrangement of balconies and loggias, the different designs of the façade of each building and the varied colour patterns used give each building an individual appearance. Nearby is a 17th century five-cupola church with a tent-shaped bell-tower, which was once the local church of the village of Troparyovo.

At the intersection of Lenin Avenue and Vernadsky Avenue stands the last group of buildings on the Troparyovo estate. The group is dominated by a 22-storey **hotel**, which can accommodate 2,000. Its main façade with its horizontal lines of windows, granite stylobate and 24-metre entrance cover looks out on to Lenin Avenue in the direction of Vnukovo Airport. Its sides run along Lenin and Vernadsky Avenues, and the 16-storey buildings adjacent to it follow the bends in the two avenues. The open spaces of Troparyovo have been turned into parks and pathways link all the apartment blocks in Troparyovo with each other and with the Prospekt Vernadskovo and Yugo-Zapadnaya Metro Stations. Above the overfalls there are ramps, staircases and bridges.

Many of the buildings on Vernadsky Avenue are connected in one way or another with the sciences. The first blocks near the beginning of the street are part of Moscow State University and in Troparyovo many higher education establishments and research institutes have been built. These include the Lenin Teachers' Training Institute, the Institute of International Relations, the Academy of Sciences Institute of Mechanics, institutes of radiotechnology, electronics, automation, light chemical technology, and the national economic management.

The town centre of Troparyovo is located near the Yugo-Zapadnaya Metro Station. It has a large department store, a restaurant, cinema, library and various other service and administrative establishments.

Thus we come to the end of the final itinerary. We would like to think that this guide has been of use to you in your excursions round the city. We hope that your stay in the Soviet capital has been an enjoyable experience and that you will come back and visit Moscow again. For quick and easy reference we have included a final section headed *Practical Information.*

Practical Information

How to get to Moscow
On arrival
Intourist at your service
A few useful points
Some useful telephone numbers
Post-office, telegraph and telephone services
For those who like to walk
Notes for the motorist
System of motorways numeration
Public transport
Hotels
Intourist cultural centre
Museums
Theatres
Cinemas
Stadiums
Restaurants
Souvenirs to buy
Some useful addresses
If you are in Moscow for a day or two
Arts festivals
Your trip continued
Old Russian towns not far from Moscow

HOW TO GET TO MOSCOW

Air service to Moscow from
Helsinki	— 1 hour 40 minutes
Warsaw	— 2 hours
Stockholm	— 2 hours
Berlin	— 2 hours 25 minutes
Budapest	— 2 hours 30 minutes
Prague	— 2 hours 35 minutes
Sofia	— 2 hours 40 minutes
Bucharest	— 2 hours 25 minutes
Istanbul	— 3 hours
Vienna	— 2 hours 45 minutes
Frankfurt-am-Main	— 3 hours
Brussels	— 3 hours 20 minutes
London	— 3 hours 40 minutes
Paris	— 3 hours 50 minutes
Cairo	— 4 hours 45 minutes
Athens	— 5 hours
Lisbon	— 5 hours 15 minutes
Bagdad	— 4 hours 30 minutes
Delhi	— 5 hours 55 minutes
Algiers	— 6 hours 10 minutes
Peking	— 7 hours 35 minutes
Kabul	— 6 hours 30 minutes
Ulan-Bator	— 9 hours 20 minutes
Tokyo	— 9 hours 40 minutes
Dakar	— 10 hours 35 minutes
Washington	— 13 hours 30 minutes
Hanoi	— 13 hours 45 minutes
Montreal	— 10 hours 15 minutes
Singapore	— 12 hours 35 minutes
Brazzaville	— 16 hours 55 minutes
Havana	— 17 hours

—**Frontier Stations**: Skafferhulle (Norway), Vaihikkale (Finland), Kuznica-Bialystok, Medyka and Terespol (Poland), Vicşani and Jąsi (Romania), Cierna (Czechoslovakia), Záhony (Hungary), Akyaka (Turkey), Jolfa (Iran), Suchbaatar (Mongolia) and Manzhouli (China).

—**Motorists** can travel to Moscow via Finland (903 km from Moscow), Poland (1,035 km), Hungary and Czechoslovakia (2,035 km), Romania (1,410 km). Border Crossings: Brusnichnoye (Vyborg), Torfyanovka (Vyborg), Brest (Brest), Shechyni (Lvov), Uzhgorod (Uzhgorod), Chop (Chop), Porubnoye (Chernovtsy), Leusheni (Kishinev).

Intourist

On Arrival. To ensure that you are met on arrival at the station or airport by Intourist, Sputnik or other representatives who will help you through the various formalities you are advised to check whether the advanced notice has been sent as to the time and place of your intended arrival.

Should it happen that the appropriate representatives are not there to meet you, simply approach any airport or station official and say the one word "Intourist". There are Intourist offices at every international airport, railway station and seaport terminal, and these can provide you with any services you require including transport to your hotel.

Intourist at your service. Intourist All-Union Joint Stock Company (Head office: 16 Prospekt Marksa, Prospekt Marksa Metro Station) handles all arrangements for tourist travel in the USSR. It runs many hotels, restaurants and transport services and has at its disposal a large staff of interpreter-guides. There are Intourist offices in many towns and cities in the USSR and abroad.

Sputnik. (International Youth Travel Bureau of the USSR) (Head Office: 15 Vorobyovskoye Shosse, Leninskiye Gory Metro Station) is concerned with travel for young people. Sputnik runs a whole network of holiday camps, hotels and camp-sites located in picturesque surroundings. It also organizes trips and excursions, meetings with young people and discussions.

Service bureaux in the hotels are open from 9 a. m. to 9-10 p. m. They are there to make your stay in the USSR as pleasant as possible and render all assistance in connection with tourist services. The bureaux book travel reservations, order theatre and cinema tickets, give information on excursion schedules and itineraries, hotel and restaurant services and take care of all formalities.

A few useful points

—A detailed list of customs and currency regulations can be found in the Intourist booklet "Memo for a Foreign Tourist".

—The check-out time in hotels is 12.00 noon.
—The cost of porterage at airports and railway stations is 30 kopecks per article of luggage.

Photography. In Moscow and elsewhere in the USSR you are allowed to take pictures, cinefilms and make drawings of architectural monuments, streets, squares, apartment blocks, civic buildings, theatres, museums and landscapes. However, as in other countries there are certain objects which it is not permitted to photograph in the USSR. These include ports, bridges, tunnels, radio stations, and closed areas. Taking films from a plane is also not permitted. At industrial plants, on collective and state farms and in government institutions photography is only allowed with the permission of the appropriate administration.

—The basic unit of Soviet currency is the rouble, consisting of 100 kopecks. There are notes in denominations of 1, 3, 5, 10, 25, 50, and 100 roubles and coins of 1, 2, 3, 5, 10, 15, 20, 50 kopecks and 1 rouble.

—Moscow time is two hours ahead of European time. When it is 12.00 noon in Moscow, then in Helsinki, Sofia, Bucharest, Warsaw, Cairo and Athens it is 11 a.m.; in Prague, Belgrade, Berlin, Budapest, Paris, Rome, Stockholm and Vienna, it is 10 a.m.; London— 9 a.m. (winter only); New York it is 4 a.m.; Buenos Aires and Mexico 3 a.m.; Delhi, 2.30 p.m.; Tokyo, 6 p.m.; Canberra, 7 p.m.

—Most people in the Soviet Union work a five-day week with Saturday and Sunday off. The working day is usually from 8-9 a.m. to 5-6 p.m. and is reduced by one hour before national holidays. Most shops and factories are closed one hour for lunch between 12.00 noon and 3 p.m.

—Holidays (days off) in the USSR are: January 1—New Year; March 8—Women's Day; May 1 and 2—International Workers' Solidarity Day; May 9—Victory Day; October 7—Constitution Day; November 7 and 8—Revolution Day.

Some Useful Telephone Numbers

Ambulance—03
Fire—01
Police—02
Telegrammes—2 25 20 02
Inter-City Telephone—06, 07, 08
Moscow Telephone Directory—09
Time—1 00
Taxi—2 25 00 00
Train Services Enquiries—2 66 90 00
Aeroflot Enquiries—1 55 09 02
Lost Property: Metro—2 22 20 85; taxi—2 33 42 25; tram, bus, trolleybus—2 33 00 18 ext. 1 39.

Post-Office, Telegraph and Telephone Services. The system used in addressing letters in Moscow is the same as that employed in other countries. There are post-offices at all hotels.

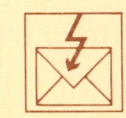

Addresses you might need

K-600 Post-Office, 3 Ul. Gorkovo (located in Intourist Hotel). "Moscow, K-600" is the postal address for all foreign tourists in the USSR. It is convenient because you do not always know in advance at which particular hotel you will be staying. The K-600 post-office works daily from 9 a.m. to 8 p.m.

Moscow Central Post-Office, 26 Ul. Kirova. Telegrammes, money orders and post-restante services are 24 hours. Other services until 10 p.m.

Moscow Central Telegraph, 7 Ul. Gorkovo. Money order, telegramme, registered letter, parcel and package services are 24 hours. Post-restante is from 8 a.m. to 11 p.m. Other services until 10 p.m.

Central Inter-City Telephone, 7 Ul. Gorkovo. 24-hour service.

International telephone. 19 Ul. Gorkovo. 8 a.m. to 11.30 p.m. Bookings until 10.30 p.m.

Communications House, 22 Prospekt Kalinina. Postal services from 8 a.m. to 8 p.m. Telegraph, intercity and international telephone are 24 hours.

International Post-Office, 1 Komsomolskaya Ploshchad. Telegramme, parcel and package services and international telephone. 9 a.m. to 9 p.m.

Postal Charges	Socialist Countries, CMEA members		Other Countries	
	Letters	Cards	Letters	Cards
Ordinary Mail	4 kop.	3 kop.	15 kop.	10 kop.
Airmail	6 kop.	4 kop.	32 kop.	27 kop.
Registered Mail	10 kop.	9 kop.	45 kop.	40 kop.
Registered Airmail	12 kop.	10 kop.	62 kop.	57 kop.

Telephone calls to any part of the world can easily be made from your room in the hotel or any of the exchanges mentioned above. The cost of a three minute call to most European countries varies from 2 to 4.50 roubles, to the United States—11 roubles and Japan—10.50 roubles.

For those who like to walk. The finest way to get the feel of a foreign city is to walk. Here are one or two tips for those who prefer this means of getting to know a city.

—All the radial roads in Moscow are numbered from the centre of the city outwards.

—Odd numbers are on the left, even numbers on the right. Street numbers are usually clearly visible along front façades of the buildings. Along the Boulevard and Sadovoye Rings and the streets that run parallel to them, numbers run clockwise.

A few rules of the road to ensure pedestrian safety:
—walk only on the pavements, keeping to the right;
—remember that traffic in Moscow goes on the right and therefore before crossing you should look left and on reaching the middle of the road look right. Many roads are one-way streets;
—motor vehicles are not permitted to use their horns in the city.

Notes for the motorist

—The speed limit in Moscow is 60 kmph (35 mph);
—horns may only be used outside the city limits or in order to avoid an accident;
—give way to fire engines, ambulances and other vehicles equipped with special signals;
—do not drive in the left-hand lane, if the right-hand lane is free;

—some traffic signals have four lights instead of three. Here left turns and U-turns (U-turns are allowed wherever there are left turns) are permitted only when both green lights are on;

—a continuous white line should not be crossed. U-turns and left turns may only be made where there is a gap in such lines or where there is an appropriate sign;

—speed should be reduced on the approach to pedestrian crossings.

N. B. In the USSR you are not permitted to drink and drive.

Motor Vehicle Insurance. If you did not ensure your car on entering the Soviet Union, you may do so in Moscow at Ingosstrakh (State Foreign Insurance Company), 11 Kuibyshev St. Insurance is available for your vehicle against accident and damage and also against civil liability for damage caused to third persons, and personal accident insurance for yourself.

Insurance may be paid for in any currency, and compensation will be paid in the currency in which the insurance was taken out.

System of Motorways numeration. To facilitate driving round the city all main roads in Moscow are numbered.

All circular roads have an alphabetical index number: "A" refers to the Boulevard Ring, "B" to the Sadovoye Ring and "K" to the outer ring road.

All radial roads have a numerical index number. If the road also becomes a major highway, it also has the letter "M" prefixed to it. Thus the main road from Moscow to Leningrad is Highway 10 and its continuation within the city limits, which is called the Leningrad Highway and, nearer the centre, Leningrad Avenue is designated "M 10". List of the main radial roads in Moscow with their road number:

M 1   Kutuzov Avenue, Minsk Highway—to Smolensk, Minsk, Brest

M 4   Warsaw Highway—to Kharkov, Simferopol, Yalta

M 8   Enthusiasts' Highway—to Vladimir, Suzdal

M 9   Peace Avenue, Yaroslavl Highway—to Zagorsk, Yaroslavl

M 10 Leningrad Avenue, Leningrad Highway—to Leningrad

Public Transport

The **Metro** costs five kopecks. Put a 5 kopeck piece in the automatic entry gate. This allows you to travel to any station irrespective of distance or changes. Luggage costs 10 kopecks per piece. The Metro is open from 06.00 to 01.00

Trolleybuses. There are no conductors. Passengers put money in the slot machines and tear off a ticket themselves. Trolleybus fares are 4 kopecks irrespective of distance. Each piece of luggage costs an extra 10 kopecks. The stops are announced by the driver. Services run from 06.00 until 01.00

Buses. Bus fares are 5 kopecks, irrespective of distance. There are no conductors. Services run from 06.00 to 01.00

Trams. Tram fares are 3 kopecks. Services run from 05.30 to 01.00

Fixed route taxis (mini-buses). Travel according to a fixed route, but may stop anywhere along that route. Fare—15 kopecks in one direction only.

Taxis are easy to recognize from the check markings on the doors and the green light in the front window. Taxi ranks are designated by an orange sign with a check design. When the green light is on the taxi is free. Fares are 20 kopecks upon entry and 20 kopecks per kilometre. The cost of waiting is 2 roubles per hour. Fares are charged according to the metre.

Hotels

Aeroflot, 37 Leningradsky Prospekt, Sokol Metro Station

Belgrad*, 5, 6 Smolenskaya Ploshchad, Smolenskaya Metro Station

Berlin*, 3 Ul. Zhdanova, Dzerzhinskaya or Kuznetsky Most Metro Station

Budapesht, 2 Petrovskiye Linii, Ploshchad Sverdlova Metro Station

Bukharest, 1 Sadovnicheskaya Naberezhnaya, Novokuznetskaya Metro Station

Druzhba, 53 Prospekt Vernadskovo, Prospekt Vernadskovo Metro Station

Intourist*, 3-5 Ul. Gorkovo, Prospekt Marksa Metro Station

Kosmos*, Prospekt Mira, VDNKh Metro Station

Leningradskaya, 21/40 Kalanchevskaya Ul., Komsomolskaya Metro Station

Metropol*, 1 Prospekt Marksa, Ploshchad Sverdlova or Dzerzhinskaya Metro Station

Minsk, 22 Ul. Gorkovo, Mayakovskaya Metro Station

Mir, 9 Bolshoi Devyatinski Per., Krasnopresnenskaya Metro Station

Moskva, 7 Prospekt Marksa, Prospekt Marksa Metro Station

Mozhaiskaya*, 65 Mozhaiskoye Shosse (hotel)

Natsional*, 1 Ul. Gorkovo, Prospekt Marksa Metro Station

Ostankino, 29 Botanicheskaya Ul, VDNKh Metro Station

Pekin, 5 Bolshaya Sadovaya, Mayakovskaya Metro Station

Rossia, 6 Ul. Razina, Ploshchad Nogina Metro Station

Sevastopol*, 1a Bolshaya Yushunskaya Ul., Kakhovskaya Metro Station

Sovetskaya, 32 Leningradsky Prospekt, Dynamo Metro Station

Sport, Luzhniki, Lenin Central Stadium, Sportivnaya Metro Station

Sputnik, 38 Leninsky Prospekt, Oktyabrskaya Metro Station

Tsentralnaya, 10 Ul. Gorkovo, Pushkinskaya Metro Station

Ukraina, 2/4 Kutuzovsky Prospekt, Kievskaya Metro Station

Varshava, 1/2 Oktyabrskaya Ploshchad, Oktyabrskaya Metro Station

Yunost, 34 Frunzensky Val, Sportivnaya Metro Station

Yuzhnaya, 87 Leninsky Prospekt, Akademicheskaya Metro Station

Note: Hotels marked with * belong to Intourist

Large new hotels are being built in various parts of Moscow: Sokolniki, Khimki-Khovrino, South-West, New Kirov Avenue, Dimitrov St., near the Kursk and Byelorussian Stations, Medvedkovo, Peace Avenue, Izmailovo, Michurin Avenue, etc.

Intourist Cultural Centre. The Intourist Cultural Centre is located at the Tchaikovsky Concert Hall. Visitors from abroad come here to take part in round-table discussions and put questions to various specialists, political and state figures and journalists.

In the evenings concerts are given here by famous folk-music ensembles and choirs from all over the Soviet Union.

* * *

The Kremlin is open to visitors daily from 10 a.m. to 7 p.m. Entry is via the Borovitskiye and Troitskiye Gates. All hand luggage should be handed in to the luggage office (located at the Troitskaya Tower in the Alexander Gardens) before entry.

The Kremlin Museum is open daily except Thursdays from 10 a.m. to 6 p.m.

The Lenin Mausoleum is open to visitors on Tuesday, Wednesday, Thursday, Saturday and Sunday. Usually foreign tourists who wish to visit the mausoleum queue up between the History Museum and the Corner Arsenal Tower (on the side of the 50th Anniversary of the October Revolution Square) between 12 noon and 1 p.m. and on Sundays between 1 p.m. and 2 p.m.

Museums
History of Revolution Museums

Central Lenin Museum, 2 Pl. Revolutsii, tel. 2 95 48 08
Central Museum of the Revolution, 21 Ul. Gorkovo, tel. 2 99 96 83

Kalinin Museum, 21 Prospekt Marksa, tel. 2 02 03 67
K. Marx and F. Engels Museum, 5 Ul. Marksa i Engelsa, tel. 2 91 88 52

Krasnaya Presnya Museum-Reserve, Branch of Central Museum of the Revolution, 4 Bolshevistskaya Ul., tel. 2 52 30 35

Lenin Funeral Train Museum, Branch of Central Lenin Museum, Paveletsky Vokzal, 1 Ploshchad Lenina, tel. 2 35 28 98

Lenin House-Museum at Gorki (from Paveletsky Station to Leninskaya Station), tel. 1 36 23 33, 1 36 23 34

Underground Printing Press of the Central Committee of the RSDLP, 1905-1906, Branch of Central Museum of the Revolution, 55 Lesnaya Ul., tel. 2 51 25 93

History Museums

Central Soviet Army Museum, 2 Ploshchad Kommuny, tel. 2 81 48 77, 2 81 56 01

Museum of the History and Reconstruction of Moscow, 12 Novaya Ploshchad, tel. 2 94 84 90

Novodevichy Convent, Branch of State History Museum, 1 Novodevichy Proyezd, tel. 2 45 32 68

Panorama of the Battle of Borodino. Kutuzov's Izba, 38 Kutuzovsky Prospekt, tel. 1 48 19 67, 1 48 19 27, 1 48 19 55.

State History Museum, 1/2 Krasnaya Ploshchad, tel. 2 28 84 52

St. Basil's Cathedral (Intercession Cathedral), Krasnaya Ploshchad, tel. 2 98 37 13, 2 98 33 04

Trinity Church in Nikitniki, Branch of State History Museum, 3 Nikitnikov Pereulok (near Ul. Razina), tel. 2 98 34 51

Arts Museums

Abramtsevo Estate-Museum, Yaroslavskoye Shosse

Andrei Rublyov Museum of Old Russian Art (Andronnikov Monastery), 10 Ploshchad Pryamikova, tel. 2 78 14 89

Arkhangelskoye Estate-Museum, Leningradskoye Shosse, tel. 1 92 87 85

Golubkina Museum and Studio, 12 Ul. Shchukina, tel. 2 02 12 17. Devoted to the life and work of the sculptress Anna Golubkina, who was a pupil of Rodin and a participant in the Russian revolutionary movement. It was Anna Golubkina who made the first Russian sculpture of Karl Marx together with a whole gallery of sculptural portraits of figures from Russian culture. **(Brief information given on the museums that are not included in the itineraries.**—*Auth.*)

Kolomenskoye Museum-Reserve (16th-17th century), Branch of State History Museum, Proletarsky Prospekt, Kolomenskaya Metro Station, tel. 1 12 53 94

Konenkov Museum, 17 Ul. Gorkovo tel. 2 29 44 72

Korin House-Museum, Branch of Tretyakov Gallery, 16 Malaya Pirogovskaya Ul., tel. 2 45 11 90

Kuskovo Estate-Museum (18th century), Ceramics Museum, Ryazansky Prospekt Metro Station, tel. 1 71 03 28

Museum of Folk Art, 7 Ul. Stanislavskovo, tel. 2 90 21 14

Museum of Oriental Art, 16 Ul. Obukha, tel. 2 97 48 00

Ostankino Palace-Museum of Serf Art, 5 Pervaya Ostankinskaya Ul., tel. 2 83 46 75

Pushkin Museum of Fine Arts, 12 Volkhonka, tel. 2 03 79 98, 2 03 95 78. *Engravings and Drawings Branch,* 4 Ul. Marshala Shaposhnikova, tel. 2 03 93 76

Shchusev Museum of Architecture, 5 Prospekt Kalinina, tel. 2 91 19 78

16th-17th Century House in the Zaryadye, 10 Ul. Razina, tel. 2 98 32 35

Treatyakov Gallery, 10 Lavrushinsky Pereulok, tel. 2 33 14 66, 2 31 13 62

Tropinin Museum, Branch of Ostankino Palace-Museum of Serf Art, 10 Shchetininsky Pereulok (near Bolshaya Ordynka), tel. 2 31 17 99

Vasnetsov Flat-Museum, Branch of Museum of the History and Reconstruction of Moscow, 6 Furmanny Pereulok, tel. 2 27 21 02

Vasnetsov House-Museum, Branch of Museum of the History and Reconstruction of Moscow, 13 Pereulok Vasnetsova, tel. 2 81 13 29

Literary Museums

Bryussov House-Museum, 30 Prospekt Mira, tel. 2 80 68 77

Chekhov House-Museum, 6 Sadovaya-Kudrinskaya, tel. 2 91 61 54

Dostoyevsky Flat-Museum, 2 Ul. Dostoyevskovo, tel. 2 81 10 85

Gogol Memorial Exhibition, 7 Suvorovsky Bulvar, in Municipal Library No 2 building

Gorky Flat-Museum, 6/2 Ul. Kachalova, tel. 2 90 05 35

Gorky Museum, 25a Ul. Vorovskovo, tel. 2 90 51 30

Herzen Museum, 27 Sivtsev Vrazhek Pereulok, tel. 2 41 58 59

Lermontov Flat-Museum, 2 Malaya Molchanovka

Lev Tolstoy Museum, 11 Kropotkinskaya Ul., tel. 2 02 30 93

Lev Tolstoy House-Museum, 21 Ul. Lva Tolstovo, tel. 2 46 94 44

Mayakovsky Museum, 3/6 Proyezd Serova, tel. 2 28 32 73, 2 21 93 96

Nikolai Ostrovsky Flat-Museum, 14 Ul. Gorkovo, tel. 2 29 85 52

Pushkin Museum, 12/2 Kropotkinskaya Ul., tel. 2 02 32 93, 2 02 23 91

State Museum of Literature, 28 Ul. Petrovka, tel. 2 21 38 57, 2 21 73 95

Theatrical and Musical Museums

Bakhrushin Central Theatrical Museum, 31/12 Ul. Bakhrushina, tel. 2 31 26 23

Glinka Central Museum of Musical Culture, 4 Georgiyevsky Per., tel. 2 92 01 14

Nemirovich-Danchenko Flat-Museum, 5/7 Ul. Nemirovicha-Danchenko, tel. 2 29 54 02

Nezhdanova Flat-Museum, Fl. 9, 7 Ul. Nezhdanovoi, tel. 2 29 01 80

Skryabin Flat-Museum, 11 Ul. Vakhtangova, tel. 2 41 03 02

Stanislavsky House-Museum, 6 Ul. Stanislavskovo, tel. 2 29 28 55

Theatrical Museums: Bolshoi Theatre, Maly Theatre, Moscow Art Theatre, Vakhtangov Theatre, Central Children's Theatre and *Central Puppet Theatre* are all located at the respective theatres.

Vakhtangov Flat-Museum, 12 Ul. Vesnina, tel. 2 41 52 39

Yermolova Flat-Museum, 11 Tverskoy Bulvar, tel. 2 90 02 15

Scientific, Technical and Natural-History Museums

Academy of Sciences Botanical Gardens, Botanicheskaya Ul., Ostankino, tel. 2 19 53 30

Anthropology Museum, 18 Prospekt Marksa, tel. 2 03 50 67

Chaplygin Flat-Museum, Branch of Zhukovsky Scientific and Memorial Museum, 1a Ul. Chaplygina, tel. 2 94 51 18. The exhibition illustrates the work of Sergei Chaplygin, a prominent Soviet scientist in the field of theoretical mechanics and aerohydrodynamics.

Charles Darwin Museum, 1 Malaya Pirogovskaya Ul., tel. 2 46 64 70

Cosmonautics Museum, Prospekt Mira, Alleya Kosmonavtov, tel. 2 83 79 68. The museum is located in the stylobate of the obelisk erected in honour of space exploration.

V. Durov Nook, 4 Ul. Durova, tel. 2 81 29 14

Fersman Mineral Museum, 14/16 Leninsky Prospekt, tel. 2 34 39 00. Contains a collection of minerals rare in its completeness, unique crystals and 120,000 types of precious stones. The museum is more than 250 years old.

Geological Museum, Leninskiye Gory, MGU, tel. 139 24 40. The museum is located on the upper floors of the Moscow University building. The museum contains exhibits, graphic representations, models and paintings illustrating the formation and development of the planet Earth and its soil, mineral deposits, flora and fauna. Here visitors can see what the Earth looked like in the past and what it will look like in the future. A special section of the museum is devoted to Moscow and outlying regions. The geological museum contains a laboratory which is used by the students of Moscow University.

Horse-Breeding Museum, 44 Timiryazevskaya Ul., tel. 2 16 10 03

Korolyov House-Museum, 2/28 6th Ostankinsky Pereulok, tel. 2 83 47 70

Liskun Livestock Museum, block 2, 48 Timiryazevskaya Ul., tel. 2 16 00 14 ext. 1 63

Museum of the History of the Moscow Metro, Sportivnaya Metro Station, tel. 2 22 73 09

Paleontology Museum, 16 Leninsky Prospekt, tel. 2 34 29 85, 2 34 18 59. This is one of the oldest museums in the Soviet Union. On display here vertibrates from various geological ages including the "North Dvina Gallery", which is a unique collection of reptiles found in the Perm region, a cave bear from the ice age and a diplodocus. Soon the Museum will be housed in a new specially constructed building at Tyoply Stan, which will have room for even its largest exhibits.

Pharmaceutics Museum, 34 Ul. Krasikova, tel. 1 20 91 51. This museum is of interest not only to specialists. The museum contains exhibits illustrating the history of pharmaceutics in various countries and contains old pharmaceutical manuals, compiled hundred of years ago. There is also a section on the pharmaceutics industry in the Soviet Union today.

Planetarium, 5 Sadovaya-Kudrinskaya, tel. 2 54 18 38, 2 54 07 66

Polytechnical Museum, 3/4 Novaya Ploshchad, tel. 2 23 06 56, 2 23 42 87

Sports and Physical Culture Museum, Lenin Central Stadium, Grand Arena, tel. 2 45 87 47

Timiryazev Biological Museum, 15 Malaya Gruzinskaya Ul., tel. 2 52 07 49

Exhibits illustrate the physiology of plants and animals together with modern selection methods in plant growing and stock rearing.

Timiryazev Flat-Museum, Flat 29, 2 Ul. Granovskovo, tel. 2 02 80 64

University Botanical Gardens, Prospekt Mira, tel. 2 81 14 07; Lenin Hills, tel. 1 39 32 93

Williams Soil and Agronomy Museum, 55 Timiryazevskaya Ul., tel. 2 16 16 19

Zelinsky Memorial Study, 2 Ul. Belinskovo, tel. 2 03 72 12. The exhibition illustrates the life and work of the founder of the Russian school of organic chemists.

Zhukovsky Scientific and Memorial Museum, 17 Ul. Radio, tel. 2 67 50 54

Zoological Gardens, Bolshaya Gruzinskaya Ul., tel. 2 55 53 27, 2 54 04 61

Zoological Museum, 6 Ul. Gertsena, tel. 2 03 89 23

Exhibitions and Exhibition Halls

Building Exhibition (Affiliated to the Exhibition of National Economic Achievement), 30 Frunzenskaya Naberezhnaya, tel. 2 45 21 07

Central Exhibition Hall, 1 Ploshchad Pyatidesyatiletiya Oktyabrya, tel. 2 02 93 04, 2 02 82 52

18-19th Century Russian Literature Exhibition (in the Naryshkin Chambers, former Vysoko-Petrovsky Monastery), 28, Ul. Petrovka, tel. 2 21 38 57

Exhibition Halls of the Union of Artists of the USSR and RSFSR, 10 Krymskaya Nab., tel. 2 38 98 43; 20 Kuznetsky Most, tel. 2 28 18 44; 25 Ul. Gorkovo, tel. 2 99 77 87; 5 Ul. Chernyakhovskovo, tel. 1 51 45 61; 46b Ul. Gorkovo, tel. 2 50 14 12; 7/9 Begovaya

Ul., tel. 2 56 41 94; 11 Kuznetsky Most, tel. 2 95 42 64; 17 Ul. Zholtovskovo, tel. 2 99 81 40; 65 Ul. Vavilova, tel. 12 56 80 9; 10 Gogolevsky Bulvar, tel. 2 90 58 39; 25 Ul. Trofimova, tel. 2 79 27 34; 13 Ul. Usiyevicha, tel. 15 10 97 1; 6 Ul. Uralskaya, tel. 4 66 42 33

Exhibition of Children's Book, 43 Ul. Gorkovo

Exhibition of National Economic Achievement, Prospekt Mira, tel. 18 19 56 1, 18 19 1 62

Exhibition of Urban Development in the City of Moscow, 4 Berezhkovskaya Naberezhnaya, tel. 2 40 63 51. Contains plans and models illustrating the General Plan for the Development of the City of Moscow

Nature and Imagination Exhibition, 5 Vorovskovo, tel. 2 50 33 23

Tchaikovsky Exhibition, Ploshchad Mayakovskovo, Tchaikovsky Concert Hall

* * *

Tourists who wish to go on **excursions** to the regions around Moscow may book through the service bureau in their hotel. The following gives an indication of the length of excursions to the most popular places:

Abramtsevo–6 hours
Arkhangelskoye–4 hours 30 minutes
Borodino (Saturdays and Sundays only)–8 hours
Gorki Leninskiye–4 hours
Klin–7 hours
Zagorsk–6 hours 30 minutes

Theatres, Concert Halls and Circuses

Bolshoi Theatre, 2 Ploshchad Sverdlova, tel. 2 92 00 50, 2 95 82 84

Central Children's Theatre, 2/7 Ploshchad Sverdlova, tel. 2 92 00 69

Central Puppet Theatre (directed by Sergei Obraztsov), 3a Sadovaya-Samotyochnaya Ul., tel. 2 99 53 73, 2 99 63 13

Central Theatre of the Soviet Army, 2 Ploshchad Kommuny, tel. 2 81 51 20, 2 81 21 10

Film Actor Studio Theatre, 33 Ul. Vorovskovo, tel. 2 90 55 24

Gogol Theatre, 8a Ul. Kazakova, tel. 2 62 92 14, 2 61 55 28

Kremlin Palace of Congresses, Kremlin, Troitskiye Vorota, tel. 2 26 79 90, 2 29 79 10, 2 29 79 01
Booking Office, 1 Prospekt Kalinina, tel. 2 27 82 63

Lenin Komsomol Theatre, 6 Ul. Chekhova, tel. 2 99 96 68, 2 99 07 08

Malaya Bronnaya Drama Theatre, 2/4 Malaya Bronnaya Ul., tel. 2 90 40 93, 2 90 67 31

Maly Theatre, 1/6 Ploshchad Sverdlova, tel. 2 23 26 21; *Branch,* 69 Ul. Bolshaya Ordynka, tel. 2 31 37 28, 2 31 11 44

Mayakovsky Theatre, 19 Ul. Gertsena, tel. 2 90 46 58, 2 90 62 41

Moscow Art Theatre, Main Building, 3 Proyezd Khudozhestvennovo Teatra, tel. 2 29 25 46, 2 29 11 52; *New Building,* 24 Tverskoi Bulvar, tel. 2 03 62 22, 2 03 87 91; *Branch,* 3 Ul. Moskvina, tel. 2 29 96 31, 2 29 20 58

Moscow Operetta Theatre, 6 Pushkinskaya Ul., tel. 2 29 96 75, 2 29 04 05

Moscow Puppet Theatre, 26 Spartakovskaya Ul., tel. 2 61 21 97

Mossoviet Theatre, 16 Bolshaya Sadovaya Ul., tel. 2 99 75 69, 2 99 20 35

Pushkin Theatre, 23 Tverskoi Bulvar, tel. 2 03 85 82, 2 03 85 14

Romen Gypsy Theatre, 32 Leningradsky Prospekt, Sovetskaya Hotel, tel. 2 50 73 53, 2 50 73 34

Satire Theatre, 18 Bolshaya Sadovaya Ul., tel. 2 99 36 42, 2 99 63 05

Sovremennik Theatre, 19a Chistoprudny Bulvar, tel. 2 97 18 19

Stanislavsky and Nemirovich-Danchenko Opera and Ballet Theatre, 17 Pushkinskaya Ul., tel. 2 29 42 50, 2 29 83 88

Stanislavsky Drama Theatre, 23 Ul. Gorkovo, tel. 2 99 72 24

State Children's Musical Theatre, 5 Prospekt Vernadskovo, tel. 1 30 51 77

State Variety Theatre, 20/2 Bersenevskaya Naberezhnaya, tel. 2 31 04 69, 2 31 08 85

Taganka Theatre of Drama and Comedy, 76 Ul. Chkalova, tel. 2 72 63 00

Theatre of the Young Spectator, Ul. Gorkovo, 10 Pereulok Sadovskikh, tel. 2 99 53 60

Vakhtangov Theatre, 26 Arbat, tel. 2 41 07 28, 2 41 16 79

Yermolova Theatre, 5 Ul. Gorkovo, tel. 2 03 90 63, 2 03 79 52

Concert Hall at the Central House of Artists, 9 Pushechnaya Ul., tel. 2 21 97 44

Concert Hall at the Gnessins Music College, 30/36 Ul. Vorovskovo, tel. 2 90 24 22

Concert Hall at the House of Scientists, 16 Kropotkinskaya Ul., tel. 2 02 54 44

Concert Hall at the Moscow Palace of Pioneers, 11/1 Vorobyovskoye Shosse, tel. 1 39 19 39

Concert Hall at Oktyabr Cinema, 42 Prospekt Kalinina, tel. 2 90 17 44

Concert Hall at Varshava Cinema, 10a Leningradskoye Shosse, 1 56 44 81

The Great Hall and the Lesser Hall of the Moscow State Conservatoire, 13 Ul. Gertsena, tel. 2 99 81 83

Great Hall at the Railway Workers' Central House of Culture, 4 Komsomolskaya Ploshchad, tel. 2 62 39 00

Great Hall in the Lenin Library, 3 Prospekt Kalinina, tel. 2 22 86 03

The Hall of Columns at House of Trade Unions, 1 Pushkinskaya Ul., tel. 2 92 09 56

Krasnoznamenny Hall and Concert Hall at the Central House of the Soviet Army, 2 Ploshchad Kommuny, tel. 2 81 55 50

October Hall, tel. 2 92 71 06

"Poetry" Concert Hall, 4, Pushechnaya Ulitsa

State Central Concert Hall (Rossia Hotel), 1 Moskvoretskaya Naberezhnaya, tel. 2 98 11 24, 2 98 55 50

Tchaikovsky Concert Hall, 20 Bolshaya Sadovaya Ul., tel. 2 99 03 78

Moscow State Circus (New Circus), 17 Prospekt Vernadskovo, tel. 1 30 96 76, 1 30 02 90

Moscow State Circus (Old Circus), 13 Tsvetnoi Bulvar, tel. 2 21 58 80, 2 28 82 31

* * *

Evening performances usually commence at 7.30 p.m. and end at 10 or 11 p.m. Coats are handed in at the cloak-room in the foyer of all theatres, where they are looked after free of charge, and from where opera glass can be hired for a small charge (30 or 40 kopecks).

Cinemas

Gorizont–21 Komsomolsky Prospekt
Khudozhestvenny–14 Arbatskaya Ploshchad
Kosmos–109 Prospekt Mira
Metropol–1 Prospekt Marksa
Mir–11 Tsvetnoi Bulvar
Moskva–2 Ploshchad Mayakovskovo
Oktyabr–42 Prospekt Kalinina
Rossia–Pushkinskaya Ploshchad
Udarnik–2 Ul. Serafimovicha
Varshava–10 Leningradskoye Shosse
Zaryadye–1 Moskvoretskaya Naberezhnaya

Cinemas are open from 9.00 a.m. and the last performance ends before 12.00 midnight. With the exception of a few cinemas you can only enter the theatre during the intervals between performances. The performance usually consists of a short documentary or news film together with the main full-length feature film. As distinct from theatres outer coats are not handed in before entry into the hall. Smoking is not permitted. All the seats are numbered.

Major Stadiums and Sports Centres

Central Lenin Stadium, Luzhniki, Sportivnaya or Leninskiye Gory Metro Station

Dynamo Stadium, 36 Leningradsky Prospekt, Dynamo Metro Station

Dynamo Sports Palace, Ul. Lavochkina, Rechnoi Vokzal Metro Station

Equestrian Centre at Bitsevo Forest-Park, Kakhovskaya Metro Station and Kaluzhskaya Metro Station

Hippodrome (Horse Racing), 22 Begovaya Ul., Dynamo and Begovaya Metro Stations

Indoor Stadium and Swimming Pool, Prospekt Mira, Prospekt Mira Metro Station

Lokomotiv Stadium, 125 Bolshaya Cherkizovskaya Ul., Preobrazhenskaya Metro Station

Moskva Swimming Pool, 37 Kropotkinskaya Naberezhnaya, Kropotkinskaya Metro Station

Rowing Canal and Cycle Track at Krylatskoye, bus from Molodezhnaya Metro Station

TsSKA Sports Centre, 39 Leningradsky Prospekt, Aeroport Metro Station

Universal Sports Hall (Sports Centre of the Central Institute of Physical Culture), Izmailovo, Izmailovsky Park Metro Station

Young Pioneers Stadium and Cycle Track, 31 Leningradsky Prospekt, Dynamo or Begovaya Metro Stations

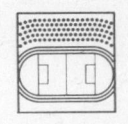

Restaurants. Lovers of Russian cuisine should try the restaurants at the **Rossia** and **Tsentralnaya** Hotels and the Restaurant **Slavyansky Bazar** (17 Ul. 25 Oktyabrya), where meals are prepared according to traditional

recipes. The restaurants **Rus** (Saltykovka Station) and **Russkaya Izba** (near Arkhangelskoye) are highly popular not only for their fine menus (*bliny, rastegai, pirogi, shchi* with mushrooms and a variety of kvasses), but also for their decor, for these restaurants are in fact genuine log *izbas* (Russian cabin) with small windows, carved porches and tiled stoves.

More than 100 different types of bread are baked in Moscow: Moskovsky, Orlovsky, Rzhanoi, Borodinsky, Peklevanny, Rizhsky—the list is endless. Many foreign tourists insist on taking a loaf of bread back with them when they leave for their relatives and friends to try. A number of foreign bakeries are already responding to the demand for Russian bread by acquiring licences for baking technology. Soviet experts have recently installed an automatic brown bread bakery in Finland.

Many Moscow restaurants specialize in the national cuisine of the various peoples of the USSR. **Aragvi** (6 Ul. Gorkovo) offers about 30 Georgian dishes (*shashlyk*, chicken *satsivi*, sturgeon on a spit, *suluguni* cheese, chicken *tabaka*) and wines (white Tsinandali and Gourdjaani, red Mukuzani, white and red Kakhetinskoye, and the equally famous semi-dry Georgian wines). For Oriental cuisine one should go to **Uzbekistan** (29 Neglinnaya Ul.) and **Baku** (24 Ul. Gorkovo). These restaurants specialize in the popular exotic cuisine from the Uzbek SSR and Azerbaijan. **Ukraina** offers Ukrainian borsch with *Pampushkas,* galushkas baked in sour cream, and the famous Crimean wines.

There are big restaurants at all Moscow hotels. The **Belgrade, Berlin, Budapest** and **Bucharest** specialize in national cuisine. So do the **Prague** (2 Ul. Arbat),

Sofia (32 Ul. Gorkovo) and **Havana** (88 Leninsky Prospekt) where you can try Czechoslovak, Bulgarian and Cuban recipes.

You can always go to the new and spacious **Arbat** restaurant at 29 Prospekt Kalinina. But if you want to visit the **Seventh Heaven** (Sedmoye Nebo) in the Ostankino TV Tower, you should make advance reservations through the service bureau.

All restaurants are open from 11 a.m. or 12 noon till 11 p.m. or midnight. There are no nightclubs in Moscow. At the **Intourist, Metropol** and **Natsional** hotels, bars are open till 2 a.m.

Souvenirs. Soviet folk craftsmen are often awarded prizes at international and national exhibitions. Traditional folk crafts—wood and bone carvings, painted wooden articles, metal stampings, enamel, filigree, embroideries, Russian lace, painted ceramics—make original and usually inexpensive souvenirs. Items from Palekh, Mstera, Fedoskino, Khokhloma, Gzhel, Hotkovo, Semyonovo are always popular with tourists. A bottle of vodka, a can of Russian caviar or a box of tea will also remind you of Moscow. Still and movie cameras make good gifts—they are inexpensive and of high quality. We also recommend watches made in Moscow: the manufacturers guarantee high quality and precision. One can hardly suit all tastes, but anyone would gratefully accept a record of Russian folk or classical music. You will surely find a souvenir you will like at one of the stores listed below:

Records	*Melodia,* 40 Prospekt Kalinina
Toys	*Dom Igrushki,* 8 Kutuzovsky Prospekt
Sheet music	14 Ul. Neglinnaya 15 Ul. Gorkovo 13 Ul. Gertsena
Books	*Dom Knigi,* 26 Prospekt Kalinina *Druzhba* (books from socialist countries), 15 Ul. Gorkovo *Moskva,* 8 Ul. Gorkovo *Knizhnaya Lavka Pisateley,* 18 Kuznetsky Most *Inostrannaya Kniga* (foreign books), 17 Zubovsky Bulvar, 18 Kuznetsky Most *Svetoch,* 1/2 Ul. Solyanka *Second-hand books in foreign languages,* 16 Ul. Kachalova
Cosmetics	*Siryen,* 44 Prospekt Kalinina 6 Ul. Gorkovo

Wines and liquors   4 Ul. Gorkovo
19 Kutuzovsky Prospekt
7 Stoleshnikov Pereulok

Gifts, arts and crafts   *Podarki,* 29 Prospekt Kalinina
4 Ul. Gorkovo
37 Ul. Gorkovo
Russky Suvenir, 9 Kutuzovsky Prospekt
6 Ukrainsky Bulvar
12 Ul. Petrovka

Cameras	*Yupiter,* 27 Prospekt Kalinina 25 Ul. Gorkovo 15 Ul. Petrovka 44 Komsomolsky Prospekt

Crystal and glass   15 Ul. Gorkovo
8/2 Ul. Kirova

Jewelry   *Malakhitovaya Shkatulka,* 24 Prospekt Kalinina
12 Ul. Gorkovo
9 Kutuzovsky Prospekt

Stamps for collectors   31/22 Ul. Chekhova
92 Leninsky Prospekt
59 Prospekt Vernadskovo

Department stores   State Department Store (GUM),
3, Krasnaya Ploshchad
Central Department Store (TsUM),
2 Ul. Petrovka
Moskva, 56 Leninsky Prospekt
Detsky Mir (goods for children),
2 Prospekt Marksa
Moskvichka (goods for women),
23 Prospekt Kalinina

Socialist countries sell their products in their own Moscow stores. **Wanda** (30 Bolshaya Polyanka) and **Polskaya Moda** (7 Ul. 26 Bakinskikh Komissarov) offer clothes, accessories, souvenirs, leather goods, cosmetics and other items from Poland. **Leipzig** (8 Ul. Akademika Vargi) sells toys, musical instruments, small leather goods and other products from the GDR. Czechoslovak **Vlasta** and Bulgarian **Varna** are on the same street (82 and 34 Leninsky Prospekt). **Balaton** (8 Michurinsky Prospekt) sells Hungarian products. **Havana** (17 Komsomolsky Prospekt) offers Cuban cigars. **Bukur** (Romania) is at 39 Pyatnitskaya Ul. and **Jadran** (Yugoslavia) at Estate No. 3 Tyoply Stan. There are foreign currency **Beriozka** shops at the hotels Metropol, Natsional, Berlin, Rossia, Ukraina, Leningradskaya, and at 9 Kutuzovsky Prospekt, 31 Ul. Kropotkinskaya, 25A Luzhnetsky Proyezd. Here you can buy furs, knitwear, crystal, china, amber, watches, Soviet-published books in foreign languages and other items.

Stores usually open at 11 a.m. and close at 7 p.m. (the hours for big department stores are 8 a.m. to 8 p.m.). Saturdays stores close two hours earlier than on weekdays, and are closed Sundays, except food stores which are open seven days a week.

Some useful addresses:

Union of Soviet Societies for Friendship and Cultural Relations with Foreign Countries–14 Prospekt Kalinina

Soviet Peace Committee–10 Kropotkinskaya Ulitsa

Soviet Women's Committee–6 Ulitsa Nemirovicha-Danchenko

USSR Committee of Youth Organisations–7/8 Ulitsa Bogdana Khmelnitskovo

Soviet Peace Fund–10 Ulitsa Kropotkinskaya

Soviet Committee for Cultural Relations with Compatriots Abroad–10 Bolshoi Kharitonyevsky Pereulok

Union of Red Cross and Red Crescent Societies–5 Pervy Cheryomushkinsky Proyezd

Soviet War Veterans' Committee–4 Gogolevsky Bulvar

Soviet European Security Committee–3 Kropotkinskaya Ulitsa

Soviet Afro-Asian Solidarity Committee–10 Kropotkinskaya Ulitsa

Znaniye (Knowledge) *Society*–4 Proyezd Serova

All-Union Central Council of Trade Unions–42 Leninsky Prospekt

Friendship House–16 Prospekt Kalinina

Union of Soviet Architects–3 Ulitsa Shchuseva

Union of Soviet Journalists–8a Suvorovsky Bulvar

Union of Soviet Composers–8/10 Ulitsa Nezhdanovoi

Union of Soviet Writers–52 Ulitsa Vorovskovo

Union of Soviet Film Workers—13 Vassilyevskaya Ulitsa

Union of Soviet Artists—10 Gogolevsky Bulvar

* * *

USSR Bank for Foreign Trade (Vneshtorgbank)—12 Neglinnaya Ulitsa, Korpus BV

USSR Insurance Company (Ingosstrakh)—12 Ulitsa Pyatnitskaya

Intourist—16 Prospekt Marksa

Intourist Central Travel Bureau—2 Ploshchad Sverdlova

Intourist Excursion Bureau—1 Ulitsa Gorkovo

Sputnik—International Youth Travel Agency—15 Vorobyovskoye Shosse

If you are in Moscow for a day or two, we recommend a three-hour tour of the city offered by Intourist.

If you stop in Moscow for one day only, you can see the Kremlin and Red Square. The guided tour is also three hours.

If you stay for the second day, be sure to visit the Exhibition of National Economic Achievement. Here you can glimpse practically all aspects of the contemporary life and economic and cultural progress of Moscow and the entire country. The tour takes four hours.

One simply cannot leave Moscow without a visit to the Tretyakov Gallery or the Bolshoi. Elsewhere in this book we have described other Moscow theatres and museums you might choose to visit.

Many tourists believe that the Moscow Metro (subway) is a good guide to the city. Any of the crosstown lines offers you information about the Soviet capital's centre and its new districts. Explanations will be provided by the tour guide if you go with a tourist group or by any guidebook (including the one you are reading) if you go on your own.

In summer you can also go sightseeing by boat. From May through September or October small boats (river streetcars, as Muscovites call them) shuttle along the River Moskva. The trip is a bit slow but very pleasant on a hot summer day, showing you the city's sights, historical monuments, old and new architecture.

There are two boat routes:

Number 1 (1 hour 36 minutes one way): Kiev Station–Lenin Hills–Gorky Park–Crimean Bridge–Bolshoi Kamenny Bridge–Bolshoi Ustinsky Bridge–Krasnokholmsky Bridge–Novospassky Bridge

Number 2 (1 hour): Kiev Station–Krasnaya Presnya Park–Kuntsevo–Krylatskoye

This trip will take you to Fili–Kuntsevo Park and to the beaches of Krylatskoye

Trips to arts festivals–*Moscow Stars (May 5-15)* and *Russian Winter (December 25–January 5)*–have become very popular with foreign tourists. Visitors are provided with first class and tourist class hotel accommodations and meals. A trip to a Russian Winter festival will save you money. Winter is not a tourist season, and Intourist offers large discounts on trips from October 1 to April 30: up to 15 per cent on individual tours, up to 25 per cent on trips for medical treatment and on group tours of all tourist classes.

To continue your trip you can go from Moscow on a tour of the Soviet Union, visiting such unique areas as the Black Sea coast of the Crimea and the Caucasus, cities on the Volga and in Central Asia, old Russian towns.

Old Russian towns around Moscow. Take the *Moscow-Gorky Highway* from the Outer Ring Road to go to *Vladimir* (128 km from Moscow) and *Suzdal* (218 km). The *Yaroslavl Highway* will take you to *Pereyaslavl-Zalessky* (141 km), *Rostov (Yaroslavsky)* (207 km) and *Yaroslavl* (260 km), and the *Simferopol Highway* to the *Lev Tolstoy Yasnaya Polyana Museum-Estate* (200 km from Moscow, near Tula).

Name index

A

Abrikosov Aleksei—172
Aksakov Sergei—126, 186, 256, 294
Alevisio Novi—54
Andreyev Nikolai—95, 99, 102, 126, 128, 173, 186
Anikushin Mikhail—128

B

Bakhrushin Aleksei—152
Barma—74
Barbusse Henri—22
Bauman Nikolai—318, 320
Bazhenov Vassily—82, 89, 113, 143, 176, 286, 300, 312, 358
Belinsky Vissarion—264
Belopolsky Yakov—375, 378, 381
Bétancourt Augustin—93
Blok Alexander—126, 185
Bolotnikov Ivan—17, 356
Bove Osip—61, 93, 94, 97, 98, 113, 193, 301, 376
Brezhnev Leonid—354
Bryussov Valery—286

C

Camporessi Francesco—178, 301, 321
Catherine II—50, 266, 358
Chaliapin Fyodor—98, 138, 152, 251, 264, 296
Chapayev Vassily—171
Chechulin Dmitri—85, 218, 234
Chekhov Anton—128, 129, 140, 252, 256, 264, 305
Chernyshevsky Nikolai—17, 94, 186, 314
Chichagov Dmitri—57, 101, 253

D

Darwin Charles—172
Deineka Alexander—70
Dimitrov Georgi—118, 119, 226
Dionysius—115
Dobrynin Pyotr——153, 163
Dolgoruky Yuri—11, 225, 284
Donskoy Dmitri—13, 47, 55, 106, 331
Dostoyevsky Fyodor—274
Dumas père—208
Durov Vladimir—272
Dzerzhinsky Felix—102, 103, 148, 284, 285

E

Engels Frederick—94, 124
Erisman Fyodor—171

F

Fadeyev Alexander—208
Fedorov Ivan—82, 92, 102
Fioravanti Aristotle—52
Fomin Ivan—148, 224
Frunze Mikhail—165, 171, 178, 275

G

Gagarin Yuri—77, 291, 292, 377
Gelfreikh Vladimir—89
Gilardi Domenico—95, 127, 139, 150, 275, 276, 320
Gilyarovsky Vladimir—133, 264
Gnesina Yelena—209
Gogol Nikolai—124-126, 141, 172, 181, 199, 296, 299

Goldenweizer Alexander—200
Gorky Maxim—128, 129, 133, 158, 207, 236, 258, 264
Gotwald Klement—226
Granovsky Timofei—176
Griboyedov Alexander—127, 131, 138, 169
Grigoriev Afanasi—112, 168, 275

H

Herzen Alexander—17, 92, 95, 125, 186, 198

I

Istomin Nazari—54
Ivan III—14, 55, 58, 89
Ivan IV the Terrible—53-55, 74, 77, 85

K

Kachalov Vassily—152, 201, 207, 253
Kalinin Mikhail—92, 126, 175, 259
Kalita Ivan—13, 52, 55, 71
Kamensky Valentin—128
Karbyshev Dmitri—132, 133
Kavos Albert—98
Kazakov Matvei—83, 95, 129, 149, 154, 176, 199, 239, 265, 270, 287, 312, 368
Kerbel Lev—100
Khachaturyan Aram—98, 200
Kibalnikov Alexander—301
Klein Roman—156, 184, 263
Klodt Pyotr—238
Kon Fyodor—14, 124, 353
Konenkov Sergei—227, 232, 367, 382
Korin Pavel—192, 257
Korolyov Sergei—77, 144, 291, 320
Kosmodemyanskaya Zoya—131, 132, 216, 244
Kovalyova-Zhemchugova Praskovya—177, 281
Kropotkin Pyotr—170

Krupskaya Nadezhda—130, 131, 259, 300, 305
Kuibyshev Valerian—83
Kun Bela—177
Kutuzov Mikhail—183, 187, 193

L

Le Corbusier—299, 300
Lenin Vladimir—63-67, 72, 73, 94, 98-101, 125, 133, 143, 151, 170, 176, 240, 256, 259, 267, 285, 330, 336
Lermontov Mikhail—28, 98, 127, 144, 172, 183
Levitan Isaac—115, 170, 264, 296, 300, 305
Lunacharsky Anatoly—126
Lyusinova Lyusik—163

M

Mamontov Savva—251
Manizer Matvei—118, 166
Marx Karl—13, 94
Mayakovsky Vladimir—104, 126, 264, 346
Melnikov Konstantin—171, 305
Merkurov Sergei—58, 101, 127, 169, 276
Meyerhold Vsevolod—201
Mickiewicz Adam—226
Minin Kozma—15, 75, 77
Minkus Mikhail—89
Mndoyants Ashot—70, 182, 183, 294
Mochalov Pavel—99, 154
Mordvinov Arkady—190, 222
Motorin Ivan—56
Mukhina Vera—200, 209, 236, 246, 294
Myaskovsky Nikolai—186

N

Napoleon—53, 77, 187, 191, 193
Nemirovich-Danchenko Vladimir—83, 226, 252, 253
Nezhdanova Antonina—98, 152, 200

Nikolayeva-Tereshkova Valentina—226, 291
Nogin Victor—105

O

Ogarev Nikolai—17, 95, 203
Ogurtsov Bazhen—50, 56, 59
Opekushin Alexander—228, 272
Ordzhonikidze Grigory—106
Ostrovsky Alexander—114, 158
Ostrovsky Nikolai—226
Ostuzhev Alexander—99, 253

P

Paustovsky Konstantin—259, 261
Perovskaya Sofia—315
Peter the Great—16, 50, 61, 67, 77, 82, 142, 173, 260, 309, 317
Pinchuk Vladimir—67
Pogodin Mikhail—126, 172, 201
Polenov Vassily—115, 152, 185, 296
Polubes Stepan—314, 329
Polzunov Ivan—77
Posnik—74
Posokhin Mikhail—70, 182, 183, 287, 294
Pozharsky Dmitri—15, 75, 77
Pudovkin Vsevolod—209
Pugachov Yemelyan—77, 82
Pushkin Alexander—98, 126, 127, 154, 168, 181, 185, 206, 226

Q

Quarenghi Giacomo—83, 143, 321

R

Rakhmaninov Sergei—98, 200, 251
Rastrelli Bartolomeo—57
Razin Stepan—77, 84
Reed John—105
Repin Ilya—115, 118, 125, 152, 158, 169, 232, 264, 296
Regberg Ilya—62, 191, 223
Rolland Romain—22, 207
Rublyov Andrei—54, 115, 331

Rubo Franz—192
Rudnev Lev—171
Ruffo Marco—47, 58
Ryleyev Kondrati—124, 143, 203
Rumyantsev Nikolai—89, 312

S

Sadoul Georges—207
Schmidt Nikolai—215
Sechenov Ivan—171
Serafimovich Alexander—66, 118
Serov Valentin—116, 152, 170, 232
Shadr Ivan—144, 201, 217, 236
Shaw Bernard—22, 207
Shchepkin Mikhail—99, 126, 154, 296
Sherwood Vladimir—76
Shchukin Boris—185
Shchuko Vladimir—89, 292
Shchusev Aleksei—73, 96, 103, 114, 117, 144, 176, 181, 303
Shehel Fyodor—207
Shostakovich Dmitri—202
Skryabin Alexander—181, 185
Sobinov Leonid—98, 152, 201, 253
Solario Pietro-Antonio—50, 58
Speransky Sergei—67
Stamo Yevgeni—70, 381, 388
Stanislavsky Konstantin—83, 127, 202, 226, 252, 296
Stankevich Nikolai—186
Stendhal—129
Sukhe-Bator—100
Surikov Vassily—115, 158, 296
Suvorov Alexander—275
Sverdlov Yakov—64, 97, 100
Sytin Ivan—112

T

Tchaikovsky Pyotr—90, 138, 200, 248
Tkhor Boris—98, 172, 182, 287, 294
Theophanes the Greek—54
Thorez Maurice—226
Timiryazev Klement—127, 176, 261
Togliatti Palmiro—226

Tolstoy Lev—98, 109, 129, 164, 169, 171, 264
Tomsky Nikolai—95, 125, 181, 193, 244
Tretyakov Pavel—114
Tropinin Vassily—117, 152
Turgenev Ivan—125, 126, 141, 162, 186, 256, 296, 300, 312

U

Ulyanova-Yelizarova Anna—178
Ulyanova Maria—259
Ushakov Simon—59, 87, 115, 174

V

Vakhtangov Yevgeny—181, 185
Vasnetsov Apollinary—115, 149, 152
Vasnetsov Victor—114, 152
Vesnin Leonid—351
Vesnin Victor—351
Vitali Ivan—58, 100, 193, 320, 328
Vorovsky Vatslav—208, 267
Vrubel Mikhail—100, 116, 152, 157, 296
Vuchetich Yevgeny—103, 246

Y

Yablochkina Alexandra—99, 253
Yermolova Maria—127, 152, 296
Yesenin Sergei—126, 202, 264, 349

Z

Zagorsky Vladimir—200, 203
Zarudny Ivan—82, 131, 317
Zholtovsky Ivan—95, 238, 272

REQUEST TO READERS

Progress Publishers would be glad to have your opinion of this book, its translation and design and any suggestions you may have for future publications.

Please send all your comments to 17, Zubovsky Boulevard, Moscow, USSR.

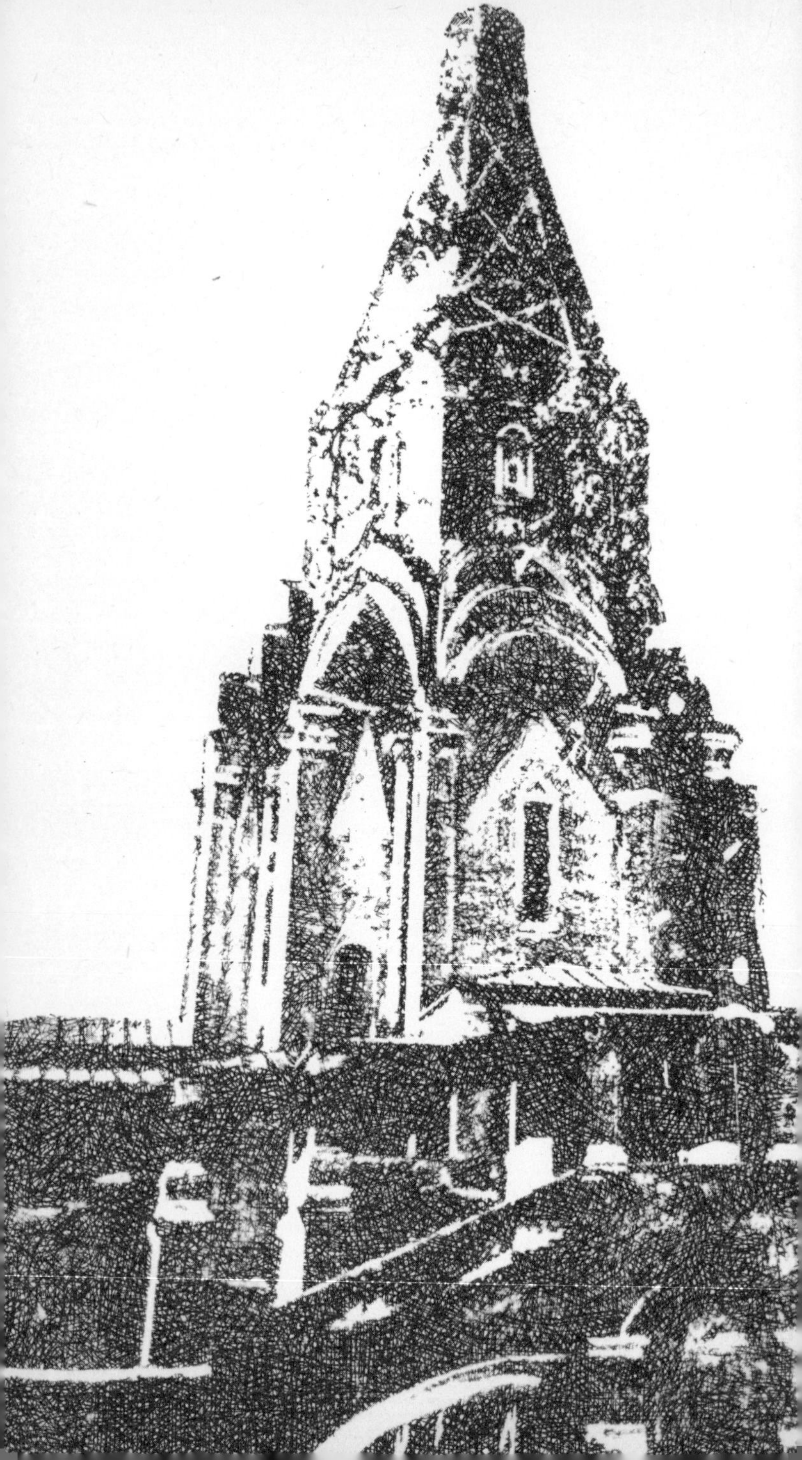